LIBRARY OF NEW TESTAMENT STUDIES
621

Formerly the Journal for the Study of the New Testament Supplement Series

Editor
Chris Keith

Editorial Board
Dale C. Allison, John M.G. Barclay, Lynn H. Cohick, R. Alan Culpepper, Craig A. Evans, Robert Fowler, Simon J. Gathercole, Juan Hernandez Jr., John S. Kloppenborg, Michael Labahn, Love L. Sechrest, Robert Wall, Steve Walton, Catrin H. Williams

THE PATH TO SALVATION IN LUKE'S GOSPEL

What Must We do?

MiJa Wi

t&tclark

LONDON • NEW YORK • OXFORD • NEW DELHI • SYDNEY

T&T CLARK
Bloomsbury Publishing Plc
50 Bedford Square, London, WC1B 3DP, UK
1385 Broadway, New York, NY 10018, USA
29 Earlsfort Terrace, Dublin 2, Ireland

BLOOMSBURY, T&T CLARK and the T&T Clark logo
are trademarks of Bloomsbury Publishing Plc

First published in Great Britain 2019
Paperback edition first published 2021

Copyright © MiJa Wi, 2019

MiJa Wi has asserted her right under the Copyright,
Designs and Patents Act, 1988, to be identified as Author of this work.

For legal purposes the Acknowledgements on p. x constitute
an extension of this copyright page.

All rights reserved. No part of this publication may be reproduced or
transmitted in any form or by any means, electronic or mechanical,
including photocopying, recording, or any information storage or retrieval
system, without prior permission in writing from the publishers.

Bloomsbury Publishing Plc does not have any control over, or responsibility for,
any third-party websites referred to or in this book. All internet addresses given
in this book were correct at the time of going to press. The author and publisher
regret any inconvenience caused if addresses have changed or sites have
ceased to exist, but can accept no responsibility for any such changes.

A catalogue record for this book is available from the British Library.

A catalog record for this book is available from the Library of Congress.

ISBN: HB: 978-0-5676-8737-1
PB: 978-0-5677-0031-5
ePDF: 978-0-5676-8738-8
eBook: 978-0-5676-8740-1

Series: Library of New Testament Studies, 2513-8790, volume 621

Typeset by Deanta Global Publishing Services, Chennai, India

To find out more about our authors and books visit
www.bloomsbury.com and sign up for our newsletters.

CONTENTS

List of Tables	ix
Acknowledgements	x
List of Abbreviations	xi

Chapter 1
INTRODUCTION — 1
- 1.1 Justification for the Thesis — 2
- 1.2 Definition of Poor and Rich — 9
  - 1.2.1 Excursus: Poverty Scale (PS) — 11
- 1.3 Interpretive Method — 14
- 1.4 The Relation of the Gospel of Luke to Acts — 18
- 1.5 Outline of the Thesis — 19

Part One
SOCIO-ECONOMIC CONTEXTS OF LUKE'S GOSPEL

Chapter 2
WEALTH: LAND, TAX, DEBT — 23
- 2.1 Introduction — 23
- 2.2 Landholding Patterns in Roman Palestine — 24
  - 2.2.1 Herod the Great — 25
  - 2.2.2 Galilee: Herodian Economics — 26
  - 2.2.3 Judaea — 27
- 2.3 Profile of Landowners — 29
  - 2.3.1 Herodian Family — 30
  - 2.3.2 Local Wealthy Aristocrats — 31
  - 2.3.3 High Priestly Families — 33
- 2.4 Tenants, Tax and Debt — 35
  - 2.4.1 Profile of Tenants and Rent — 36
  - 2.4.2 Burdens of Tax — 37
  - 2.4.3 Problem of Debt — 39
- 2.5 Conclusion — 41

Chapter 3
LIFE ESSENTIALS: FOOD AND CLOTHING — 43
- 3.1 Introduction — 43
- 3.2 Food — 44
  - 3.2.1 Daily Bread — 45
  - 3.2.2 Food Crisis: Famine and Hunger — 48
  - 3.2.3 Food and Economic Disparity — 51
- 3.3 Clothing — 54
  - 3.3.1 Daily Clothing — 55
  - 3.3.2 Clothing and Economic Disparity — 56
- 3.4 Conclusion — 58

Part Two
SALVATION OF THE POOR AND THE RICH

Chapter 4
SALVATION IN THE GOSPEL OF LUKE — 63
- 4.1 Introduction — 63
- 4.2 Salvation and Mercy — 64
- 4.3 Salvation as Release — 66
- 4.4 Salvation as Reversal — 70
- 4.5 Salvation as Repentance — 73
- 4.6 Salvation as Restoration — 77
- 4.7 Conclusion — 79

Chapter 5
SALVATION OF THE POOR: DIVINE MERCY AND JUSTICE (LK. 4.18-19; 7.22; 7.11-17; 16.19-31) — 81
- 5.1 Introduction — 81
- 5.2 The Good News of τὴν Βασιλείαν τοῦ Θεοῦ (Lk. 4.18-19; 7.22) — 81
- 5.3 Miracle and Compassion (Lk. 7.11-17) — 86
  - 5.3.1 Literary and Narrative Contexts and Text — 86
  - 5.3.2 Miracle, Faith and Salvation — 90
- 5.4 Reversal and Justice (Lk. 16.19-31) — 92
  - 5.4.1 Literary and Narrative Contexts and Text — 92
  - 5.4.2 Reversal, Piety, Salvation of Lazarus — 98
- 5.5 Salvation of the Poor: Divine Mercy and Justice — 100
- 5.6 Conclusion — 101

Chapter 6
WHAT MUST WE DO?: HUMAN EMBODIMENT OF DIVINE MERCY I (LK. 3.1-20) — 103
- 6.1 Introduction — 103
- 6.2 A Chiastic Reading of Lk. 3.1-20 — 104
- 6.3 The Historical–Political Context of John's Teaching (Lk. 3.1-2, 19-20) — 106
- 6.4 The Soteriological Context of John's Teaching (Lk. 3.3-6, 18) — 108
- 6.5 The Eschatological Context of John's Teaching (Lk. 3.7-9, 15-17) — 114
- 6.6 What Must We Do?: Bearing Fruit(s) of Mercy and Justice (Lk. 3.10-14) — 116
- 6.7 Conclusion — 121

Chapter 7
WHAT MUST I DO?: HUMAN EMBODIMENT OF DIVINE MERCY II (LK. 10.25-37; 18.18-30) — 123
- 7.1 Introduction — 123
- 7.2 Τί Ποιήσας Ζωὴν Αἰώνιον Κληρονομήσω (Lk. 10.25; 18.18) — 124
- 7.3 Mercy (Ἔλεος) and Eternal Life (Ζωή Αἰώνιος) (Lk. 10.25-37) — 127
- 7.4 Almsgiving (Ἐλεημοσύνη) and Eternal Life (Ζωή Αἰώνιος) (Lk. 18.18-30) — 131
- 7.5 Law, Mercy and Almsgiving and Eternal Life — 135
- 7.6 Conclusion — 136

Chapter 8
WHAT MUST I DO?: HUMAN EMBODIMENT OF DIVINE MERCY III (LK. 12.16–21; 16.1-9) — 138
- 8.1 Introduction — 138
- 8.2 Points of Contacts: The Parables of the Rich Fool (Lk. 12.16-21) and the Unjust Steward (16.1-9) — 139
- 8.3 Storing up Treasure and the Demise of the Rich Fool (Lk. 12.16-21) — 140
  - 8.3.1 Literary and Narrative Contexts of the Parable of the Rich Fool — 140
  - 8.3.2 Wealth and Death — 142
- 8.4 Use of Unjust Wealth (Τοῦ Μαμωνᾶ τῆς Ἀδικίας) and Eternal Dwelling (Αἰώνιος Σκηνή) (Lk. 16.1-9) — 144
  - 8.4.1 Various Readings of the Parable of the Unjust Steward — 144
  - 8.4.2 Wealth and Eternal Dwelling — 146
- 8.5 Proper Use of Wealth: Is Almsgiving Redemptive? — 149
- 8.6 Conclusion — 152

Chapter 9
SALVATION OF THE RICH: RESTORED PEOPLE OF GOD (LK. 14.1-24) — 154
9.1 Introduction — 154
9.2 The Messianic Banquet in Jewish Apocalyptic Traditions — 155
9.3 The Messianic Banquet in Luke's Narrative Contexts — 159
   9.3.1 Reclining at Table of the Kingdom: Lk. 13.22-30 — 159
   9.3.2 Juxtaposition of the Earthly and Heavenly Banquets I (Lk. 15.1-32) — 161
   9.3.3 Juxtaposition of the Earthly and Heavenly Banquet II (Lk. 16.19-31) — 162
9.4 The Parable of the Great Banquet (Lk. 14.1-24) — 164
   9.4.1 Who will Eat at the Banquet of the Kingdom? — 165
   9.4.2 Blessed are the Rich? — 168
   9.4.3 Various Readings of the Parable of the Messianic Banquet — 169
   9.4.4 Who are Present at the Banquet? — 171
9.5 Conclusion: Salvation, the Messianic Banquet and the Place of the Poor and the Rich — 172

Chapter 10
CONCLUSION — 174
10.1 Summary and Conclusions — 174
10.2 Contributions — 176
10.3 Limitations and Further Studies — 177
10.4 Implications for the World Today — 177

Bibliography — 179
   Primary Sources — 179
   Secondary Sources — 180
Index — 198
Ancient Index — 205

LIST OF TABLES

Table 1.1	The daily calorie intake and the average price of wheat	12
Table 1.2	Friesen's Poverty Scale (PS)	13
Table 9.1	Lists of the Invitees in Luke's Gospel and of the excluded in 1QSa	167

ACKNOWLEDGEMENTS

This thesis represents a slight revision of my doctoral work submitted to the University of Manchester in 2017. This research would not have been possible without the support of many people. I wish to express my deepest gratitude to Dr Kent Brower, my main supervisor, for his unceasing encouragement and patient guidance throughout the research and for his willingness to take extra miles whenever necessary. His and Mrs Francine Brower's loving kindness shown to me has been invaluable not only to make progress of my research but also to shape my personhood. I would also like to thank Dr Svetlana Khobnya for her helpful comments as a supervisor and for her friendship. I also wish to express my appreciation to Dr John Wright for his willingness to read the thesis at the final stage of my research and for his valuable critiques and to Mrs Elaine Noble who proofread it with expertise and grace. I also owe special thanks to Prof John Nolland and Dr Dwight Swanson as my examiners for their helpful comments and to Prof Chris Keith and Dr Christopher M. Hays for their guidance and encouragements during the publishing process.

I would also like to thank the research community at NTC (Nazarene Theological College Manchester) and to Ehrhardt Seminar at University of Manchester whose comments have been formative for the research. I also wish to thank Didsbury House Group members of Longsight Community Church of the Nazarene who studied Luke's Gospel with enthusiasm during my research. I have learnt much from them in our weekly discussion. With a pleasant surprise, I had joy of being part of another community, YeDam Church Manchester, in my later stage of research. Their fellowship and prayers are much appreciated.

Without generous gift from the Souter Charitable Trust Postgraduate Student Fellowship through Nazarene Theological College, it would not have been possible to conduct this research at all. Special thanks to those generous supporters. My parents have been a source of encouragement and great support ever since I started this journey in theological education. Studying the Bible for so long must have made little sense to them who do not yet share the faith which has led me thus far. Yet, their Christlike love and grace has always been an example to follow.

Finally, I wish to express my deepest love and gratitude to Kyong Im Lee, a friend over seventeen years, who is more a sister than a friend, and to Eun Ho Kim, a life partner and friend, whose presence and support I cherish. To them, I dedicate this thesis.

LIST OF ABBREVIATIONS

Primary Sources

1 En.	1 Enoch (Ethiopic Apocalypse)
1QM	War Scroll
11QMelch	Melchizedek
1QS	Rule of the Community
1QSa	Rule of the Congregation
2 Bar.	2 Baruch (Syriac Apocalypse)
2 Macc	2 Maccabees
4 Macc	4 Maccabees
4Q521	Messianic Apocalypse
4QMMT	Miqsat Ma'aseh ha-Torah
Agr.	*De agricultura (De re rustica)*
Ann.	*Annales*
Ant.	*Jewish Antiquities*
Aug.	*Divus Augustus*
Bell. Cat.	*Bellum catalinae*
Cat.	*Cataplus*
Cat. Maj.	*Cato Major*
CD	Damascus Document
Cic.	*Cicero*
CIL	*Corpus Inscriptionum Latinarum*
Deipn.	*Deipnosophistae*
Dig.	*Digest*
Ep.	*Epistulae*
Fug.	*Fugitivi*
Gall.	*Gallus*
Gos. Thom.	Gospel of Thomas
Hist.	*Historiae*
Hom. Gen.	*Homiliae in Genesim*
ILS	*Inscriptiones Latinae Selectae*
Jos. Asen.	Joseph and Aseneth
Jub.	Jubilees
J.W.	*Jewish War*
Let. Aris.	Letter of Aristeas
Mor.	*Moralia*
Mur	Murabba'at
NRSV	The New Revised Standard Version
Off.	*De officiis*

P.Oxy.	The Oxyrhynchus Papyri
Pesah.	Pesahim
Pss. Sol.	Psalms of Solomon
Res gest. divi Aug.	Res gestae divi Augusti
Rust.	De re rustica
Sat.	Satirae
Sir	Sirach
Sol.	Solon
Spec.	De specialibus legibus
T. Ab.	Testament of Abraham
Tg. Isa.	Targum Isaiah
Tob	Tobit
Vit. Apoll.	Vita Apollonii

Secondary Sources

AASOR	Annual of the American Schools of Oriental Research
AB	Anchor Bible
ABD	Anchor Bible Dictionary
AcTSup	Acta Theologica Supplementum
ANRW	Aufstieg und Niedergang der römischen Welt
AWOL	The Ancient World Online
BBR	Bulletin for Biblical Research
BDAG	Danker, Frederick W., Walter Bauer, William F. Arndt, and F. Wilbur Gingrich. *Greek-English Lexicon of the New Testament and Other Early Christian Literature.*
BHGNT	The Baylor Handbook on the Greek New Testament
Bib	Biblica
BibInt	Biblical Interpretation
BibInt	Biblical Interpretation Series
BZNW	Beihefte zur Zeitschrift für die neutestamentliche Wissenschaft
CBQ	Catholic Biblical Quarterly
CBQMS	Catholic Biblical Quarterly Monograph Series
CRINT	Compendia Rerum Iudaicarum ad Novum Testamentum
CUP	Cambridge University Press
CurBR	Currents in Biblical Research
DJD	Discoveries in the Judaean Desert
DSD	Dead Sea Discoveries
EgT	Eglise et théologie
EphM	Ephemerides Mariologicae
ExAud	Ex Auditu
ExpTim	Expository Times
HBT	Horizons in Biblical Theology
HNT	Handbuch zum Neuen Testament
IAC	Institute for Antiquity and Christianity

ICC	International Critical Commentary
IJT	Indian Journal of Theology
Int	Interpretation
JBL	Journal of Biblical Literature
JECS	Journal of Early Christian Studies
JESHO	Journal of the Economic and Social History of the Orient
JETS	Journal of the Evangelical Theological Society
JNES	Journal of Near Eastern Studies
JRS	Journal of Roman Studies
JRT	Journal of Religious Thought
JSHJ	Journal for the Study of the Historical Jesus
JSJ	Journal for the Study of Judaism in the Persian, Hellenistic, and Roman Periods
JSJSup	Supplements to the Journal for the Study of Judaism
JSNT	Journal for the Study of the New Testament
JSNTSup	Journal for the Study of the New Testament Supplement Series
JSOTSup	Journal for the Study of the Old Testament Supplement Series
JSP	Journal for the Study of the Pseudepigrapha
JSPSup	Journal for the Study of the Pseudepigrapha Supplement Series
JTS	Journal of Theological Studies
KEK	Kritisch-exegetischer Kommentar über das Neue Testament
LCL	Loeb Classical Library
LNTS	The Library of New Testament Studies
NBBC	New Beacon Bible Commentary
NEA	Near Eastern Archaeology
Neot	Neotestamentica
NICNT	New International Commentary on the New Testament
NIGTC	New International Greek Testament Commentary
NovT	Novum Testamentum
NovTSup	Supplements to Novum Testamentum
NSBT	New Studies in Biblical Theology
NTL	New Testament Library
NTS	New Testament Studies
OPIAC	Occasional papers of the Institute for Antiquity and Christianity
PRSt	Perspectives in Religious Studies
RevExp	Review and Expositor
RIDA	Revue Internationale des droits de l'Antiquité
R&E	Review and Expositor
RLT	Revista Latinoamericana de Teología
SBL	Society of Biblical Literature
SBLDS	Society of Biblical Literature Dissertation Series
SBLECL	Society of Biblical Literature Early Christianity and Its Literature
SBLMS	Society of Biblical Literature Monograph Series
ScrB	Scripture Bulletin
SNTSMS	Society for New Testament Studies Monograph Series
SNTSU	Studien zum Neuen Testament und seiner Umwelt
SP	Sacra Pagina

SPCK	Society for Promoting Christian Knowledge
SSEJC	Studies in Scripture in Early Judaism and Christianity
SJT	*Scottish Journal of Theology*
SE	*Studia Evangelica*
TDNT	*Theological Dictionary of the New Testament*
TDOT	*Theological Dictionary of the Old Testament*
TS	*Theological Studies*
TynBul	*Tyndale Bulletin*
WBC	Word Biblical Commentary
WBC	*The Women's Bible Commentary*
WJK	Westminster John Knox
WTJ	*Westminster Theological Journal*
WUNT	Wissenschaftliche Untersuchungen zum Neuen Testament
ZNW	*Zeitschrift für die neutestamentliche Wissenschaft und die Kunde der älteren Kirche*

Other

ANE	Ancient Near Eastern
ES	Economic Scale
HB	Hebrew Bible
LXX	Septuagint
NM	Nazareth Manifesto
NT	New Testament
PS	Poverty Scale
STP	Second Temple Period
TN	Travel Narrative

Chapter 1

INTRODUCTION

Luke's noted concern for socio-economic issues is axiomatic in Lukan studies as the plethora of works in this area shows. Most studies are directed towards Luke's theology of the poor or Luke's wealth ethics. Rarely, however, have scholars discussed Luke's interest in socio-economic issues in relation to his message of salvation despite their close links in the Gospel.[1] Few works directly tackle the salvation of the poor and the rich, and the use of wealth in the light of salvation in Luke's Gospel.[2] In fact, Luke frequently communicates the message of salvation in socio-economic terms. Concerning soteriological inquiries, Luke's response conveys economic connotations in perspective (Lk. 3.10-14; 10.25, 28, 37; 18.18, 22). Conversely, how one uses material goods determines one's eternal destiny (Lk. 12.15, 20-21; 16.9). Socio-economic issues not only serve as an essential part of Lukan salvation but also shape his understanding of salvation in the Gospel. Hence this thesis explores Luke's incorporation of socio-economic issues into his message of salvation and Luke's soteriological concerns for the rich as well as the poor.

---

1. Thomas E. Phillips, *Reading Issues of Wealth and Poverty in Luke-Acts* (Lewiston, NY: Edwin Mellen, 2001), 109–15. Phillips, employing Wolfgang Iser's theory which highlights 'interaction between text and reader', connects Luke's use of economic terms for soteriological purposes (52). However, his study as a whole is directed towards wealth ethics. For brief, but perceptive discussion of salvation of poor and rich, see Philip Francis Esler, *Community and Gospel in Luke-Acts: The Social and Political Motivations on Lucan Theology*, SNTSMS 57 (Cambridge: CUP, 1987), 187–200. See also Anthony Giambrone, *Sacramental Charity, Creditor Christology, and the Economy of Salvation in Luke's Gospel*, WUNT 2.439 (Tübingen: Mohr, 2017). Giambrone offers 'theologically oriented exegesis' of Luke's message on wealth and thus takes it beyond ethical application.

2. Several works allude to the connection between the use of wealth and repentance, and thus suggest the possibility of salvation for the rich. Nonetheless, this conclusion is often inferred from the examination of use of wealth or repentance. See Walter Pilgrim, *Good News to the Poor: Wealth and Poverty in Luke-Acts* (Minneapolis: Augsburg, 1981), 146; Phillips, *Issues*, 269; Guy D. Nave, Jr, *The Role and Function of Repentance in Luke-Acts* (Atlanta: SBL, 2002), 185–9; Fernando Méndez-Moratalla, *The Paradigm of Conversion in Luke*, JSNTSup 252 (London: T&T Clark, 2004), 205–7.

This thesis aims to address several issues. First, what does it mean when Luke's Gospel postulates good news to the poor (Lk. 4.18-19; 7.22; cf. 1.52-53; 6.20-21; 7.11-17; 16.19-31)? Who are the poor and what is good news? Second, what is the significance of the recurring question: Τί ποιήσωμεν (Lk. 3.10, 12, 14; also in 10.25; 12.17; 16.3; 18.18; cf. Acts 2.37; 16.30), which apparently combines salvation with 'doing'? Is Luke's preponderant use of ἔλεος (ἐλεέω, ἐλεημοσύνη Lk. 1.50, 54, 58, 72, 78; 10.37; 11.41; 12.33; 16.24; 17.13; 18.38; cf. 6.36) in the context of salvation significant in this regard? Third, can the rich be saved, even with Luke's unfavourable depiction (Lk. 6.24-25; 1.51-53; 12.16-21; 14.16-24; 16.19-31; 18.18-25; cf. 19.1-10)? If so, how? Finally, these still beg one final question: Do the salvation of the poor and the rich relate to each other? If so, how does Luke's Gospel envisage their gathering? While these questions will be revisited and refined throughout the thesis, this chapter deals with some preliminary issues for the whole thesis.

1.1 Justification for the Thesis

Good news to the poor (πτωχοί) (Lk. 4.18; 7.22) is an axiom upon which Luke's Gospel builds. Lukan studies on 'poor and rich' primarily define the poor in the light of the good news. François Bovon's review of research on 'poor and rich' in Luke-Acts affirms that scholars have addressed this topic substantially.[3] Bovon, however, raises a significant question: 'Is it healthy' to produce another exegetical work on this issue?[4] This is indeed a crowded area of research; however, continued scholarly works evince both the unresolved problems and the relevancy of this issue for Lukan studies. The spectrum of scholarly opinions on 'poor and rich' and (either lack of or surplus of) wealth is wide and diverse. It ranges from the 'centrality of the poor'[5] to Luke as 'the evangelist of the rich'[6] and from the elimination of wealth[7] to its accommodation.[8]

---

3. François Bovon, *Luke the Theologian: Fifty-five Years of Research (1950–2005)*, 2nd and rev. edn (Waco: Baylor University, 2005), 442–8, 546–51.

4. Bovon, *Theologian*, 550.

5. Joel B. Green, 'Good News to the Poor: A Lukan Leitmotif', *RevExp* 111.2 (2014): 173.

6. Luise Schottroff and Wolfgang Stegemann, *Jesus and the Hope of the Poor*, trans. Matthew J. O'Connell (Maryknoll: Orbis, 1986), 117.

7. James A. Metzger, *Consumption and Wealth in Luke's Travel Narrative*, BibInt 88 (Leiden: Brill, 2007), 176.

8. See Kyoung-Jin Kim, *Stewardship and Almsgiving in Luke's Theology*, JSNTSup 155 (Sheffield: Sheffield Academic, 1998), 109. He observes that Luke's total renunciation is to be understood in the context of total renunciation of ownership and suggests almsgiving as the right use of possession; Kiyoshi Mineshige distinguishes between the renunciation of possessions and almsgiving. The former applies to the first disciples who radically changed their lifestyle while the latter applies Christians in general. *Besitzverzicht und Almosen bei*

More importantly, previous works focused on resolving seemingly problematic issues which emerge from the programmatic role of good news to the poor (Lk. 4.18; 7.22) in Luke-Acts. If Luke's πτωχοί are the beneficiaries of salvation, they either have spiritual or moral qualities. This refers to their belief. It is often questioned whether material poverty and wealth might be the sole factors which determine one's salvation.[9] Nor can the scope of salvation be reduced only to the socio-economically impoverished.

This thesis, however, suggests that the issues need to be addressed from a different angle. The vital role of Lk. 4.18-19 (7.22) does not and should not confine good news only to the poor regardless of how one defines them. Although this programmatic passage underscores Jesus' primary concern for the poor, salvation is not limited to the poor in Luke.[10] Previous studies have not sufficiently addressed the 'poor and rich' in the context of Luke's message of salvation which centres on divine mercy (ἔλεος) and its human embodiment. Divine mercy and its human embodiment in fact shed light on the salvation of the rich as well as the poor and on the restorative and redemptive use of wealth, namely, almsgiving (ἐλεημοσύνη).[11]

In what follows, I will offer a brief survey of scholarly readings of 'poor (πτωχοί) and rich (πλούσιοι)' in Luke's Gospel. Defining the poor is a 'vexing question'.[12] The spiritual and religious understanding of them has never faded while their socio-economic status seems more remarked on.[13] Scholars have asserted that the humble

---

Lukas: Wesen und Forderung des lukanischen Vermögensethos, WUNT 163 (Tübingen: Mohr, 2003), 262-4; Christopher M. Hays, *Luke's Wealth Ethics: A Study in Their Coherence and Character*, WUNT 275 (Tübingen: Mohr, 2010), 185-6. Kim, Mineshige and Hays to some degree follow Hans-Joachim Degenhardt's much contested two-tiered wealth ethics – small circle of disciples and followers. See Degenhardt, *Lukas Evangelist der Armen: Besitz und Besitzverzicht in Den Lukanischen Schriften: Eine Traditions- und Redaktionsgeschichtliche Untersuchung* (Stuttgart: Katholisches Bibelwerk, 1965), 27-33.

9. Degenhardt, *Lukas*, 51. Outi Lehtipuu, 'The Rich, the Poor, and the Promise of an Eschatological Reward in the Gospel of Luke', in *Other Worlds and Their Relation to This World: Early Jewish and Ancient Christian Traditions*, ed. Tobias Nicklas et al., JSJSup 143 (Leiden: Brill, 2010), 231.

10. Degenhardt, *Lukas*, 51. See also Lehtipuu, 'Reward', 246. She identifies the poor with the believers.

11. Mineshige, *Almosen*, 262. On the soteriological aspect of almsgiving, see Klaus Berger, 'Almosen für Israel: Zum Historischen Kontext der Paulinischen Kollekte', *NTS* 23 (1977): 180-204; Halvor Moxnes, *The Economy of the Kingdom: Social Conflict and Economic Relations in Luke's Gospel* (Eugene: Wipf and Stock, 1988), 119-23; Roman Garrison, *Redemptive Almsgiving in Early Christianity*, JSNTSup 77 (Sheffield: Sheffield Academic, 1993), 60-6; Gary Anderson, *Charity: The Place of the Poor in the Biblical Tradition* (New Haven: Yale University, 2013), 62-7, 70-1.

12. John Nolland, *Luke 1–9:20*, WBC 35_A (Dallas: Word Books, 1989), 197.

13. John R. Donahue, 'Two Decades of Research on the Rich and the Poor in Luke-Acts', in *Justice and the Holy: Essays in Honor of Walter Harrelson*, ed. Douglas A. Knight and Peter J. Paris (Atlanta: Scholars, 1989), 142-3.

circumstances of the poor lead them to trust in God. I. Howard Marshall's view on the poor as the pious is typical in this regard.[14] In a similar vein, Luke T. Johnson argues that Luke employs the terms, 'poor and rich', for a literary purpose.[15] Johnson argues that Luke uses the terms symbolically to denote their spiritual attitude, and thus they do not carry socio-economic meanings.[16] Johnson sets 'the pattern of the Prophet and the People' in his reading of 'poor and rich' in Luke-Acts. Those who accept the prophet are the poor and those who reject the rich.[17]

David P. Seccombe contends that the poor in Luke's Gospel are Israel who needs salvation while the rich are those who refuse to repent.[18] He asserts the following:

> The poor is a traditional characterization of Israel understood in terms of its suffering and humiliation at the hands of nations and as a result of its own disordered internal life. ... There is nothing socio-economic or socio-religious about Luke's use of 'poor' terminology in the passages. ... The poor are Israel and the answer to their poverty is the messianic Kingdom.[19]

Due to his overemphasis on an Isaianic understanding of the poor, he suppresses their socio-economic meaning despite its evident presence in the texts (e.g. Lk. 7.11-17; 14.16-24; 16.19-31).[20] Rather, he unduly applies the notion of the poor as Israel to texts that mention the poor.

Employing a literary approach, John Roth categorizes the poor as a character type which depicts unfortunate stereotypes in the LXX.[21] They are not actors, but acted upon, and thus 'conventional recipients of God's saving action'.[22] In doing this, he tackles the long-standing conundrum, that is, Luke's pervasive use of the terms 'poor (πτωχοί) and rich (πλούσιοι)' and the warning against wealth in the Gospel that virtually disappear in Acts.[23] His study offers a Christological solution

---

14. Marshall, *The Gospel of Luke: A Commentary on the Greek Text*, NIGTC (Exeter: Paternoster, 1978), 635.

15. Luke T. Johnson, *The Literary Function of Possessions in Luke-Acts*, SBLDS 39 (Missoula, MT: Scholars, 1977), 130.

16. While he specifies the poor as the outcasts, he observes, '[Their] poverty is not an economic designation, but a designation of spiritual status.' See Johnson, *Literary*, 139.

17. Johnson, *Literary*, 121, 126.

18. David P. Seccombe, *Possessions and the Poor in Luke-Acts*, SNTSU 6 (Linz: A. Fuchs, 1982), 28 (On the poor, 23–96; on the rich, 225).

19. Seccombe, *Possessions*, 94–5.

20. For instance, Lk. 16.19-31 is 'a back-drop to the story of the rich man', for he argues, 'There is no cause for us to think [the literal poor] existed socially among the lower strata of society.' Seccombe, *Possessions*, 171–89 (187).

21. S. John Roth, *The Blind, the Lame, and the Poor: Character Types in Luke-Acts*, JSNTSup 144 (Sheffield: Sheffield Academic, 1997), 95–141.

22. Roth, *Blind*, 140–3 (143).

23. Ibid., 18–19.

for the absence of the terms in Acts. Jesus is no longer God's eschatological benefactor of the poor, but a risen Lord in Acts.²⁴ While the works of Seccombe and Roth mainly focus on the poor, Halvor Moxnes features Luke's description of the rich as 'negative examples', somewhat similar to the Pharisees – φιλάργυροι (Lk. 16.14).²⁵ His contextual studies of first-century Palestine peasant society stand solid: the rich in that society oppressed the poor.²⁶ Thus, rich Christian sounds almost oxymoronic to him. The rich in Luke's narrative world are outsiders, urban elites and unbelievers.

Similarly, Outi Lehtipuu observes that the poor and the rich in Luke's Gospel are characters in 'a socially – and ideologically – constructed reality'.²⁷ She raises and revisits disturbing problems of the salvation of the poor and the rich in Lk. 16.19-31 in which Jesus bases their salvation seemingly on their economic status.²⁸ It is indeed problematic to modern readers that the poor are rewarded for their poverty and the rich are condemned for their wealth. Instead of challenging the issues further, however, she opts for a spiritual understanding of 'poor and rich'. The poor are 'the good and humble' and Luke's audience identify themselves with the poor.²⁹ The rich are the proud and their salvation necessarily involves repentance. Hence an understanding of 'poor and rich' based on their spiritual and moral qualities upholds the traditional notion of salvation which hinges on human response, namely, πίστις and μετάνοια.³⁰ Luke, however, rarely highlights the spiritual qualities of the poor in relation to their salvation. Rather, he shifts focus to God's mercy and justice which captures the nature of good news.³¹ Chapter 5 ('Salvation of the Poor') will discuss this issue more fully.

The centrality of good news to the poor is the main concern of Walter Pilgrim's study. He notes that Jesus' movement emerges in the lower strata of society.³² He also finds a close link between the '*anawim* piety' and the Gospel traditions.³³ He merges a socio-economic meaning of 'poor and rich' with their spiritual connotations.³⁴ The

---

24. Ibid., 220-1.
25. Moxnes, *Economy*, 145, 164. The rich are those outside of the believing community.
26. Ibid., 164.
27. Lehtipuu, 'Reward', 245.
28. Lehtipuu, *The Afterlife Imagery in Luke's Story of the Rich Man and Lazarus*, NovTSup 123 (Leiden: Brill, 2007), 5, 159, 177-8; 'Reward', 231-2.
29. Lehtipuu, 'Reward', 246.
30. See Bovon, *Theologian*, 277; David A. Neale, *None But the Sinners: Religious Categories in the Gospel of Luke*, JSNTSup 58 (Sheffield: Sheffield Academic, 1991), 153; Méndez-Moratalla, *Conversion*, 219.
31. Jacques Dupont, *Les Béatitudes*, Tome II: *La Bonne Nouvelle* (Paris: J. Gabalda et Cⁱᵉ Éditeurs, 1969), 89-90.
32. Pilgrim, *Good News*, 39-55. His sketch of political and historical situation of Palestine is built upon scant evidence.
33. Ibid., 41-57.
34. Ibid., 83.

term 'poor' reflects both socio-economic realities and deep spiritual needs.[35] Joel B. Green's two short essays offer a more wide-ranging definition of the poor.[36] He warns against applying a modern financial understanding of the poor to the ancient context in which social and religious overtones are loaded with its use.[37] Thus, according to Green, the poor to whom good news is proclaimed (Lk. 4.18; 7.22) are socially outcasts, economically destitute and religiously sinners.[38] While his notion has merit, one should note that Luke never assigns the term 'poor' to tax collectors, sinners, women, Samaritans or Gentiles.

Jacques Dupont highlights the socio-economic overtones of 'poor and rich'. He observes the relatedness of the term 'poor' with the afflicted and the hungry from extensive semantic studies.[39] Πτωχός generally means a person who is reduced to begging;[40] however, he suggests that the biblical usage of the word, πτωχός, in the LXX brings new resonances.[41] He draws a parallel to the grouping of the poor with orphans and widows as victims of injustice with that of the afflicted and the hungry in Luke.[42] This grouping specifies the meaning of the poor as 'des gens qui se trouvent dans une situation misérable et digne de compassion'; thus, its spiritual understanding seems rather difficult.[43] His remark on the blessedness of the poor in Luke's Gospel is illuminating:

> Il n'y a pas lieu de faire des pauvres, des affligés et des affamés autre chose que n'indiquent les mots qui désignent ces malheureux. La raison de leur privilège se trouve, non en eux, mais en Dieu et dans la manière dont Dieu entend exercer sa royauté au profit des faibles et des malheureux.[44]

---

35. See Mikeal C. Parsons, *Luke*, Paideia (Grand Rapids: Baker Academic, 2015), 81.

36. Joel B. Green, 'Good News to Whom? Jesus and the "Poor" in the Gospel of Luke', in *Jesus of Nazareth Lord and Christ: Essays on the Historical Jesus and New Testament Christology*, ed. Joel B. Green and Max Turner (Grand Rapids: Eerdmans, 1994), 59–74; 'Leitmotif', 173–9.

37. Green, 'Leitmotif', 175.

38. Green, 'To Whom?', 68–74.

39. Dupont, *Bonne Nouvelle*, 379.

40. It is frequently noted that πτωχός is a beggar while πένης refers to a daily labourer. See Aristophanes, *Plut.* 552-4. See also Margaret Atkins and Robin Osborne, eds, introduction to *Poverty in the Roman World*, by Robin Osborne (Cambridge: CUP, 2006), 11.

41. Dupont, *Bonne Nouvelle*, 22–9.

42. Ibid., 50.

43. Ibid. Similarly, Thomas Hoyt, in his study of the Beatitudes, observes that Luke features 'economic and physical meaning of πτωχός', and thus focuses on 'external plights of humankind'. 'The Poor/Rich Theme in the Beatitudes', *JRT* 37 (1980): 40, 41.

44. Dupont, *Bonne Nouvelle*, 142.

Similarly, Thomas Malipurathu's observation on Luke's grouping of the poor with 'the hungry' and 'the weeping' in the Beatitudes (Lk. 6.20-21) leads him to conclude the following: 'The biblical poor were primarily the sociologically poor' despite the wide 'acceptance of [their] spiritual connotation' in biblical traditions.[45]

Another stream of works which features a socio-economic definition of 'poor and rich' reconstructs Luke's *Sitz im Leben*. Esler and Schottroff and Stegemann rightfully ask, 'What is it like to be poor and rich in the first century?'[46] Their studies consider historical contexts seriously and prefer an exclusive socio-economic understanding of the poor (πτωχοί) as beggars. What is at stake, however, is their reconstruction of Luke's historical community/ies).[47] For Esler, the poor and the rich are members of Luke's own community[48] while, for Schottroff and Stegemann, the poor are Jesus' disciples who literally abandoned everything, but who are not to be found in Luke's community.[49]

In sum, this brief survey shows (1) religious and literary readings of 'poor and rich' in Luke's Gospel unduly highlight spiritual overtones of עֲנָוִים while underestimating its original socio-economic reference to the indebted, the landless and daily labourers in the HB and the historical contexts in which the term is embedded.[50] Moreover, the renderings of אֶבְיוֹן, דַּל and עָנִי as πτωχός in the LXX are fluid.[51] The identification of the poor as the pious and of the rich as the wicked

---

45. Thomas Malipurathu, *'Blessed Are You Poor!' Exploring the Biblical Impulses for an Alternative World Order* (Ishvani Kendra, India: SPCK, 2014), 59-73 (59). See also Eben Scheffler, 'Luke's View on Poverty in its Ancient (Roman) Economic Context: A Challenge for Today', *Scriptura* 106 (2011): 121.

46. Esler, *Community*, 169; Schottroff and Stegemann, *Poor*, 16-17.

47. Esler argues that the legitimization of Christianity, 'sectarian strategies', shapes the theology of Luke-Acts. *Community*, 46-70; Schottroff and Stegemann, *Poor*, 16-17. The main issue of the Lukan community was wealth. See also Robert J. Karris, 'Poor and Rich: The Lukan *Sitz im Leben*', in *Perspectives on Luke-Acts*, ed. Charles H. Talbert (Edinburgh: T&T Clark, 1978), 118, 123-4. For Karris, persecution was the key issue in Luke's community.

48. Esler, *Community*, 183-7.

49. Schottroff and Stegemann, *Poor*, 90.

50. See Degenhardt, *Lukas*, 49. He notes that the sociological meaning of עָנִי shifted to the spiritual one in the HB. This, however, is to ignore its sociological meaning which remains in the HB. For instance, see Deut. 15.11 and 24.12, 14, 15 where עָנִי is used in the context of indebtedness. Also, understanding πτωχοί in the light of עֲנָוִים in Isa. 61.1-2 brings undue emphasis on spiritual meaning. See Esa J. Autero, *Reading the Bible across Contexts: Luke's Gospel, Socio-Economic Marginality, and Latin American Biblical Hermeneutics*, BibInt 145 (Leiden: Brill, 2016), 144-6.

51. Although the verbal form, עָנָה, denotes to humble oneself, עָנִי is not always rendered as πτωχός in the LXX. See Augustin George, 'Poverty in the Old Testament', in *Gospel Poverty: Essays in Biblical Theology*, ed. Augustin George et al., trans. Michael Guinan (Chicago: Franciscan Herald, 1977), 4-6; Donald E. Gowan, 'Wealth and Poverty in the Old

is not explicit at all in Luke's Gospel. Rather, the piety of the poor is often silenced while the possibility of salvation for the rich is open. Nickelsburg's comparative study on riches and the rich in 1 Enoch and Luke's Gospel is apposite in this regard.[52] He notes that the texts converge on their negative attitude towards riches. Luke, however, sharply diverges from 1 Enoch in that his message constantly opens the possibility of salvation for the rich instead of pronouncing 'inevitable doom' against them.[53]

(2) An inclusive definition of the poor as the socially, economically and religiously marginalized perhaps offers a more acceptable option in the light of Jesus' ministry in the wider narrative contexts.[54] It also takes into account both historical and narrative contexts. While this inclusive notion of the poor is plausible, I will discuss its legitimacy in the following section (see 1.2).

(3) A socio-economic reading of 'poor and rich' challenges how Luke's Gospel appropriates their salvation. Finding an answer from Luke's *Sitz im Leben* is appealing, yet its reconstruction seems neither possible nor constructive (see 1.3). Rather salvation of the poor emerges in the context of divine mercy and justice and of the divine answer to the injustice of the world to which Dupont draws attention.[55] Moreover, a close link appears between a real experience of hunger and an eschatological expectation of abundant food and meals.[56] This sheds light not only on one's understanding of the poor and the hungry but also on one's theological reading of the text in its historical context.

(4) Finally, alongside this, the use of wealth and its relation to repentance and salvation need further investigation considering Luke's recurring question: Τί ποιήσωμεν. Yet, one needs to take a step further from almsgiving towards the gathering of the poor and the rich around the table. Salvation of the poor and the rich culminates at the banquet with the Messiah. Luke's two most distinctive

---

Testament: The Case of the Widow, the Orphan, and the Sojourner', *Int* 41.4 (1987): 341–53; David L. Baker, *Tight Fists or Open Hands?: Wealth and Poverty in Old Testament Law* (Cambridge: Eerdmans, 2009), 189–93.

52. George W.E. Nickelsburg, 'Riches, The Rich, and God's Judgment in 1 Enoch 92–105 and the Gospel according to Luke', *NTS* 25.3 (1979): 324–44; 'Revisiting the Rich and the Poor in 1 Enoch 92–105 and the Gospel according to Luke', in *George W.E. Nickelsburg in Perspective: An Ongoing Dialogue of Learning*, ed. Jacob Neusner and Alan Avery-Peck, JSJSup 80 (Leiden: Brill, 2003), 547–71.

53. Nickelsburg, 'Riches', 341.

54. Johnson, *The Gospel of Luke*, SP (Collegeville: Liturgical, 1991), 79; Robert C. Tannehill, *The Narrative Unity of Luke-Acts: A Literary Interpretation*, vol. 1: *The Gospel According to Luke* (Philadelphia: Fortress, 1986), 129.

55. Dupont, *Bonne Nouvelle*, 89–90.

56. Peter-Ben Smit, *Fellowship and Food in the Kingdom: Eschatological Meals and Scenes of Utopian Abundance in the New Testament*, WUNT 2.234 (Tübingen: Mohr, 2008), 54–62.

interests of 'poor and rich' and banquet themes thus converge at Lk. 14.1-24 with the rich imagery of the messianic banquet.

1.2 Definition of Poor and Rich

Having noted the need for this thesis, I shall now offer a definition of the poor and the rich. The terms 'πτωχός' and 'πλούσιος' form one of the most common antitheses in both Jewish and Graeco-Roman literature.[57] Luke's references are no exception.[58] From Luke's use of πτωχός in the Gospel, two things are worth noting.

First, Luke refers to the poor as a category of people in the plural (πτωχοί) seven times out of ten. The poor in five out of the seven references represent several groups of people, namely, the captives (αἰχμάλωτοι), the blind (τυφλοί), the oppressed (τεθραυσμένοι) in Lk. 4.18; those who are hungry (οἱ πεινῶντες) and weep (οἱ κλαίοντες) in 6.20; the blind (τυφλοί), the lame (χωλοί), the lepers (λεπροί), the deaf (κωφοί), the dead (νεκροί) in 7.22; and the crippled (ἀνάπειροι), the lame (χωλοί), the blind (τυφλοί) in 14.13, 21.[59] The grouping in Lk. 4.18 is 'paralleled by the reference to the "severe famine" in Elijah's day (4.25)'.[60] The poor are aligned with the hungry (Lk. 6.20; cf. 1.53) and with the disabled (4.18; 7.22; 14.13, 21). Also noteworthy is the physical location of the group mentioned in Lk. 14.21. They are to be found along the lanes of the city where the poor dwell.[61]

---

57. See George, 'Poverty', 4–21; Gowan, 'Wealth', 341–53; Roth, *Blind*, 95–141. For the poor in Ancient Near Eastern (ANE) traditions, see F. Charles Fensham, 'Widow, Orphan, and the Poor in Ancient Near Eastern Legal and Wisdom Literature', *JNES* 21 (1962): 129–39; Dupont, *Bonne Nouvelle*, 53–90; Baker, *Tight Fists*, 189–93. In Roman Palestine and the Graeco-Roman world in general, see Gildas Hamel, *Poverty and Charity in Roman Palestine, First Three Centuries C.E.* (Berkeley: University of California, 1990). Atkins and Osborne, *Poverty*. The essays included in this volume cover various aspects of poverty in Rome. Among those particularly helpful are Neville Morley's 'The Poor in the City of Rome', 21–39; Greg Woolf's 'Writing Poverty in Rome', 83–99. See also C.R. Whittaker, 'The Poor', in *The Romans*, ed. Andrea Giardina, trans. Lydia G. Cochrane (Chicago: Chicago University, 1993), 272–309. In Pauline studies, See Justin J. Meggitt, *Paul, Poverty and Survival* (Edinburgh: T&T Clark, 1998); Bruce Longenecker, *Remember the Poor: Paul, Poverty and the Greco-Roman World* (Grand Rapids: Eerdmans, 2010). In early Christianity, David L. Mealand, *Poverty and Expectation in the Gospels* (London: SPCK, 1980).

58. Lk. 1.53 (πεινάω; πλούσιος); 6.20, 24; 14.12, 13, 21; 16.19, 20; 18.22, 23; 19.2, 8; 21.1, 2.

59. For the general attitude towards the disabled in the Graeco-Roman world, see Robert Garland, *The Eye of the Beholder: Deformity and Disability in the Graeco-Roman World* (London: Duckworth, 1995), 2, 30.

60. Scheffler, 'Poverty', 121.

61. See Richard L. Rohrbaugh, 'The Pre-Industrial City in Luke-Acts: Urban Social Relations', in *The Social World of Luke-Acts: Models for Interpretation*, ed. Jerome H. Neyrey (Peabody: Hendrickson, 1991), 133–6.

Hence what marks Luke's grouping of the poor is their experience of hunger, physical disability and physical location. The remaining two references to the poor as plural (Lk. 18.22; 19.8) are used as antithetical terms for the rich and the objects of almsgiving.

Second, Luke refers to only two individuals as πτωχός – the poor man, Lazarus (Lk. 16.20, 22) and the poor widow (21.2). He hardly designates the tax collectors or sinners as πτωχοί only because they are socially and religiously marginalized. Neither does he call the pious or the believers πτωχοί.[62] Lazarus is a beggar (πτωχός) who experiences hunger and nakedness on a daily basis.[63] The widow is poor as all that she had was two *lepta* (Lk. 21.2). This was not quite enough to provide a single meal as the following section (Poverty Scale) will demonstrate. Hence Scheffler notes, 'Nothing in Luke's use of the term [πτωχός] compels us to assign any meaning other than its basic economic reference of "poor, destitute", even "begging poor".'[64] Moreover, Steve Friesen's categories of the PS suggest that those who are below subsistence level are 'unattached widows, orphans, beggars, disabled, unskilled day labo[u]rers and prisoners'.[65]

Likewise, Luke's use of πλούσιοι stamps their socio-economic location. First, the rich are those who are well-fed and well-dressed (Lk. 6.24; 16.19). They are often found at banquets (Lk. 14.12; 16.19). Second, they are landowners and creditors with abundance of goods and money (Lk. 12.16; 16.1). What marks them as rich is their material wealth (Lk. 12.17-18; 16.1; 18.22, 24; 19.8; 21.1). Third, Luke's negative attitude towards them is clearly noted from the pronouncement of woes (Lk. 1.53; 6.24; 16.23-25; 18.25). Nevertheless, the possibility of their salvation often remains open. While their use of wealth – food, clothing, land, money and goods – in relation to the poor is critical, they are not necessarily equated as the wicked. Thus, this thesis refers to 'poor and rich' primarily if not solely in socio-economic terms. This definition will be further developed in the discussion of the issues related to land and food and clothing in the following two chapters (Chapters 2 and 3). This definition offers a main thread running through

---

62. Luke's use of terminology is not indiscriminate. Similarly, none needs to be defined as or become a sinner to be saved. For example, sinners are contrasted with the righteous or the Pharisees while the poor with the rich. Neither does Luke equate the sinners with the rich nor the righteous with the poor. See Neale, *Sinners*, 191–4. His study aptly demonstrates a shift of understanding of sinners from the objects of judgement to that of God's mercy and salvation in Luke's Gospel. However, he falls into this generalization of the sinners in his reading of the texts: 'All are "sinners" in need of forgiveness' (152–3).

63. Lazarus's physical disability is also alluded to in the parable (ἐβέβλητο Lk. 16.20). Scheffler argues that the poor in Luke's Gospel can be best understood in Luke's description of Lazarus. 'Poverty', 122.

64. Scheffler, 'Poverty', 121.

65. Steven J. Friesen, 'Poverty in Pauline Studies: Beyond the So-called New Consensus', *JSNT* 26.3 (2004): 341.

the thesis as it discusses the salvation of the poor and the rich (Chapters 5 and 9) and the redemptive aspect of wealth (Chapters 6, 7 and 8) in Luke's Gospel.

1.2.1 Excursus: Poverty Scale (PS)

In Douglas Oakman's short essay, 'The Buying Power of Two *Denarii* (Lk. 10.35)', he poses intriguing questions:

> Exactly how much money was a *denarius* and how much would it buy? ... Was a *denarius* per day adequate, ... to feed wife and children, purchase clothing and other household necessities, get next year's crops out, take care of any family livestock, pay taxes, Temple dues, rents, and so on? ... 'How far would the *denarius* stretch in the first century?'[66]

The significance of these questions lies not so much in determining the real value of money in the first century, but in providing a tangible description of poverty. Here the widow's two *lepta*[67] (Lk. 21.2-4), the Samaritan's two *denarii* (10.35)[68] and the woman's ten *drachmae*[69] (15.8-10) are the test cases to measure poverty in Luke's Gospel. In order to assess the worth of two *lepta*, two *denarii* and ten *drachmae*, I will examine the prices of necessities and estimate the living costs of the non-elites in the early Roman Empire.

Despite the difficulty in calculating the value of money in antiquity,[70] studies on the 'purchasing power of ancient money' have been fruitful in measuring prices quantitatively.[71]

Duncan-Jones's extensive work demonstrates the prices in Italy and North Africa. He observes a relative stability of prices during the first two centuries CE and analyses the prices of necessities and subsistence costs.[72] Stegemann and Stegemann have applied quantitative sources to estimate the cost of living in the

---

66. Douglas Oakman, 'The Buying Power of Two *Denarii* (Luke 10.35)', *Jesus and the Peasants* (Eugene: Cascade, 2008), 40-1.

67. In the Synoptic Gospels, three types of bronze coins are mentioned: *assarion* (ἀσσάριον), *quadrans* (κοδράντης) and *lepton* (λεπτόν). See Mt. 5.26; 10.29; Mk 12.42; Lk. 12.6, 59; 21.2. cf. Plutarch, *Cic.* 1.29.4.

68. The *denarius* was used as a standard payment for tax, wage or debt in the Roman economy. See Mt. 18.28; 20.2, 9, 13; 22.19; Mk 12.15; Lk. 7.41; 20.24.

69. The *drachma* is equivalent to the *denarius*. Josephus, *Ant.* 3.195.

70. Prices and costs differ from one location to another. Moreover, there were numerous variables which affected changes in prices and the cost of living.

71. Richard Duncan-Jones, *The Economy of the Roman Empire: Quantitative Studies*, 2nd edn (Cambridge: CUP, 1982), 11.

72. Duncan-Jones, *Quantitative*, 6-11, 33-59, 144-7.

Table 1.1 The daily calorie intake and the average price of wheat

	Duncan-Jones	Scheidel and Friesen	Stegemann and Stegemann
Calories / day	3,000–3,500	1,500–2,000	2,500
Price (*denarius*) / *modius*	0.5–1	0.5–0.75	1.5–2
Cost of wheat / month	2.5–5	1–1.875	
Cost for a family of four / year	ca. 120–240	ca. 48–90	250–300

first-century Roman Empire.[73] Finally, Scheidel and Friesen's most recent study which estimates the size of the Roman economy and the income distribution in order to scale the poverty level of the Empire adds valuable sources to this analysis.[74] Here I will first note the daily minimum calorie intake and the average price of wheat per *modius* (=6.67 kg) in *denarius* with the subsistence cost of living. Table 1.1 is the simplified figure, based on the works above-mentioned.

Duncan-Jones's living costs are twice as high as those of Scheidel and Friesen. Stegemann's estimation is even higher than Duncan-Jones's since his price for wheat is 1.5 to 2 *denarii*. However, when Scheidel and Friesen's cost of food expenditure other than wheat is included, the annual cost for a family of 4 is between 177 ('bare bones' level) and 297 *denarii*.[75] Hence the cost of the very minimum existence for a family of 4 ranges from 177 to 300 *denarii* per year.

Based upon the estimates provided, let us examine the widow's two *lepta*. A *lepton* is equal to 1/128 *denarius*. Two *lepta* is then 1/64 *denarius*. Taking the lowest price of wheat which is 0.5 *denarius* per *modius*, two *lepta* could buy about 200g of wheat.[76] This would be barely enough for another meal. It strikingly evokes the handful of flour of the widow of Zarephath (Lk. 4.25-27; 1 Kgs 17.8-12). She had a handful of wheat flour (ἄλευρον 1 Kgs 17.12 LXX) in a jar as the last meal for her and her son. Both poor widows offered all that they had to live on.

---

73. Ekkehard W. Stegemann and Wolfgang Stegemann, *The Jesus Movement: A Social History of its First Century*, trans. O.C. Dean, Jr (Edinburgh: T&T Clark, 1999), 79–85.

74. Walter Scheidel and Steven J. Friesen, 'The Size of the Economy and the Distribution of Income in the Roman Empire', *JRS* 99 (2009): 61–91; Friesen, 'Poverty', 323–61. See also John Barclay, 'Poverty in Pauline Studies: A Response to Steven Friesen', *JSNT* (2004): 363–6; Peter Oakes, 'Constructing Poverty Scales for Graeco-Roman Society: A Response to Steven Friesen's "Poverty in Pauline Studies"', *JSNT* (2004): 367–71. Both Barclay and Oakes critique that Friesen's treatment of economy in his poverty scale is solely economic, and thus isolated from other factors such as the social status issue.

75. Scheidel and Friesen, 'Economy', 68.

76. Two lepta = ca. 0.015 *denarius* (one *modius* = 6670g). Two hundred grams is a bit more than a cup of flour. It can be calculated into 666 calories, based on Peter Garnsey, *Food and Society in Classical Antiquity* (Cambridge: CUP, 1999), 19–20.

The Samaritan's two *denarii* cover more than a month of wheat if we take the lowest price and minimum intake of calories.[77] Yet, since the money was given to the inn keeper, a better understanding of the Samaritan's two *denarii* might come from an inscription from Aesernia in central Italy which records a bill settlement between an innkeeper and a guest.

> Innkeeper, let us settle the bill.
> You had one half-litre of wine, one [*aes*[78]]'s worthy of bread, and two [*aeris*] for the pillow. Fine.
> And eight [*aeris*] for the girl. This also is fine.
> Hay for your mule-two [*aeris*]. That mule will do me in. (*ILS* 7478, *CIL* IX 2689)[79]

This gives an estimated expense for wine and bread of one *aes* which is equal to 1/16 *denarius*[80] and for the room (?) of 1/8 *denarius* if a pillow is accepted.[81] Therefore, two *denarii* might provide about ten days of simple lodging with bread and wine. The Samaritan who gives two *denarii*, either a month's worth of wheat or ten days' worth of room and board, for the wounded stranger is not only compassionate but also a person with relative wealth.

Finally, how much is one *drachma* worth to a village woman? Taking the minimum scale (0.5 *denarius* per *modius*), she may buy wheat for a week to feed

Table 1.2 Friesen's Poverty Scale (PS)[82]

PS 1–3	Imperial, Regional, Provincial Municipal Elites
PS 4	Moderate surplus resources (some merchants and traders, military veterans)
PS 5	Stable near subsistence level (many merchants and traders)
PS 6	At subsistence level (small farm families, labourers, wage earners)
PS 7	Below subsistence level (unattached widows, orphans, beggars, disabled, unskilled day labourers, prisoners)

77. Oakman suggests that 'the two *denarii* of the Samaritan might feed the wounded man for around 24 days'. See 'Two *Denarii*', 45.

78. *Aes* means a bronze coin in Latin. It is equivalent to ἀσσάριον (=1/16 *denarius*) after it was re-tariffed in the second century BCE. See Michael Crawford, 'Money and Exchange in the Roman World', *JRS* 60 (1970): 40.

79. Neil Elliott and Mark Reasoner, eds, *Documents and Images for the Study of Paul* (Minneapolis: Fortress, 2011), 252.

80. Duncan-Jones, *Quantitative*, 46.

81. The word in the inscription is not clear. Stegemann suggests 'meat' instead of 'pillow'. *Movement*, 40.

82. Friesen, 'Poverty', 341. This is a simplified form. See also Longenecker, *Remember*, 44–57. Although Longenecker proposes a modified economic scale (ES), it only differs from Friesen's PS and Friesen and Scheidel's scale in terms of the distribution of percentage (PS 4–7; ES 4–7).

her family with one *drachma*. Her ten *drachmae* savings might provide about two and half months of wheat for her family in times of difficulties. If we place these three people in Friesen's PS (Table 1.2),[83] the widow is undoubtedly at starvation level (PS 7) while the Samaritan seems to have enough surplus to offer two *denarii* which is more than a month's worth of wheat to a stranger (PS 5). The woman with ten *drachmae* might be slightly above subsistence level (PS 6).

These observations suggest that Luke does not provide a binary world[84] of extremely rich and of extremely poor, but a multilayered one. For instance, we see a rich man who had at least ten slaves and was able to entrust each with a hundred *denarii* (Lk. 19.11-15). Considering the number of slaves and one thousand *denarii* (ten *minas*) at his disposal, we could locate him possibly in PS 3–4.[85] We also see the extremely poor as noted (PS 7). Yet, there are others in between: a creditor who lent hundreds of *denarii* to debtors (PS 4), the Samaritan who had enough surplus (PS 5), the woman with some savings (PS 6). Hence we find non-elites in their diverse economic situations.

1.3 Interpretive Method

The methodology to be employed in this thesis is twofold. First, it primarily takes a narrative approach as 'a reading strategy', that is, reading Luke's Gospel narratively as a whole.[86] This strategy prioritizes the whole narrative of Luke's Gospel, placing secondary importance on Luke's sources.[87] I mainly refer to two extant potential sources, the Gospels of Matthew and Mark.[88] Though not limiting Luke's sources

---

83. Friesen, 'Poverty', 341.

84. Meggitt, *Poverty*, 50. He states, 'Over 99% of the Empire's population could expect little more from life than abject poverty'.

85. Luke's depiction of the rich is still in a touchable scale compared to Matthew's which employs an astronomical amount. See also Duncan-Jones, *Quantitative*, 343 [Appendix 7]. He lists the size of private fortunes in terms of half to one million *denarii*.

86. See Mark Allen Powell, 'Narrative Criticism: The Emergence of a Prominent Reading Strategy', in *Mark as Story: Retrospect and Prospect*, ed. Kelly R. Iverson and Christopher W. Skinner (Atlanta: SBL, 2011), 22.

87. The text claims itself as an orderly account (διήγησις Lk. 1.1) while acknowledging its awareness of reliable sources (1.2).

88. I opt for the simple theory, Markan priority, and the so-called Farrer-Goulder hypothesis on the synoptic problem despite its challenges. See Austin Farrer, 'Dispensing with Q', in *Studies in the Gospels: Essays in Memory of R. H. Lightfoot*, ed. D.E. Nineham (Oxford: Blackwell, 1955), 55-8; Michael D. Goulder, *Luke: A New Paradigm*, vol. 1, JSNTSup 20 (Sheffield: Sheffield Academic, 1989), 22-6; Mark Goodacre, *The Case against Q: Studies in Markan Priority and the Synoptic Problem* (Harrisburg: Trinity, 2002), 19–45; *The Synoptic Problem: A Way through the Maze* (Sheffield: Sheffield Academic, 2001), 56–83, 154–6. For different solutions, Delbert Burkett, *Rethinking the Gospel Sources: From Proto-*

to these two Gospels, it seems more valid to take Matthew and Mark than Q – a hypothetically reconstructed source.[89] In general, however, Matthew and Mark are referred to and compared with Luke as literary parallels, not necessarily as sources.[90]

This thesis, then, draws attention to literary patterns (how it is organized) such as repetitions, themes and temporal and spatial markers within the larger Lukan narratives to interpret the text (what is written).[91] For instance, the recurring theme of salvation as mercy (ἔλεος) particularly in the beginning of the Gospel and the recurring question: Τί ποιήσωμεν; throughout the Lukan narratives serve as guides to lead the discussion of the critical issues in this thesis, namely, the soteriological concerns expressed in socio-economic terms. Alongside the consideration of narrative contexts, the LXX, the HB, the Second Temple literature and Graeco-Roman literature provide a frame of reference to literary contexts in interpreting Luke's Gospel. The aim is not necessarily to find a literary dependency, but to look for the use of 'common motifs and images' in its literary contexts to illuminate the meaning of the text.[92] To this end, Lukan accounts of miracle and reversal motifs and eschatological banquet imagery are examined in their literary contexts, particularly in Chapters 5 and 9.

Mark to Mark (London: T&T Clark, 2004), 1–6, 58–9, 92, 118, 141–2. Burkett argues for 'proto-Mark' as common sources (141). Michael F. Bird, *The Gospel of the Lord: How the Early Church Wrote the Story of Jesus* (Grand Rapids: Eerdmans, 2014), 186–7. Bird suggests Luke's use of 'L', 'Mark', 'Matthew' and 'Q'.

89. James M. Robinson, Paul Hoffmann and John S. Kloppenborg, eds, *The Critical Edition of Q*, Hermeneia (Minneapolis: Fortress, 2000). Contra Q hypothesis as 'a hypothesis', see Farrer, 'Dispensing with Q', 66; Goodacre, *Against Q*, 5–10.

90. For instance, Chapter 7 discusses Lk. 10.25-28 and 18.18-30 in parallel with Mt. 22.34-40 and 19.16-30 and Mk 12.28-34 and 10.17-31.

91. Powell, 'Toward a Narrative-Critical Understanding of Luke', *Int* 48 (1994): 344. On literary patterns, it does not aim to build any set pattern which overarches the whole narrative. Rather, it pays due attention to various patterns emerging from the text and to the flow of the narrative. See the works on literary patterns and structure in Luke's Gospel. Charles H. Talberts, *Literary Patterns, Theological Themes and the Genre of Luke-Acts*, SBLMS 20 (Missoula, MT: Scholars, 1974); Douglas S. McComiskey, *Lukan Theology in the Light of the Gospel's Literary Structure* (Carlisle: Paternoster, 2004). For the patterns in Luke's Travel Narrative (TN), see M.D. Goulder, 'The Chiastic Structure of the Lucan Journey', *SE II*, ed. F.L. Cross (Berlin: Akademie-Verlag, 1964); David P. Moessner, *Lord of the Banquet: The Literary and Theological Significance of the Lukan Travel Narrative* (Harrisburg: Trinity, 1989).

92. Lehtipuu, *Afterlife*, 45–53. She notes: 'Instead of fixed parallels and direct dependency, we should speak of intertextual relations, common motifs and images that were used in the cultural milieu in the first century Mediterranean world' (45).

Also, intertextual 'allusions' and 'echoes' are noted in addition to any direct citations from the LXX.[93] With the criteria of hearing echoes suggested by Hays,[94] the intertexts mentioned in this thesis are supported by historical, literary and thematic aspects.[95] For instance, the scriptural tradition of Jubilee is noted in the reading of Luke's texts (Lk. 3.1-20; 4.18-19; 6.27-38) in Chapters 4, 5 and 6, based on the significant verbal echoes (e.g. ἀφίημι) and historical contexts examined in Chapters 2 and 3. The echoes of Leviticus 19 are heard in the literary and thematic coherence of being merciful in Lk. 6.36 and 10.25-37 in Chapters 4 and 7. Intertextual echoes can also be heard without any verbal echoes.[96] For instance, Luke makes no reference to Deut. 15.11 in his account of a woman anointing Jesus in Lk. 7.36-50 unlike other Gospels. However, thematic echoes of Deuteronomy 15 are loudly heard in the parable in Lk. 7.41-42 and in the later account in Acts 4.34 which cites Deut. 15.4.

Second, this thesis takes a historical–critical approach in examining the socio-economic contexts of Luke's Gospel. A narrative approach is often criticized for ignoring history despite restated affirmation of the importance of the historical and socio-economic realities behind the text by narrative critics.[97] Luke's Gospel is indeed a document 'with external, historical referents' as it explicitly sets the message in the historical and political contexts of its day.[98] Hence understanding the historical, cultural and socio-economic realities behind the text is crucial to finding meaning in the text. However, the primary goal of examining historical contexts is 'less' about validating their historicity and 'more' about finding their significance for the narrative.[99]

In this regard, Chapters 2 and 3 sketch the first-century socio-economic world in which Luke's Gospel is written. The discussion of land and food and clothing, which utilizes archaeological and literary evidence, will on the one hand provide the background in which the text becomes more fully intelligible in its socio-

---

93. Richard B. Hays, *Echoes of Scripture in the Letters of Paul* (New Haven: Yale University, 1989), 29; *Echoes of Scripture in the Gospels* (Waco: Baylor University, 2016), 10.

94. R. Hays, *Echoes in Paul*, 29–32; *The Conversion of the Imagination: Paul as Interpreter of Israel's Scripture* (Cambridge: Eerdmans, 2005), 34–45.

95. Ibid., 28.

96. Kenneth D. Litwak, *Echoes of Scripture in Luke-Acts: Telling the History of God's People Intertextually*, JSNTSup 282 (London: T&T Clark, 2005), 64.

97. Powell, *What is Narrative Criticism?: A New Approach to the Bible* (London: SPCK, 1993), 97; Petri Merenlahti and Raimo Hakola, 'Reconceiving Narrative Criticism', in *Characterization in the Gospels: Reconceiving Narrative Criticism*, ed. David Rhoads and Kari Syreeni (London: T&T Clark, 2004), 268; Green, 'Narrative Criticism', in *Methods for Luke*, ed. Joel B. Green (Cambridge: CUP, 2010), 84–6.

98. Green, 'Narrative', 84; *The Theology of the Gospel of Luke* (Cambridge: CUP, 1995), 1–16. Green aptly calls attention to how Luke begins his narrative, and thus to the 'worlds' of Luke (2).

99. Ibid., 88.

economic context[100] and, on the other hand, shed further light on any theological readings of the text.[101] For instance, release (ἄφεσις) of the captives (Lk. 4.18) draws a vivid image of God's deliverance and liberation of his people. Yet, it cannot be read apart from the problematic reality of the indebtedness of the poor and of the landless under exploitative structures. Similarly, the messianic banquet (Lk. 13.25-30; 14.15) and the anticipation of abundant food (1.53; 6.21; 15.16-17; 16.21) not only portray an eschatological and theological world but also reflect the real concerns of the hungry, the scarcity of food and socio-economic disparity.

Paying due attention to the historical context encourages the reconstructing of Luke's community/ies) (Luke's *Sitz im Leben*) behind the text. But, as noted earlier, this effort has produced multivalent hypothetical communities of Luke under different and often opposite situations.[102] Johnson's caution against looking for Luke's historical community is insightful. He notes the issue of the genres of the Gospels which questions the legitimacy of reconstructing specific community/ies) behind the Gospels.[103]

Above all, the contours of debate concerning the Gospel community/ies) have somewhat subsided with the effects of Richard Bauckham's proposal regarding the Gospel audiences. He convincingly argues that the Gospels are written for a 'general Christian audience'.[104] If it can be safely said that Luke's Gospel is written for Christian communities in the late first-century Roman Empire, then, attention is fittingly given to the broad historical and socio-economic contexts

---

100. Peter Oakes, 'Methodological Issues in Using Economic Evidence in Interpretation of Early Christian Texts', in *Engaging Economics: New Testament Scenarios and Early Christian Reception*, ed. Bruce W. Longenecker and Kelly D. Liebengood (Grand Rapids: Eerdmans, 2009), 9–34.

101. Smit aptly draws attention to the connection between real experience of hunger and theological expectation of banquets. *Food*, 54.

102. See fn. 47 of this chapter.

103. Johnson, 'On Finding the Lukan Community: A Cautious Cautionary Essay', in *Contested Issues in Christian Origins and the New Testament: Collected Essays* (Leiden: Brill, 2013), 129–43. See also Graham Stanton, *Jesus and Gospel* (Cambridge: CUP, 2004), 192–3.

104. Richard Bauckham, ed., introduction to *The Gospels for All Christians: Rethinking the Gospel Audiences*, by Richard Bauckham (Edinburgh: T&T Clark, 1998), 1. See also Esler, 'Community and Gospel in Early Christianity: A Response to Richard Bauckham's *Gospels for All Christians*', *SJT* 51.2 (1998): 235–48; Bauckham, 'Response to Philip Esler', *SJT* 51.2 (1998): 249–53; Edward W. Klink III, 'The Gospel Community Debate: State of the Question', *CurBR* 3.1 (2004): 60–85. Note also Michael Wolter's critique of Bauckham's argument. While agreeing with a wider audience of the Gospels, he cautions, (1) It does not suggest that Luke emerges from nowhere, but he must have belonged to a community. (2) The distinction between real and intended readers must be made in that there must have been a specific intended readership. *Das Lukasevangelium*, HNT 5 (Tübingen: Mohr, 2008), 22–3.

of the first-century Graeco-Roman world, rather than to the reconstruction of a hypothetical community behind Luke's text.[105]

1.4 The Relation of the Gospel of Luke to Acts

The unity of Luke-Acts constitutes one final issue that we must address. This thesis assumes and affirms the narrative, thematic and authorial coherence of Luke-Acts despite the limitation of this thesis to the Gospel of Luke. The relationship between Luke and Acts has been revisited from authorial,[106] generic,[107] narrative,[108] theological[109] and reception–historical perspectives[110] since Parsons and Pervo's challenge to the scholarly assumption which follows Cadbury's long-standing 'hyphenated' Luke-Acts.[111] However, Bird's survey of recent discussion on the issue

---

105. By this, I do not aim to draw a specific narrative world of Luke's Gospel either. For instance, Moxnes sketches a Luke's community drawn from the narrative, noting that he does not look for 'a specific setting' but 'typical' life setting in a Graeco-Roman city. Moxnes, 'The Social-Context of Luke's Community', *Int* 48 (1994): 379–89 (381). In this regard, Bauckham's observation is to the point: 'Probably most Christian communities in the period when the canonical Gospels were being written were located in cities, … included some people, even if not many, from both ends of the socio-economic spectrum.' Bauckham, 'For Whom?', 24.

106. Patricia Walters, *The Assumed Authorial Unity of Luke and Acts: A Reassessment of the Evidence* (Cambridge: CUP, 2008), 3–8, 190–4. Her study challenges the authorial unity and suggests two different authors as a 'viable' option (194).

107. Richard Pervo, 'Israel's Heritage and Claims upon the Genre(s) of Luke and Acts: The Problems of a History', in *Jesus and the Heritage of Israel: Luke's Narrative Claim upon Israel's Legacy*, ed. David P. Moessner (Harrisburg: Trinity, 1999), 127–43. Pervo challenges the generic unity, noting 'There is tension between evident generic disunity and indisputable thematic unity' (135).

108. Tannehill, *Unity*, 2 vols (Philadelphia: Fortress, 1986, 1990); Marshall, 'Acts and the "Former Treatise"', in *The Book of Acts in Its Ancient Literary Setting*, ed. Bruce W. Winter and Andrew D. Clarke, vol. 1 of *The Book of Acts in Its First Century Setting*, ed. Bruce W. Winter (Grand Rapids: Eerdmans, 1993), 163–82; Johnson, 'Literary Criticism of Luke-Acts: Is Reception-History Pertinent?' *JSNT* 28 (2005): 159–62.

109. Marshall, '"Israel" and the Story of Salvation: One theme in Two Parts', *Heritage*, 340–57; 'How does One Write on the Theology of Acts?' in *Witness to the Gospel: The Theology of Acts*, ed. I. Howard Marshall and David Peterson (Cambridge: Eerdmans, 1998), 3–16. While rejecting the possibility of isolating the two different theologies of Luke and Acts from one another, he fully acknowledges: 'It is proper to consider [the] theology [of Acts] separately from that of the Gospel' (16).

110. C. Kavin Rowe, 'History, Hermeneutics and the Unity of Luke-Acts', *JSNT* 28 (2005): 131–57.

111. Mikeal C. Parsons and Richard I. Pervo, *Rethinking the Unity of Luke and Acts* (Minneapolis: Fortress, 1993), 3. They particularly question and re-examine the generic,

demonstrates that scholarly opinion on the unity of Luke-Acts remains firm.[112] Instead of joining the detailed argument on the issue, a brief rationale for limiting this thesis to Luke's Gospel while affirming the unity of Luke-Acts will suffice.

Simply put, Acts does not employ the term 'poor and rich'. The studies of Luke's wealth ethics often and rightly deal with both the Gospel and Acts despite the absence of the terms. However, the ways in which the Gospel expresses salvation are different although the significance of salvation and the concern for the poor continue in Acts.[113] First, in Acts, the salvation of the poor and the rich does not appear to be a primary issue; incorporation of the Gentiles into salvation constitutes the main question. While Luke's interest in the salvation of the Gentiles is noted from the beginning of the Gospel,[114] it does not fully develop until Acts.

Second, Luke's Gospel frequently employs mundane and socio-economic terms to communicate the message of salvation, whereas belief in Jesus, the Lord and the Saviour, (e.g. πίστευσον ἐπὶ τὸν κύριον Ἰησοῦν Acts 16.31) encapsulates salvation in Acts.[115] However, this does not suggest any thematic or theological disunity of Luke-Acts. In fact, the salvation of the poor and the rich is rather assumed in the community life of the believers in Jerusalem in Acts.[116] The believing community in Acts 2.44-46 and 4.32-37 is identified as the gathering of the poor and the rich, landless and landowners and haves and have-nots. Hence, with the affirmation of the unity of Luke-Acts, this thesis examines salient aspects of Luke's message of salvation in the Gospel.

1.5 Outline of the Thesis

This thesis has two parts. Part I takes a focused approach to specific socio-economic issues, namely, land (Chapter 2) and food and clothing (Chapter 3). The

---

narrative and theological unity of Luke and Acts. See Henry J. Cadbury, *The Making of Luke-Acts* (London: Macmillan, 1927), 11.

112. Bird, 'The Unity of Luke-Acts in Recent Discussion', *JSNT* 29.4 (2007): 434–5.

113. For the theological unity, see Marshall, 'Story of Salvation', 347–9 (348). Jesus is 'the proclaimed' and 'the proclaimer' in Luke-Acts. For special concern for the widows, see Acts 6.1; 9.39, 41; for healing ministry, see Acts 3.2-8; 8.5-8; 9.32-35; 14.8-10. Moreover, redemptive almsgiving is also hinted at in Acts 10 (cf. Acts 9.36-43). Although the terms are absent in Acts, those in need and widows as objects of almsgiving are clearly present (Acts 2.45; 4.35; 6.1; 9.39). See also Jacques Dupont, 'The Poor and Poverty in the Gospels and Acts', *Gospel Poverty*, 25; Autero, *Contexts*, 162.

114. Most notably, see Lk. 2.32; 3.23-38 (Luke's genealogy which traces back to Adam); 4.25-30 (God's favour on the Gentiles); 10.30-37; 17.11-19 (Luke's interest in Samaritans).

115. Ben Witherington, 'Salvation and Health in Christian Antiquity: The Soteriology of Luke-Acts in Its First Century Setting', *Witness*, 159–60.

116. The linguistic, thematic and theological unity is explicitly detected between Lk. 3.1-20 and Acts 2.29-40. See Tannehill, *Unity: Acts*, 29, 40.

significance of examining socio-economic issues at the beginning of this thesis (Part I) lies in their implications for the theological reading of Luke's Gospel in later chapters (Part II). Building on the analysis of Part I, Part II explores Luke's message of salvation in relation to socio-economic issues through a close examination of the texts.

Chapter 2 examines land in terms of landholding patterns, landowner and tenants and the issues related to land, namely, tax and debt. The examination unfolds oppressive socio-economic relations which are deeply embedded in the political–religious structures and illuminates socio-economic contexts of Luke's Gospel. Chapter 3 discusses two key socio-economic indicators, which are food and clothing. As they are stereotypical markers of wealth in antiquity, hunger and nakedness mark poverty. They describe the socio-economic condition of the people of the day. Economic disparity turns out to be a disturbing reality. This will shed further light on Luke's message of salvation in its socio-economic context. Hence the sketch of Luke's socio-economic context in Part I enhances the discussion of Part II which studies Luke's message of salvation in relation to socio-economic issues (Chapter 4) and the interpretation of the texts (Chapters 5, 6, 7, 8 and 9).

Chapter 4 examines major themes of salvation in Luke's Gospel which are linked to the following chapters (Chapters 5, 6, 7, 8 and 9). Chapter 5 draws attention to the salvation of the poor as Luke's Gospel promulgates it from the beginning of Jesus' ministry (Lk. 4.18-19). With noted concern given to the socio-economic aspects of the poor, Chapter 5 underscores the salvation of the poor in terms of divine mercy and justice (thus, reversal) in response to the problems of injustice of the world in which they live (Lk. 7.11-17; 16.19-31).

From a slightly different angle, Chapters 6, 7 and 8 explore salvation as the human enactment of divine mercy (thus, repentance) and examine the passages where Luke's paradigmatic question 'What must we/I do?' occurs (Lk. 3.1-20; 10.25-37; 12.16-21; 16.1-9; 18.18-30). The question is almost always responded to in socio-economic terms. Chapter 6 examines John the Baptist's teaching in Lk. 3.10-14, highlighting repentance in terms of doing mercy and justice. Chapter 7 inquires what the Law says to this question in the passages of Lk. 10.25-27 and 18.18-30. In both passages, the Law points to ἔλεος and ἐλεημοσύνη. Chapter 8 approaches the question by exploring the (im)proper use of wealth and salvation in Lk. 12.16-21 and 16.1-9. Hence the question in the passages under discussion is appreciated in relation to repentance, the Law and the (im)proper use of wealth.

Lastly, Chapter 9 develops from Chapters 6, 7 and 8 and directly responds to Chapter 5. It discusses the salvation of the rich in relation to that of the poor. While Lk. 14.15 pronounces the blessedness of the rich in their relation to the poor, the passage specifically draws the imagery of the messianic banquet in terms of divine reward. It anticipates the restored people, 'poor and rich', gathering around the table with the Messiah in the coming kingdom. Hence Part II features the salvation of the rich as well as the poor in terms of divine mercy, its human enactment and divine reward which is summed up as the restoration of the people of God.

Part One

SOCIO-ECONOMIC CONTEXTS OF LUKE'S GOSPEL

Chapter 2

WEALTH: LAND, TAX, DEBT

2.1 Introduction

This chapter examines land, the principal source of wealth of the state and of personal fortunes, and the issues pertaining to it – taxes and debt. Land is vital in Roman society.[1] It, first and foremost, produces food and generates wealth – taxes and rent – at the expense of the tenants and peasants.[2] Landed wealth is also closely linked with status.[3] Trimalchio, a fictitious character in *Satyricon*, adopted the lifestyle of the elite society of his time and took the mentality of the landowner through purchasing large estates with the wealth he gained from trade as a freedman.[4] He became a man of property, and thus joined the landed aristocracy at least in his lifestyle.[5]

Within the Jewish tradition, however, land signifies covenant rather than status. It is an identity marker which ties the people to their God.[6] Nonetheless,

---

1. M.I. Finley, ed., introduction to *Studies in Roman Property*, by M.I. Finley (Cambridge: CUP, 1976), 1; Finley, *Ancient Economy*, 2nd edn (London: Penguin, 1992), 89–91; Peter Garnsey and Richard Saller, *The Roman Empire: Economy, Society and Culture* (London: Duckworth, 1987), 64.

2. Garnsey and Saller, *Empire*, 109–10; Dorothy J. Crawford, 'Imperial Estates', *Roman Property*, 35–6.

3. Garnsey and Saller, *Empire*, 44–5; Finley, *Economy*, 50–1, 95.

4. Petronius, *Satyricon* 48, 53, 76; Paul Veyne, 'Vie de Trimalcion', *Annales. Économies, Sociétés, Civilisations* 16.2 (1961): 236, 240. See also Cicero, *Off.* 1.151.

5. In a legal sense, Trimalchio as a freedman could not attain political office. Yet, he openly boasts and indulges his lifestyle in the pattern of elite society of his time.

6. Walter Brueggemann, *The Land* (Philadelphia: Fortress, 1977), 3–4; Christopher J.H. Wright, *God's People in God's Land: Family, Land and Property in the Old Testament* (Grand Rapids: Eerdmans, 1990), 12; W.D. Davies, *The Gospel and the Land: Early Christianity and Jewish Territorial Doctrine* (Berkeley: University of California, 1974), 15–35. Note that the significance of land as a geographical and physical entity seems to experience a major shift to a cosmic, eschatological and spiritual one in NT times as Davies observes. The locus of covenant centres on the person, Jesus, instead of a place. *Land*, 366–70.

the economic value of land as wealth and property plays a central role in ancient agrarian societies regardless of the socio-political and religious background. Hence identifying the landed and the landless and examining socio-economic relations between them are germane in discussion of the socio-economic context of Luke's Gospel.

To this end, I will first sketch the land ownership and landholding patterns in Roman Palestine – Galilee and Judaea in particular – during the late Second Temple Period (STP) (63 BCE–70 CE). Next, I will identify the profile of landowners based on the general landscape of the period. Lastly, I will discuss the relationship between workers and landlords in terms of rent, tax and debt. These findings have implications for the historical – political and socio-economic contexts of Luke's Gospel.

2.2 Landholding Patterns in Roman Palestine

In the STP (530 BCE–70 CE), foreign rulers held ultimate jurisdiction over the land of Judaea except during the reign of the Hasmonaean Dynasty (140 BCE–63 BCE). Pompey's conquest of Syria (63 BCE) marked the end of the Hasmonaean kingdom and the beginning of Roman Palestine. Pompey limited the territories in Judaea. He reduced the Judaean kingdom drastically in size to Galilee, a part of Samaria, Judaea and eastern Idumea.[7] This arrangement may have given rise to a large number of landless and homeless Jews as those residing in the expanded territories during the Hasmonaean period now had to leave the areas or live as residents of gentile territories.[8]

Julius Caesar reversed Pompey's arrangements and restored the former Hasmonaean estates to the control of Jewish rulers, Hyrcanus and Antipater.[9] Whether this restoration of the territory to Jewish control brought changes in landholding patterns is unclear. Nevertheless, it seems evident that the Jewish

---

7. E. Mary Smallwood, *The Jews under Roman Rule: From Pompey to Diocletian: A Study in Political Relations* (Leiden: Brill, 1981), 27–9; Martin Goodman, *The Ruling Class of Judaea: The Origins of the Jewish Revolt against Rome A.D. 66–70* (Cambridge: CUP, 1987), 9.

8. Jack Pastor, *Land and Economy in Ancient Palestine* (London: Routledge, 1997), 89; Smallwood, *Jews*, 29. Smallwood notes that the diminished border of Judaea impinged on the economic life of the Jewish people due to its isolation from the coastal regions and the heavy taxation imposed upon it. See also S. Applebaum, 'Economic Life in Palestine', in *The Jewish People in the First Century II*, ed. S. Safrai and M. Stern (Amsterdam: CRINT, 1976), 637. Applebaum suggests that Pompey's land arrangement considerably increased the number of 'landless Jewish peasants' as he sees this phenomenon as 'a key to an understanding of the entire development of the agrarian problem in Judaea down to the great rebellion of 70 CE'.

9. Josephus, *Ant.* 13.395-397; 14.190-195.

temple elite and aristocracy benefited greatly. Hyrcanus, the high priest and the ethnarch and his sons were guaranteed the tithes paid to the temple; the lands possessed by their forefathers, the Hasmonaeans, were restored.[10] The wealth of Antipater and his sons grew to such a great extent out of the revenues that people complained about their accumulation of wealth.[11] Concomitantly, the Jewish authorities freely collected the tax 'levied on the whole country' and 'a variable land-tax' for the Roman authorities.[12]

2.2.1 Herod the Great

When the Roman Emperor appointed Herod the Great (37–4 BCE) as a client king of Judaea, a Judean king with an Idumaean father now oversaw land. Herod, well known for his massive building works including the expansion of the Temple in Jerusalem[13] and lavish public spending,[14] owned considerable estates. The size of his property must have been vast. He settled the veterans from his military campaigns – six thousand inhabitants according to Josephus – with the allotment of rich lands near Samaria.[15]

Land ownership, on the one hand, was passed from 'one ruling house to another – the Hellenistic monarchies, to the Hasmonaeans and the Herodians'.[16] Landholding patterns, on the other hand, indicate that 'the best lands became part of the royal possessions, either through confiscation or because their owners could not meet the heavy taxes which Herod exacted from the country people'.[17] Moreover, perpetual droughts and famine during Herod's reign (25–24 BCE) contributed to the increase of the landless class.[18] From earlier on, famine was one of the major factors which made small landowners into landless or debt-bondage slaves.[19] Hence several factors point to the increase of large landholdings at the expense of small landowners in this period.

---

10. Josephus, *Ant.* 14.202-212.
11. Josephus, *Ant.* 14.163.
12. Smallwood, *Jews*, 38–41.
13. Josephus, *Ant.* 16.142-145. Some of his major building works include Caesarea, Antipatris, Capharsaba and Cyprus.
14. Josephus, *Ant.* 16.136-149. Herod hosted perpetual festivals and games, sumptuously entertained guests and lavished them with generous gifts.
15. Josephus, *Ant.* 15.296; *J.W.* 1.403.
16. Seán Freyne, *Galilee: From Alexander the Great to Hadrian 323 BCE to 135 CE* (Edinburgh: T&T Clark, 1980), 163.
17. Freyne, *Galilee*, 164. See also Applebaum, 'Economic', 662. Applebaum observes, 'Down to 4 BCE the combination of Roman tribute and Herodian taxation, with religious dues, would have been extremely oppressive.'
18. Josephus, *Ant.* 15.299-300, 302-304. Regarding Herod's relief work during the famine, Applebaum suggests that it might not have been a free gift but 'a repayable loan'. 'Economic', 664.
19. Neh. 5.3.

2.2.2 Galilee: Herodian Economics

Upon Herod's death (4 BCE), his three sons became rulers of the Judaean state with reduced political powers as the ethnarch (Archaeleus 4 BCE–6 CE) and the tetrarchs (Herod Antipas 4 BCE–39 CE; Philip 4 BCE–34 CE). While Archaeleus, the ruler of Judaea and Samaria, was soon deposed (6 CE) and replaced by a Roman governor, Galilee remained under Herod Antipas's rule till 39 CE.[20] In many ways, Antipas continued what Herod the Great initiated.[21] He rapidly urbanized and Romanized Galilee.[22] He built and populated two major cities, Sepphoris and Tiberius.[23] The land in Galilee was intensely exploited to such a degree that 'almost every available plot of land in Galilee' was cultivated during this period.[24] Did this change of landscape in Galilee bring changes in landholding patterns? If the question is placed in a broader spectrum, do Herodian economics bring positive effects to the situation of the masses?

In an appraisal of Herodian economics, scholars have put forward two opposite views. One highlights the negative side of the Herodian economy due to heavy taxation and a monetized economy;[25] the other suggests that an economic boom resulted from creating employment through constant building works, developing arable land and maintaining political stability. Pastor and Jensen argue for this view.[26] They suggest an alternative appraisal of Herodian economics against a more traditional view which highlights the detrimental effects on the rural economy. It seems true that Herodian economic policies were successful at least to serve the Herodian rulers and leaders. Nonetheless, it is open to question to what degree

---

20. John H. Hayes and Sara R. Mandell, *The Jewish People in Classical Antiquity: From Alexander to Bar Kochba* (Louisville: John Knox, 1998), 146–50. See also Pastor, *Land*, 98–9, 110–15.

21. Freyne, 'Herodian Economics in Galilee', in *Modelling Early Christianity: Social-scientific Studies of the New Testament in its Context*, ed. Philip F. Esler (London: Routledge, 1995), 28.

22. Freyne, *Galilee*, 121–38; Morten Hørning Jensen, *Herod Antipas in Galilee*, WUNT 215 (Tübingen: Mohr, 2006), 251. Jensen, however, suggests a much more moderate view of the urbanization of Sepphoris and Tiberias under Antipas from the archaeological investigations.

23. Josephus, *Ant.* 18.27, 36-38.

24. Jonathan L. Reed, *Archaeology and the Galilean Jesus: A Re-examination of the Evidence* (Harrisburg: Trinity, 2000), 88.

25. Many scholars maintain that Herod's economic policies impoverished the populace and the landless class due to heavy taxes to pay for lavish spending. See Applebaum, 'Economic', 665-7; Freyne, *Galilee*, 183-4. See Josephus, *Ant.* 16.154-155. Tacitus, *Ann.* 2.42: 'The provinces … of Syria and Judaea, exhausted by their burdens, implored a reduction of tribute.'

26. Pastor, *Land*, 110-15; Jensen, *Antipas*, 249-51. For instance, Pastor argues that Herod's extensive building works boosted the economy through creating employment which allowed extra income to the populace.

the Herodians in general eased the economic situation of the masses through urbanization and development.

Applebaum and Freyne argue that urbanization and monetization induced distressful conditions of the peasantry.[27] They suggest a close link between landholding patterns and Antipas's urbanization project. The surrounding countryside had to feed the urban population who did not work on the land. The monetized economy of the Herodian Period, spurred on by the cash payment of taxes, forced the traditional peasantry to sell their food. This led to small landholdings at or near subsistence level being swallowed up by large proprietors.

A shift in landholding patterns continued towards large estates. This in turn brought changes in agricultural structures from poly-cropping to specialization in crops for capital investments such as viticulture or the olive industry.[28] Also, considering the notoriously high tax rate during the Herodian Period,[29] we may safely say that the expansion of large estates was closely associated with the struggles of traditional peasants who subsisted on small plots of land.

2.2.3 Judaea

While Galilee remained under Herodian rule till mid-first century CE, Judaea became a Roman province early on in 6 CE. Did this change of political structure affect land ownership and landholding patterns in Judaea? Two of the salient events are pertinent to our discussion here. Quirinius, the governor of Syria, was sent to Judaea (6 CE), which was a newly organized imperial province, to take a census obviously for *tributum capitis* – 'a Roman denarius per head'[30] – and to dispose of Archaeleus's property.[31] Thus two things took place in this process: (1) direct

---

27. Applebaum, 'Economic', 664-7; Freyne, 'Herodian', 23-46. Freyne's view has shifted from a positive one to a negative one. He suggested in his earlier work that the Herodians's rule may have brought some 'stabilizing effect on the economy of Galilee'. See *Galilee*, 191-2.

28. Freyne, 'Herodian', 33-4; See John S. Kloppenborg, *The Tenants in the Vineyard*, WUNT 195 (Tübingen: Mohr, 2006), 287; Ze've Safrai, *The Economy of Roman Palestine* (London: Routledge, 1994), 126.

29. Reed, *Archaeology*, 72-3; Douglas Oakman, *Jesus and the Economic Questions of His Day* (Queenston, Canada: Edwin Mellen, 1986), 72. Josephus and Tacitus provide several indirect evidences of Herodian taxation: (1) the tribute paid to Rome, (2) complaints of people over heavy taxation after Herod's death and (3) general accounts of the lavish lifestyle of the Herods. See Josephus, *Ant.* 14.200-204; 15.132; 16.154-155; 17.318; Tacitus, *Ann.* 2.42.

30. Smallwood, *Jews*, 151-3. See Mt. 22.17-18; Mk 12.14; Lk. 20.22, 24-25. Josephus, *Ant.* 17.354; 18.1-2.

31. Josephus records that Quirinius's main purpose for his visit to Judaea was 'to take an account of their substance, and to dispose of Archelaus's money' (ἀποδωσόμενος τὰ Ἀρχελάου χρήματα) (*Ant.* 18.2). Here ἀποδίδωμι indicates either to lease the property or to sell the property. See Applebaum, 'Economic', 658. Although Applebaum prefers property

Roman taxation and (2) shift of the ownership of royal estates from Archaeleus's families to the imperial authorities.

Although this political change did not effect a major shift in the land ownership of private estates in Judaea till 70 CE,[32] the *tributum capitis*, which was imposed on every person in addition to a land-tax, the *tributum soli*, became a heavy burden especially for the peasantry.[33] The Roman direct taxation was one of the main causes of the revolt led by Judas.[34] After King Agrippa I's short reign (41–44 CE), the Judaean state remained under the rule of Roman governors from 44 CE till 70 CE. The Roman land policy, however, was to leave land ownership in local hands unless the land was conquered in war.[35]

Hence there seemed no drastic changes of land ownership to the hands of Romans in Judaea and Galilee before the War (66–70 CE).[36] It mostly remained with local Jewish landowners despite political changes while royal estates which belonged to the Hasmonaeans were sold or leased as imperial property. Upon the War,[37] however, both small and large landholdings were greatly affected. After 70 CE the Judaean land was considered to be the 'property of the Roman state' – *ager publicus populi Romani*.[38]

Landholding patterns continued to shift towards large estates during the late STP despite the persistent survival of traditional small landowners according to literary and archaeological evidence.[39] Although it is difficult to distinguish small landholdings from leased estates in archaeological surveys, the coexistence of

---

leased to sold, either case points to maintaining the tenancy or leasing structure with possible modified terms followed by shifted land ownership.

32. Goodman, *Ruling*, 59; Oakman, *Economic*, 69.

33. It seems hard to pinpoint upon whom the *tributum soli* fell. Smallwood notes that it was 'payable by only well-to-do'. *Jews*, 160. Conversely, Oakman indicates that the burden fell upon the Jewish peasantry. *Economic*, 68–9.

34. Josephus, *Ant.* 18.1-4. Acts 5.37.

35. A.N. Sherwin-White, *Roman Foreign Policy in the East: 168 B.C. to A.D. 1* (London: Duckworth, 1984), 232. Josephus, *J.W.* 6.333.

36. See Oakman, *Economic*, 46.

37. In relation to our discussion, the cause of the War has been explained as the socio-economic conditions during this period. See Goodman, *Ruling*, 109–33. Contra Pastor in agreement with Jonathan J. Price, who looks for the cause in 'ideological and practical complaints'. See Pastor, *Land*, 136–7; Price, *Jerusalem Under Siege: The Collapse of the Jewish State 66–70 C.E.* (Leiden: Brill, 1992), 45–50.

38. Oakman, *Economic*, 67; Pastor, *Land*, 160; Freyne, *Galilee*, 166–9.

39. Reed, *Archaeology*, 88; Kloppenborg, *Tenants*, 287; Freyne, 'Herodian', 34–5; Yizhar Hirschfeld, 'Ramat Hanadiv and Ein Gedi: Property versus Poverty in Judea before 70', in *Jesus and Archaeology*, ed. James H. Charlesworth (Grand Rapids: Eerdmans, 2006), 384–92. Hirschfeld strongly suggests that there were large landowners who held the quality lands from Herod's time and onward, from the archaeological findings.

small and large landholdings seems plausible.⁴⁰ Lin Foxhall, however, suggests that even large estates were often divided into small plots for intense exploitation of land.⁴¹

For the summary of this section, Applebaum's observation of landholding patterns from the late Hasmonaeans and onward is apt:

> Two parallel processes were at work in the country in the first century BCE; on the one hand, the growth of large estates which assimilated complete villages in tenancy, and on the other hand, the conversion of single farmsteads into agglomerations of a number of homes by the addition of settlers or by natural increase of population.⁴²

What is inferred then is that heavy taxes and food shortages (due to famine at times) made it very difficult for small landowners to preserve their small properties. Large landholdings grew at the expense of the small landowners.

2.3 Profile of Landowners

Our discussion thus far points to no drastic shift of land ownership from the locals to the Romans in Galilee and Judaea despite the changes of political regimes. Yet it suggests a continuous expansion of large estates during the period. This raises a further enquiry: Who were the large landowners? Before drawing a profile of large landowners, a brief note is necessary on the ethnic identity of those who inhabited in Galilee and Judaea. Archaeological findings suggest that the majority of the inhabitants at the heart of Galilee and Judaea were Jewish while the coastal Hellenized cities had a predominant gentile population perhaps after Pompey's resettlement.⁴³ There were few gentile residents in Jerusalem, the indisputable cultural and religious centre of the Jews. Even the two most Hellenized cities in Galilee, Sepphoris and Tiberius,⁴⁴ were mainly Jewish in terms of their residents, not to mention the surrounding villages.⁴⁵ Hence most large landowners in Galilee and Judaea appeared to be Jewish.

---

40. Freyne, 'Herodian', 34–5.
41. Lin Foxhall, 'The Dependent Tenant: Land Leasing and Labour in Italy and Greece', *JRS* 80 (1990): 97.
42. Applebaum, 'Economic', 643.
43. Ibid., 632.
44. Josephus records that Antipas brought the inhabitants, mainly Galileans both rich and poor, by force to Tiberius but under attractive conditions – making slaves freedmen, providing land and housing – because the city was on top of old graves which made the inhabitants ritually unclean (*Ant.* 18.36-38).
45. Mark Alan Chancey and Adam Lowry Porter, 'Archaeology of Roman Palestine', *NEA* 64.4 (2001): 179–80. Chancey and Porter affirm that archaeological findings of 'ritual

Here three major groups of large landowners will be further identified as (1) members of the Herodian family who ruled during the period, (2) local wealthy aristocrats who were affiliated to the Herodian rulers and (3) the high priestly families as religious leaders who controlled the flow of wealth through the Temple throughout the period.

2.3.1 Herodian Family

Herod and his families owned large estates. Herod acquired and accumulated estates from inheritance,[46] from confiscation[47] and from his kingship.[48] Herod seems to have owned lands everywhere – Jericho, Caesarea, Galilee, Idumaea, Samaria – cities and countryside alike.[49] It is even suggested that more than half of the kingdom belonged to Herod.[50] Royal estates during the Herodian Period extended far beyond Galilee and Judaea. They were frequently found outside central Galilee and Judaea in the villages of the Great Plain in Galilee, in West Samaria where a number of towers were excavated and in Jericho.[51] All these estates were particularly identified by Josephus and Aristeas as the most fertile lands.[52] They also produced valuable products such as wine, olive oil and balsam.

Josephus also records that Herod's sister, Salome, owned estates in Jamnia and the Jordan Valley which were left to Julia, Caesar's wife, upon her death (*Ant*. 18.31). Antipas was no exception in owning large estates since he was able to distribute land to those whom he forced to move to Tiberias.[53] Interestingly, Luke mentions Joanna, the wife of Herod's steward (ἐπίτροπος)[54] Chuza (Lk. 8.3). He could have been 'either manager of a royal estate or manager of the estates and finances of Antipas's whole realm' and '[a member] of Herod's court at Tiberias'.[55] Thus, the Herodian families as the royals of the period naturally became large landowners.

---

baths and fragments of stone vessels found near the acropolis' attest to a predominant Jewish population. Thus, they are sceptical of the city's predominantly Graeco-Roman character. Yet, both cities politically promoted the Roman regime and culturally adopted Hellenism despite the predominant presence of the Jewish population. See Freyne, *Galilee*, 123, 133; Jensen, *Antipas*, 135–6. Josephus, *J.W.* 3.30-32.

46. Josephus, *Ant.* 14.8-10, 80-81.
47. See Josephus, *Ant*.15.5-7; 17.305, 307; Applebaum, 'Economic', 657; Pastor, *Land*, 101.
48. Pastor, *Land*, 100–1; Freyne, *Galilee*, 163–4; Josephus, *Ant*. 15.342-345.
49. Applebaum, 'Economic', 657–8.
50. Pastor, *Land*, 103.
51. Applebaum, 'Economic', 657–8.
52. Josephus, *J.W.* 3.42, 517-519; 4.473; *Let. Aris.*, 112–13.
53. Pastor, *Land*, 133. He indicates that Tiberias is most likely part of royal land.
54. Also in Mt. 20.8.
55. Bauckham, 'Paul and Other Jews with Latin Names in the New Testament', in *Paul, Luke and the Graeco-Roman World: Essays in Honour of Alexander J. M. Wedderburn*, ed. Alf Christophersen et al., JSNTSup 217 (London: T&T Clark, 2003), 220.

2.3.2 Local Wealthy Aristocrats

Leading aristocrats whose economic basis was built on land were also large landowners. Occasionally part of the royal estates or land which had been confiscated were granted as gifts to political adherents of the regime. Josephus mentions that Ptolemy, Herod's friend, owned a village called Arus.[56] Costobarus, one of Herod's chief men, hid the sons of Babas, chief enemies of Herod, in his own farms (ἐν οἰκείοις χωρίοις) with an expectation of advantages once the political power changed.[57] Politically associated leading aristocrats – possibly the Herodians[58] – were wealthy men who owned large estates. Not surprisingly, these principal men were urban dwellers most probably in Sepphoris, Tiberias and Jerusalem. Josephus lists men of high standing (εὐσχήμων)[59] in Tiberias and refers to Crispus who has 'estates beyond Jordan'.[60] These men were pro-Roman and loyal to the ruling party (Agrippa II).

In another place, Josephus mentions 600 principal men of the city (τοὺς πρώτους τῆς δήμου) in Tiberias.[61] As a result of Antipas's settlement arrangement in Tiberias, there were some wealthy people who came to live there. Nobles, military commanders and leading people of Galilee (τοῖς μεγιστᾶσιν αὐτοῦ καὶ τοῖς χιλιάρχοις καὶ τοῖς πρώτοις τῆς Γαλιλαίας) were present at Antipas's birthday banquet (Mk 6.21). There seems no doubt that these principal men were wealthy landowners.[62] They were very likely absentee landowners who resided in urban centres but had their landed wealth in the countryside.[63] Luke mentions absentee landowners who entrusted their properties to managers.[64] The Synoptic Gospels take for granted that large absentee landowners lease their estates.[65]

---

56. Josephus, *J.W.* 2.69.
57. Josephus, *Ant.* 263-265.
58. Matthew and Mark mention the Herodians (Ἡρῳδιανοί) who plotted against Jesus. Also, both Gospels connect Herodians with the Pharisees in their collaborated scheme to trap Jesus (Mt. 22.16; Mk 3.6; 12.13). Josephus refers to Ἡρῴδην as Herod's party or those on Herod's side. *Ant.* 14.335, 479.
59. Also in Mk 15.43; Acts 13.50; 17.12.
60. Josephus, *Life* 33.
61. Josephus, *J.W.* 2.641; *Life* 64.
62. Pastor, *Land*, 134; Applebaum, 'Economic', 663. Applebaum notes that 'city-councillor' is 'often synonymous with "man of wealth"'.
63. Absentee landlords were common in Roman society and the land was often managed by slaves or tenants. Finley, *Economy*, 76; Hamel, *Poverty*, 152.
64. See Lk. 12.42-48; 16.1-8; cf. 14.18. Luke also mentions traditional large landowners who probably cultivated their estates as family businesses or with hired workers (12.13-21; 15.11-31). See also Mt. 21.28-29; Mk 1.20.
65. Mt. 21.33-41; Mk 12.1-9; Lk. 20.9-16; *Gos. Thom.* 65. See also Kloppenborg, *Tenants*, 279.

As is widely accepted, 'The principal economic asset of ... most ancient cities was its rural hinterland'.[66] Likewise many villages surrounded Sephhoris and Tiberias was situated on the lake and in fertile land.[67] It is not unreasonable to suggest that Galilean urban centres drew their wealth from the rural areas and fishing industry. In this respect, what were urban–rural relations like? Were they parasitic or reciprocal? Jensen's survey of urban–rural relations demonstrates what Finley indicated long ago – 'ranging over a whole spectrum, from complete parasitism at one end to full symbiosis at the other'.[68] It seems impossible to pinpoint the relations one way or the other. Nonetheless, Josephus's depiction of Galileans over against the inhabitants of the cities is interesting. As Freyne observed, the Galileans in Josephus's *Life* were 'the country people as distinct from the inhabitants of the major towns ... , but not essentially revolutionary or subversive'.[69] Their attitude towards urban dwellers, however, was unquestionably antagonistic and hostile.[70]

The situation was not much different in Judaea. Jerusalem was both a religious and economic centre. Due to its unique standing as a cultic centre, most of Jerusalem's income came from outside despite its relatively developed commerce and trade.[71] The Temple as a central axis of the city represented 'a large capital accumulation'.[72] A considerable number of wealthy aristocrats lived in Jerusalem, similar to those absentee landowners in Tiberias and Sepphoris. Goodman argues that the large landowners in Jerusalem were originally 'the creatures of Herod who had been granted land and position within the state'.[73]

Judaea was soon under the direct rule of Roman governors. The Roman authorities seemed to prefer Jewish religious leaders – high priests – to the Herodian aristocrats. Hence the Roman authorities granted power to temple leaders, that is, to the leader of the Sanhedrin as the representatives of the Jewish people.[74] The

---

66. Garnsey, 'Economy and Society of Mediolanum under the Principate', in *Cities, Peasants and Food in Classical Antiquity: Essays in Social and Economic History*, ed. Walter Scheidel (Cambridge: CUP, 1998), 45.

67. Josephus, *Life* 346; *J.W.* 3.516-521. Freyne, 'Herodian', 34, 37.

68. Finley, *Economy*, 125 (for parasitic relations). Contra Jensen, *Antipas*, 9–30. Jensen's conclusion from the archaeological surveys of two urban centres and rural areas of Galilee under Antipas suggests that it was a period of stability and rural villages in Galilee were 'expanding and thriving' during this period (249–51).

69. Josephus, *Life* 30, 123. Freyne, 'The Galileans in the Light of Josephus' *Vita*', *NTS* 26 (1980): 412; Tessa Rajak, *Josephus: The Historian and His Society*, 2nd edn (London: Duckworth, 2002), 151. Rajak comments that Josephus's Galileans are indeed 'dubious characters'.

70. Applebaum, 'Economic', 663–4.

71. Goodman, *Ruling*, 52. Note that when famine hit Judaea, Jerusalem became extremely vulnerable. Josephus, *Ant.* 20.51-52.

72. Applebaum, 'Economic', 691.

73. Goodman, *Ruling*, 40.

74. Josephus, *Ant.* 20.251.

unique position of high priests was unquestioned[75] although their legitimacy was open to question from the Herodian–Roman period.[76] The high priestly office ceased to be hereditary from this period. Nevertheless, two prestigious families produced half the high priests in this period: the Boethus and Annas (Ananus).[77]

2.3.3 High Priestly Families

This leads us to the last group of landowners: high priestly families. Many of them had their permanent residence in Jerusalem[78] as temple officials and political leaders. Frequently the high priestly families occupied chief positions in the Temple such as captain of the Temple (ὁ στρατηγὸς [τοῦ ἱεροῦ])[79] or treasurers who took care of 'landed property, wealth and treasure, administration of flood of tribute money and votive offerings as well as private capital deposited at the Temple'.[80] Moreover, they supervised markets in the Temple (e.g. animals for sacrifices), and thus exercised their influence on various matters, including economic ones. Complaints by the people reflected in the much later Talmudic literature indicate that they abused their monopoly of wealth and power:

> Woe is me because of the house of Boethus; woe is me because of their staves! Woe is me because of the house of Hanin [or Annas], woe is me because of their whisperings! Woe is me because of the house of Kathros, woe is me because of their pens! Woe is me because of the house of Ishmael the son of Phabi, woe is me because of their fists! For they are High Priests and their sons are [Temple] treasurers and their sons-in-law are trustees and their servants beat the people with staves.[81]

---

75. Josephus's account indirectly expresses the discrepancy between the high priestly position and those who occupy it. *Ant.* 15.403-405; 18.90-95; 20.6.

76. Joachim Jeremias, *Jerusalem in the Time of Jesus: An Investigation into Economic and Social Conditions during the New Testament Period* (London: SCM, 1969), 158–9. Herod began to appoint and depose high priests 'arbitrarily'. Josephus reports that there were twenty-eight high priests from Herod's reign till Titus's destruction of the Temple (*Ant.* 20.251). Even in earlier days, there were records that high priestly offices were bought by bribing the king (2 Macc. 4.7-10, 24).

77. E. Mary Smallwood, 'High Priests and Politics in Roman Palestine', *JTS* 18 (1962): 14–15. The Boethus were dominant under Herod while Annas's family kept the high priestly office under Roman governors.

78. Jeremias, *Jerusalem*, 96–7.

79. Lk. 22.4, 52; Acts 4.1; 5.24, 26. Josephus, *Ant.* 20.131.

80. Jeremias, *Jerusalem*, 97, 99, 166. He remarks on the 'great luxury' of the residences of the high priestly families.

81. B. Pesah. 57a. Translation is from Isidore Epstein, *Soncino Babylonian Talmud*. AWOL. 10 August 2015, http://ancientworldonline.blogspot.co.uk/2012/01/online-soncino-babylonian-talmud.html

Similarly, Josephus plainly reports on the great riches of the high priestly families, and how the high priests and their servants exploited the tithes which were other priests' dues:

> But as for the high priest, Ananias, he increased in glory every day, and this to a great degree … ; for he was a great hoarder up of money: … he also had servants who were very wicked, who joined themselves to the boldest sort of the people, and went to the thrashing-floors, and took away the tithes that belonged to the priests by violence, and did not refrain from beating such as would not give these tithes to them. So the other high priests acted in the like manner, as did those his servants, without any one being able to prohibit them; so that [some of the] priests, that of old were wont to be supported with those tithes, died for want of food.[82]

Hence the outrage from the outset of the War (66–70 CE) against the high priest, Ananias, was not surprising.[83]

Large landowners were political rulers and temple aristocracy. Indeed, ancient economies were intrinsically embedded in their socio-political structure.[84] Priestly groups in ancient societies were often 'in a unique position to make demands on the economic surplus'.[85] Josephus, who drew his lineage from both royal and priesthood lines, was a priest and owned estates near Jerusalem.[86] Hence it is not difficult to assume that influential priestly families in the period had landed wealth

---

82. Josephus, *Ant.* 20.205-207. The poor priests most probably lived in the villages of Judaea like Zechariah who came for his service to the Temple temporarily (Lk. 1.23, 39-40).

83. Josephus, *J.W.* 2.426. They set fire to the house of Ananias, the high priest and later killed him with his brother. Note James S. McLaren, 'Corruption among the High Priesthood: A Matter of Perspective', in *A Wandering Galilean: Essays in Honour of Seán Freyne*, ed. Zuleika Rodgers et al., JSJSup 132 (Leiden: Brill, 2009), 146–56. He argues that Josephus's account (*J.W.* 2.426-442) and rabbinic tradition (*Pesah.* 57a) do not necessarily reflect the populace's animosity towards the high priests and their corruption. Nonetheless, his reading of Josephus underestimates that the accounts reflect Josephus's, and thus the first-century Judaean aristocrats' perspective.

84. Karl Polanyi, 'The Economy as Instituted Process', in *Trade and Market in the Early Empires: Economies in History and Theory*, ed. Karl Polanyi et al. (Glencoe, IL: Falcon's Wing, 1957), 250–6.

85. Gerhard E. Lenski, *Power and Privilege: A Theory of Social Stratification* (New York: McGraw-Hill, 1966), 67.

86. Josephus, *Life* 1–2. cf. From an earlier period of Jewish history, it was testified that priests owned estates (1 Kgs 2.26; Amos 7.17). Yet, Torah does not sanction priests owning land (Deut. 10.9; 12.12; 18.1). Note that Barnabas, a Levite, owned a field which belonged to him (Acts 4.37).

near Jerusalem or in the countryside.[87] In this regard, Luke's treatment of the chief priests is intriguing. Chief priests (ἀρχιερεύς) in Luke's Gospel are grouped with elders, scribes or wealthy men (principal men) and geographically confined to Jerusalem.[88] They were depicted as the powerful in Jerusalem. They almost always appear in the context of plotting to kill Jesus.[89]

Furthermore, Jesus' parable of the tenants in the vineyard is illuminating in that the parable is told to chief priests and religious leaders in Jerusalem.[90] This parable, on the one hand, as Kloppenborg observes, reflects the economic situation of first-century Roman Palestine: (1) large landholdings with specialization in crops, especially viticulture which is the most capital intensive and (2) hostile relationship between absentee landowners and tenants.[91] The parable, on the other hand, identifies chief priests and leaders in Jerusalem who in reality are large landowners with tenants. By doing this, the parable reminds them of God's ownership of the land, one of the major themes throughout the scriptural tradition.[92]

The significance of socio-economic relations among the people is strongly recalled from its intertextual relationship with Isa. 5.1-7. In Isaiah, what immediately follows is a denouncement of the accumulation of properties and estates (Isa. 5.8-9). The two stories diverge when judgement is pronounced. Unlike Isaiah where judgement is pronounced upon the vineyard (Isa. 5.5-6) which is the house of Israel (Isa. 5.7), the Gospel specifically points to the tenants in the parable who were in reality both large landowners and religious leaders in Jerusalem (Lk. 20.16).[93]

2.4 Tenants, Tax and Debt

We have examined the expansion of large landholdings at the expense of small landowners and the identity of landowners. These findings indicate an increase of the landless who either turned to banditry,[94] or moved to cities, or became tenants (γεωργοί) or hired workers (μίσθιοι) of their own land or of large estates. I will now turn to those who worked on the land either as tenants or hired workers

---

87. M. Stern, 'Aspects of Jewish Society: The Priesthood and Other Classes', *Jewish People*, 587, 600–1.

88. Steve Mason, *Josephus, Judea, and Christian Origins: Methods and Categories* (Peabody: Hendrickson, 2009), 351–3.

89. Lk. 9.22; 19.47; 20.10; 22.2, 4, 52, 54, 66; 23.4, 10, 13; 24.20. cf. Lk. 3.1 provides a historical context of the high priesthood.

90. Lk. 20.9-16//Mt. 21:33-41//Mk 12:1-9.

91. Kloppenborg, *Tenants*, 279–314.

92. Wright, *God's People*, 12–15, 109–10; Norman C. Habel, *The Land is Mine: Six Biblical Land Ideologies* (Minneapolis: Fortress, 1995), 44–53, 98.

93. Joel B. Green, *The Gospel of Luke*, NICNT (Grand Rapids: Eerdmans, 1997), 704–5.

94. Goodman, *Ruling*, 63. Josephus, *Ant.* 20.124.

and their economic relationship with the landlords which was entangled with the issues of rent, tax and debt.

2.4.1 Profile of Tenants and Rent

While tenant farming was quite common during the period,[95] tenancy was not a 'monochrome institution'.[96] Among tenants, there were 'owner-occupiers', 'tenant-farmers' and 'farm labourers working for a wage'.[97] Small landowners may have worked as tenants of large estates while working on their own plots. 'Inheritance' and 'dowry practices' seem to have resulted in traditional landholdings being split into smaller plots, in which case peasants needed to work as tenants to feed their family members.[98]

Others became tenants of their own land either temporarily due to a debt contract[99] or permanently once their plot was absorbed into nearby large estates.[100] Compulsory labour was another possibility when peasants were indebted to creditor landlords. Hired workers also cultivated large estates under the supervision of managers or family members as the Synoptic Gospels frequently attest.[101] They were paid in food at least in part (Lk. 15.17). There were also daily labourers whose circumstances were a lot more precarious as seen from Matthew's account of workers who waited all day to be hired (Mt. 20.2-7) and slaves who worked in the field and tended sheep and yet were supposed to serve the meal for the master (Lk. 17.7).

Regarding rents, tenants paid a fixed percentage of their harvest in rent or paid a fixed amount in money or in produce. Half the produce was paid in rent while the tenancy or lease usually went for five to six years.[102] During the tenancy, the tenants maintained relative power over the land with less supervision by landlords, particularly if tenants were under fixed rents, either in kind or in cash. Yet the danger arose when unpredictable factors such as bad weather conditions affected the yield. In that case, the tenants still had to pay the fixed rents.[103] The contracts varied widely and often followed local tradition as unwritten customs of the past.

---

95. Safrai, *Economy*, 335.

96. Garnsey and Saller, *Empire*, 72. In addition, there were also wealthy tenants who leased substantial areas of land on a larger scale and managed it through slaves. See Dennis P. Kehoe, *Investment, Profit, and Tenancy: The Jurists and the Roman Agrarian Economy* (Ann Arbor: University of Michigan, 1997), 174–8.

97. Garnsey and Saller, *Empire*, 76.

98. Reed, *Archaeology*, 85.

99. Moshe Gil, 'The Decline of the Agrarian Economy in Palestine under Roman Rule', *JESHO* (2006): 306.

100. Garnsey and Saller, *Empire*, 77.

101. Mt. 21.28-29; Mk 1.20; Lk. 15.11-31.

102. Applebaum, 'Economic', 659; Safrai, *Economy*, 332.

103. Hamel, *Poverty*, 158–9.

The general rule, however, was 'one quarter for land use, one quarter for labo[u]r, another quarter for use of tools and animals and the remainder for seeds. If the landowner provided everything ... and paid taxes, the sharecropper received one fourth of the yield for the work of his family.'[104]

Archaeological surveys seem to show the increase of tenancy. Reed observes that 'the trend points to a rise of larger holdings and leasing at the expense of small holdings'.[105] Also, frequent references to vineyard (ἀμπελών) in relation to tenants (γεωργοί) in the Gospels attest to the growth of tenants and day labourers and the accumulation of land by the few in Palestine.[106]

2.4.2 Burdens of Tax

As a part of the contracts between tenants and landlords, tax was often an issue. While a poll tax, *tributum capitis*, was imposed on everyone, a land-tax, *tributum soli*, and religious tithes were more controversial. There seemed to be several tithes due every year. Following a combination of statements from Deuteronomy, Numbers and Nehemiah, one tithe was owed to the Levites (priests) and another to Jerusalem. Every third and sixth year a tithe was given to the poor.[107] Besides there was possibly a double or triple taxation during the period, that is, Roman tribute and local taxation and Temple tax. Hence Oakman observes that Jews in Roman Palestine were in a unique situation where tax burdens may have come from three parties – priests, Herodians and procurators.[108] This intolerable tax burden resulted in 'the growth of tenancy and the landless class'.[109] The Gospels portray the possibility of losing land in the process of settling debts, otherwise of resulting in imprisonment or slavery.[110]

In contrast Sanders comments that a double taxation was not peculiar or particularly oppressive in Roman Palestine as it was rather 'standard' in the Roman Empire. He estimates that the tax was less than 30 per cent of the income based on the above-mentioned tithe system, Temple tax and Roman tax (12.5 per cent of the crops).[111] The difficulty of pinpointing the percentage of tax during the period remains due to lack of evidence. Nonetheless, a crucial question for our discussion is this: On whom were religious tithes and Roman tax imposed, tenants

---

104. Hamel, *Poverty*, 155–6.

105. Reed, *Archaeology*, 87.

106. Kloppenborg, *Tenants*, 290–300. Mt. 21.33-41//Mk 12.1-9//Lk. 20.9-16.

107. E.P. Sanders, *Judaism: Practice and Belief 63 BCE–66 CE* (London: SCM, 1992), 148–9. Deut. 14.28-29; 26.12; Num. 18.21-32; Neh. 10.37-39; Jub. 32.9-15. Josephus, *Ant.* 4.69, 205, 240. cf. Tob. 1.6-8.

108. Oakman, 'Jesus and Agrarian Palestine: The Factor of Debt', *Peasants*, 19.

109. Oakman, 'Debt', 25.

110. Ibid., 27. Mt. 5.25; 18.23-25; Lk. 12.58.

111. Sanders, *Judaism*, 160–9. cf. Applebaum, 'Economic', 665–7; Oakman, *Economic*, 72. Oakman's estimation ranges from one-half to two thirds.

or landlords? Finley observes that the burden of taxation 'lay most heavily, directly or indirectly, on those who work the land' in the Roman Empire.[112]

Likewise, there seems no doubt that the Roman legal system favoured the landed.[113] Roman law played a crucial role in protecting the property of the landed.[114] The pattern of social–economic disparity is strengthened and maintained through the property (land), the law and occupation (landlord and tenants). The legal system protected the land, the chief source of wealth and its inheritance. Land further generates wealth at the expense of the peasants and tenants.[115] Thus, not only is the pre-industrial Roman economy deeply embedded in the social and political system but the whole system reinforces the interests of those who have wealth, status and power.

The situation was more complex among the Jews in Roman Palestine. As prescribed in the Torah, Jewish landlords, not to mention religious leaders,[116] were expected to champion the rights of the landless.[117] Though not all, many absentee landowners, including chief priests in Jerusalem, were leading aristocrats in urban centres – Tiberias and Sepphoris. Landlords constituted councils which regulated taxation in local terms.[118] The Sanhedrin functioned as 'a tax-collection body'.[119] The Jewish ruling class, as the landowners, often sided with Roman authority.[120]

When Judaea became a Roman province (6 CE), the direct Roman taxation gave rise to a strong opposition from all the Jews because of the fact that they should pay tax directly to the Romans. However, large landowners soon became persuaded by Joazar, the high priest. Many consented to it while others rebelled because direct taxation was thought of as slavery. Josephus's account is as follows:

> The Jews, although at the beginning they took the report of a taxation heinously, yet did they leave off any further opposition to it, by the persuasion of Joazar, who was the son of Boethus, and high priest; so they, being over-persuaded by Joazar's words, gave an account of their estates, without any dispute about it. Yet was there one Judas, a Gaulonite, of a city whose name was Gamala, who, taking with him Sadduc, a Pharisee, became zealous to draw them to a revolt, who

---

112. Finley, *Economy*, 91.
113. Finley, 'Private Farm Tenancy in Italy before Diocletian', *Roman Property*, 109; Kehoe, *Investment*, 181–3.
114. Garnsey and Saller, *Empire*, 110.
115. Ibid., 109–10.
116. The high priestly families were the most prominent ruling class during the late STP in Judaea as noted. Although their power was limited to religious office, they remained influential. See Goodman, *Ruling*, 29–50; Jeremias, *Jerusalem*, 193–8.
117. Note Lev. 25.25-8, 35-55; Deut. 15.1-18; Exod. 22.25-7.
118. Hamel, *Poverty*, 149; Applebaum, 'Economic', 663.
119. Goodman, *Ruling*, 116.
120. Pastor, *Land*, 145–6; Jeremias, *Jerusalem*, 195–6.

both said that this taxation was no better than an introduction to slavery, and exhorted the nation to assert their liberty. (*Ant.* 18.3-4)

Hence the landlords manipulated the matters over land for their own benefit. A strong animosity of tenants against landlords thereby is not surprising. Revolts after the death of Herod centred on the royal estates, and thus probably were led by the tenants of the estates. The large landowners were the first to be attacked by the rebels.[121] After all, it was the peasantry who most suffered from a poll tax which was imposed equally on every person. Whether peasants survived or became tenants or day labourers, they were burdened with heavy taxes.

2.4.3 Problem of Debt

The relationship between tenants and landlords was even more complicated as debts often bound tenants to landlords.[122] As noted, crop failure due to various factors left the peasantry with little choice but to become debtors and remain as tenants of their own land or of large estates.[123] The Gospels frequently attest the prevalence of indebtedness.[124] Likewise Josephus gives an account of the rebels who burnt the archives of debt contracts in Jerusalem:

> They carried the fire to the place where the archives were reposited, and made haste to burn the contracts belonging to their creditors, and thereby to dissolve their obligations for paying their debts; and this was done in order to gain the multitude of those who had been debtors, and that they might persuade the poorer sort to join in their insurrection with safety against the more wealthy; so the keepers of the records fled away, and the rest set fire to them. (*J.W.* 2.427)

This account indicates that a considerable number of debtors and creditors dwelt in first-century Jerusalem although Josephus explains that the rebels burnt the debt contracts to attract the poor to their party.[125]

---

121. Mt. 21.33-41//Mk 12.1-9//Lk. 20.9-16. Josephus, *Ant.* 17.274-277; *J.W.* 2.57, 2.652. Kloppenborg, *Tenants*, 324-5; Hamel, *Poverty*, 157-8; Applebaum, 'Economic', 658. Applebaum notes that the revolts took place in Peraea and Jericho where the royal estates were located.

122. Goodman, *Ruling*, 67.

123. Hamel, *Poverty*, 156-7; Goodman, *Ruling*, 57, 67. Goodman notes, 'The only logical reason to lend was thus the hope of winning the peasant's land by foreclosing on it when the debt was not paid off as agreed' (57).

124. Mt. 5.26; 18.23-35; Lk. 7.41-42; 12.59; 16.1-9. Luke mentions a moneylender (δανιστής) alongside debtors (χρεοφειλέτης).

125. Goodman, *Ruling*, 57.

Another legal document found in the Judaean Desert provides several illuminating aspects on debt transactions during the reign of Nero.

> The year two of the Emperor Nero at Siwaya, Absalom, son of Hannin, from Siwaya, has declared in my presence that there is on account with me, Zechariah, son of Yohanan, son H ... [ ], living at Cheaslon, the sum of twenty *zuzin*. The sum I am to repay b[y But if] I have not paid (?) by this time, I will reimburse you with (interest of) a fifth and will settle in entirety, even if this is the Year of Release. And if I do not do so, indemnity for you (will be) my possessions, and whatever I acquire (will be) at your disposal.
> Zechariah, son of Yohanan, for himself.
> Joseph, so[n of   ], wrote (this), witness.
> Jonathan, son of John, witness.
> Joseph, so[n of J]udan, witness.[126]

This document reveals two pertinent points for our discussion. First, the debtor will reimburse the amount which is twenty *zuzin* with a fifth [possibly interest]. If he fails to do so by a certain time, all his possessions will be at the creditor's disposal. There was interest involved in the debt – a violation of the Torah – and all the debtor's possessions were pledged in the process. Thus, it may reflect the practice of mortgaging land for debts, in which case the creditor could easily take over the land.[127] Second, debts also functioned as a tool which landowners could use to control tenants.[128] Landlords regulated the pressure to exact debt payment from tenants and to make the most profit from this dependent relationship.[129] Hence their relationship was socio-economically exploitative.

Finally, payment of taxation might well have worsened the cycle of indebtedness. Philo provides a vivid account of this:

> When some of [tax collector's] debtors whose default was clearly due to poverty took flight in fear of the fatal consequences of his vengeance, he carried off by force their womenfolk and children and parents and their relatives and beat and subjected them to every kind of outrage and contumely in order to make them either tell him the whereabouts of the fugitive or discharge his debt themselves. As they could do neither the first for want of knowledge, nor the second because they were as penniless as the fugitive. (*Spec. Leg.* 3.159)

---

126. DJD 2 (Mur 18). The English translation of the text is from Pastor, *Land*, 148.

127. Gil, 'Agrarian', 306.

128. Similar practice is also attested from Pliny's writing: 'The previous owner quite often sold off the tenants' pledges for their debts; and while he reduced the debt of the tenants for a time, he depleted their resources for the future, on account of the loss of which they began to run up their debts again' (*Ep.* 3.19.6).

129. Foxhall, 'Tenants', 113. Columella, *Rust.* 1.7.1–3.

Luke also treats debts and tax as normal aspects of life. John the Baptist's teaching in Lk. 3.10-14 is particularly pertinent in this respect. His message concerns the poor (Lk. 3.11) and challenges injustice done to them (Lk. 3.13-14). The scriptures frequently portray the possibility of losing land due to the indebtedness.[130] Thus, Oakman observes, 'The abolition of debt was frequently encountered as a revolutionary slogan of the disfranchised, usually accompanied by a demand for the redistribution of land.'[131] In this regard, the ministry of ἄφεσις in Jesus' programmatic statement (Lk. 4.18-19) resonates with the scriptural tradition of the Jubilee (Leviticus 25; Deut. 15.1-18; cf. Isa. 58; 61.1-2) (see Chapters 4 and 5).

Hence debts in ancient society often handicapped the peasants' sustainability. The burden of debt repayments with taxes and rents controlled peasant labour.[132] Debt is also a dividing marker between the rich and the poor as well as between cities which keep the records of debts and the villages where majority poor peasants dwell.[133]

2.5 Conclusion

To sum up, the socio-economic reality of Roman Palestine can be identified in three terms: (1) the 'concentration of land ownership', (2) the 'increase of tenants and day labourers' and (3) the 'over indebtedness' of peasants.[134] These suggest, first of all, the concentration of wealth on those who are both politically powerful and religiously entitled. Socio-economic privilege is entangled with political–religious power as the examination of the profile of landowners shows. Second, the growth of large estates and large landowners reflects the growth of the landless.

Third, the problem of debt lies at the centre of this vicious circle. It impels the peasants, always vulnerable to crop failure, to become 'tenants or day labourers' or to fall into the 'debtor's prison or slavery'.[135] It serves as not only the main cause of the growth of large landowners and of landless peasants but also the outcome of the growth of the landless. Hence this overall sketch of land, and the issues pertaining to it, points to (1) the economic disparity between the rich and the poor, embedded within social, political and religious factors[136] and (2) the socio-economic and religious–political exploitation of the poor by the powerful.

---

130. Oakman, *Peasants*, 27. Lk. 12.58; Mt. 5.25; 18.23-25. Also see Lev. 25.25-28, 35-54; Deut. 15.1-18.
131. Oakman, *Peasants*, 13.
132. K.C. Hanson and Douglas Oakman, *Palestine in the Time of Jesus: Social Structures and Social Conflicts* (Minneapolis: Fortress, 1998), 75, 111.
133. Oakman, *Peasants*, 17.
134. Stegemann, *Movement*, 100.
135. Ibid.
136. Finley, *Economy*, 152.

In what sense then does this conclusion shed light on the socio-economic world of Luke's Gospel and its message? First, Luke's socio-economic world is also coloured by political and religious injustice. Luke's reference to political–religious rulers in the beginning of the Gospel not only assumes an oppressive political system that transfers wealth from the poor to the rich but also implies an economic exploitation through taxation (Lk. 1.5; 2.1-2; 3.1-2; cf. 3.12-14). Towards the end of the Gospel, Luke's critique against the political–religious system is brought to the fore. The Parable of the Tenants (Lk. 20.9-18) disapproves of the religious leaders and their socio-economic exploitation of land. Luke placed the story of the widow's two *lepta* (Lk. 21.1-4) between the reproval of the scribes' devouring of widows' houses (20.46-47) and the foretold destruction of the Temple (21.5-6).

Second, Luke's Gospel, while taking for granted the existence of hired labourers, tenants and slaves (Lk. 15.11-32; 17.7-10; 20.9-16; cf. 16.1-9) and owners of large estates (Lk. 8.3; 12.16; 14.18; 15.12, 15, 17, 25; 16.1; 20.9), highlights the generosity of the creditor who cancelled (χαρίζομαι) the debts in the face of the problem of indebtedness (Lk. 7.41-42), the generosity of the Samaritan in the face of the hostile society (10.30-35) and the generosity of the poor widow in the face of the prevailing injustice (21.1-4). Hence what is at issue in Luke's Gospel is how one who holds the land deals with others in distress. The Jubilee tradition (Lev. 25.25-55; Deut. 15.1-18; cf. Lk. 4.18-19; Isa. 58.6; 61.1-2) explicitly prescribes such practices. Moreover, considering the recurring issue of debts in the Gospel, it can be hardly missed that ἄφεσις of debts was an underlying concern.

Sharing freely with others stands out against these oppressive and exploitative economic relations. This is clearly noted in the teachings of Jesus (Lk. 6.27-38; 4.18-19; cf. 2.1-3) and John the Baptist (Lk. 3.10-14; cf. 1.5) which concern the sharing of life essentials for the benefit of the poor.[137] Thus, I will now turn to explore these life essentials: food and clothing.

---

137. Oakman, 'Countryside in Luke-Acts', *Social World*, 174.

Chapter 3

LIFE ESSENTIALS: FOOD AND CLOTHING

3.1 Introduction

As noted (Chapter 2), the land was the key source of wealth in ancient Roman society.[1] Food, 'being the most important product of the land', was the most distinctive economic indicator.[2] The second-century Roman Jurist Gaius notes that the verb *vivere* ('to be alive') is related to the word 'food'; then, he adds clothes to the things without which no one can live.[3] Sallust also mentions food and clothing as the necessities for human subsistence.[4] The Jewish tradition is no exception on this matter. Pairing food to the hungry with clothing to the naked is proverbial in the scriptural tradition.[5] Food and clothing are the two elements compared with life and body in Matthew and Luke.[6] Indeed, the lack of food was a threat to physical survival; hunger was not an uncommon experience in antiquity.[7] Similarly, the lack of clothing in winter days and during the night could put the lives of many in serious peril.[8]

This chapter concerns the primary functions of food and clothing for physical needs and protection. I will examine daily food and clothing and the experience of hunger and nakedness in antiquity. Each examination will shed further light on the economic disparity between the rich and the poor as food and clothing function as key indicators which describe one's economic condition. I will also examine Luke's references to food and clothing as a reader might hear them within

---

1. Finley, *Economy*, 89.
2. Garnsey, *Food*, 23.
3. Gaius, *Dig.* 50.16.234.2. Translation is from Rena van den Bergh, 'The Plight of the Poor Urban Tenant', *RIDA* 50 (2003): 449.
4. Sallust, *Bell. Cat.* 48.
5. 2 Chron. 28.15; Job 22.6-7; 24.10; Isa. 58.6-7; Ezek. 18.7; Tob. 1.17, 4.16; Mt. 25.35-38, 42-44; Jas 2.15.
6. Mt. 6.25-34; Lk. 12.22-31.
7. See Gen. 47.15; Neh. 5.2.
8. Exod. 22.26-27; Job 24.7. Josephus, *Ant.* 4.269; 15.310.

a Graeco-Roman context. This may, in turn, enhance our understanding of Luke's message of salvation in the following chapters (Part II).

3.2 Food

Peter Garnsey defines food both as 'nutrition, needed by the body for its survival' and as a symbolic object.[9] He also notes that historians and archaeologists have attended to 'the material aspects of food' while devoting less attention to its symbolic aspects.[10] On the contrary, biblical studies have exhibited particular concern to the theological implications of food and meals. Indeed, what to eat and with whom to eat matter especially in the Jewish tradition within which early Christianity was originated. Food is directly related to purity.[11] Communal meals not only function as boundary markers but also serve as symbolic worlds.[12] Hence consumption of food is more than a matter of the satiation of hunger.

Luke is no exception in this respect.[13] Food and meals are prevalent themes in Luke's Gospel.[14] Their literary and theological significance have been widely

---

9. Garnsey, *Food*, xi.
10. Ibid.
11. Mary Douglas, *Purity and Danger: An Analysis of Concepts of Pollution and Taboo* (London: Routledge, 1966), 41–57; 'Deciphering a Meal', in *Implicit Meanings: Essays in Anthropology* (London: Routledge, 1975), 249–75. Douglas's study explains the dietary laws in Leviticus and Deuteronomy in relation to symbolic boundaries and holiness.
12. Eating with tax collectors and sinners (Lk. 5.29-32); washing hands before the meal (11.38). See Marcus J. Borg, *Conflict, Holiness, and Politics in the Teachings of Jesus* (Harrisburg: Trinity, 1998), 88–134. He argues that table fellowship was 'a public embodiment of holiness'. Hence Jesus' sharing meals with tax collectors and sinners which endangered the purity of the community were at the heart of conflicts with his opponents.
13. For the symbolic and theological significance of meals on the Lukan studies, see Esler's discussion on table fellowship, *Community*, 71–109; Willi Braun's discussion on the symbolic nature of Luke 14, construed in a similar setting of Graeco-Roman symposia, *Feasting and Social Rhetoric in Luke 14*, SNTSMS 85 (Cambridge: CUP, 1995); Craig L. Blomberg, *Contagious Holiness: Jesus' Meals with Sinners*, NSBT 19 (Downers Grove: InterVarsity, 2005), 130–63; Richard P. Thompson, 'Gathered at the Table: Holiness and Ecclesiology in the Gospel of Luke', in *Holiness and Ecclesiology in the New Testament*, ed. Kent Brower and Andy Johnson (Grand Rapids: Eerdmans, 2007), 76–94.
14. Luke uses 'eat' related verbs – ἐσθίω, πίνω, κατακλίνω, συνανακεῖμαι, ἀναπίπτω – sixty-two times. Besides, food-related words such as βρῶμα, τροφή, σῖτος, σιτομέτριον, ἄρτος and ἰχθύς occur thirty-one times excluding water, meat and some other foodstuffs. Robert J. Karris notes that Luke employs at least forty-five different words in relation to food. *Eating Your Way through Luke's Gospel* (Collegeville: Order of Saint Benedict, 2006), 14–21.

noted.[15] Table fellowship is one of the most characteristic, yet disputed issues in Jesus' ministry.[16] Food and meals also recur as topics in the parables and teachings of Jesus. Most significantly, the imagery of abundant food anticipates an eschatological reversal while that of meals foreshadows the upcoming messianic banquet. Despite these rich theological implications of food and meals, Luke also refers to food in relation to physical needs.[17] Concern for daily food and the experience of hunger prominently appear in the Gospel.[18] Considering the relative scarcity of food and the frequent experience of food crises in antiquity, food was an absolute necessity.[19]

Hence this section examines (1) the staple foods and the standard diet, (2) the experience of hunger and famine and (3) food and economic disparity. Each examination considers Luke's accounts of both surplus and lack of food to shed light on the economic reality in which the Gospel is embedded.

3.2.1 Daily Bread

The ancient Roman obsession with food is best described in Juvenal's *panem et circenses* (*Sat.* X. 78) – the only two things that concern the Roman plebeians.[20]

---

15. John Paul Heil discusses twelve major meal scenes from Luke's Gospel. *The Meal Scenes in Luke-Acts: An Audience-Oriented Approach*, SBLMS 52 (Atlanta: SBL, 1999), 21–234. Dennis E. Smith, *From Symposium to Eucharist: The Banquet in the Early Christian World* (Minneapolis: Fortress, 2003), 253–77; Smith, 'Table Fellowship as a Literary Motif in the Gospel of Luke', *JBL* 106.4 (1987): 613–38; E. Springs Steele, 'Luke 11.37-54: A Modified Hellenistic Symposium', *JBL* 103.3 (1984): 379–94; Thompson, 'Gathered', 76–94.

16. Eating with tax collectors and sinners: Lk. 5.29-32; 15.1-2; 19.1-10; eating with the Pharisees (and scribes or lawyers): 7.36-50; 11.37-52; 14.1-24; eating at Peter's and Martha's: 4.38-39; 10.38-42.

17. In Luke's Gospel, food is primarily substance; thus, what satisfies the hunger (Lk. 1.53; 3.11; 4.2-4; 6.1-3, 21; 9.17; 11.3; 12.22-23; 15.16; 16.21). There are rather limited uses of food (bread, meal) specifically for symbolic purposes (Lk. 5.29; 7.33; 14.7-24; 15.23; 22.18-19). Although these two functions often converge, its primary function as nutrition should be examined first to shed light on the other.

18. Πεινάω in Lk. 1.53; 4.2; 6.3, 21, 25. Λιμός in 4.25; 15.14, 17; 21.11. Χορτάζω in 6.21; 9.17; 15.16; 16.21.

19. Garnsey, *Food*, 10. His remark is apposite here: 'The role of food in moral discourse in Greece and in Rome was of little relevance to ordinary people and was not intended to be.' The symbolic aspects of food were of significance among the few while nutritional value was paramount among the many who experienced hunger.

20. Juvenal, *The Sixteen Satires*, trans. Peter Green (Harmondsworth: Penguin, 1967), 207. Fronto also features *annona et spectaculis* (*Principia Historiae* 2.17) as two rudiments for the success of the Roman government. *The Correspondence of Marcus Cornelius Fronto*, 2.217. Yet, Whittaker states that this phrase reflects the standpoint of the Roman rich

This well-known phrase discloses that life of the many hung on grain or bread.[21] Grain was the basic necessity for the ordinary people. Fernand Braudel calls 'wheat, olives and vines' the triad of food in the Mediterranean world.[22] Wheat is the first item discussed by the second-century physician Galen in his *On the Properties of Foodstuffs*.[23] Among wheat, white bread made from well-sifted hulled wheat flour was a prestige food while bread made from bran which Galen calls, 'impure' flour, was lower quality, yet more common.[24] Wheat flour was often mixed with bran, chaff and other impurities.[25]

Barley was considered an inferior grain to wheat.[26] It was far less nutritious, Galen comments.[27] Columella says that it was suitable food for cattle.[28] Barley bread (μᾶζα) was somewhat typical of bread for the poor in ancient literature,[29] yet it was a common staple food for Greeks.[30] Only John's Gospel specifies that it was five barley loaves (πέντε ἄρτους κριθίνους) which fed the crowd (Jn 6.9, 13).[31] Barley (κριθή) was usually half the price of wheat[32] while Revelation lists the price of barley three times as cheap as that of wheat (Rev. 6.6).

Other than wheat and barley, Cato's allocation of subsistence food to his slaves helps us understand the diet of the masses. It includes grain, salt, a little bit of

---

towards the plebeians. Besides, the very poor, foreigners and widows were not even considered in the grain dole policy. 'Poor', 272.

21. It also reflects the political power of those who are in control of food. See Paul Veyne, *Bread and Circuses: Historical Sociology and Political Pluralism*, trans. Brian Pearce (London: Penguin, 1990), 417–18.

22. See also Deut. 28.51. Fernand Braudel, *The Mediterranean and the Mediterranean World in the Age of Philip II*, trans. Siân Reynolds, 2 vols (Berkeley: University of California, 1995), 236.

23. Galen, *On the Properties of Foodstuffs* VI, 481–90.

24. Galen, *Foodstuffs*, 481–2.

25. Hamel, *Poverty*, 55. See also Magen Broshi, *Bread, Wine, Walls and Scrolls*, JSPSup 36 (Sheffield: Sheffield Academic, 2001), 125. Broshi notes that the bread for the poor was often described as 'black bread' since it was made from the 'minimally sifted flour'.

26. Broshi, *Bread*, 124; Josephus, *J.W.* 5.427. Origen's allegorical interpretation of the Law as 'barley' and of the Gospel as 'wheat' indicates that barley was thought inferior at least in the third century of Alexandria (*Hom. Gen.* 12.5).

27. Galen, *Foodstuffs*, 507.

28. Columella, *Rust.* 2.9.14; Origen, *Hom. Gen.* 12.5.

29. Lucian, *Fug.* 14; Athenaeus, *Deipn.* 2.55a, 60c, 60d.

30. Garnsey, *Food*, 119.

31. cf. 2 Kgs 4.42-43. Hamel, *Poverty*, 34–5. For the references to barley flour or bread, see Num. 5.15; Judg. 5.8 LXX; Judg. 7.13; Ezek. 4.12.

32. Garnsey, *Food*, 32; Daniel Sperber, 'Costs of Living in Roman Palestine', *JESHO* 8 (1965): 257.

olive oil and fish-pickle or vinegar,[33] but no 'meat or cheese'.[34] Meat was very rare in the diet of the common people. Hence the diet of the many was often very simple: coarse bread or porridge made from millet. Water was the usual drink while cheap, diluted wine was available at times.[35] In addition to wheat or barley bread and water, dried figs, some native vegetables or crushed olives and salted fish could have added to ordinary meals for the many.[36] Garnsey estimates 75 per cent of calorific needs came from grain in antiquity.[37]

What then is the daily food in Luke's Gospel? Does the Gospel indicate any staple food? Luke mentions grain (σῖτος) and olive oil (ἔλαιον) in the context of debt (Lk. 16.6, 7). Jesus' disciples were rubbing heads of grain (στάχυς) to fill their hunger (Lk. 6.1). Nevertheless, bread (ἄρτος) is the most predominant food in terms of what satisfies one's hunger and what one finds in ordinary meals. To eat bread (φαγεῖν ἄρτον) is used both for a Sabbath meal (Lk. 14.1) and the eschatological meal (14.15).[38] The Lord's Supper which is also served as a real meal consists of breaking bread and drinking wine (Lk. 22.17-19).[39] Daily bread meant daily food (Lk. 11.3).

Alongside bread, Luke mentions fish and eggs for which children ask their fathers in Jesus' teaching on prayer (Lk. 11.11-12).[40] While fish is common in Galilee,[41] Luke's reference to eggs is rather surprising. Eggs were relatively rare and considered a delicacy.[42] Only Luke among the Gospel writers mentions the fattened calf (τὸν μόσχον τὸν σιτευτόν), and thus the consumption of meat in the great celebration (Lk. 15.27, 30).[43] Butchering a calf meant that the feast was for

33. Cato, *Agr.* 56–60.
34. Naum Jasny, 'The Daily Bread of the Ancient Greeks and Romans', *Osiris* (1950): 228.
35. Reay Tannahill, *Food in History* (London: Eyre Methuen, 1973), 93.
36. Athenaeus, *Deipn.* 16c; Lucian, *Fug.* 14.
37. Garnsey, *Cities*, 236, 241. cf. Broshi estimates that bread constituted about 50 per cent of the caloric intake in Roman Palestine. *Bread*, 121.
38. cf. Lk. 24.30, 35.
39. Matthias Klinghardt, 'A Typology of the Communal Meal', in *Meals in the Early Christian World*, ed. Dennis E. Smith and Hal Taussig (New York: Macmillan, 2012), 10.
40. Oakman argues that comparing serpent and scorpion with fish and eggs demonstrates Jesus' criticism of money in that the former two were 'suggestive of common scourges of the Galilee'. However, he seems to read too much into the text by commenting on Jesus' attitude to money here. See 'Money in the Moral Universe of the New Testament', *Peasants*, 94.
41. Josephus's description of the lake of Gennesareth also attests to the fishing industry. *J.W.* 3.506-508. See Freyne for further details on the fishing industry in Galilee, *Galilee*, 173-4.
42. Eggs often occur in the discussion of the diners' table with various meat, honey, fruit and herbs. See Athenaeus, *Deipn.* 129c, 131e, 149f; Petronius, *Satyricon* 46. Chicken and eggs were food which could be presented to the guest proudly.
43. For Josephus's reference to μόσχος, see *Ant.* 1.197; 6.339. cf. Gen. 18.8; 1 Sam. 28.24.

the whole community.⁴⁴ Luke's food coincides with the diet of the many which was mainly bread, but at times could have fish or wine. His inclusion of eggs and meat gives a glimpse of the diet of the wealthy.

3.2.2 Food Crisis: Famine and Hunger

Frequent occurrences of eating in the Gospel do not necessarily reflect an abundance of food. Rather, they indicate a common experience of hunger in that bread often comes in the context of hunger. In Greek, λιμός means both 'hunger' and 'famine'.⁴⁵ Hence the meaning of λιμός ranges from hunger caused by a food shortage to catastrophic famine.⁴⁶ Food crisis was an ongoing issue of the Roman Empire.⁴⁷ Although most accounts of food crises focused on the extent to which Rome was hit, we should not underestimate its wider impact.

Either the imports from North Africa or Egypt or from the surrounding countryside where considerable land belonged to the absentee landowners provided grain for Rome and other major cities (see Chapter 2).⁴⁸ Galen mentions the extent to which the city dwellers took all the grain from the fields, leaving barely anything edible for the country people.⁴⁹ How frequent then was famine in the first-century Roman world? To what extent did people undergo food crises?

During the Julio-Claudian Emperors' rule (27 BCE–68 CE), at least ten famines or severe food crises were recorded. Josephus gives an account of one famine which lasted at least two years in Judaea (26–24 BCE). When famine after perpetual droughts came upon the land,⁵⁰ people began, 'out of necessity, to eat many things that did not used to be eaten'.⁵¹ Josephus seems to indicate that people ate impure food in times of food crises. From a slightly different perspective, Galen provides a list of food which people ate when hit by famine: 'carob', 'tare', 'vetch' and 'oats' which he notes are food for animals, thus not suitable for humans and which could

---

44. Kenneth E. Bailey, *Poet & Peasant and Through Peasant Eyes: A Literary-Cultural Approach to the Parables in Luke* (Grand Rapids: Eerdmans, 1983), 186. He notes, 'To kill a calf and not invite the community would be an insult to the community and a waste for the family.'

45. 'λιμός', *BDAG*: 476. See Lk. 15.14, 17.

46. Garnsey, *Famine and Food Supply in the Graeco-Roman World: Response to Risk and Crisis* (Cambridge: CUP, 1988), 8–9, 37.

47. Garnsey, *Food*, 2. He argues that famine as a real catastrophe was less frequent while food crises were common occurrences. See also Garnsey and Saller, *Empire*, 100.

48. Ramsay MacMullen, *Roman Social Relations: 50 B.C. to A.D. 284* (London: Yale University, 1974), 5–6.

49. Cited by MacMullen, *Relations*, 33.

50. Josephus, *Ant.* 15.299–310. This famine affected all the surrounding areas. Herod was finally able to buy corn from Egypt to relieve the famine.

51. Josephus, *Ant.* 15.303.

cause numerous ulcers, and wild animals like 'bear', 'lion' and 'old donkey'.[52] Here Galen's remark on ulcers, caused by famine, is worth noting in that he elsewhere connects malnutrition to various physical diseases:[53]

> The famines (λιμοι) occurring in unbroken succession over a number of years among many of the peoples subject to the Romans have demonstrated clearly … , the important part played in the genesis of diseases by the consumption of unhealthy foods. … The country people finished the pulses during the winter, and so had to fall back on unhealthy foods during the spring; they ate twigs and shoots of trees and bushes and bulbs and roots of indigestible plants; they filled themselves with wild herbs and cooked fresh grass. (*Foodstuffs* VI 749)[54]

Cassius Dio, a Roman historian, refers to an empire-wide famine in 22 BCE.[55] The funerary inscription of Augustus records the same event and how the emperor delivered the entire city from the food shortage at his own expense.[56] Severe food crises struck Rome between 5 CE and 7 CE. A food crisis started in 5 CE after earthquakes, reached its worst in 6 CE and hit Rome once more in 7 CE after having subsided in the spring of the same year.[57] The remedies for severe food crises were regulating the price of grain, free grain distribution (grain dole) and the expulsion of slaves in markets, gladiators and all foreigners from Rome.[58] During 38–39 CE, a year-long drought caused food shortages[59] while the food crisis (39–41 CE) under Gaius was believed to be caused by his bizarre deeds.[60]

When a severe famine struck Jerusalem, Queen Helena of Adiabene brought grain from Egypt and dried figs from Cyprus to support people in the city. Her son, King Izates, sent a great sum of money to Jerusalem as well.[61] Likely, the same

---

52. Galen, foreword to *On the Properties of Foodstuffs* (*De alimentorum facultatibus*), by John Wilkins, trans. Owen Powell (Cambridge: CUP, 2003), xi–xii.

53. Galen, *Foodstuffs*, 686. See also Hamel's discussion on malnutrition and disease, *Poverty*, 53.

54. Cited in Garnsey and Saller, *Empire*, 97.

55. Cassius Dio, *Roman History*, 54.1.1–2.

56. Res gest. divi Aug. 5.22: 'I did not decline at a time of the greatest scarcity of grain the charge of the grain-supply, which I so administered that, within a few days, I freed the entire people, at my own expense, from the fear and danger in which they were.'

57. Dio, *History*, 55.26.1–5, 27.1, 31.3–4.

58. Dio, *History*, 55.26.1–3. Suetonius, *Aug.* 42.3: 'Once indeed in a time of great scarcity when it was difficult to find a remedy, [Augustus] expelled from the city the slaves that were for sale, as well as the schools of gladiators, all foreigners with the exception of physicians and teachers.'

59. Josephus, *Ant.* 18.285.

60. Dio, *History*, 59.17.2.

61. Josephus, *Ant.* 20.51-53, 101. Hamel estimates the years of famine between 46 CE and 48 CE. *Poverty*, 50.

event was mentioned in Acts 11.28 where Agabus prophesied that there would be a worldwide famine. The same verse testifies that it took place in the days of Claudius (41–54 CE).[62] A scarcity of food in 51 CE was due to a bad harvest caused by 'long-continued droughts'.[63] The Great Fire was responsible for another food crisis in Rome in 64 CE. During 68–70 CE, war and flood deprived people of food.[64] Josephus's vivid description demonstrates the dire consequences of the famine and particularly the vulnerability of women, children and the aged while Jerusalem was besieged during the War:

> Then did the famine widen its progress, and devoured the people by whole houses and families; the upper rooms were full of women and children that were dying by famine, and the lanes of the city were full of the dead bodies of the aged; the children also and the young men wandered about the marketplaces like shadows, all swelled with the famine, and fell down dead. (*J.W.* 5.512-513)

> [When the deserters of the city] came first to the Romans, they were puffed up by the famine, and swelled like men in a dropsy; after which they all on the sudden overfilled those bodies that were before empty, and so burst asunder, excepting such only as were skilful enough to restrain their appetites, and by degrees took in their food into bodies unaccustomed thereto. (*J.W.* 5.549)

Luke refers to the worldwide famine in the time of Elijah and God's mercy shown to the widow at Zarephath (Lk. 4.25-26; 1 Kgs 18.2). The famine arose in the land where the prodigal son stayed (Lk. 15.14). Out of hunger, Luke states, he was longing to be fed with the pods which the pigs ate. This pod (κεράτιον Lk. 15.16) is what Galen calls 'carob' which was sometimes eaten by people during a period of famine. He describes carobs as the following:

> [Carobs (κεράτια)] are a food that is unwholesome and woody, and necessarily difficult to concoct for nothing woody is easy. But the fact that they also are not excreted quickly is a considerable defect with them. So that it would be better for us not even to import them from the eastern regions where they are produced. (*Foodstuffs* VI 615)

Galen's description of the food consumed during famine often describes the diet of the country people, and thus their suffering from lack of food. However, the situation of the urban poor was not very different. Those who were not far above

---

62. Josephus also records that there was a great famine under Claudius. *Ant.* 3.320. It is plausible that Claudius expelled foreigners, thus, Jews (Acts 18.2), as Augustus did when a food crisis was severe.

63. Tacitus, *Ann.* 12.43. Famine in 51 CE may refer to the same event which Josephus and Luke in Acts refer to under Claudius if it lasted for years or affected different areas for a period of time.

64. Tacitus, *Hist.* 1.86.

subsistence level were vulnerable to food crises in general.[65] Particularly widows, orphans, foreigners and those with physical disabilities were extremely helpless in times of crisis.

Within this context, what was the experience of hunger in Luke's Gospel? Jesus was hungry after forty days of fasting and tempted to make stones into bread (Lk. 4.1-3). His disciples ate heads of grain while they were walking through the grain field on the Sabbath. Their action was legitimized by David's eating of the sacred bread out of hunger (Lk. 6.1-4).[66] Jesus' announcement of blessing upon the hungry follows this incident (Lk. 6.21; cf. 1.53). As noted (see Chapter 1), there is no need to detach the word 'hungry' (οἱ πεινῶντες) from its literal meaning.[67] You who are hungry now will be fed (χορτασθήσεσθε) (Lk. 6.21).[68] The hungry crowd ate and all were satisfied (ἐχορτάσθησαν) (Lk. 9.17). For the prodigal son who was longing to be fed (χορτασθῆναι) even with swine's food (Lk. 15.16), the fattened calf was awaiting. Lazarus who was longing to be fed (χορτασθῆναι) with what fell from the rich man's table (Lk. 16.21) was found at Abraham's bosom, ready to be filled with good things.[69]

The Lord's Prayer includes asking God each day (καθ' ἡμέραν) for daily (ἐπιούσιον) subsistence (Lk. 11.3).[70] Luke's use of the present imperative form, δίδου with καθ' ἡμέραν, underscores the daily need of food. By stark contrast, the rich man who was feasting sumptuously every day (καθ' ἡμέραν) is found in agony with thirst (Lk. 16.19, 24). Jesus' teaching on not to worry about what to eat is followed by the story of the rich man who stored enough food to live on, but no life to enjoy it (Lk. 12.16-31). Jesus, his disciples and the many in the Gospel were not unfamiliar with hunger. Food was necessary to survive. Yet the message is clear that food is not something to be obsessed with (Lk. 12.22-24).

3.2.3 Food and Economic Disparity

While hunger was the common experience of the many, landowners frequently practised hoarding grain in grain storage in antiquity. A surplus of grain was stored for plain necessity in the first place. It was also kept for profitable sale or for export.[71] It is not clear for what purpose the rich landowner in Lk. 12.16-21

---

65. Garnsey, *Cities*, 238. He notes that the residents of Rome who were not included in the grain dole, but had to buy all their food in the market were more vulnerable.
66. cf. Mt. 12.1.
67. Dupont, *Bonne Nouvelle*, 50, 142.
68. Lk. 6.21; 9.17; 15.16; 16.21.
69. Lk. 1.53; 6.21. cf. Pss. 107.9; 146.5-9.
70. Ἐπιούσιος means (1) necessity for existence, (2) for current day or today, (3) for the following day and (4) for the future. *BDAG*: 296-7. See also Green, *Luke*, 442.
71. Garnsey, *Famine*, 75-6. See Livy, *History of Rome*, 4.12. Minucius, Perfect of the Corn-Market (*praefectus annonae crearetur*), forced those who stored grain to sell all the grain to the state except a month's supply to relieve the food crisis in 440-390 BCE.

was thinking of storing his surpluses by building a larger barn in the text which will be examined later (Chapter 8). Nonetheless, the parable clearly demonstrates the surpluses[72] and self-centredness of the rich man.[73] On the contrary, somewhat typical of the urban poor, Lucian's Micyllus, a cobbler, in *Gallus*, could barely earn his daily bread even with working from early in the morning.[74] Hunger was his usual experience.[75] Food took a great percentage of what the ordinary urban residents earned. Their little purchasing power without direct access to food and the high rent, particularly in Rome, made the urban poor more vulnerable.[76] For the fieldworkers in the countryside, 'food was actually all or a great part of their salary'.[77]

Similarly, peasants who produced food had to give up the surplus or their portion of food for tax or other necessities.[78] Wheat, the grain that most small-scale peasants grew, provided the lowest profit margin for its grower.[79] Grapes yielded the greatest profits, but were also the most cost-intensive. It was estimated that viticulture was at least ten times more profitable than wheat in Roman Palestine.[80] Thus, the large-scale landowners produced grapes, mainly for export.[81] Considering the tax and rent which the peasants and the tenants were responsible for (see Chapter 2), they could hardly have had any surplus to prepare for harvest failure. When shortages came, their vulnerability became evident.

Inevitably, the problem of debt creeps into this process and exacerbates the situation. Once again what worsens the economic disparity was debt. In times of food crisis, many were left with no choice but to become indebted.[82] Those with little saved money exchanged it for food. Any livestock or small piece of land was sold in exchange for bread. Those who had nothing but themselves were sold as

---

72. Bailey, *Peasant*, 63–4. Sir. 11.18-20 reflects the typical attitude toward wealth in the wisdom tradition as reward. Conversely, poverty and hunger are due to idleness in Prov. 19.15.

73. Jesus' criticism of hoarding food by the rich landowner is evident. The parable is sandwiched between Jesus' response to a man's request about inheritance and Jesus' teaching on not to worry. Hence the fuller meaning of the parable should be discussed in a broader context (see Chapter 8).

74. Lucian, *Gall*. 1.

75. Meggitt, *Poverty*, 59. Lucian, *Cat*. 20.

76. Morley, 'Poor', 37. See also Juvenal for the high rent in Rome, *Sat*. III, 223–5.

77. Hamel, *Poverty*, 37.

78. Garnsey, *Food*, 25–9.

79. Safrai, *Economy*, 355–6.

80. Ibid., 356.

81. Cato, *Agr*. 1.7: 'A vineyard comes first if it produces bountifully wine of a good quality; … ; fourth, an oliveyard; fifth, a meadow; sixth, grain land.' See also Duncan-Jones, *Quantitative*, 39; Safrai, *Economy*, 132–4.

82. Garnsey, *Famine*, 180. cf. Gen. 47.13-26; Neh. 5.1-13.

slave workers.⁸³ This practice of debt slavery existed even before 600 BCE.⁸⁴ Hence food shortages, for which many fell into debt slavery, coexisted with food surpluses with which the rich accumulated wealth.⁸⁵

Luke also refers to grain (σῖτος) and olive oil (ἔλαιον) in the context of debt in Lk. 16.1-9 as noted. The manager of another rich man thought to himself, Τί ποιήσω (Lk. 16.3), and arrived at a quite different solution from the rich landowner (Lk. 12.7). He called his master's debtors (χρεοφειλέται) and reduced the debts by 20 per cent and 50 per cent.⁸⁶ The rich man most probably was an absentee landowner who appointed a well-trained agent to manage his property.⁸⁷ The amount of debt looks extremely high.⁸⁸ For example, a hundred *cors* (κόρος) of wheat may well value about one talent (six thousand *denarii*).⁸⁹ The huge amount of debt might have included a considerable percentage of interest added to the original debt.⁹⁰ Moxnes highlights 'the unjust system of exacting interest' against

83. Philo on the remission of debt and of indebted slavery (*Spec. Leg.* 2.71–85). cf. Lev. 25.39-43; Deut. 15.12-18. The famine account in Gen. 47.13-26 strangely seems to provide a similar setting. People brought money in exchange for grain, then livestock, land and themselves for food. Finally, all the people and land belonged to Pharaoh. Then, people were to give one fifth of the yields to Pharaoh.

84. Plutarch, *Sol.* 15. See Garnsey, *Famine*, 74–5, 111. Garnsey argues that the law enforced by Solon (early 600 BCE) banning 'debt-slavery' and 'the export of agricultural crops' was issued in the context of a food crisis. Similarly, Nehemiah also indicates debt-slavery being practised among the Jews (5.1-5). Note also Columella, *Rust.* 1.3.12. He refers to rich landowners using citizens enslaved by debt as their fieldworkers in the first century.

85. Concerning food storage and regulation of the price of grain by the rich, Peter Brown offers a valuable analysis although his work concerns much later period. See *Through the Eye of a Needle: Wealth, the Fall of Rome, and the Making of Christianity in the West, 350-550 AD* (Princeton, NJ: Princeton University, 2012), 13–14.

86. Χρεοφειλέτης only occurs in Lk. 7.41 and 16.15. The former speaks of the debtors who owed money (500 *denarii* and 50 *denarii*) and the latter who owed in commodity (hundred measures of olive oil and hundred *cors* of wheat).

87. Joseph A. Fitzmyer, *The Gospel according to Luke X–XXIV*, AB (New York: Doubleday, 1985), 1097–8.

88. Bailey suggests that they were tenants who 'paid a fixed portion of the crop to be grown'. *Peasant*, 92. However, Hays argues that they were not tenants but merchants since χρεοφειλέτης (debtor), not γεωργός (tenant as in 20.9-16), is used as in 7.41. *Ethics*, 141–2.

89. One κόρος is equal to ten Attic *medimni*. See Josephus, *Ant.* 15.314. One Attic *medimnum* is about six *modii*. Hence a hundred *cors* of wheat amount to six thousand *modii*. Based on the price of wheat as one *denarius* per *modius*, it is about six thousand *denarii* (or one talent).

90. Fitzmyer, *Luke*, 1097–8; Moxnes, *Economy*, 140–1. For the Jewish practice of ursury, see Fitzmyer, 'The Story of the Dishonest Manager (Luke 16:1–13)', *TS* 25.1 (1964): 35, 40; J. Duncan M. Derrett, 'Fresh Light on St. Luke XVI', *NTS* 7 (1960): 209–10.

the plight of the peasants and tenants.[91] The message of ἄφεσις of debt resounds in all the debt-related settings in the Gospel (Lk. 7.41-42; 16.5-7; cf. 4.19; 11.4). I will now turn to the second of the food and clothing pair.

3.3 Clothing

What does it mean to have two tunics (χιτῶνας)? John the Baptist said to those who came to be baptized: whoever has two [tunics][92] must share with anyone who has none (Lk. 3.11). While clothing was an expensive item in antiquity, it was also a necessity for human subsistence. Clothing marked status, especially among the elites, the Roman citizens and the rich.[93] For the rest, it was primarily for 'protection' and 'human dignity'.[94] Hence clothing or lack of clothing revealed the socio-economic conditions of the people.

Once again a typical urban poor person, Lucian's Micyllus, describes himself as shivering on a winter day, barefoot (ἀνυπόδητος) and half-naked (ἡμίγυμνος).[95] Josephus also mentions people suffering from lack of clothing during the winter days.[96] Hence this section examines (1) daily clothing of the common people and (2) economic disparity observed from different descriptions of clothing to shed light on their implications for Luke's message in its socio-economic context.

---

91. Moxnes, *Economy*, 141. Taking interest may have been a persistent practice although it was against the Law (Exod. 22.25; Lev. 25.36-37). Nehemiah under Persian rule (the fifth century BCE) records people's complaints about the interest taken by their own nobles and officials and his charges against them in Neh. 5.11 (restore to them, this very day, their fields, their vineyards, their olive orchards, and their houses, and the interest on money, grain, wine and oil that you have been exacting from them).

92. Tunic (χιτών) is an undergarment. NRSV renders χιτών as a coat; however, Luke with other Gospel writers distinguishes tunic (χιτών) from cloak or outer garment (ἱμάτιον). See Mt. 5.4; 10.10; Mk 6.9; Lk. 6.29; 9.3; Jn 19.23.

93. For clothing as a status marker, see Joseph H. Hellerman, *Reconstructing Honor in Roman Philippi: Carmen Christi as Cursus Pudorum*, SNTSMS 132 (Cambridge: CUP, 2005), 12-19. Although he asserts, 'Clothing functioned as a constant reminder of rank on all social levels', his discussion focuses on the clothing of the Roman citizens and the elites. See also Meyer Reinhold, *History of Purple as a Status Symbol in Antiquity*, Collection Latomus 116 (Bruxelles: Latomus, 1970), 48-61 (ch. 5: The Roman Empire). Purple clothing in the literature of this period was used as 'symbols of royalty, mythological heroes, gods and goddesses and general affluence', 48. See also Dio, *History*, 42.40.4-5. Lk. 15.21-22. cf. Gen. 41.42; Est. 8.15.

94. Hamel, *Poverty*, 57. Note the social aspect of clothing. Luke describes the Gerasene demoniac who did not wear ἱμάτιον as clothed and in his right mind (ἱματισμένον καὶ σωφρονοῦντα) once he was healed (Lk. 8.35). Also in Mk 5.15.

95. Lucian, *Cat.* 20. See also Job 24.7.

96. Josephus, *Ant.* 15.310. Herod the Great (25–24 BCE) provided people with food first and then with clothing during the prolonged drought (*Ant.* 15.299-311).

3.3.1 Daily Clothing

Two standard items of clothing were the tunic (χιτών) which was put on next to the skin and the cloak or mantle (ἱμάτιον) which was wrapped around as an outer garment. Most people wore belts (ζωνή) and sandals (ὑπόδημα or σανδάλιον).[97] John the Baptist was wearing a garment made from camel's hair and a leather belt around his waist (τὸ ἔνδυμα αὐτοῦ ἀπὸ τριχῶν καμήλου καὶ ζώνην δερματίνην περὶ τὴν ὀσφὺν αὐτοῦ) (Mt. 3.4).[98] Jérôme Carcopino mentions 'a simple loin cloth' which may have been the only undergarment in the earlier times of the Roman Empire.[99] Perhaps this was the clothing for fieldworkers,[100] fishermen or slaves while working. To be dressed only with this type of inner garment (tunic) was considered being naked (γυμνός).[101] When serving the master, the slave was told to dress himself (περιζώννυμι) (Lk. 17.8).[102] Carcopino further describes a tunic as 'a kind of long shirt of linen or wool formed of two widths sewed together [which] was slipped over the head and fastened around the body by a belt'.[103]

Elisabeth Crowfoot comments that the small child's linen tunic found in the Wâdī ed-Dâliyeh followed a similar pattern of the everyday Roman tunic: 'Two rectangular sheets, joined ... on the shoulders, leaving a hole for the neck.'[104] The discovery suggests that the clothing of the Roman period was made of linen and wool, but not of mixed material of the two.[105] Similarly, Yadin notes that the textiles found in the Cave of Letters were also not mixed of linen and wool unlike those in the Ancient Near Eastern (ANE) towns.[106] Hence tunics were usually made of linen, cotton and wool. Flax was cultivated in Palestine[107] and cotton also became popular during the first centuries.[108] Imported silk was available during the period,

---

97. Hamel, *Poverty*, 58.

98. Also in Mk 1.6.

99. Jérôme Carcopino, *Daily Life in Ancient Rome: The People and the City at the Height of the Empire*, ed. Henry T. Rowell, trans. E.O. Lorimer (London: Routledge, 1968), 153.

100. Mt. 24.18; Mk 13.16.

101. Hamel, *Poverty*, 62. See Jn 21.7 (Peter put on an outer garment [τὸν ἐπενδύτην διεζώσατο] for he was stripped [ἦν γὰρ γυμνός] for work).

102. Also in Lk. 12.35, 37.

103. Carcopino, *Life*, 153.

104. Elisabeth Crowfoot, 'Textiles', in *Discoveries in the Wâdī ed-Dâliyeh*, ed. Paul W. Lapp and Nancy L. Lapp, AASOR 41 (Cambridge, MA: American School of Oriental Research, 1974), 62. See also Yigael Yadin, *The Finds from the Bar Kokhba Period in the Cave of Letters* (Jerusalem: Israel Exploration Society, 1963), 204.

105. Crowfoot, 'Textiles', 60.

106. Yadin, *Letters*, 170.

107. Frederick C. Grant, *The Economic Background of the Gospels* (London: Oxford University, 1926), 61. See also Safrai, *Economy*, 192. He comments on the textile industry in Palestine.

108. Hamel, *Poverty*, 59.

yet only affordable by the few.¹⁰⁹ Wearing two tunics was not uncommon in the Roman period as Mark's Gospel indicates.¹¹⁰ Suetonius mentions that Augustus wore four tunics in winter times.¹¹¹ Practically, having two tunics allows a person to wash one while wearing the other 'without being put to shame'.¹¹²

Cloaks or mantles (ἱμάτια) were usually made of wool. Unlike the toga which was in a semicircular shape for the Roman citizens, the cloak (ἱμάτιον) was a rectangular sheet with four corners.¹¹³ The cloak seemed to gain more popularity in the imperial period.¹¹⁴ The male cloak found at the Cave of Letters (ca. 95–135 CE) showed that the clothing worn by the Jews of the first and second century was 'of white or yellow wool with reddish brown or blackish-blue notched bands woven into the fabric'.¹¹⁵ Although there was no sharp distinction between male and female clothing in terms of its shape, Yadin notes that male cloaks were 'lighter in colour' than those of the women.¹¹⁶

Practically, cloaks were indispensable items to protect the body on cold days since tunics were sleeveless or covered only the upper part of the arms.¹¹⁷ Moreover, they were used as blankets while sleeping. Hamel notes, 'To own one cloak could often mean that it was the only one in the household.'¹¹⁸ Hence to clothe the naked should be understood in this respect.¹¹⁹ The scriptural concern which prohibited the keeping of a cloak as a pledge till the sun went down was to protect a poor person from spending the night without covering (Exod. 22.26-27). Similarly, Job 24.7 LXX describes the poor going to sleep without a cloak (γυμνοὺς πολλοὺς ἐκοίμισαν ἄνευ ἱματίων).

3.3.2 Clothing and Economic Disparity

Clothing was a valuable item in antiquity. Estimates for the cost of the high priest's vestments range from 10,000 to 20,000 *denarii* in the first century CE.¹²⁰ Luxurious

---

109. John Peter Wild, 'The Eastern Mediterranean, 323 BC–AD 350', in *The Cambridge History of Western Textiles I*, ed. David Jenkins (Cambridge: CUP, 2003), 108.
110. Carcopino, *Life*, 153. Mk 6.9.
111. Suetonius, *Aug.* 82.1.
112. Hamel, *Poverty*, 68.
113. Yadin, *Letters*, 219–21.
114. Douglas R. Edwards, 'Dress and Ornamentation', *ABD*: 235; Carcopino, *Life*, 154-5. Suetonius, *Aug.* 40.5.
115. Edwards, 'Dress', 235. He cites Yadin, *Letters*, 169–203.
116. Yadin, *Letters*, 229.
117. Carcopino, *Life*, 154.
118. Hamel, *Poverty*, 71.
119. One of the acts of charity Tobit lists is 'Give his ἱμάτιον to the naked.' Tob. 1.17; 4.16.
120. Sperber, 'Costs', 252. The price seems to indicate the full set of the priestly garments. See Josephus, *Ant.* 11.331. He describes the priests being clothed with fine linen and the

clothes were kept in vaults with money and other precious goods.¹²¹ However, the economic value of the common people's clothing is of our interest here. The price of decent tunics ranged from twelve to twenty-five *denarii* in the second century CE in Roman Palestine. Cloaks cost from twenty to fifty *denarii* in the first two centuries.¹²² Compared with the price of wheat per *modius* (6.67 kg) which ranged from 0.5 to 1 *denarius*¹²³ and the daily wage which was one *denarius*,¹²⁴ clothing was indeed very expensive. Hence it may have been common for many people to wear the same tunic throughout the year.¹²⁵

Cato's allowance for his slaves again offers a good glimpse into the clothing of the ordinary people: 'A tunic 3½ feet long and a blanket every other year. When you issue the tunic or the blanket, first take up the old one and have patchwork made of it. A stout pair of wooden shoes should be issued every other year' (*Agr.* 59). If this reflects the common condition of the ordinary people, the Gospels' frequent accounts of mending and patching the clothing were not surprising.¹²⁶ Tunics and cloaks were altered or divided into pieces for various purposes.¹²⁷ It was common to pass on clothing or lend it to others.¹²⁸ It could also be stolen as Matthew and Luke mention.¹²⁹ For instance, the man in the Parable of the Good Samaritan (Lk. 10.30) was stripped by the robbers.

Due to the cost of cloth, the longer the clothing, the more the cost. Intriguingly enough, wearing long robes is one of Jesus' negative remarks concerning the scribes (Mk 12.38//Lk. 20.46). The length, material, colour and quality of the clothing described the socio-economic condition of a person. The clothing made of fine linen (βύσσος), silk or purple cloth (πορφύρα) seemed to be a typical description of the rich.¹³⁰ The rich man in Luke was clothed in purple and fine linen (ἐνεδιδύσκετο πορφύραν καὶ βύσσον Lk. 16.19). Micyllus describes Simon who became rich by inheriting a fortune as 'clothed in purple and scarlet'.¹³¹ Jesus says that a man dressed in a soft cloak (ἄνθρωπον ἐν μαλακοῖς ἱματίοις ἠμφιεσμένον) is found in king's courts (Lk. 7.25).

---

high priest in purple and scarlet clothing. See also *Ant.* 3.151-171. Exod. 28.35, 36.35; 1 Chron. 15.27; 2 Chron. 5.12.

121. Josephus, *J.W.* 2.282.
122. Sperber, 'Costs', 252. cf. Plutarch, *Cat. Maj.* 1.4.3.
123. Duncan-Jones, *Quantitative*, 146.
124. Mt. 20.2; Tob. 5.15.
125. Hamel, *Poverty*, 66.
126. Mt. 9.16; Mk 2.21; Lk. 5.36. See also Whittaker, 'Poor', 286.
127. Crowfoot, 'Textiles', 62. Mt. 27.35; Mk 15.24; Lk. 23.34; Jn 19.23-24.
128. Hamel, *Poverty*, 58–9.
129. Mt. 5.40; Lk. 6.29.
130. Silk was cited in order to criticize the extravagance of the wealthy. See Dio, *History*, 43.24.2. Lk. 7.25; 16.19. Lucian, *Gall.* 6, 12; *Cat.* 14.
131. Lucian, *Gall.* 14.

Conversely Juvenal mentions a coarse cloak which was still a decent garment in rural villages.[132] The clothing of the poor was often referred to as dirty rags.[133] Juvenal gives a detailed account of a poor man's clothing in his *Satire*: 'The poor man's an eternal butt for bad jokes, with his torn and dirt-caked top-coat, his grubby toga, one shoe agape where the leather's split – those clumsy patches.'[134] The poor man, Lazarus, was covered with sores instead of clothes (Lk. 16.20).

Hence Carcopino's comment on the stereotyped costumes of the actors in the theatres of the Roman Empire is helpful here: 'Costumes draped in Greek or Roman fashion gave an immediate clue to the *dramatis personae*: ... purple for the rich, red for the poor, a short tunic for the slave.'[135] Description of one's clothing indicates one's socio-economic status. Luke's portrayal of the rich man's linen and purple clothes in contrast to that of Lazarus highlights their economic disparity in addition to their contrasting nutritional condition.

3.4 Conclusion

As shown in this chapter, food was scarce in antiquity. The diet of the many was simple and repetitive: bread and water. Jesus' diet must have not been very far from this. In first-century Roman Palestine, Safrai comments that a little bit of meat and wine could be called a 'gluttonous meal'.[136] Recurrent food crises triggered the experience of hunger among the many who earned barely enough for their daily bread. The lack of food forced the poor to eat what was considered impure or unsuitable and malnutrition made the poor prone to various diseases. Conversely, it was common practice for the rich to store food surpluses not only for their own necessity but also for the accumulation of their wealth by profiting from selling grain in times of food shortage.

Alongside food, clothing was a distinctive socio-economic marker which ancient literature customarily used. Worn-out and patched clothing which was often referred to as rags was rather common for the many, not necessarily for the extremely poor. Clothing in general was not a matter of choice, but a necessity to cover the body. What is observed then is the problem of the lack and abundance of food juxtaposed to the opulence and austerity of clothing. The disparity between rich and poor is vast. Luke's Gospel also describes the scarcity of food and the experience of hunger side by side with the surplus of food and sumptuous banquets. Similarly, nakedness is contrasted with luxurious clothing.

---

132. Juvenal, *Sat.* III, 170.
133. Lucian, *Gall.* 9, 14. Note also a stark contrast between the clothing of the rich (ἐν ἐσθῆτι λαμπρᾷ) and that of the poor (ἐν ῥυπαρᾷ ἐσθῆτι) in 2.2.
134. Juvenal, *Sat.* III, 147–150.
135. Carcopino, *Life*, 222–3.
136. Safrai, *Economy*, 131. cf. Mt. 11.19; Lk. 7.34.

3. Life Essentials: Food and Clothing

What, then, are the implications of this thesis of food and clothing for Luke's Gospel? First, ἄφεσις of debt is once again urged as noted (Chapter 2). A rich man's manager who shrewdly cancelled some portion of debt was praised (Lk. 16.1-9). Debt inevitably exploited the vulnerable at the expense of their very existence under the oppressive system, taking frequent food crises into consideration.

Second, the disparity between lack and abundance foreshadows the upcoming reversal (Lk. 1.52-53; 6.20-21, 24-25; 16.19-31). The hungry are being satisfied and will be satisfied. The rich will be sent away empty. The injustice of the world where lack and surplus coexist will be redressed with divine reversal. At the same time, divine intervention calls for human enactments of mercy and justice towards the poor and the needy here and now (Chapters 5 and 8).

Third, sharing food and clothing is a desideratum. Radical generosity is expected in line with divine mercy (ἔλεος) which is expressed in Lk. 6.36 (γίνεσθε οἰκτίρμονες καθὼς [καὶ] ὁ πατὴρ ὑμῶν οἰκτίρμων ἐστίν) (Chapter 4).[137] John the Baptist exhorts the crowd who asks Τί οὖν ποιήσωμεν, (Lk. 3.11) to share with those who have none (Chapter 6). Owning two tunics is not far from a subsistence level.[138] Jesus tells those for whom clothing may be their very necessity not to withhold the tunic from the one who takes away the cloak (Lk. 6.29). Conversely, the criticism is sharp in the Parable of the Rich Fool (Lk. 12.16-21) who thought of storing all his food surpluses (Chapter 8). Jesus' criticism of the scribes who wear long garments (στολή)[139] extending to the feet can also be understood within this context (Lk. 20.46).

Lastly, feeding the hungry and clothing the naked in this world have implications for one's eternal destiny (Lk. 3.7-14; 12.33; 16.9; 18.22; 19.8-9). Conversely, failure to do so leads one to an undesirable end (Lk. 12.20; 16.23-31) (Chapters 6, 7 and 8). Above all, the promise of satiation of the hungry draws the imagery of the messianic banquet. Participating in the messianic banquet is a possibility for the rich who satiate the hunger of the poor (Lk. 14.12-15) (Chapter 9).

In conclusion, the examination of the physical aspects of food and clothing as key economic indicators offers a firm ground for the discussion of not only Luke's message of salvation in terms of release, reversal, repentance and restoration, in the next chapter (Chapter 4), but also the texts and their theological implications in the remaining chapters (Chapters 5, 6, 7, 8 and 9).

---

137. Lk. 3.10-14; 6.29-30, 34-35, 38; 10.30-37; 18.22.
138. Mt. 10.10; Mk 6.9; Lk. 9.3.
139. Στολή refers to the priestly garment in Exod. 28.2-4; 29.5, 21, 29; 31.10 LXX. Josephus, *Ant.* 3.151-158.

Part Two

SALVATION OF THE POOR AND THE RICH

Chapter 4

SALVATION IN THE GOSPEL OF LUKE

4.1 Introduction

Salvation is arguably the central theme of Luke's theology.[1] A brief survey of σῴζω-group words, such as διασῴζω, σωτήρ, σωτηρία and σωτήριον,[2] in Luke evinces it. Moreover, Luke deploys almost all the expressions which describe God's saving activity: deliverance, redemption, visitation, God's reign/kingdom, forgiveness of sins, repentance, conversion, peace and eternal life.[3] These rich and diverse references to salvation also reflect its multifaceted meanings.

This chapter explores the major themes of salvation in Luke in the light of the previous discussion of the socio-economic contexts (Part I) under four aspects: (1) Release, (2) Reversal, (3) Repentance and (4) Restoration. The critical question for our discussion here is this: 'Is Luke's noted concern for social and economic

---

1. Marshall, *Historian*, 93; Green, 'The Message of Salvation in Luke-Acts', *ExAud* 5 (1989): 21; Christoph W. Stenschke, *Luke's Portrait of Gentiles Prior to Their Coming to Faith*, WUNT 2.108 (Tübingen: Mohr, 1999), 1; Brendan Byrne, *The Hospitality of God: A Reading of Luke's Gospel* (Collegeville: Liturgical, 2000), 195. As a conclusion to his concise commentary of Luke's Gospel, Byrne features salvation as the central theme. Kevin L. Anderson, '*But God Raised Him from the Dead': The Theology of Jesus' Resurrection in Luke-Acts* (London: Paternoster, 2006), 22. He states, 'Luke-Acts is above all about a narrative about salvation.'

2. Σῴζω occurs thirteen times, διασῴζω one time, σωτήρ two times, σωτηρία four times and σωτήριον two times. cf. λύτρωσις two times. Noun forms occur all in the birth narratives except in Lk. 19.9.

3. Note ῥύομαι in Lk. 1.74, λύτρωσις (ἀπολύτρωσις) in Lk. 1.68; 2.38; Acts 21.28, ἀφέσει ἁμαρτιῶν in Lk. 1.77; 3.3; 24.47 (cf. 5.20, 23, 24; 7.48, 49; 11.4); Acts 2.38; 5.31; 10.43; 13.38; 26.18, μετάνοια in Lk. 3.3, 8; 5.32; 15.7; 24.47; Acts 5.31; 11.18; 13.24; 19.4; 20.21; 26.20, ἐπιστρέφω in Lk. 1.16 (cf. 17.4); Acts 3.19; 9.35; 11.21; 14.15; 15.19; 26.18, 20; 28.17, εἰρήνη in Lk. 1.79; 2.14, 29; 7.50; 8.48; 24.36 (cf. 10.5); Acts 10.36 and ζωή αἰώνιος in Lk. 10.25; 18.18, 30; Acts 13.46, 48. Note also that ἐπισκέπτομαι in Lk. 1.68, 78; 7.16; Acts 15.14 and ἱλάσκομαι in Lk. 18.13 which strongly allude to the Jewish scriptural traditions are also related to God's salvation and forgiveness.

issues incorporated into his understanding of salvation?'[4] First, I will offer a brief observation on salvation and mercy (ἔλεος) in Luke to show the ways in which the above-mentioned four aspects of salvation centre around divine mercy (ἔλεος) and its human embodiment. Next, I will examine each aspect of salvation with its close incorporation into socio-economic issues. Lastly, I will draw the conclusion as a foundation for the detailed explorations which follow in Chapters 5, 6, 7, 8 and 9.

4.2 Salvation and Mercy

Luke begins his Gospel with heavily loaded soteriological expressions which recall scriptural promises of salvation.[5] The beginning recalls God's saving activities: λύτρωσις (ἀπολύτρωσις), ῥύομαι, ἀφέσει ἁμαρτιῶν[6] all of which arise from and are closely linked with God's mercy (ἔλεος). Divine ἔλεος in the beginning of the Gospel can best be understood in the sense of חֶסֶד[7] which occurs in the context of God's saving activity promised to his people in the HB.[8] The Magnificat (Lk. 1.46-55) juxtaposes divine power (ὁ δυνατός, κράτος vv. 49, 51) with ἔλεος (vv. 50, 54). God reverses the position of the lowly and the powerful, and of the hungry and the rich (vv. 52–53). Moreover, divine ἔλεος (ποιῆσαι ἔλεος, σπλάγχνα ἐλέους vv. 72, 78) in the Benedictus (Lk. 1.68-79) points directly to the coming saviour (κέρας σωτηρίας, ἀνατολὴ ἐξ ὕψους vv. 69, 78).[9] Ἔλεος denotes God's saving covenantal faithfulness whose end is not only the redemption of the people of God but also their restoration.

---

4. Timothy W. Reardon, 'Recent Trajectories and Themes in Lukan Soteriology', *CurBR* 12.1 (2012): 78.

5. Bauckham, 'The Restoration of Israel in Luke-Acts', in *Restoration: Old Testament, Jewish and Christian Perspectives*, ed. J.M. Scott, JSJSup 72 (Leiden: Brill, 2001), 439–66; Tannehill, *Unity: Luke*, 15–44. Tannehill aptly titles his discussion of Lk. 1.5-2.40 'Previews of Salvation'.

6. See fn. 3 of this chapter. See also R. Hays, *Echoes in the Gospels*, 191–201.

7. Bultmann, 'ἔλεος, ἐλεέω', *TDNT* 2:483; Denis S. Kulandaisamy, 'The Tender Mercy of God in the Magnificat (Lk. 1:46-55)', *EphM* 66 (2016): 69–70.

8. Bultmann, 'ἔλεος, ἐλεέω', 2:480. Note that Bultmann observes חֶסֶד (ἔλεος in Greek) as 'the act or demonstration of assisting faithfulness'.

9. Fitzmyer, *Luke*, 384, 386–7; Parsons, *Luke*, 47, 48. The infinitive ποιῆσαι ἔλεος (Lk. 1.72) explains a horn of salvation (1.69). For the messianic use of κέρας σωτηρίας and ἀνατολὴ ἐξ ὕψους (Lk. 1.69, 78), see Bauckham, 'Restoration', 452–3; Fitzmyer, *Luke*, 387; Gregory R. Lanier, 'The Curious Case of צֶמַח and ἀνατολή: An Inquiry into Septuagint Translation Patterns', *JBL* 134.3 (2015): 505–27. See Jer. 23.5; Zech. 3.8; 6.12 for the messianic use of ἀνατολή (צֶמַח) in the LXX. See also 2 Sam. 2.10; 22.3; Pss. 18.2; 89.25; 132.17; Ezek. 29.21.

Likewise, Jesus' saving activity responds to the request for mercy.[10] Jesus announces good news to the poor, release (ἄφεσις) to the captives and the oppressed and the reversal of fortunes (Chapter 5). Jesus' Sermon on the Plain culminates in Lk. 6.36 (γίνεσθε οἰκτίρμονες καθὼς καὶ ὁ πατὴρ ὑμῶν οἰκτίρμων ἐστίν). While οἰκτίρμων with πολυέλεος and ἐλεήμων portrays the quintessential characteristics of God in his saving and forgiving grace to his people in the LXX,[11] the structure of Lk. 6.36 calls for participation in God's mercy – *imitatio Dei*.[12] The paradigm-setting expression of this is found in Lev. 19.2 LXX (ἅγιοι ἔσεσθε, ὅτι ἐγὼ ἅγιος, κύριος ὁ θεὸς ὑμῶν). There the holiness of God expressed in the community entails loving neighbours and strangers through the merciful and just dealings and the care of the poor (Lev. 19.9-10, 13-18, 33-37).

Similarly, Lk. 6.36 demands the human enactment of the divine ἔλεος. God's covenantal ἔλεος (חֶסֶד) is intertwined with social relationship among humans. Thus, the immediate context of the Sermon on the Plain (Lk. 6.17-49) features lending generously and giving freely (δανίζετε μηδὲν ἀπελπίζοντες, δίδωμι 6.35, 38). Lending (δανείζω) and showing mercy (ποιέω ἔλεος) also closely relate in the LXX (Ps. 111.4-5; Prov. 19.17; Sir. 29.1-2). In particular, Deut. 15.1-18 provides a rich context for lending generously and giving freely followed by divine reward.

In the wider context of Luke's narratives, the human response to divine mercy can be best described as μετάνοια (ἐπιστρέφω).[13] This is not an abstract concept, but is expressed in transformative and practical deeds in interpersonal relations, namely showing mercy and doing justice.[14] It is vividly portrayed in John the Baptist's teaching (Lk. 3.10-14) at the outset of Luke's Gospel (Chapter 6).

---

10. See Lk. 17.13; 18.38, 39 and 7.13 (σπλαγχνίζομαι). Note also οἰκτίρμων in Lk. 6.36 and ἱλάσθητί μοι in 18.13. James R. Harrison observes that Luke's use of the unusual verb, ἱλάσκομαι, instead of ἐλεέω in 18.13 highlights 'the unusualness' of divine mercy exercised towards 'the "unworthy"' against Graeco-Roman understanding of *clementia* which is conditioned by the worthiness of the recipients. 'Who Is the "Lord of Grace?"': Jesus' Parables in Imperial Context', in *Borders: Terminologies, Ideologies, and Performances*, ed. Annette Weissenrieder, WUNT 366 (Tübingen: Mohr, 2016), 386, 410–12.

11. Exod. 34.6; Deut. 4.31; Neh. 9.17, 31; 2 Chron. 30.9; Pss. 68.17; 77.38; 85.15; 102.8; 110.4; 144.8; Joel 2.13; Jon. 4.2 (God's mercy extends to the Ninevites); Sir. 2.11. See R. Hays, *Echoes in the Gospels*, 214–15. Hays highlights Ps. 144.8-9 where χρηστός and οἰκτιρμός occur in a close parallel as in Lk. 6.35-36.

12. See Parsons, *Luke*, 111. He notes Sir. 4.10 which echoes υἱὸς ὑψίστου in Lk. 6.35. Also see Eryl Wynn Davies, 'Walking in God's Ways: The Concept of *Imitatio Dei* in the Old Testament', in *In Search of True Wisdom: Essays in Old Testament Interpretation in Honour of Ronald E. Clements*, ed. Edward Ball, JSOTSup 300 (Sheffield: Sheffield Academic, 1999), 99–115.

13. μετάνοια in Lk. 3.3, 8; 5.32; 15.7; 24.47; Acts 5.31; 11.18; 13.24; 19.4; 20.21; 26.20, ἐπιστρέφω in Lk. 1.16 cf. 17.4; Acts 3.19; 9.35; 11.21; 14.15; 15.19; 26.18, 20; 28.17, πίστις in Lk. 5.20; 7.9, 50; 8.48; 17.19; 18.42; Acts 3.16; 14.9.

14. Nave, *Repentance*, 158–9.

Furthermore, it is the Samaritan in Lk. 10.30-35 who not only shows compassion (ἐσπλαγχνίσθη v. 33) but also enacts mercy (ἔλεος) in tangible actions (vv. 34–35). Luke's emphasis of almsgiving (ἐλεημοσύνη) as the human embodiment of divine mercy (ἔλεος) should be understood along a similar line (Chapters 7 and 8). Just as divine mercy and justice promises the kingdom to the poor, so for those who practise ἔλεος and ἐλεημοσύνη towards the poor, Luke's Gospel promises the divine reward in diverse terms: υἱοὶ ὑψίστου, εἰρήνη, ζωή αἰώνιος, σκηνή αἰώνιος, θησαυρός ἐν τοῖς οὐρανοῖς, ἡ βασιλεία τοῦ θεοῦ and eating ἐν τῇ βασιλείᾳ τοῦ θεοῦ.[15]

Among these, the imagery of the messianic banquet is noteworthy in three aspects: (1) the banquet first and foremost welcomes the poor with rich food; (2) the banquet is also open to those who show mercy and do justice particularly to those in need; (3) the banquet ultimately looks forward to the gathering of the poor and the rich around the table together as the restored people of God (Chapter 9). While Luke's Gospel often portrays these divine rewards in the future, the present fulfilment of God's promise particularly pronounced to the poor (Lk. 6.20-21) through the ministry of Jesus should be noted.[16] The *eschaton* has been inaugurated through the person and ministry of Jesus. York affirms, 'The future has broken into the present [in Jesus].'[17]

This brief observation sets the ground for Luke's multifaceted expressions of salvation which are deeply rooted in divine mercy (ἔλεος) and its human embodiment. I will now turn to the examination of the four aspects of salvation in Luke's Gospel in its socio-economic contexts: (1) Release, (2) Reversal, (3) Repentance and (4) Restoration.

4.3 Salvation as Release

Ἄφεσις most frequently refers to forgiveness (ἄφεσις) of sins. David Neale's study examines sinners in Luke's Gospel, and thus draws particular attention to forgiveness (ἄφεσις) of sinners.[18] Neale develops 'Luke's rhetoric of salvation'

---

15. υἱοὶ ὑψίστου in Lk. 6.35, εἰρήνη in Lk. 1.79; 2.14, 29; 7.50; 8.48; 24.36; cf. 10.5; Acts 10.36, ζωή αἰώνιος in Lk. 10.25; 18.18, 30; Acts 13.46, 48, σκηνή αἰώνιος in Lk. 16.9, θησαυρός in heaven in Lk. 12.33; 18.22, ἡ βασιλεία τοῦ θεοῦ in Lk. 12.32; 18.24, 25 and eating ἐν τῇ βασιλείᾳ τοῦ θεοῦ in Lk. 13.28, 29; 14.15.

16. Contra Lehtipuu, 'Reward', 246. She suggests that the promise to the poor is 'an eschatological reward'. Her argument is only partly true: the fulfilment of the hungry being fed and the weeping consoled is inaugurated through the ministry of Jesus throughout the Gospel of Luke. Note also the fulfilment of Lk. 6.21 in Lk. 7.13-15; 9.16-17; 15.14-17, 23, 27, 30.

17. John O. York, *The Last Shall Be First: The Rhetoric of Reversal in Luke*, JSNTSup 46 (Sheffield: Sheffield Academic, 1991), 55.

18. Neale, *Sinners*, 191–4.

which is centred on sinners, forgiveness and repentance, and asserts the following: 'Luke's apparent purpose is to convince his audience that all are sinners in need of forgiveness and to establish repentance as the only remedy for that condition.'[19] However, his overemphasis on ἄφεσις of sinners not only underplays Luke's concern for socio-economic issues but also obscures the underlying meaning of ἄφεσις of debt.[20] He too quickly transforms ἄφεσις of debt into forgiveness of sin and shifts the focus from the impoverished to the sinners. But the echoes of ἄφεσις in the context of the cancellation of debt can hardly be missed, considering the problem of indebtedness in Luke's context as examined (Chapters 2 and 3) and his concern for the poor throughout the Gospel.

The repeated use of ἄφεσις in the Nazareth Manifesto (NM) (Lk. 4.18-19) is paradigmatic. It captures not only the nature of Jesus' ministry but also what salvation means in Luke's Gospel. First, Jesus' announcement is identified as τοῖς λόγοις τῆς χάριτος (Lk. 4.22). The meaning of τῆς χάριτος here is much discussed.[21] It might be read either as a subjective or an objective genitive.[22] Thus, it means gracious words or words about God's grace. Nolland argues that χάρις in Luke denotes 'a tangible divine power dramatically present with Jesus and the Church of Acts'.[23] Whichever the case may be, what is significant for our discussion is Luke's use of χάρις in relation to Jesus. Χάρις was upon him as he grew up (Lk. 2.40, 52), and his words and deeds are described in terms of χάρις (τοῖς λόγοις τῆς χάριτος 4.22, τυφλοῖς πολλοῖς ἐχαρίσατο βλέπειν 7.21). Moreover, Luke employs χάρις in rather unusual places. Χάρις (Lk. 6.32, 33, 34) is used alongside μισθός (6.35)[24] and

---

19. Neale, *Sinners*, 152-3.

20. In doing this, Neale also shifts the meaning of ἄφεσις from a covenantal and communal understanding to individualized one. Neale, *Sinners*, 152-3.

21. Whether it is the hearers' acknowledgement or the narrator's is debated. If it is the hearer's, the following comment does not seem congruent. Fitzmyer, Green, Carroll and Parsons note that the comments of the hearers are in fact positive. Fitzmyer, *Luke*, 535; Green, *Luke*, 214-15; John T. Carroll, *Luke*, NTL (Louisville: WJK, 2012), 113; Parsons, *Luke*, 82. On the contrary, Nolland argues that it is the narrator's comment. Thus, χάρις here carries a 'dynamic sense' in terms of divine power rather than winsomeness (48). See Nolland, 'Words of Grace (Luke 4,22)', *Bib* 65.1 (1984): 48-9. cf. Τῷ λόγῳ τῆς χάριτος αὐτοῦ in Acts 14.3; 20.32.

22. Carroll, *Luke*, 110, 113; Green, *Luke*, 214-15; Fitzmyer, *Luke*, 535. cf. Nolland suggests 'words endued with the power of God's grace'. *Luke 1–9:20*, 198.

23. Nolland, 'Luke's Use of ΧΑΡΙΣ', *NTS* 32.4 (1986): 619.

24. Matthew consistently uses μισθός. Nathan Eubank suggests that μισθός in Matthew is not a reward but a wage which describes the following: 'God gives for the work that he demands, work that is described as necessary to enter the kingdom' (70). However, Luke's employment of χάρις and μισθός in 6.32-35 makes this translation of μισθός difficult. *Wages of Cross-Bearing and Debt of Sin: The Economy of Heaven in Matthew's Gospel*, BZNW 196 (Berlin: De Gruyter, 2013), 68-70.

χαρίζομαι (cancelling debts in 7.42, 43) alongside ἀφίημι (forgiving sins in 7.47, 48, 49). Here χάρις is juxtaposed with its human embodiment.

Second, the combined citation of Isa. 61.1-2 and 58.6 LXX in Lk. 4.18-19 carries heavy allusion to the Jubilee tradition with the repetition of ἄφεσις.[25] While Isa. 61.1-2 alludes to an 'eschatological and messianic' expectation of Jubilee, the context of Isa. 58.6 clearly draws out the economic expression of the tradition.[26] Ἄφεσις in the LXX occurs where legislation of the Jubilee is pronounced (Exod. 21.2-3; 23.10-11; Leviticus 25; Deut. 15.1-18). Whether ἄφεσις of land or debt is proclaimed, the central concern for the Jubilee is twofold. It champions the rights of the impoverished and particularly those who fall into (debt) slavery (Exod. 21.2-3; Lev. 25.39-54; Deut. 15.12-18).[27] It enjoins the well-off to be merciful and generous towards the indebted. Thus, ἄφεσις primarily deals with the problem of debt in economic terms.

Similarly, a short-lived legislation of Jubilee in Jer. 34.8-16 is directed for the ἄφεσις of the impoverished, and thus of those who sold themselves into slavery due to indebtedness.[28] Ἄφεσις in the context of Jesus' ministry expresses the very nature of divine mercy. It finds firm ground in a socio-economic sense before it becomes too quickly spiritualized into a concern for ἄφεσις of sins.

Moreover, Luke intertwines release (ἄφεσις) from sin (ἁμαρτία) with release from debt (Lk. 11.4; 7.41-50).[29] The Lord's Prayer in Lk. 11.4 reads as follows: Καὶ **ἄφες** ἡμῖν τὰς **ἁμαρτίας** ἡμῶν, καὶ γὰρ αὐτοὶ **ἀφίομεν** παντὶ **ὀφείλοντι** ἡμῖν (emphasis added). When compared with Mt. 6.12,[30] Luke's use of sin (ἁμαρτία) is noteworthy. Gary Anderson observes the semantic links between sin and debt in the HB (particularly from its Aramaic translation) and in later rabbinic thought.[31] He notes how the concepts of sin and debt become blurred particularly during the

---

25. Contra ἄφεσις in Lk. 3.3 and 4.18 in the light of the ministries of John the Baptist and Jesus is often discussed in the context of 'exile-new exodus'. See David W. Pao, *Acts and the Isaianic New Exodus* (Grand Rapids: Baker, 2002), 77–84. He argues that what is noted from Luke 4 for the later Lukan narratives is not much about the Jubilee, but more about the Isaianic New Exodus.

26. John Sietze Bergsma, *The Jubilee from Leviticus to Qumran: A History of Interpretation* (Leiden: Brill, 2007), 298.

27. In Exodus 21, 23 and Leviticus 25, it is the land to which ἄφεσις is proclaimed for the benefit of the poor, the slaves and the wild animals. In Deuteronomy 15, ἄφεσις of debt is noted.

28. Those who sold themselves into slavery due to debt are widely attested. 2 Kgs 4.1-2; Amos 2.6; Isa. 50.1; Neh. 5.1. See Jeffries M. Hamilton, *Social Justice and Deuteronomy: The Case of Deuteronomy 15*, SBLDS 136 (Atlanta: Scholars, 1992), 3–4, 30; Baker, *Tight Fists*, 138–40.

29. See Raymond E. Brown, 'The Pater Noster as an Eschatological Prayer', *TS* 22.2 (1961): 200–4.

30. Mt. 6.12 (καὶ ἄφες ἡμῖν τὰ ὀφειλήματα ἡμῶν, ὡς καὶ ἡμεῖς ἀφήκαμεν τοῖς ὀφειλέταις ἡμῶν). See Gary Anderson, *Sin: A History* (New Haven: Yale University, 2009), 27–37.

31. Anderson, *Sin*, 27–32.

STP.³² His observation explains Matthew's use of ὀφείλημα which indicates both sin and debt (Mt. 6.12), but it does not clarify Luke's use of both sin (ἁμαρτία) and debt (ὀφείλοντι indebted) (Lk. 11.4). Rather Luke distinguishes ἄφεσις of sin from debt, retaining the economic meaning of debt instead of collapsing it into a metaphorical meaning of sin. This distinction highlights ἄφεσις of debt in human relations in response to ἄφεσις of sin.³³ Hence Luke's prayer stresses the mutual relationship between God's ἄφεσις of sin and the human response of ἄφεσις of debt.

Luke's parable (Lk. 7.41-42), which illuminates the story of Simon the Pharisee and the woman (7.36-50), uses the cancellation of debt (χαρίζομαι) to illustrate Jesus' ἄφεσις of sin. As mentioned, the act of the moneylender (δανιστής) is described as χαρίζομαι,³⁴ which elsewhere refers to Jesus' gracious act of bestowing sight to the blind (Lk. 7.21).³⁵ In the light of the previous discussion of Deut. 15.1-18 and the Jubilee, Luke's omission of Deut. 15.11 in this account appears surprising at first hand, noting that all the other Gospels draw on a similar tradition and refer to Deut. 15.11.³⁶

However, this absence is more apparent than real. Luke's account draws on the main theme of Deuteronomy 15 in terms of generosity and cancelling debts.³⁷ With Jesus' question to Simon (Lk. 7.42), the focus of the story turns to the response of both debtors who are granted favour from the moneylender. The woman's actions (Lk. 7.44-46; cf. 7.37-38) are revisited in the light of the parable.³⁸ The parable in Lk. 7.36-50 juxtaposes the moneylender's gracious act of cancelling debts (χαρίζομαι) with Jesus' forgiving (ἀφίημι) sins. It sheds further light on the response which is described as tangible acts of love (ἀγαπάω).³⁹ Hence Luke's juxtaposition of ἄφεσις of sin and debt strengthens the mutual relationship of religious and economic matters while debt retains its financial meaning.

---

32. Anderson, *Sin*, 34–7. He notes the way in which 11QMelch understands the idea of דרור in Lev. 25.10; Isa. 61.1 and שמטה in Deut. 15.1 in relation to sin (11QMelch 1.6). Contra Eubank, *Wages*, 53-4. He notes that Matthew's pairing of ἀφίημι and ὀφείλημα strongly indicates its financial meaning rather than a spiritualized one.

33. Note Sir. 28.2 ('Forgive your neighbor the wrong he has done, and then your sins will be pardoned when you pray'). See Nolland, *Luke 9:21–18:34*, WBC 35ᵦ (Dallas: Word Books, 1993), 618.

34. As noted, Luke uses χάρις in Lk. 6.32, 33, 34 instead of μισθός (Mt. 5.46; cf. Lk. 6.23, 35).

35. James A. Sanders, 'Sins, Debts and Jubilee Release', in *Text as Pretext: Essays in Honour of Robert Davidson*, ed. Robert P. Carroll, JSOTSup 138 (Sheffield: Sheffield Academic, 1992), 277. He notes that χαρίζομαι is here used as a synonym of ἀφίημι.

36. Other canonical Gospels refer to Deut. 15.11 in the account of a woman anointing Jesus with precious oil. Mt. 26.6-13 (26.11)//Mk 14.3-9 (14.7)//Jn 12.1-8 (12.8).

37. Sanders, 'Sins', 273–4. What is striking is Luke's reference to Deut. 15.4 in Acts 4.34.

38. John J. Kilgallen, 'Forgiveness of Sins (Luke 7:36–50)', *NovT* 40 (1998): 114.

39. Jesus' delineation of the woman's acts is summed up as love in Lk. 7.42, 47.

Jesus' ministry of ἄφεσις in Lk. 4.18-19 (cf. 7.22) includes physical healing.[40] The disabled with their close association with the poor in Luke's Gospel lived at the margins of society (see Chapter 1).[41] Jesus' healing brings 'release – liberation' to them.[42] Lk. 13.10-17 refers to the healing (θεραπεύω v. 14) of a bent-over woman as release ([ἀπο]λύω vv.12, 15) from the bondage (δέω, δεσμόν v. 16) of Satan. The visible physical and particularly socio-economic effects of salvation 'here and now' sign the invisible deliverance from Satan.[43] In this respect, Esler aptly draws attention to the tangible benefits of salvation which Jesus brings, asserting that salvation for the poor must entail this-worldly physical deliverance, for instance, ἄφεσις of debt.[44] Hence what is noted is the integrated nature of release (ἄφεσις) in its spiritual and physical aspects. The invisibility of ἄφεσις of sins is manifested with the visible actions of healing (Lk. 5.18-26). Ἄφεσις of sin is tied to that of debt. The spiritual aspects of ἄφεσις assume and entail socio-economic dealings, and vice versa.

4.4 Salvation as Reversal

Joel Green features Luke's way of understanding salvation as 'reversal of positions'.[45] Reversal is both explicitly and implicitly a recurring theme throughout Luke's Gospel.[46] At the outset of the Gospel, the Magnificat (Lk. 1.46-55) manifests the intrinsic nature of reversal in three critical ways. First, Lk. 1.46-55 predominantly points to God (κύριος, σωτήρ, δυνατός vv. 46, 47, 49) as the subject. Except for μεγαλύνει and ἠγαλλίασεν (v. 46), all the verbs refer to God in the third person

---

40. The Hebrew text of Isa. 61.1 does not have recovering of sight to the blind.
41. Lk. 4.18; 5.12; 7.22; 8.43-44; 14.13, 21; 16.20-21; 17.11-19; 18.35-43.
42. John T. Carroll, 'Sickness and Healing in the New Testament Gospels', *Int* 49.2 (1995): 134–5. See also Donald E. Gowan, 'Salvation as Healing', *ExAud* 5 (1989): 10–12. cf. John J. Plich, 'Sickness and Healing in Luke-Acts', *Social World*, 181–209 (esp. 204–9); Bruce J. Malina, *The New Testament World: Insights from Cultural Anthropology* (Atlanta: John Knox, 1981), 61–2.
43. Esler, *Community*, 194.
44. Ibid., 191–7.
45. Green, 'Salvation', 27. He argues that Luke's use of σῴζω – both physical and spiritual – needs to be understood within a broader context of reversal in that Jesus' life reflects the heart of this theme. Thus, Green finds a close link between Jesus' exaltation and Lukan soteriology. Similarly, York observes the most important reversal in the life of Jesus. *Last*, 171–2.
46. York, *Last*, 9–10. His study divides the Lukan reversal passages into two categories: explicit reversal (Lk. 1.53-55; 6.20-26; 16.19-31; 18.9-14) and implicit reversal (2.34; 3.4-6; 7.36-50; 10.25-37; 14.7-24; 15.11-32; 18.18-30).

singular.⁴⁷ Second, God's doing is emphasized with the repetition of ποιέω (vv. 49, 51).⁴⁸ The first ποιέω points to great (μέγας v. 49) things done by the Mighty One (ὁ δυνατός v. 49) to Mary, a lowly servant (ταπείνωσις, δούλη v. 48),⁴⁹ and the second one refers directly to the reversal of the powerful and the rich and of the lowly and the hungry (vv. 51-53). God's saving activity is highlighted in terms of reversal.

Lastly, yet most importantly, God's saving action further unfolds as mercy (ἔλεος).Ἔλεος (vv. 50, 54) encloses the divine action expressed in terms of reversal (Lk. 1.51-53).⁵⁰ Luke also spells out what God has done for Elizabeth (Lk. 1.25) as his ἔλεος (1.58). Zechariah praises God for what he has done, that is, ἐποίησεν λύτρωσιν (Lk. 1.68) and ποιῆσαι ἔλεος (1.72). Once again God's saving activity is firmly grounded in his mercy (ἔλεος). Hence the Magnificat reveals that reversal is initiated by God. It is not human initiative, but God's doing. Moreover, his saving activity, featured as divine reversal, is grounded in his mercy.

Reversal occurs through divine initiative, yet whose status and fortunes are reversed? Lk. 1.52-53 contrast the powerful (δυνάστας) to the lowly (ταπεινούς), and the rich (πλουτοῦντας) to the hungry (πεινῶντας). The transposing verbs also explicitly invert directions:

καθεῖλεν **δυνάστας** ἀπὸ θρόνων
καὶ ὕψωσεν **ταπεινούς**,
πεινῶντας ἐνέπλησεν ἀγαθῶν
καὶ **πλουτοῦντας** ἐξαπέστειλεν κενούς. (Lk. 1.52-53 emphasis added)

The terms 'δυνάστης' and 'ταπεινός' are already mentioned in Lk. 1.48-49 with reference to God and Mary. The word 'δυνάστης' denotes one's position and power

---

47. See ἐπέβλεψεν (v. 48), ἐποίησέν (vv. 49, 51), καθεῖλεν (v. 52), ὕψωσεν (v. 52), ἐνέπλησεν (v. 53), ἐξαπέστειλεν (v. 53) and ἀντελάβετο (v. 54). The aorist tense of the verbs is much contested. The three suggestions are offered: (1) gnomic aorist as describing God's recurring action, (2) simple aorist as describing a past event and (3) prophetic perfect as describing a future event. For the first option, Walter Radl, *Das Evangelium Nach Lukas 1,1–9,50* (Freiburg im Breisgau, Germany: Herder, 2003), 82-3; the second, Raymond E. Brown, *The Birth of the Messiah: A Commentary on the Infancy Narratives in the Gospels of Matthew and Luke* (New York: Doubleday, 1999), 362-3; the third, Stephen Farris, *The Hymns of Luke's Infancy Narratives: Their Origin, Meaning, and Significance*, JSNTSup 9 (Sheffield: JSOT, 1985), 115-16.

48. York, *Last*, 49.

49. Ibid., 47-8.

50. See Mark Coleridge's discussion of divine power 'governed' by his mercy in Lk. 1.51-54. *The Birth of the Lukan Narrative: Narrative as Christology in Luke 1-2*, JSNTSup 88 (Sheffield: Sheffield Academic, 1993), 91-2.

as ruler.⁵¹ In contrast, the lowly (ταπεινούς) are the powerless. Moreover, ταπεινός here, despite its possible reference to one's spiritual status before God, primarily assumes one's low status in a literal sense.⁵² Whether it denotes Mary or Israel, the context is clear that they are located at the opposite end from power. Thus, both δυνάστης and ταπεινός suggest their objective status, not a figurative state of mind or spiritual state.⁵³ The literal sense of their meanings is further strengthened by the following two contrasting terms: 'πεινάω' and 'πλουτέω'.

Considering the common experience of hunger among the many (see Chapter 3), the use of the hungry (πεινάω) instead of the poor (πτωχός) as the antithesis of the rich (πλουτέω) sharpens the contrast.⁵⁴ The passage announces God's provision to those for whom hunger is a daily experience while the rich are sent away empty. Moreover, the identical words (ἐμπίπλημι, πεινάω) used in Lk. 6.25 correspond to the fate of the rich in 1.53. This inversed fate of the hungry and the rich is further elaborated in Luke's Beatitudes (Lk. 6.20-21, 24-25). Jesus pronounces blessings to the poor (πτωχοί), the hungry (πεινῶντες) and those who weep (κλαίοντες) while the rich (πλούσιοι), the well-fed (ἐμπεπλησμένοι) and those who laugh (γελῶντες) await their opposite fate. This reversal statement is vividly visualized in the Parable of Lazarus and the Rich Man (Lk. 16.19-31).

All these passages (Lk. 1.52-53; 6.20-21, 24-25; 16.19-31) call attention to the most disturbing reality, that is, 'the problem of abundance and lack', and thus of injustice.⁵⁵ Hence reversal manifests divine mercy and justice for those who suffer, namely, the poor, the hungry and those who weep, and against the injustice of the world. It is 'a matter of rejoicing' for the lowly and powerless like Mary and good news to the poor.⁵⁶

But what if 'the final consolation of the poor awaits them only after death[?]'⁵⁷ Indeed, an 'eschatological overtone' shades the Lukan passages of reversal.⁵⁸ The Parable of Lazarus and the Rich Man portray reversed fortunes only after their death. So are the Beatitudes (Lk. 6.21, 25) largely future oriented. Luke's frequent

---

51. The term, 'δυνάστης', refers to the official of Queen Candace in Acts 8.27 and to a prince of Arabia in Josephus, *Ant.* 13.118.

52. Klaus Wengst, *Humility: Solidarity of the Humiliated*, tran. John Bowden (London: SCM, 1988), 42. He notes, 'The description of Mary as a maid or slave points to the social sphere.' He further comments, 'The one who utters the Magnificat cannot be a person of high standing.'

53. R. John Vijayaraj, 'Human Rights Concerns in the Lukan Infancy Narratives (Luke 1:5–2:52)', *IJT* 46/1-2 (2004): 5.

54. Malipurathu, *Blessed*, 59–60. Although hunger can be used metaphorically for desiring God, 'it was not a known metaphor for a spiritual condition, nor was "hungry" ever considered a standard description for the "pious"' (60). See also Smit, *Food*, 126.

55. Smit, *Food*, 128.

56. Farris, *Hymns*, 124.

57. Lehtipuu, 'Reward', 246.

58. Ibid., 230.

remarks on divine reward such as eternal life (Lk. 10.28; 18.30), messianic banquet (13.28-29; 14.15), eternal dwelling (16.9) and treasure in heaven (18.22) seem to point to the future. Thus, Lehtipuu concludes, 'All Luke promises the poor is an eschatological reward.'[59]

Yet, ἡ βασιλεία τοῦ θεοῦ is announced as a present reality (ἐστίν) to the poor (Lk. 6.21). The poor belong to the kingdom now (νῦν Lk. 6.21, 25). Luke's narrative contexts show the fulfilment of the promises. Those who are hungry now (Lk. 6.21) are being satisfied (9.17; cf. 15.16; 16.21) and those who weep now (6.21) are being comforted (7.13-15, 38, 50; 8.49-56). Jesus' ministry fulfils them now in the Gospel in view of the eschatological fulfilment of the promise at the end of the age. Perhaps the contested use of the aorist tense in the Magnificat captures the ongoing tension observed in the Lukan reversal passages. Although York and Farris opt for different understandings of the aorist, together they highlight the eschatological tensions of reversal in the Magnificat.[60] Hence the future reversal has its sign in present reality.[61] The ministry of Jesus has inaugurated the future; the end of the age has already arrived in the person of Jesus while it is yet to be fully fulfilled and consummated.

4.5 Salvation as Repentance

While reversal as the message of salvation underscores its divine initiative and the lowly and the poor as its beneficiaries, repentance (μετάνοια; ἐπιστρέφω)[62] moves the focus towards human appropriation in response to divine action. Repentance is undoubtedly demanded of both because of a spiritual state of sinfulness and

---

59. Lehtipuu, 'Reward', 246.

60. York's note on an apocalyptic understanding of Lk. 1.48-54 converges with Farris's observation of the eschatological tension in the passage. York, *Last*, 52, 54–5; Farris, *Hymns*, 115–16.

61. York, *Last*, 56.

62. שוב which carries a general sense of repentance in the HB is most commonly translated into ἐπιστρέφω in the LXX instead of μετάνοια. However, increased use of μετάνοια to render שוב is attested. Thus, the two terms are 'convergent'. See Joel B. Green, *Conversion* (Grand Rapids: Eerdmans, 2015), 50–2. For further discussion on the terms, see Bertram, 'ἐπιστρέφω', *TDNT* 7:722–9; J. Behm, 'μετανοέω, μετάνοια', *TDNT* 4:989–1022; Nave, *Repentance*, 111–18; James G. Crossley, 'The Semitic Background to Repentance in the Teaching of John the Baptist and Jesus', *JSHJ* 2.2 (2004): 138–57; Méndez-Moratalla, *Conversion*, 15–18; David S. Morlan, *Conversion in Luke and Paul: An Exegetical and Theological Exploration* (London: Bloomsbury, 2013), 54–68. Note also almost half of the occurrences of μετανοέω and μετάνοια are found in Luke-Acts in the NT. Fourteen out of thirty-four of μετανοέω and eleven out of twenty-two of μετάνοια occur in Luke-Acts. See Torsten Jantsch, *Jesus, der Retter: Die Soteriologie des lukanischen Doppelwerks*, WUNT 381 (Tübingen: Mohr, 2017), 62. The case is similar with ἐπιστρέφω.

moral-ethical failure as Stenschke shows in his study of Luke's anthropology in relation to salvation.[63] Moreover, Luke's portrayal of repentance in socio-economic terms is evident in the Gospel. Thus, Luke's programmatic question, Τί ποιήσωμεν (Lk. 3.10, 12, 14), is crucial (Chapter 6). It not only expresses the eagerness for salvation but also expects the unfolding of what repentance entails, that is, ethical and behavioural change. The significance of John the Baptist's teaching is particularly noted in the discussion on repentance.[64] While the passage (Lk. 3.1-20) will be examined in Chapter 6 in detail, the point at issue here is the extent to which repentance is embodied in transformed behaviour in socio-economic relations.

Nave's study of 'the meaning of repentance' (μετανοέω, μετάνοια) repeatedly highlights its ethical characteristics.[65] He finds a paradigmatic role of John the Baptist's teaching (Lk. 3.10-14) in understanding repentance. Thus, repentance entails bearing the fruit which indicates the change of 'ethical social behaviour'.[66] The response of the disciples to Jesus' call is encapsulated in the phrase: they left everything (ἀφέντες πάντα Lk. 5.11, καταλιπὼν πάντα 5.28). Repentance provides a way to avoid the grim fate through a change of lifestyle in relation to the poor in the Parable of Lazarus and the Rich Man (Lk. 16.19-31). It takes a concretized form of mercy and justice towards the poor as it is closely tied to Moses and the Prophets in the parable. Luke expresses repentance in terms of transformed 'ethical behaviour that treats others fairly, justly and equitably'.[67] This particularly points to a proper use of possessions. In response to divine saving activity grounded in

---

63. Stenschke, *Portrait*, 383-5; 'The Need for Salvation', *Witness*, 132-4, 142. His survey underscores the Gentiles' need of salvation due to their moral failure and more importantly to their spiritual one. He argues that they are not in need of simple moral correction but of salvation. cf. Jantsch, *Jesus, der Retter*, 75-6. He highlights that repentance is demanded of sinners whose disposition is evil and wrong.

64. Nave, *Repentance*, 29. He argues that fruits and deeds worthy of repentance (ποιήσατε οὖν καρποὺς ἀξίους τῆς μετανοίας Lk. 3.8 and ἄξια τῆς μετανοίας ἔργα πράσσοντας Acts 26.20) show Luke's intentional emphasis on repentance. Similarly, Green also notes that Lk. 3.1-14 sets a framework for understanding the Lukan theme of repentance. Yet his argument diverges from Nave in that the passage is significant in two aspects both of which are closely tied to Isaianic prophecy: (1) its introduction to the image of restoration and (2) its theme of journey. *Conversion*, 17.

65. Nave, *Repentance*, 39-145. From his extensive investigation of the words, he suggests, 'Μετανοέω and μετάνοια essentially mean a change in thinking that usually leads to a change in behavior and or way of life' (145). Thus, he concludes that Luke's use of the word is in closer proximity to Graeco-Roman literature than Jewish one. Against this, Green critiques that Nave ignores 'Luke's concept of [the] covenantal basis' of repentance. *Conversion*, 52.

66. Nave, *Repentance*, 147.

67. Ibid., 164-89 (169).

mercy, repentance 'represents a voluntary human response ... as a method of correcting economic and social disparity among people'.[68]

Tannehill, however, cautions against what he sees as an overemphasis in understanding repentance as fruit and deeds of human actions. He accepts that ethical transformation marks repentance in Luke, yet he warns that salvation is not contingent upon human appropriation but divine mercy which comes prior to repentance.[69] He aptly draws attention back to divine initiated repentance. For Luke, even the possibility of repentance is grounded in the prior mercy of God. God's call for his people to *imitatio dei* (Lev. 19.2; Lk. 6.36) is based on God's saving mercy. However, repentance as human embodiment and enactment of divine mercy is not incongruent with salvation initiated by God.

John Barclay's paradigm shifting study on 'gift', which he interchangeably uses with grace and mercy, illuminates this point.[70] He rightly rejects 'the notion of "pure" gift, a gift without return' in his study of gift in antiquity. Gift and its reciprocal nature in both Graeco-Roman and Jewish contexts expects a return in certain forms.[71] Repentance, therefore, is both a gift of God and a response to this gift. It does not remain as an abstract term, but embodies ethical and behavioural changes in communal settings.[72] Recipients of this gift of repentance are expected to enact mercy (ἔλεος) as ὁ πατὴρ ὑμῶν οἰκτίρμων ἐστίν (Lk. 6.36) in tangible forms again marked with a socio-economic accent: loving enemies, doing good and lending generously (6.27-35).[73]

Repentance is also a transforming process, and thus its dynamic nature can be featured as 'a journey'.[74] Green observes that repentance as a journey implicates (1) 'the trajectory of one's life path', (2) 'the practices that are integral to this journey' and (3) 'the quality of one's travelling companions along the way'.[75] The practices embodying divine mercy evidence the orientation of one's journey and mark one's belonging. While journey is a central motif in the Lukan narratives,[76] this is particularly incorporated into the introduction of John the Baptist's ministry in

---

68. Nave, *Repentance*, 159.

69. Robert C. Tannehill, 'Repentance in the Context of Lukan Soteriology', in *The Shape of Luke's Story: Essays on Luke-Acts* (Eugene: Cascade, 2005), 88–90.

70. John M.G. Barclay, *Paul and the Gift* (Grand Rapids: Eerdmans, 2015), 183–8, 313.

71. Barclay, *Gift*, 64.

72. Green, *Conversion*, 45. Green comments, 'Embodiment is key.' See also Barclay, *Gift*, 574. In his conclusion, he notes, '[The divine gift of grace] has its necessary embodiment in the life of transformed communities.'

73. Lk. 6.27-35 not only implies that socio-economic issues are involved but also explicitly mentions radical giving and lending.

74. Green, *Conversion*, 17. Green uses conversion instead of repentance. Nonetheless, he rejects the distinction between the two terms.

75. Ibid.

76. In Luke-Acts, πορεύομαι occurs in 88 of 153 uses in the NT and πορεία occurs in Lk. 13.22. Also ὁδός occurs in 40 of 101 uses in the NT. A journey motif and the way signify

Lk. 3.4-6 (Isa. 40.3-6 LXX) (see Chapter 6). Not only does it refer to the way (ὁδός), it also pictures the image of transformation on the way. While the expressions of πληρόω and ταπεινόω (Lk. 3.5a) allude to the transposition of the powerful and the lowly in the Magnificat (1.52-53), σκολιός and εὐθεῖα (Lk. 3.5b) portray the image of transformation, and thus repentance.[77]

Luke's citation of Isa. 40.3-6 LXX has drawn scholarly attention to the Isaianic new exodus theme in the Lukan narratives.[78] Green observes that repentance as a journey is a journey to restoration.[79] Repentance is not only 'the response appropriate to God's initiative in restoration' but also 'the response that marks one as a member of the restored community'.[80] This theologically loaded new exodus motif is detected in Lk. 3.1-20. Nevertheless, the issue pertinent to our discussion is the way in which Luke unpacks its socio-economic implications in Lk. 3.10-14 and in his wider narratives.

The central section (Lk. 9.51–19.44) follows Jesus' physical and theological journey to Jerusalem.[81] At the outset and at the end of the journey, Jesus is met with the quest for eternal life: Τί ποιήσας ζωὴν αἰώνιον κληρονομήσω (Lk. 10.25; 18.18) (Chapter 7). Despite the lack of reference to repentance in these two accounts, the question echoes the inquiry of those who come to John the Baptist (Lk. 3.10-14). Doing (ποιέω) is stressed in terms of one's relation to the needy (ποιήσας τὸ ἔλεος Lk. 10.37) and to the poor (διάδος πτωχοῖς 18.22). Moreover, τί ποιήσω in Lk. 12.17 and 16.3 points in a similar direction (Chapter 8). Decisions made upon what to do with wealth affects one's destiny. Thus, the question of 'what

---

both geographical moves and theological implications. Concerning Luke's reference to the way (ὁδός), see Chapter 6.

77. Tannehill, *Unity: Luke*, 48.

78. See for the new exodus motif in Luke-Acts, Max Turner, *Power from on High: The Spirit in Israel's Restoration and Witness in Luke-Acts* (Sheffield: Sheffield Academic, 1996), 248–9; Pao, *Exodus*, 38–41; Peter Mallen, *The Reading and Transformation of Isaiah in Luke-Acts* (London: T&T Clark, 2008), 14–19; R. Hays, *Echoes in the Gospels*, 217–30; Green, *Conversion*, 69–81. Their argument is largely based on N. T. Wright's view that Israel in the STP was still in an exilic condition, 'under the oppression of foreign overlords' and hoped for the new exodus. See Wright, *The New Testament and the People of God* (London: SPCK, 1992), 269. He further argues that forgiveness of sins means return from exile. 'Exile will be undone when sin is forgiven' (273).

79. Green, *Conversion*, 69.

80. Ibid., 81–2.

81. The theological significance of Luke's Travel Narrative (TN) has been studied in the light of Deuteronomy. Moessner parallels the frame of Jesus' journey to Jerusalem (Lk. 9.51; cf. 9.31) with Israel's journey, particularly 'Moses and the exodus journey of Deuteronomy'. *Banquet*, xx. Also C.F. Evans, 'The Central Section of St. Luke's Gospel', in *Studies in the Gospels: Essays in Memory of R. H. Lightfoot*, ed. D.E. Nineham (Oxford: Basil Blackwell, 1955), 42–50. Evans suggests that Luke's Gospel is 'a Christian Deuteronomy' (42) and Luke arranges the Gospel following 'a Deuteronomic sequence' (50).

must we/I do?' in Luke's Travel Narrative (TN) (9.51-19.44) consistently recalls the message of repentance in Lk. 3.10-14 and challenges people on their journey to walk in the way of God, that is, being merciful.

4.6 Salvation as Restoration

The previous discussion of salvation as release, reversal and repentance point to and culminate in the restorative aspect of salvation. Release (ἄφεσις) from sin and debt marks a restoration in both covenantal and communal terms. Reversal redresses injustice, and thus restores justice. Repentance (μετάνοια, ἐπιστρέφω) enacts God's restoration through transformed relations with one another. The hopes and promises of restoration project an overall image of salvation. In what follows, I will examine the ways in which Luke's Gospel anticipates restoration.

First, understanding salvation as the restoration of Israel is deeply rooted in its covenantal relationship.[82] Ravens finds continuity between Israel's story and 'God's coming salvation' in Luke's infancy narratives.[83] Similarly Bauckham observes that Luke 1–2 skilfully incorporate a 'comprehensive programme of restoration of Israel'.[84] He also notes the 'unexpected route to Israel's restoration' from Jesus' death, resurrection and ascension[85] and the significance of the twelve in the programme of the restoration of Israel in Luke-Acts.[86] While salvation as restoration of Israel underscores the overall scheme of salvation in Luke-Acts from historical and theological perspectives,[87] Luke apparently sets the groundwork and the scope of Jesus coming in a bigger context than historical Israel.[88] Hence Gunter

---

82. This again has been promoted and strongly argued by N. T. Wright. Wright highlights salvation as creation of a new Israel as the renewed people of God who respond to God's faithful covenant. In this respect, Luke also reflects Jewish belief, that is, the redemption of Israel will benefit the whole world. *People*, 268–9, 334–81.

83. David Ravens, *Luke and the Restoration of Israel*, JSNTSup 119 (Sheffield: Sheffield Academic, 1995), 48–9.

84. Bauckham, 'Restoration', 439–63.

85. Ibid., 467–8. Here he points to the fulfilment of the new exodus. Contra Ravens argues that salvation is not freshly understood in the light of Jesus' death and resurrection, but is continuously centred on the God of Israel in Luke-Acts. *Restoration*, 168–9.

86. Ibid., 467–73 (467).

87. For instance, Ravens thinks that Israel denotes the undivided Davidic Kingdom. Thus, he notes the importance of the Samaritans who claim to be the descendants of the northern tribes. *Restoration*, 167–9. In a similar vein, Bauckham portrays the scheme of salvation in terms of the return of exiles by which he means the regathering and restoring of the twelve tribes, though not in a literal sense.

88. See Luke's worlds in Lk. 2.1; 3.1-2, Simeon's prophecy in 2.32 and the genealogy in 3.23-38.

Wasserberg argues that Luke interprets the Christian salvific event as the universal fulfilment of the Jewish promise of salvation.[89] Salvation as the restoration of Israel carries a bigger picture of God's renewal and the restoration of creation with Jesus.

Second, restoration features a communal aspect of salvation.[90] This shifts the focus from individual salvation to communal one which includes individuals by being a member of the community.[91] Johnson calls it a social dimension of salvation.[92] The essential meaning of salvation is 'inclusion within God's people'.[93] For instance, he links Jesus' healing accounts to restoration within a society.[94] Thus, the stress is on restoration, not on release from disease. Salvation means 'belonging to a certain community' here and now.[95] In a similar vein, Byrne expresses salvation as hospitality through which he reads Luke's Gospel – 'being welcomed into the community of salvation'.[96] This leads to our last point, that is, Luke's unique way of portraying salvation in the imagery of banquets.

Jesus' meal scenes most saliently portray restoration in Luke's Gospel. While Jesus eats with his friends and enemies, he welcomes, challenges and thus gathers people along the journey. With the ongoing imagery of banquets (particularly in Lk. 13.22–16.31), Jesus challenges the rich to invite the poor to their banquets as an apt response to the divine invitation and in view of ἡ βασιλεία τοῦ θεοῦ (Lk. 14.1-24) (Chapter 9). Hence the divine gift of salvation is depicted as an invitation to the messianic banquet. The imagery of banquets captures the reversed fate of the vindicated and condemned.

Yet Luke intriguingly leaves the door open,[97] and thus the possibility of salvation remains open for those who enact divine mercy. The imagery portrays not only the salvation of the poor and the hungry satisfied with abundant food but also the

---

89. Gunter Wasserberg, *Aus Israels Mitte - Heil für die Welt: Eine narrativ-exegetische Studie zur Theologie des Lukas*, BZNW 92 (Berlin: De Gruyter, 1998), 3.

90. Ravens, *Restoration*, 148–50. His reading of Luke's Gospel in relation to Jesus' ministry features more the restoration of sinners and the lost to the community than the pronouncement of forgiveness. Repentance (μετάνοια) is not directly linked to the forgiveness (ἄφεσις) of sins, but to the restoration of sinners to God and to the people of Israel.

91. Luke T. Johnson, 'Social Dimension of Sōtēria in Luke-Acts and Paul', *Essays*, 184, 189. While Ravens picks up Wright's covenantal understanding of the salvation of Israel, Johnson develops Wright's this-worldly and social dimension of salvation in early Christianity.

92. Johnson, 'Sōtēria', 184.

93. Ibid., 190.

94. Ibid., 189. Lk. 4.39; 5.14, 25; 6.9; 7.10; 8.39, 48-56; 14.4; 17.19.

95. Ibid., 196. Closer to Johnson's focus on the social dimension of salvation, Byrne and Bovon also draw attention to the communal aspect of salvation in Lukan soteriology. See Byrne, *Hospitality*, 195–7; Bovon, *Theologian*, 300–4.

96. Byrne, *Hospitality*, 195.

97. Lk. 14.12-14; 15.31-32; 16.27-31. cf. 13.25-30.

possibility of salvation for the rich in their relation to them. The enactment of divine mercy in a communal setting intrinsically involves the restoration of the people of God, that is, the gathering of the restored people of God.

One final observation needs to be reinforced, however, in that Luke does not offer an 'unconditional' notion of restoration. The divine gift of salvation as restoration assumes both active participation and divine reward.[98] Barclay's observation on gift and reward is again worth noting here.

> God's grace is not the opposite of recompense, but is *simultaneously* gift and reward. There is no antithesis here between gift and merit; grace and recompense stand in conjunction, not opposition. This is not to make the gift as less a gift or something akin to pay. Those who deserve gifts are still the recipients of gifts, given voluntarily and without legal requirement. They do not *cause* the gift to be given (that is always a matter of the benefactor's will), but they prove themselves to be its suitable recipients and thus provide the *condition* for its proper distribution. (Italic his)[99]

Luke never suppresses the idea of divine recompense and reward. Rather he features the concept in manifold ways and in close relation to the notion of salvation. Eating at the messianic banquet is a reward, particularly promised to the rich who celebrate their earthly banquets with the poor.

4.7 Conclusion

To sum up, this chapter affirms that 'Luke's noted concern for social economic issues [is indeed] incorporated into his understanding of salvation.'[100] The Lord's prayer in Luke's Gospel intertwines release (ἄφεσις) from sin and debt (Lk. 11.4). Merciful acts of releasing debts are analogized with Jesus' forgiving acts (Lk. 7.41-42). When reversal is pronounced and portrayed in the Gospel, it is heavily toned with socio-economic issues (Lk. 1.52-53; 6.20-21, 24-25; 16.19-31). Luke thus frequently welds religious concepts to socio-economic matters.[101]

Repentance is appreciated in terms of transformed socio-economic relations (Lk. 3.10-14; 5.28, 32). Divine rewards are promised to those who give freely and lend generously to the poor and who show mercy to the needy and do justice to others (Lk. 6.35, 38; 10.25-28, 37;12.32-33; 14.12-14; 16.9; 18.22, 28-30). Most crucially, the rich who invite the poor to their earthly banquets will participate in the messianic banquet. Thus, the imagery of banquet anticipates the poor and the rich as the restored people gathered around the table.

---

98. Barclay, *Gift*, 563.
99. Ibid., 316.
100. Reardon, 'Trajectories', 78.
101. York, *Last*, 60.

All the four aspects of salvation are derived from divine mercy (ἔλεος) and manifested in its human embodiment, particularly in the context of socio-economic relations. Reversal most vividly demonstrates divine justice particularly for the poor and against the injustice of the world. Salvation as release (ἄφεσις) and repentance (μετάνοια; ἐπιστρέφω) assumes divine mercy, and yet calls for its embodied form in a tangible transformation of lives in relation to others. Finally, restoration of the people of God concerns not only the historical and theological restoration of Israel, but also communal aspects of salvation. Luke portrays a vivid picture of restoration with the imagery of the messianic banquet, anticipating the gathering of the people, both the poor and the rich, around the table.

This chapter thereby draws on the discussion of socio-economic contexts (Chapters 2 and 3) to explicate the message of salvation in Luke's Gospel. At the same time, it offers a layout for the discussion of Luke's Gospel in the following chapters: (1) salvation of the poor in terms of divine mercy and justice (Chapter 5), (2) 'What must we/I do?' in terms of the human embodiment of divine mercy (Chapters 6, 7, 8) and (3) salvation of the rich in terms of the messianic banquet (Chapter 9).

Chapter 5

SALVATION OF THE POOR: DIVINE MERCY AND JUSTICE (LK. 4.18-19; 7.22; 7.11-17; 16.19-31)

5.1 Introduction

This chapter draws attention to the salvation of the poor. First and foremost, good news to the poor is the axiom which culminates in Jesus' mission statement in Luke's Gospel (see Chapter 1). Thus, the nature and the beneficiaries of this good news will be examined from Lk. 4.18-19 and 7.22 and their literary contexts. Next, I will examine the two passages, Lk. 7.11-17 and 16.19–31, which concern the widow and the fatherless and the poor, namely the triad of the helpless in the light of divine mercy and justice.[1] Lk. 7.11-17, the story of the widow at Nain whose son was dead at an early age, will be considered in terms of miracle, faith and salvation in order to see whether human appropriation is necessary for the salvation of the poor. Lk. 16.19-31, the parable of the poor man, Lazarus, and the rich man, will be examined in terms of reversal, piety and salvation. Lastly, I will revisit the salvation of the poor as divine mercy and justice, asking the following question: in the light of Luke's linking of socio-economic issues to salvation, can salvation be solely a divine gift without human appropriation?

5.2 The Good News of τὴν Βασιλείαν τοῦ Θεοῦ (Lk. 4.18-19; 7.22)

Jesus' ministry, encapsulated in Lk. 4.18-19 and reaffirmed in Lk. 7.22, not only demonstrates the identity of the Messiah but also reveals the nature of his mission. In these passages, the poor are the primary beneficiary of the good news. These two programmatic accounts thus capture the content of salvation: preaching good news to the poor (εὐαγγελίσασθαι πτωχοῖς Lk. 4.18; 7.22). Jesus' reading of Isaiah in Lk. 4.18-19 omits 'the day of vengeance of our God' (Isa. 61.2b) but adds to 'let

---

1. These two passages are selected as they offer the most vivid examples of the poor despite other instances where the text embraces the poor without using the term (e.g. Lk. 3.10-11; 4.25-26; 18.1-8).

the oppressed go free' (Isa. 58.6). This seemingly intentional alteration brings a double effect.

First, the omission weakens 'a negative aspect of the Isaianic message' while the addition strengthens the message of 'release'.[2] Second, as noted in Chapter 4, the combination of Isa. 61.1-2a and 58.6 brings the Jubilee traditions of the HB (Leviticus 25; Deut. 15.1-18; Exod. 21.2-4; 23.10-11) to the fore.[3] The correspondence of release (ἄφεσις, דְּרוֹר) in Lev. 25.10 and Isa. 61.1 weaves Jubilee images into the eschatological reign of God.[4] The release (ἄφεσις, שְׁמִטָּה) of debt (Deut. 15.1-11) and emancipation of slaves (Deut. 15.12-18), who most likely become indentured labourers due to indebtedness, feature socio-economic concerns towards those at the margins of society.[5] Strong messages admonishing mercy and justice towards the oppressed and the poor in Isaiah 58 also resonate with the images of Jubilee.[6] Hence God's sovereignty, expressed in his care for the poor, namely, the widow, the fatherless and the sojourner, demands that his people show mercy and do justice to them.[7] It is within these underlying themes of the Jubilee traditions that Jesus' proclamation of the NM is placed.

Lk. 7.22 (//Mt. 11.2-5) also strongly recalls Isaianic passages, especially Isa. 35.5-6, 29.18 and Isa. 61.1 LXX, each of which refers to the blind, the lame, the deaf and the poor in the context of eschatological expectations.[8] A similar expectation of a messianic figure is noted in 4Q521 (Messianic Apocalypse) which heavily draws on passages from Psalm 146 and Isaiah 61. In addition to an explicit mention of the Messiah (מָשִׁיחַ 4Q521 2 II 1), 4Q521's description of certain activities associated with a messianic figure is illuminating:

> (6) and his spirit will hover over the poor, and he will renew the faithful by his might. ... (8) releasing captives, giving sight to the blind and raising up those who are bo[wed down]. ... (12) for he will heal the wounded, give life to the dead and preach good news to the poor (13) and he will [sat]isfy the [weak] ones and lead those who have been cast out and enrich the hungry.[9]

---

2. Green, *Luke*, 209–10.
3. Sharon H. Ringe, *Jesus, Liberation, and the Biblical Jubilee: Images for Ethics and Christology* (Philadelphia: Fortress, 1985), 16–32; Nolland, *Luke 1–9:20*, 197; Wolter, *Lukasevangelium*, 192.
4. Ringe, *Jubilee*, 28–30.
5. Hamilton, *Deuteronomy*, 135–6.
6. Baker, *Tight Fists*, 97.
7. See Lev. 25.35-46; Deut. 15.7-14. Both passages highlight just and generous dealings with the poor, based on God's sovereignty.
8. Also possibly Isa. 26.19 LXX (ἀναστήσονται οἱ νεκροί). See Joseph Blenkinsopp, *Opening the Sealed Book: Interpretations of the Book of Isaiah in Late Antiquity* (Grand Rapids: Eerdmans, 2006), 135; George J. Brooke, *The Dead Sea Scrolls and the New Testament: Essays in Mutual Illumination* (London: SPCK, 2005), 162.
9. Translation is from John Collins, 'The Works of the Messiah', *DSD* 1.1 (1994): 99.

Interesting links between Lk. 7.22 and 4Q521 suggest that Luke and the author of 4Q521 share 'a common set of messianic expectations'.[10] Resurrecting the dead, not found in Isa. 61.1, is mentioned in both texts. Lk. 7.22 immediately follows the account of Jesus' raising of the widow's dead son (7.11-17). Similarly, Jesus' proclamation in Lk. 4.18-19 is further elaborated by reference to Elijah's visit to the Sidonian widow whose dead son Elijah raises and Elisha's healing of Naaman the leper (4.25-27).[11]

The structures of Lk. 4.18-9 and 7.22 also reveal the nature of Jesus' messianic ministry. Lk. 4.18-19 highlights **me** as the anointed one who <u>proclaims</u>, lists *the beneficiaries* of his ministry and stresses the nature of his ministry as *release* (ἄφεσις).[12] Followed by the summary of Jesus' ongoing ministry (Lk. 7.21), his answer to John the Baptist's question regarding his identity as the coming one (ὁ ἐρχόμενος)[13] is given in the repeated plural nouns with the present tense verbs in 7.22.[14]

πνεῦμα κυρίου ἐπ' ἐμὲ
οὗ εἵνεκεν ἔχρισέν **με**
    <u>εὐαγγελίσασθαι **πτωχοῖς**</u>,
ἀπέσταλκέν **με**,
    <u>κηρύξαι</u> *αἰχμαλώτοις* ***ἄφεσιν***
    καὶ *τυφλοῖς* ἀνάβλεψιν,
    ἀποστεῖλαι *τεθραυσμένους* ἐν ***ἀφέσει***,
    <u>κηρύξαι</u> ἐνιαυτὸν κυρίου δεκτόν. (Lk. 4.18-19)
    τυφλοὶ ἀναβλέπουσιν,
    χωλοὶ περιπατοῦσιν,
    λεπροὶ καθαρίζονται
    καὶ *κωφοὶ* ἀκούουσιν,
    νεκροὶ ἐγείρονται,
    <u>**πτωχοὶ** **εὐαγγελίζονται**</u>. (Lk. 7.22)[15]

What is highlighted from the juxtaposition of the two passages is εὐαγγελίσασθαι πτωχοῖς which captures the pinnacle of Jesus' messianic ministry. Both passages have strong allusions to the Isaianic message of God's salvific activities which feature his special concern for the poor, the disabled, the captives and the oppressed.

---

10. James D. Tabor and Michael O. Wise, '4Q521 "on Resurrection" and the Synoptic Gospel Tradition: A Preliminary Study', *JSP* 10 (1992): 161.

11. 1 Kgs 17.8-24; Lk. 7.11-17; 2 Kgs 5.1-19; Lk. 17.11-19.

12. Green, *Luke*, 210.

13. Tannehill, *Unity: Luke*, 80. Tannehill notes, 'John's question concerns the Messiah.' See also Fitzmyer, preface to *The One Who is to Come* (Grand Rapids: Eerdmans, 2007), vii.

14. Tannehill, *Unity: Luke*, 79.

15. The structural emphasis is adapted from Green, *Luke*, 210.

A further examination is necessary of the use of good news and its relation to the poor in the Isaianic context. First, Luke's predominant use of the verb εὐαγγελίζω is worth noting in that the same verbal form frequently occurs in Isaiah LXX. It is found only once in Matthew among the Gospels.[16] Conversely, Luke never uses a noun form, εὐαγγέλιον, in the Gospel unlike its frequent occurrences in Matthew and Mark.[17] Εὐαγγέλιον is also very rare in the LXX and never used in Isaiah LXX.[18]

Second, the ways in which Isaiah LXX uses εὐαγγελίζω are crucial. Isaiah LXX refers to εὐαγγελίζω in four different places (40.9; 52.7; 60.6; 61.1).[19] בָּשַׂר is used also in Isa. 41.27, but rendered as παρακαλέω in the LXX. In Isa. 40.9 and 41.27, good news is promised to Jerusalem without specifying its content. Yet, the message which is to comfort the people is implied from both passages as the rendering of בָּשַׂר in Isa. 41.27 LXX indicates. In Isa. 52.7 LXX the message becomes explicit. The messenger brings and announces good news (בָּשַׂר, εὐαγγελίζω), peace (שָׁלוֹם, εἰρήνη) and salvation (יְשׁוּעָה, σωτηρία). The crux of good news is encapsulated in the last phrase: your God reigns (מָלַךְ אֱלֹהָיִךְ, Βασιλεύσει σου ὁ θεός).[20] This directs our attention back to the Gospel. Blenkinsopp states that ἡ βασιλεία τοῦ θεοῦ in the Gospels is an 'abstract formulation of the statement "Your God reigns".[21]

Ἡ βασιλεία τοῦ θεοῦ has been understood as both/either reign as God's kingly rule and/or realm as the kingdom.[22] Dale C. Allison observes that these meanings are hard to disentangle while highlighting the spatial reality of ἡ βασιλεία τοῦ θεοῦ.[23] It is a place to enter in the future and the power which has already brought into action. A brief examination of τὴν βασιλείαν τοῦ θεοῦ in the Gospels reveals

---

16. Εὐαγγελίζω occurs twenty-six times in Luke-Acts while Matthew uses it only once (11.5). See Schilling, 'בשר', *TDOT* 2:316. He notes that the use of the word in Isaiah 61 indicates clearly the message of salvation. He further suggests that Luke's citation of Isa. 61.1 LXX illuminates the rendering of בשר as εὐαγγελίσασθαι in Isa. 61.1 LXX.

17. Εὐαγγέλιον is used twice in Acts (15.7; 20.24), none in Luke. However, it occurs twelve times in Matthew and Mark.

18. 2 Sam. 4.10 LXX.

19. See Craig A. Evans for full discussion of good news in Isaiah and the Gospels, 'The Function of Isaiah in the New Testament', in *Writing and Reading the Scroll of Isaiah: Studies of an Interpretive Tradition*, ed. Craig C. Broyles and Craig A. Evans, vol. 2 (Leiden: Brill, 1997), 653–91. He notes the following: The good news in Isaiah is 'theocentric' and entails 'healing and restoration'. He further suggests repentance as 'a prerequisite' for the good news (657).

20. Note that the LXX renders מָלַךְ (reigns) as βασιλεύσει (will reign).

21. Blenkinsopp, *Opening*, 135.

22. 'βασιλεία', *BDAG*: 134–5.

23. Dale C. Allison, Jr, *Constructing Jesus: Memory, Imagination, and History* (London: SPCK, 2010), 168–9.

that the Gospel writers use it both ways without constraint.[24] However, it means God's kingly reign when used in combination with εὐαγγελίζω in Luke's Gospel.

Luke frequently intertwines proclaiming good news with ἡ βασιλεία τοῦ θεοῦ.[25] In doing so, he specifies the nature of the kingdom or God's reign as good news. After announcing the NM, Jesus reasserts his mission in Capernaum as proclaiming the good news of God's reign (εὐαγγελίσασθαί ... τὴν βασιλείαν τοῦ θεοῦ Lk. 4.43). What is added to the good news is ἡ βασιλεία τοῦ θεοῦ. A similar pattern is found in Lk. 7.22 and 8.1. Jesus' ministry is listed in Lk. 7.22, echoing the NM, and then it is summarized as the good news of ἡ βασιλεία τοῦ θεοῦ in 8.1. One last time where this combination is found is in Lk. 16.16 where the new age is announced as the continuation of the Law and the Prophets.

Lastly, both ἡ βασιλεία τοῦ θεοῦ in the Gospel and βασιλεύσει σου ὁ θεός in Isaiah LXX point to God as a king. Royal concern for the poor is not only found in the HB but widely shared among the ANE traditions. Widows and orphans are the most vulnerable members of the ANE patriarchal societies. The protection of widows, orphans and the poor is stressed in religious and legal spheres. Specific gods or goddesses are designated as their protectors.[26] In Israel, although God is the only granter of justice to the poor,[27] kings as representatives of God's rule are expected to show special concern for them as their helpers, protectors and deliverers.[28]

---

24. For instance, ἡ βασιλεία τοῦ θεοῦ indicates a reward to be granted in Lk. 6.20; 12.31; 18.17, a place to enter in 18.24, 25 or a place where the messianic banquet takes place in 13.28; 14.15 and a reign which is to be proclaimed in 4.43; 8.1. Yet, there are places where its meaning may denote all the above. For more detailed discussion of the use of ἡ βασιλεία τοῦ θεοῦ in the Synoptic Gospels, see Allison, *Constructing*, 178–84.

25. Lk. 4.43; 8.1; 16.16; cf. Mt. 4.23; 9.35; 24.14. See Hans Conzelmann, *The Theology of Saint Luke*, trans. Geoffrey Buswell (London: Faber and Faber, 1960), 114. Acts also combines εὐαγγελίζω with peace, Jesus, resurrection and the kingdom of God. But they are usually used as objects of εὐαγγελίζω or with the preposition περί. Thus, what is proclaimed is specified as Jesus or his resurrection. Note also Lk. 9.2, 6 where proclaiming God's reign and preaching good news are used interchangeably. Tannehill's observation on Luke's combination of these two is also helpful. *Unity: Luke*, 77–81.

26. See Fensham, 'Widow', 129–39; Dupont, *Bonne Nouvelle*, 53–90; Baker, *Tight Fists*, 189–93.

27. Pss. 68.6-7; 76.8-10; 82; 103.6; 132.14-18; 140.13; 146.7-10; Isa. 14.30; 29.19-21; 25.4-5, 8; 35.2-10; 40.9-11; 41.17; 46.13; 51.5; 61.1, 7-8, 11; 67.1; Deut. 10.17-18; 15.7, 9; 24.14, 19-21 and so on.

28. Walter Houston, 'The King's Preferential Option for the Poor: Rhetoric, Ideology, and Ethics in Psalm 72', *BibInt* 7 (1999): 341–67; W. Dennis Tucker, Jr. 'Democratization and the Language of the Poor in Psalms 2–89', *HBT* 25 (2003): 161–78. Note that each member of the community is also called to do justice and show mercy towards the poor based on God's justice and mercy shown to them in their shared history.

In this respect, the coming of ἡ βασιλεία τοῦ θεοῦ announces good news particularly to the poor. It brings deliverance, release and rescue to widows, orphans and the poor. Jesus as the bringer and enactor of the good news of ἡ βασιλεία τοῦ θεοῦ fulfils scripture in his ministry and teaching. The content of his mission, summed up as the good news of ἡ βασιλεία τοῦ θεοῦ, is stated and restated throughout the Gospel.[29] Hence the good news of ἡ βασιλεία τοῦ θεοῦ captures a vital aspect of the salvation of the poor. It highlights God and Jesus, the One who is sent by God, and their action while the spiritual and moral qualities of the poor as the beneficiaries of salvation become less relevant.

I will now turn to two passages which specifically feature the widow, the fatherless and the poor and disclose their salvation in the light of divine mercy and justice. The first concerns the story of the revival of the only son of the widow (χήρα) at Nain in Lk. 7.11-17, and the second concerns Lazarus, who is called a poor man (πτωχός) in 16.19-31.

5.3 Miracle and Compassion (Lk. 7.11-17)

5.3.1 Literary and Narrative Contexts and Text

Since the story of Jesus' raising of widow's son at Nain (Lk. 7.11-17) is unique in Luke's Gospel, attention has been drawn to its literary affinities with a miraculous act of Apollonius (Ἀπολλωνίου θαῦμα)[30] and more frequently with Elijah's raising of the widow's son at Zarephath (1 Kgs 17.7-24).[31] The former gives an account of the resuscitation of a newly married girl who was seemingly dead and who was lamented by her bridegroom in the presence of the whole Rome.[32] The comparison is merited by the fact that the story is about the resuscitation of a young girl done by a wonder worker. Apart from this, however, links to the Lukan story are scant.[33] The tale was written later than the Gospel although it may have been known in the first century.[34]

---

29. Note Peter's summary of Jesus' ministry to Cornelius's household in Acts 10.38.
30. Philostratus, *Vit. Apoll.* 4.45.
31. cf. 2 Kgs 4.8-37.
32. Philostratus repeatedly uses δοκέω to describe the death of the girl: τεθνάναι ἐδόκει, τοῦ δοκοῦντος θανάτου. Then, he ends this miraculous account by casting doubts on whether the girl was dead (ἀπεσβηκυῖαν τὴν ψυχὴν) or still alive (σπινθῆρα τῆς ψυχῆς εὗρεν ἐν αὐτῇ).
33. See further discussion on the relationship of this account to the Lukan passage. Fitzmyer, *Luke*, 656–7; Graham H. Twelftree, *Jesus the Miracle Worker* (Downers Grove: InterVarsity, 1999), 307.
34. The work was written in the third century although Apollonius was active in the first century.

The affinities found to the LXX tradition are closer.³⁵ The identical phrase, Ἔδωκεν αὐτὸν τῇ μητρὶ αὐτοῦ (1 Kgs 17.23 LXX), is found in Lk. 7.15. The two stories indicate the gate of the city (πυλών, πύλη τῆς πόλεως) as the place where the prophets encountered the widows.³⁶ Thematically, both feature the raising of widows' sons and by these miraculous works, Elijah and Jesus are acknowledged as prophets sent by God. Nonetheless, dissimilarities are also noticeable. The ways in which Jesus raised the widow's son are distinctive from those of the stories of Apollonius and of Elijah. Jesus said to the young man ἐγέρθητι in a public setting, following which the dead man sat up and began to speak. By contrast, Apollonius uttered some secret words to the dead girl, and Elijah cried out to God in private to restore the boy's life.

Luke's narrative context strongly evokes the previous reference to Elijah's ministry to the widow at Zarephath (Lk. 4.25-26) which is mentioned as part of Jesus' mission statement. The story is placed right before the summary account of Jesus' ministry (Lk. 7.22) as mentioned.³⁷ Both point to the identity of Jesus and to the nature of his mission. Hence not only does the passage highlight Jesus' ministry of raising the dead as a 'messianic sign'³⁸ but it also refers to Jesus' announcement of the 'epoch of salvation' of which the primary statement is good news to the poor as noted earlier.³⁹ Moreover, reading the passage together with the account of a Gentile centurion (Lk. 7.1-10) provides a closer parallel with Jesus' message at Nazareth (4.24-27) where Naaman, a Gentile general, and the widow are mentioned as beneficiaries of God's messengers.⁴⁰

Within its immediate context, the passage is interestingly sandwiched between two well-known accounts, that of the centurion (Lk. 7.1-10) and of a woman known as a sinner (7.36-50) where πίστις is featured in relation to (δια)σῴζω.⁴¹ Crucially, our passage is silent on the faith, piety, humility or gratitude of either the widow or her son. The situation of the widow is highlighted, epitomizing the helpless and the impoverished. The σῴζω group word does not occur either, yet

---

35. See seven parallels between Elijah and Jesus' miracles, suggested by Craig A. Evans, 'The Function of the Elijah/Elisha Narratives in Luke's Ethics of Election', in *Luke and Scripture: The Function of Sacred Tradition in Luke-Acts*, ed. Craig A. Evans and James A. Sanders (Minneapolis: Fortress, 1993), 76–7.

36. Note τὸν πυλῶνα τῆς πόλεως in 1 Kgs 17.10 LXX and τῇ πύλῃ τῆς πόλεως in Lk. 7.12.

37. Tannehill, *Unity: Luke*, 72, 79–80, 88.

38. Alan Richardson, *The Miracle-Stories of the Gospels* (London: SCM, 1948), 113.

39. Green, *Luke*, 210–12.

40. Thomas L. Brodie, 'Towards unravelling Luke's use of the Old Testament: Luke 7:11–17 as an *imitatio* of 1 Kings 17:17-24', *NTS* 32 (1986): 250. He suggests reading Luke's two miraculous accounts in 7.1-10 and 11-17 with the broader context of the accounts in 1 Kgs 17.1-24.

41. Lk. 7.3, 9, 50. Note that the faith, piety and humility of the centurion and the faith and gratitude of the woman are the two distinctive aspects of the two accounts.

the salient phrase – ἐπεσκέψατο ὁ θεὸς τὸν λαὸν αὐτοῦ (Lk. 7.16)[42] – strongly indicates God's salvific activity done through Jesus. Hence careful examination of the text will further illuminate the dynamics of the story. Attention will be given to some significant words and phrases which capture its central message in three sections: (1) 7.11-12, (2) 7.13-15 and (3) 7.16-17.[43]

7.11-12
Καὶ ἐγένετο ἐν τῷ ἑξῆς ἐπορεύθη εἰς πόλιν καλουμένην Ναῒν
καὶ **συν**επορεύοντο **αὐτῷ** οἱ μαθηταὶ αὐτοῦ καὶ **ὄχλος πολύς**.
ὡς δὲ ἤγγισεν τῇ πύλῃ τῆς πόλεως,
καὶ ἰδοὺ ἐξεκομίζετο τεθνηκὼς *μονογενὴς υἱὸς τῇ μητρὶ αὐτοῦ* καὶ αὐτὴ ἦν *χήρα*,
καὶ **ὄχλος** τῆς πόλεως **ἱκανὸς** ἦν **σὺν αὐτῇ**.

7.13-15
καὶ ἰδὼν <u>αὐτὴν</u> ὁ κύριος ἐσπλαγχνίσθη ἐπ' <u>αὐτῇ</u>
καὶ εἶπεν <u>αὐτῇ</u>· **μὴ κλαῖε**.
καὶ προσελθὼν ἥψατο τῆς σοροῦ, οἱ δὲ βαστάζοντες ἔστησαν,
καὶ εἶπεν· νεανίσκε, **σοὶ λέγω, ἐγέρθητι**. καὶ ἀνεκάθισεν ὁ νεκρὸς καὶ ἤρξατο λαλεῖν, καὶ ἔδωκεν αὐτὸν <u>τῇ μητρὶ αὐτοῦ</u>.

7.16-17
ἔλαβεν δὲ **φόβος** πάντας καὶ **ἐδόξαζον τὸν θεὸν** λέγοντες
ὅτι *προφήτης μέγας ἠγέρθη ἐν ἡμῖν*
καὶ ὅτι **ἐπεσκέψατο ὁ θεὸς** τὸν λαὸν αὐτοῦ.
καὶ ἐξῆλθεν ὁ λόγος οὗτος ἐν ὅλῃ τῇ Ἰουδαίᾳ περὶ αὐτοῦ καὶ πάσῃ τῇ περιχώρῳ.

The first section describes two main figures: Jesus and the widow. Both are followed by large crowds and the two groups meet at the city gate (πύλη τῆς πόλεως). The dead person, the only son of his mother and the widow are introduced. The second section draws three parallels: (1) Jesus speaks to the widow and to her son; (2) Jesus has compassion on her and restores her son to her; (3) the Lord (ὁ κύριος) is the one who not only has compassion on the widow but also commands the dead man (ὁ νεκρὸς) to rise. The last section records the whole group's response. All (πάντας) celebrate the miraculous act which is interpreted and reported as a divine intervention, placing a particular emphasis on God.

Several details need further investigation. First, the text centres on the widow as Jesus saw *her* and had compassion on *her*, the crowd was with *her* and Jesus gave the raised son to *his mother*.[44] Jane Schaberg remarks, 'Most of the poor in every

---

42. Ἐπισκέπτομαι in Lk. 1.68, 78.
43. See Walter Vogels, 'A Semiotic Study of Luke 7:11-17', *EgT* 14 (1983): 273-92.
44. Green, *Luke*, 292.

age are women and the children who are dependent on them.'⁴⁵ This reflects the distressing reality of women in antiquity, especially widows who were deprived of male protectors. Thus, widows were grouped with vulnerable ones in their legal, social and economic relations; namely, the destitute, the fatherless, the sojourners and hired labourers in the scriptural tradition.⁴⁶ Luke's frequent reference to widows is also worth noting. Widows are depicted as those at the margins of society in the context of injustice and exploitation.⁴⁷ They are in abject poverty and the objects of charity (see Chapter 1 [PS]).⁴⁸

The gravity of the situation cannot be overemphasized. Unlike Luke's portrayal of some pious widows,⁴⁹ nothing is mentioned about her faith or piety. The text simply focuses on her tragic situation. Jesus speaks not only to the widow but also to the young man. The story thus concerns the restoration of life to both the widow and to her son who died at an early age. They are the poorest among the poor as the widow's distressful situation, complicated by the death of her dependent, fatherless son, indicates.

Second, ὁ κύριος which is 'Luke's first indisputable [Christological] use' of the word in Lk. 7.13 is noteworthy.⁵⁰ Luke deliberately uses ὁ κύριος instead of ὁ Ἰησοῦς in this account as it points to the subsequent question of John the Baptist on Jesus' identity as the Messiah, the coming one.⁵¹ In the text, the crowd acknowledges Jesus as the great prophet (προφήτης μέγας) which may allude to the eschatological prophet mentioned in Deut. 18.15, 18 and Acts 3.21.⁵²

Lastly, Luke's use of the word ἐπισκέπτομαι (Lk. 7.17) deserves most attention. It is particularly significant in its connection to salvation. It resonates with God's saving activity in the scriptural tradition when God is the subject of the action.⁵³

---

45. Jane Schaberg, 'Luke', in *WBC*, ed. Carol A. Newsom and Sharon H. Ringe (London: SPCK, 1992), 277.

46. H. Hoffner, 'אַלְמָנָה', *TDOT* 1:288; G. Stählin, 'χήρα', *TDNT* 9:445.

47. Note the Sidonian widow in abject poverty with her son in Lk. 4.25-26, a persistent widow asking for justice in 18.3-5 and widows' houses being devoured in 20.47.

48. Note a poor widow's offering in Lk. 21.2 and widows as the objects of charity in Acts 6.1; 9.39, 41.

49. Piety of Anna and that of two other widows (18.3, 5 and 21.2) are implied in the text.

50. Kavin Rowe, *Early Narrative Christology: The Lord in the Gospel of Luke* (Grand Rapids: Baker, 2009), 117.

51. Lk. 7.18-20 (ὁ ἐρχόμενος). cf. 3.17-18 (ἔρχεται). Rowe, *Christology*, 118–20; Green, *Luke*, 295–6.

52. Bovon, *Luke 1: A Commentary on the Gospel of Luke 1:1–9:50*, Hermeneia (Minneapolis: Augsburg, 2002), 270; Johnson, *Luke*, 119.

53. ἐπισκέπτομαι (פָּקַד) is used to refer to divine intervention for blessing or judgement. Note some manuscripts (f¹³ it sy^h) add εις αγαθον which makes the character of the visitation even clearer. See H.W. Beyer, 'ἐπισκέπτομαι', *TDNT* 2:605. See Gen. 21.1; 50.24, 25; Exod. 3.16; 4.31; 13.19; Ruth 1.6 and Acts 15.14 for the use of ἐπισκέπτομαι with God as the subject. In Acts 15.14, it refers to God's salvation initiated and brought to the Gentiles.

People's response demonstrates that what they witnessed is not only God's blessing on the individuals but also God's saving activity enacted on his people.[54] It recalls Zechariah's prophecy (Lk. 1.67-79) where he proclaims God's visitation (ἐπισκέπτομαι) to and redemption (λύτρωσις) of his people. Moreover, understanding God's visitation (ἐπεσκέψατο ὁ θεὸς Lk. 7.16) in relation to the Lord's compassion (σπλαγχνίζομαι 7.13) strongly evokes Zechariah's words: σπλάγχνον, ἐλέους θεοῦ, ἐπισκέπτομαι (Lk. 1.78). Thus, what was done by the compassionate Lord (Lk. 7.13) towards the widow and her fatherless son is clearly understood as God's saving mercy (ἔλεος).

Moreover, the story echoes the NM as it identifies the bringer, the beneficiaries and the content of the good news. In other words, it encapsulates the good news to the poorest of the poor, proclaimed and enacted by Jesus. The whole incident is summed up as God's gracious visitation to the helpless. With this in mind, we can now explore the relationship between the faith and salvation of the poor.

5.3.2 Miracle, Faith and Salvation

This story is one of the six uniquely Lukan miracle stories out of twenty miracles in the Gospel.[55] The significance of the Lukan miracle accounts is frequently noted at two points. First, the miracles are closely tied to the salvific work of God. Second, human faith plays a pivotal role between miracles and salvation.[56] The first point is agreed. Luke makes it quite evident that Jesus' healing ministry and miracles are to be understood in the light of a messianic sign which comes with ἡ βασιλεία τοῦ θεοῦ.[57] The second point is rather problematic. Miracles are evidently used as an effective device to bring people to faith in Acts.[58] Yet Jesus' miraculous acts in the Gospel do not always relate to faith or salvation.[59] Perhaps a more appropriate question for the miracles in Luke's Gospel is to what extent does faith effect miracles that result in salvation?

Theissen defines faith as 'the boundary-crossing motif' for the miracle to take place.[60] Faith in the Gospels may include not only trust but also pleas or cries for

---

Conversely, Lk. 19.44 uses it in the context of pronouncing judgement on Jerusalem. When humans are the subject, it means to visit the needy. See Mt. 25.36, 43; Acts 7.23; 15.36; Jas 1.27.

54. See Beyer, 'ἐπισκέπτομαι', *TDNT* 2:602.
55. There are about twenty miracle stories in Luke's Gospel. Six are uniquely Lukan: Lk. 5.1-11; 7.11-17; 13.10-17; 14.1-6; 17.11-19; 22.51.
56. Twelftree, *Miracle*, 144.
57. Blenkinsopp, *Opening*, 135.
58. Acts 3.6-9; 9.33-35, 40-42; 13.10-12; 16.30, 33; 19.13-20. See Paul J. Achtemeier, 'The Lucan Perspective on the Miracles of Jesus: A Preliminary Sketch', *JBL* 95.4 (1975): 553.
59. cf. Lk. 17.11-19 is a most salient example where miracle, faith and salvation are closely intertwined.
60. Gerd Theissen, *The Miracle Stories of the Early Christian Tradition* (Minneapolis: Fortress, 1983), 75-7.

help. Theissen's survey, on the one hand, distinguishes the faith connected to miracles of the NT tradition from other ancient miracle stories. It, on the other hand, highlights that faith in the Lukan miracle accounts is particularly 'grateful faith'.[61] The Samaritan leper's story (Lk. 17.11-19) is frequently referred to as a proof text to point out that his grateful faith leads him to salvation unlike nine others who experienced a mere physical healing (αὐτοὺς ἐκαθαρίσθησαν 17.14).[62] It is only when the Samaritan leper returned to show his gratitude after finding himself healed (ἰδὼν ὅτι ἰάθη Lk. 17.15) that Jesus pronounced that his faith has saved him (ἡ πίστις σου σέσωκέν σε 17.19).[63]

Slightly different though, Marshall comments that the issue is not so much the lack of faith of the nine lepers but their lack of gratitude. He notes, 'To faith must be added thanksgiving' for a physical healing to be an experience of salvation.[64] Twelftree cites Marshall's comment on several occasions to highlight that faith is the required element of the miracles.[65] Achtemeier goes further to assert that this story is reshaped to highlight faith in relation to miracle.[66] Admittedly, grateful faith or gratitude added to faith functions as a vehicle to bring salvation in this account.

However, two other Lukan miracle accounts – the healing of the woman bent over for eighteen years (Lk. 13.10-17) and of the man with dropsy (14.1-6) – are worth considering alongside the raising of the widow's son at Nain (7.11-17). How does faith work in these miracle narratives? First of all, the passive roles given to the beneficiaries are noted although the joyful response of the crowd is added to the miracles as they are done in public settings.[67] The widow and her fatherless son at Nain are presented as the archetypal poor. The woman who was bound for eighteen years is the captive whom Jesus came to set free. The man with dropsy

---

61. Theissen, *Miracle*, 135. His observation of Luke's distinctive way of narrating miracles is helpful (130–8).

62. Thus, it is argued that Luke distinguishes physical health (καθαρίζω in 17.14, 17; ἰάομαι in 17.15) from salvation (σῴζω in 17.19). Luke may have 'systematically' avoided his use of σῴζω when referring to merely physical healings as John Navone suggests. *Themes of St. Luke* (Rome: Gregorian University, 1971), 145. Or perhaps Luke simply changes to similar words – θεραπεύω, ἰάομαι, σῴζω, καθαρίζω – to avoid repetition for a literary purpose (See Lk. 5.12, 13, 15, 17; 7.3, 7; 8.43, 47, 48, 50; 17.14, 15, 17, 19).

63. Ἡ πίστις σου σέσωκέν σε occurs four times in Lk. 7.50; 8.48; 17.19; 18.42, once in Mt. 9.22 and twice in Mk 5.34; 10.52 and. cf. Lk. 8.50b (μὴ φοβοῦ, μόνον πίστευσον, καὶ σωθήσεται).

64. Marshall, *Luke*, 649, 652.

65. Twelftree, *Miracle*, 163, 175, 184, 185.

66. Achtemeier, 'Miracles', 554.

67. The bent-over woman responds to the healing by praising God (Lk. 13.13).

whose disease causes insatiable thirst was present in a meal setting at a Pharisee's house and healed.[68]

Second, the two healing stories in Luke 13 and 14 correspond at various points both linguistically and thematically. Both take place on the Sabbath and both point to healings in the context of release – (ἀπο)λύω. (Ἀπο)λύω (Lk. 13.12, 15, 16) is empathetically repeated in connection with eighteen years (13.4, 11) and δέω (δεσμός) (13.16). Jesus released (ἀπέλυσεν in 14.4) the dropsical man after healing. This alludes to the NM where the message which is also proclaimed on the Sabbath emphasizes release – ἄφεσις.[69] Lastly, these three miracle accounts are on the landscape of God's salvation enacted by Jesus. In these three accounts, the faith or piety of the distressed seems less relevant. Instead, the stories highlight the troubled circumstances of the beneficiaries and the compassion of the one who brings and enacts salvation. We will now turn to our second passage which deals with the salvation of the poor man Lazarus.

5.4 Reversal and Justice (Lk. 16.19-31)

5.4.1 Literary and Narrative Contexts and Text

Several ancient stories have the theme of reversed life after death in which they depict the sinners being punished while the just are rewarded.[70] An ancient Egyptian story, *Setne Khamwas and Si-Osire (Setne II)*, has been suggested as the

---

68. The physical conditions of the woman in Luke 13 and the man in Luke 14 draw much attention from physiognomic or metaphorical uses in the Graeco-Roman literary settings. For instance, Mikeal C. Parsons suggests that Graeco-Roman physiognomic traditions offer a better understanding to the physical condition of the woman described as 'unable to stand up straight' or 'having a "spirit of weakness"' which denotes moral weakness or 'evil disposition'. See *Luke*, 217–19; *Body and Character in Luke and Acts: The Subversion of Physiognomy in Early Christianity* (Waco, TX: Baylor University, 2011), 83–95. Also, dropsy in Luke 14 has been noted as a widely used term for 'greed and wealth'. Hence Hartsock argues that the presence of the dropsical man is used to attack the Pharisees for their insatiable greed. See Chad Hartsock, 'The Healing of the Man with Dropsy (Luke 14:1-6) and the Lukan Landscape', *BibInt* 21 (2013): 341–54. See also Green, *Luke*, 543, 546–7; Braun, *Feasting*, 22–42. While these seem plausible, primary attention should be given to their distressful physical conditions (see Chapter 9).

69. (ἀπο)λύω in Lk. 13.12, 15, 16 and 14.4. Sabbath in 13.10, 14, 16 and 14.1, 3, 5. Also in 4.16, 18.

70. For the popular reversal motifs of rich and poor in ancient folk tales, see C.F. Evans, 'Uncomfortable Words', *ExpTim* 81 (1970): 229. Note also Ronald F. Hock's suggestion: 'It is legitimate to cast the comparative net wide enough to include at least the traditional culture of Greco-Roman society.' 'Lazarus and Micyllus: Greco-Roman Background to Luke 16:19-31', *JBL* 106 (1987): 456. See also Nickelsburg, 'Riches', 324–44.

basis for this reversed motif in Luke's Parable of Lazarus and the Rich Man.[71] Two points of contact are found. Both stories depict the funerals (deaths) of poor and rich men, and their reversed fortunes in the afterlife.[72] However, the Egyptian story makes it clear that the reversal depends on good deeds done on earth.

Ronald Hock calls attention to a Graeco-Roman background of the parable by comparing Lazarus and a poor cobbler Micyllus from Lucian's *Gallus* and *Cataplus*.[73] Similar to Luke's description of the rich man, Lucian uses conventional ways of describing the rich men, Simon and Megapenthes.[74] Yet the reason for the reversed fate of the poor man, Micyllus, and the rich man, Megapenthes, in the afterlife is seemingly based on their moral character.[75] Reversal motif and judgement in the afterlife are also common in Jewish traditions.[76] However, these extensive parallels of ancient traditions where moral life in this world is counted to determine the fate in the afterlife have been rather unwisely used to fill the gap where Luke's parable remains silent.[77]

The parable most vividly embodies the Magnificat (Lk. 1.46-53) and the Beatitudes (6.20-21, 24-25) as noted (see Chapter 4). Linguistic echoes are clearly heard.

---

71. *Setne Khamwas and Si-Osire (Setne II)* 1, 15–33; 2, 1–15 in Miria Lichtheim, *Ancient Egyptian Literature: A Book of Readings*, vol. 3: *The Late Period* (Berkeley: University of California, 2006), 139–41. Lichtheim notes that the manuscript is from the first century CE and the story of the reversed fortunes reflects the common Greek thoughts fused into Egyptian stories. *Egyptian*, 9, 125–6.

72. See Bauckham for the detailed discussion of the Egyptian parallel to Luke's parable, 'The Rich Man and Lazarus: The Parable and the Parallels', *NTS* 37.2 (1991): 225–31.

73. Hock, 'Micyllus', 457–63.

74. Lucian, *Cat.* 14, 20; *Gall.* 6, 12.

75. Lucian's *Cataplus*, though not explicitly, provides the reasons for Micyllus to be destined to the Isles of the Blest alongside Cyniscus, the philosopher, in the narrative (*Cat.* 23). In the case of Megapenthes, the tyrant, the judgement finds clear grounds for his doom (*Cat.* 24–8). See Hock, 'Micyllus', 459. He attempts to fill the gap about which Luke's parable is silent concerning the reversal from Lucian's *Cataplus*.

76. Yet the reversed fate is not necessarily between rich and poor, but between righteous and unrighteous in Jewish traditions. See Larry Kreitzer, 'Luke 16:19–31 and 1 Enoch 22', *ExpTim* 103 (1992): 139–42. Rudolf Bultmann, *The History of the Synoptic Tradition*, trans. John Marsh (Oxford: Blackwell, 1972), 203. He finds Deut. 30.11-14 being illustrated in the parable in terms of Moses and the Prophets. Abraham and Eliezer in Genesis 15 is also suggested as an OT background setting for the parable by C.H. Cave, 'Lazarus and the Lukan Deuteronomy', *NTS* 15 (1969): 324–5; J. Duncan M. Derrett, *Law in the New Testament* (London: Darton, Longman & Todd, 1970), 86–8. For the illustration of Hades, see 1 En. 22, of afterlife and judgement, see *4 Ezra* 7.73-104 and of paradise, see *T. Ab.* 20.14.

77. Bauckham, 'Lazarus', 232. His reading of the first part of the parable (16.19-26) is particularly helpful. He observes that the gap which Luke leaves in the parable is one of the salient points of departure from other ancient stories.

16.25 τέκνον, μνήσθητι ὅτι ἀπέλαβες **τὰ ἀγαθά** σου ἐν τῇ ζωῇ σου, καὶ Λάζαρος ὁμοίως τὰ κακά· νῦν δὲ ὧδε **παρακαλεῖται**, σὺ δὲ ὀδυνᾶσαι.
6.24 Πλὴν οὐαὶ ὑμῖν τοῖς πλουσίοις, ὅτι ἀπέχετε τὴν **παράκλησιν** ὑμῶν.
1.53 πεινῶντας ἐνέπλησεν **ἀγαθῶν** καὶ πλουτοῦντας ἐξαπέστειλεν κενούς.

It is thematically connected to the previous story of the steward (Lk. 16.1-9) as both begin with an introduction to a rich man (ἄνθρωπός τις ἦν πλούσιος 16.1, 19) and concern the issue of wealth and its use.[78] The Pharisees and scribes are the intended audience of both Luke 15 and 16. Although Jesus directs attention to the disciples as he begins the story of the steward (Lk. 16.1), the Pharisees are present until 17.1 (16.14). Jesus' response to the derision of the Pharisees foreshadows an upcoming reversal in the parable: what is exalted before people is an abomination before God (Lk. 16.15).

What troubles commentators most is the section on the law, the kingdom and divorce (Lk. 16.16-18) which seemingly has little to do with the two parables in chapter 16.[79] Johnson's observation is illuminating in this regard. Abomination (βδέλυγμα) (Lk. 16.15), found in the Torah, particularly Deut. 24.4 and 25.16, points to condemnation on the remarriage of a divorced man to his former wife and on dishonest financial dealings.[80] The term is most often used to condemn idolatry.[81] It is also found in the context of religious observation and injustice done to the powerless in Isaiah 1.[82] Thus, this rather strange use of βδέλυγμα here links to the previous parable on financial dealings with reference to mammon (μαμωνᾶς), the teaching on divorce and the Parable of Lazarus and the Rich Man which ends with references to Moses and the Prophets (Lk. 16.29, 31).

The frequent references to the law in this chapter are also intriguing in that the law is juxtaposed with the good news of ἡ βασιλεία τοῦ θεοῦ (Lk. 16.16). This verse plays a central role for Conzelmann to demarcate the first two epochs of the history of salvation.[83] For Matthias Klinghardt, the difference between John the Baptist and Jesus who proclaims the good news of ἡ βασιλεία τοῦ θεοῦ in Lk. 16.16 lies in

---

78. Kreitzer, 'Luke 16:19–31', 140. He states that there is 'the essential compatibility' between the two parables (16.1-8a and 19-31). Marshall, *Luke*, 624.

79. Jacques Dupont, *Les Béatitudes*, Tome III: *Les Évangélistes* (Paris: J. Gabalda et Cie Éditeurs, 1973), 164. Dupont notes that 16.14-18 raises the most difficult question in his discussion of the rich man and Lazarus. Marshall, *Luke*, 624; Fitzmyer, *Luke*, 1114.

80. Johnson, *Luke*, 255. See also George Brooke, 'Luke-Acts and the Qumran Scrolls: The Case of MMT', in *Luke's Literary Achievement: Collected Essays*, ed. C.M. Tuckett, JSNTSup 116 (Sheffield: Sheffield Academic, 1995), 78. He notes the parallels between 4QMMT[a] and Luke-Acts on the issues of money and divorce.

81. βδέλυγμα in Deut. 27.15; 29.17; 32.16 LXX; 1 Kgs 11.5 LXX; Dan. 9.27; 11.31 LXX is used in the context of idolatry. cf. Mt. 25.15; Mk 13.14.

82. βδέλυγμα in Isa. 1.13 LXX. The prophet condemns the observation of religious festivals full of injustice and inequity but admonishes Israel to seek justice (Isa. 1.10-23).

83. Conzelmann, *Theology*, 16.

the dissolution of boundaries.⁸⁴ The eternal validity of the law remains because it serves the law of salvation.⁸⁵ In the discussion of the law in Lk. 16.16-18, he highlights the renunciation of possessions as comprehensive obedience to the law which ensures an eschatological reward.⁸⁶ He also links the opposition pronounced in Lk. 16.14-15 to the issue of purity in the light of Lk. 11.39, arguing that Pharisaic alms overcomes the contamination of impurity.⁸⁷ He further suggests that the prohibition on marriage arrangements in Lk. 16.18 which is originally applicable only to priests applies to Luke's community.⁸⁸ Hence Luke's teaching of the law is closely intertwined with the renunciation of possessions and purity. Unfortunately, however, his overall examination of the law is built upon and supported by the assumption that Luke is addressing his message to a church in danger of division.⁸⁹

In the light of the following verse (Lk. 16.17) and Luke's overall attitude towards the law, S. G. Wilson observes that the law is affirmed, yet with emphasis given to 'doing the law', not to abrogating it.⁹⁰ Hence the kingdom and the law coexist. However, Wilson wrongly harmonizes the two under the theme of 'a call to repentance'.⁹¹ He argues, 'Since "preaching of the kingdom" in Luke means primarily a call to repentance, the function of the Law and the Prophets is understood similarly.'⁹² This is not justified as Luke never combines the kingdom with repentance. Rather, the kingdom and the law are juxtaposed in several places in Luke. When the lawyer (Lk. 10.25-37) and the rich ruler (18.18-30) asked Jesus what they must do to inherit eternal life,⁹³ Jesus points to the law not to disprove

---

84. Matthas Klinghardt, *Gesetz und Volk Gottes: Das Lukanische Verständnis des Gesetzes nach Herkunft, Funktion und Seinem Ort in der Geschichte des Urchristentums*, WUNT 32 (Tübingen: Mohr, 1988), 79.

85. Klinghardt, *Gesetz*, 82.

86. Ibid., 81.

87. Ibid., 28. His discussion of Lk. 16.16-18 in the light of Lk. 11.39-41 and 14.13-21 is helpful.

88. Ibid.

89. Ibid., 24–9. One of his main arguments is Luke's understanding of the law and its relation to the debate between Jewish (law abiding) and Gentile believers. While investigating this, he forcefully compares the role of tax collectors and sinners against the Pharisees in Luke's Gospel to that of the Gentiles in Acts.

90. S.G. Wilson, *Luke and the Law*, SNTSMS 50 (Cambridge: CUP, 1983), 18. He agrees with Conzelmann at this point who argues, 'Until now there was "only" the Law and the Prophets, but from now on there is "also" the preaching of the Kingdom.' Conzelmann, *Theology*, 23.

91. Wilson, *Law*, 44.

92. But see my previous discussion (5.2). Luke combines the kingdom with good news while Matthew and Mark combine it with repentance.

93. Ζωὴν αἰώνιον (18.18, 30) is interchangeably used with entering εἰς τὴν βασιλείαν τοῦ θεοῦ (18.24, 25) and σῴζω (18.26). Note also Lk. 10.25-29 finds two points of contact with 16.14-18, which are the issues of the law and the self-justification of the lawyer and the Pharisees.

its validity but to highlight the central concern of the law towards the needy and the poor (see Chapter 7).[94]

In this respect, the parable's double references to Moses and the Prophets (Lk. 16.29, 31) are closely tied to its concern for the poor.[95] Both the law and the good news of ἡ βασιλεία τοῦ θεοῦ (Lk. 16.16) point to their particular concern for the poor which is essentially based on God's justice declared in Moses and the Prophets.[96] Likewise, the parable, on the one hand, depicts the eschatological reversal of fortunes as a central message of ἡ βασιλεία τοῦ θεοῦ. It, on the other hand, draws attention back to Moses and the Prophets.

The structure of the parable deserves a brief observation. The story can be divided into two parts: Lk. 16.19-26 and 16.27-31.[97] While Lk. 16.19-23 narrates the lives of Lazarus and the rich man and the deaths of both, the rest of the parable records the conversation between the rich man and Abraham. All of the rich man's requests are refused with the last section of the parable drawing attention back to the rich man's house. The parts are highlighted as follows:

Description	Content	Space / Time
Life of the rich man	luxurious clothing/feasting	rich man's house (gate)
Life of the poor man	sores and hunger; dogs	/ this world
Death of the poor man	angels	Abraham's bosom / afterlife
Death of the rich man	burial; tormenting	Hades / afterlife
Dialogue		
Rich man's petition	thirst; sending Lazarus to him	Hades / afterlife
Abraham's refusal	reversal and chasm	
Rich man's petition	sending Lazarus to his brothers	rich man's house / this world
Abraham's refusal	Moses and the Prophets	
Rich man's petition	resurrection and repentance	rich man's house
Abraham's refusal	Moses and the Prophets	/ this world

The two lives and deaths are pictured in stark contrast (Lk. 16.19-23). Luke employs a conventional way of depicting the poor and rich in terms of food and clothing (see Chapter 3).[98] The rich man is extremely wealthy in every way: house,

---

94. Lk. 10.28 confirms that obeying the law ensures eternal life (cf. Lev. 18.5); however, what is lacking is mercy towards the needy. Similarly, Lk. 18.22 suggests that what the ruler lacks in his keeping the law is his concern for the poor.

95. Green, *Luke*, 600.

96. Also in Lk. 10.25-37; 16.1-31; 18.18-30. See Josh Stigall, "'They have Moses and the Prophets": The Enduring Demand of the Law and Prophets in the Parable of the Rich Man and Lazarus', *R&E* 112.4 (2015): 553.

97. It is unnecessary to conclude that the second part of the parable is not original as suggested by John D. Crossan. 'Parable and Example in the Teaching of Jesus', *NTS* 18.3 (1972): 298–9.

98. The ways in which Luke describes the rich man's clothing (ἐνεδιδύσκετο πορφύραν καὶ βύσσον) and daily sumptuous feasting (εὐφραινόμενος καθ' ἡμέραν λαμπρῶς) are very

food, clothing and family (five brothers) while all the poor man owns is his name, Lazarus. He is thrown (ἐβέβλητο) at the gate (πυλῶνα) of the rich man's house and longs for (ἐπιθυμῶν χορτασθῆναι) food crumbs in the company of dogs.[99] His life of poverty needs no further demonstration. While the spatial proximity of Lazarus and the rich man is strikingly close, their socio-economic disparity is too wide to be overcome with the presence of the gate. This may well reflect the down to earth realities of the first-century Graeco-Roman world.[100] Their afterlife is similarly contrasted by Abraham's bosom (εἰς τὸν κόλπον Ἀβραάμ) over against Hades (ἐν τῷ ᾅδῃ) with repeated references to torment (βάσανος Lk. 16.23, 28) and agony (ὀδυνάω 16.24, 25).[101]

As the descriptive narration ends, the dialogue between the rich man and Abraham begins.[102] Lazarus is only referred to (Lk. 16.24, 25, 27, 28) without his voice being heard. Upon the rich man's appeal for mercy (ἐλεέω), Abraham provides two reasons for his refusal over which he has no control.[103] First, the reversal is affirmed echoing the Beatitudes (Lk. 6.20-24). Unlike the Egyptian story and Lucian's *Cataplus* where the reasons for the inversed fortunes are explained based on good deeds done on earth, Abraham's answer points to the disparity between the life of Lazarus and of the rich man and the divine justice exerted against this injustice.[104]

Second, the chasm which stood between Lazarus and the rich man in life not only exists but is also fixed to a degree that no one can cross even if one wishes to do so.[105] The presence of the physical gate (πυλών)[106] divides the rich man's world from that of Lazarus in life. In the afterlife, the chasm stands. While seemingly accepting his fate, the rich man appeals to Abraham for his brothers who are still living at his father's gated house. The temporal and spatial dimension of the parable

---

close to those of Lucian as noted (see Chapter 3). Lucian, *Gall.* 6, 12, 14; *Cat.* 14. See also Woolf, 'Writing', 83–99; William R. Herzog, *Parable as Subversive Speech: Jesus as Pedagogue of the Oppressed* (Louisville: John Knox, 1994), 117–21.

99. Possibly Lazarus is crippled as ἐβέβλητο suggests. Woolf, 'Writing', 95. Note his discussion of the association between beggars and dogs in antiquity.

100. Woolf, 'Writing', 84–5.

101. Abraham's bosom seems self-explanatory as the blessed state of Lazarus in the hereafter, strongly alluding to the banquet imagery (see Chapter 9). See also Jn 1.18; 13.23; 4 Macc. 13.17 for the use of κόλπος.

102. Lehtipuu, *Afterlife*, 7. She notes, 'The credibility is maintained by changing the narrative into a dialogue'.

103. Vogels notes that the passive form is used in v. 26. It suggests that not only the reversal but also the chasm is set by God. 'Having or Longing: A Semiotic Analysis of Luke 16:19–31', *EgT* 29 (1989): 33.

104. Bauckham, 'Lazarus', 232.

105. See *4 Ezra* 7.102–105 (esp. 104). The decisiveness of the Day of Judgement is mentioned.

106. It often refers to the entrance of palaces or temples. See 'πυλών', BDAG: 897.

moves back to where it began. Abraham rejects the rich man's request again this time on the basis of Moses and the Prophets, which are already available and sufficient to instruct them. Here again the parable departs from typical ancient reversal stories in that Abraham refuses to send the messenger to the living.[107]

5.4.2 Reversal, Piety, Salvation of Lazarus

While reversal is a recurring theme in the Lukan narratives (see Chapter 4),[108] it is not explained but pronounced.[109] Thus, scholars have attempted to answer why Lazarus is found at Abraham's bosom whereas the rich man is tormented in Hades. Jeremias offers the explanation for the reversal due to 'piety and humility' and 'impiety and lovelessness'.[110] Similarly Fitzmyer derives piety and humility from the poor man's name, Lazarus, as he is a uniquely named character in all of Jesus' parables.[111] However, as the beginning of the parable vividly pictures, Luke's focus once again is not on Lazarus's piety, but on his miserable life in stark contrast to the extravagant lifestyle of the rich man.[112] Repentance by the rich man is hinted at,[113] but nothing is mentioned of Lazarus's moral or spiritual conditions, only his physical misery.

Where, then, do we find an answer to Lazarus's presence at Abraham's bosom? Most likely, reversal as divine mercy and justice explains Lazarus's fortune. As mentioned in our earlier discussion of Lk. 7.11-17, God's visitation to the widow and her son is interpreted as God's visitation (ἐπισκέπτομαι) to his people. That is, the inauguration of God's reign is characterized by God's special concern for the poorest of the poor. The reversal in this parable points in a similar direction. The reversal which God initiates depicts ἡ βασιλεία τοῦ θεοῦ. It cannot be reduced to a mere moral lesson, but encapsulates the nature of ἡ βασιλεία τοῦ θεοῦ which is characterized by mercy and justice against the injustice in this world.[114] Abraham's response affirms that the reversal is not only just but also irrevocable as it is divinely sanctioned. Besides, μνήσθητι in Lk. 16.25 urges us to recall what is already pronounced by Jesus in the Beatitudes (6.20-21, 24-25) with the coming of

---

107. Bauckham, 'Lazarus', 245-6.
108. York, Last, 9-10. On Lazarus and the rich man, see 62-71.
109. Dupont, Évangélistes, 178. His note on Abraham's response in Lk. 16.25 is helpful: 'Le sous entendu est certainement qu'il est normal et juste que les choses se passent ainsi. Mais Abraham ne cherche pas à justifier; il se borne à constater.'
110. Joachim Jeremias, The Parables of Jesus (London: SCM, 1972), 185. His reading is grounded upon the folk tales of which he argues Jesus made use.
111. Fitzmyer, Luke, 1129. Lazarus (Λάζαρος), a Greek form of Hebrew Eleazar (אֶלְעָזָר), which means 'God helps' seems to be an apt name for this helpless poor man.
112. Dupont, Évangélistes, 175. He aptly notes that Luke is silent on Lazarus's piety or trust in God but speaks only of his extreme poverty.
113. Lehtipuu, Afterlife, 246.
114. See Bauckham, 'Lazarus', 232; Evans, 'Uncomfortable', 229.

ἡ βασιλεία τοῦ θεοῦ.[115] Hence the salvation of Lazarus depends solely on divine justice, not on his piety or moral qualities. This does not mean that God's justice has nothing to do with ethics, which I will discuss later (Chapters 6, 7 and 8). Rather, what is highlighted here is God's justice.

What is the significance of Moses and the Prophets which Abraham offers to the rich man's second appeal? Scriptural passages which lie behind the parable are worth noting.[116] As examined, the Jubilee traditions 'in Moses' (Exod. 21.2-4; 23.10-1; Leviticus 25; Deut. 15.1-18) provide firm grounds for Luke's concern for the poor. Also noteworthy are Isaiah 1 and Amos 5 where justice is centred at the heart of the prophets' warnings. Injustice to the needy at the gate (πύλη, πυλών) is condemned while justice at the gate is urged in Amos. It echoes what occurs at the gate of the rich man's house. Thus, the rich man's repentance in relation to Moses and the Prophets is crucial. Dupont argues that his inattentiveness to the teachings of Moses and the Prophets results in his doom.[117] Hence the repentance of the rich man based on the teachings of Moses and the Prophets is implied in the second part of the story (Lk. 16.27-31).[118]

However, it is unnecessary to argue that the parable is about the rich man and his brothers, following Jeremias.[119] This ignores Luke's concern for Lazarus and for God's justice which persistently appears throughout the story. The parable speaks not merely to the charitable works neglected by the rich man. Rather, it directs attention to divine mercy and justice which the ministry of Jesus enacts throughout the Gospel.[120] The juxtaposition of the reversal and Moses and the Prophets culminates in God's mercy and justice. Hence the parable diverges from ancient reversal stories. It features divine justice against injustice in this world, making the piety of the poor less relevant. Besides, the parable does not end with an apocalyptic dimension, but draws attention back to this world and Moses and the Prophets which the living already have.

---

115. As noted, it also echoes Mary's song in 1.53 (ἀγαθῶν; τὰ ἀγαθά in 16.25).

116. Deut. 15.4-8; 24.6; Isa. 1.5-6, 17, 23; Amos 5.12-15. See Marshall, *Luke*, 632; Herzog, *Parables*, 121; Cave, 'Lazarus', 322, 325. For a more extensive reference to the HB, see Johnson, *Luke*, 253.

117. Dupont, *Évangélistes*, 182; Green, *Luke*, 609.

118. Lehtipuu argues that the message of repentance is intensified by the theme of reversal in the parable. The rich man's failure to listen to Moses and the Prophets regarding special concerns for the poor explains his fate in Hades. *Afterlife*, 165–6, 296.

119. Jeremias, *Parables*, 186. His concluding comments on the parable are as follows: 'Hence the poor Lazarus is only a secondary figure, introduced by way of contrast. The parable is about five brothers, and it should not be styled the parable of the Rich Man and Lazarus, but the parable of the six brothers.'

120. Lk. 24.27, 44.

5.5 Salvation of the Poor: Divine Mercy and Justice

While the miracle story in Lk. 7.11-17 depicts salvation as God's compassionate visitation to the widow and her son, the Parable of Lazarus and the Rich Man highlights the reversal of fortunes as God's justice. The two passages examined intriguingly converge at several points. Both contain the theme of death and resurrection. Σῴζω-group words do not occur in either story. Nonetheless, they resonate with significant salvific themes. The beneficiaries are the widow (χήρα), her fatherless son and a poor (πτωχός) man, Lazarus. They graphically represent the poor to whom good news is proclaimed and ἡ βασιλεία τοῦ θεοῦ is promised. Both stories allude to the Magnificat (Lk. 1.52-53), the Benedictus (1.68-69), the NM (4.18-19; 7.22) and the Beatitudes (6.20-21). They portray the fulfilment of the promises mentioned at the outset of the Gospel.

Lazarus, who longs for food, is found at Abraham's bosom at the eschatological banquet (Lk. 16.22, 23). A feast is awaiting as promised in the Beatitudes (Lk. 6.20a) that the one who is hungry will be filled. The widow, the one who weeps, is now comforted by Jesus' word and deed which are elsewhere described as χάρις (Lk. 4.22; 7.21).[121] The resuscitation of her son changes her tears into laughter (Lk. 6.20b). Salvation is a very present reality to the widow and her son while it points to the future reversal in the Parable of Lazarus and the Rich Man.

Both accounts also refer to the gate (πύλη, πυλών) as the place where the stories take place. At the gate of Nain, Jesus meets the widow and her dead son, where Jesus shows compassion to the widow and restores her son to life. Conversely, at the gate of the rich man's house, Lazarus, a beggar, is thrown and desires to relieve his hunger. No mercy (ἔλεος) is shown to him at this gate. The gate generally served as public space in the ANE towns.[122] Its juridical function makes the gate the place where justice to the socially and legally deprived is promoted in the HB in particular.[123] The scriptural tradition makes it evident that God's justice (מִשְׁפָּט) represses the oppressors, but delivers the oppressed.[124] Thus, Amos condemns injustice done at the gate towards the needy (אֶבְיוֹן [πένης] Amos 5.12 [LXX]) alongside the poor (דַּל [πτωχός] 5.11 [LXX]) being trampled (בוש [κατακονδυλίζω]

---

121. G. Stählin, 'χήρα', *TDNT* 9:450. He notes, 'Tears are a stock attribute of the widow.' cf. Job 31.16; Lam. 1.2.

122. Otto, 'שַׁעַר', *TDOT* 15:395.

123. Otto, 'שַׁעַר', 15:376.

124. For the use of justice (מִשְׁפָּט) expressed with a special concern towards the powerless – widow, orphan and the poor – in the HB, see Exod. 23.6; Lev. 19.15; Deut. 10.18; 24.17; 27.19; Isa. 1.17; 3.14; 10.2; 32.7; Jer. 5.28; 22.3; Mal. 3.5; Pss. 103.6; 146.7. For the detailed discussion of justice in the HB, see Moshe Weinfeld, '"Justice and Righteousness" – צדקה משפט – The Expression and Its Meaning', in *Justice and Righteousness: Biblical Themes and their Influence*, ed. Henning Graf Reventlow and Yair Hoffman, JSOTSup 137 (Sheffield: JSOT, 1992), 228–46.

5.11 [LXX], literally means to strike with the fist) and admonishes Israel to establish justice at the gate (5.15).¹²⁵

> For I know how many are your transgressions,
> and how great are your sins –
> you who afflict the righteous, who take a bribe,
> and push aside the needy in the gate. (Amos 5.12)

> Hate evil and love good,
> and establish justice in the gate. (Amos 5.15a)

Perhaps it is not without significance that both stories are set up at the gate. The content of good news is ἡ βασιλεία τοῦ θεοῦ whose nature is summed up as justice. Dupont's comment on God's justice in the light of good news is illuminating: 'sa "justice" devient ainsi sollicitude compatissante à l'égard des faibles et des pauvres, et l'annonce de son intervention apparaît aux malheureux comme une "bonne nouvelle".'¹²⁶ God's reign which is intrinsically tied to his justice is marked by mercy (ἔλεος) towards the helpless.

5.6 Conclusion

To sum up, Luke's focus is not on the faith or piety of the poor, but on God's mercy and justice which ἡ βασιλεία τοῦ θεοῦ brings. Salvation of the poor in the passages examined (Lk. 7.11-17; 16.19-31) stresses divine mercy rather than human appropriation. Particularly because of the nature of ἡ βασιλεία τοῦ θεοῦ, it is good news to the poor. This does not idealize the poor or poverty. Their condition is not to be envied. But their plight draws God's mercy and demands his justice. Salvation of the poor is contingent upon divine ἔλεος and justice. Thus, what is needed is not a theology of the poor but a theology of God's justice.¹²⁷ God's justice speaks loudly in the scriptural tradition as it is intertwined with its cultic settings.¹²⁸ Luke indeed closely follows the tradition. His message of salvation foremost highlights

---

125. Timothy M. Green, *Hosea-Micah: A Commentary in the Wesleyan Tradition*, NBBC (Kansas City: Beacon Hill, 2006), 277-9; Weinfeld, '"Justice and Righteousness"', 238. Weinfeld argues that what is observed in Amos (3.10; 4.1; 5.11; 8.5-6) is 'oppression perpetrated by the rich landowners and the ruling circles who control socioeconomic order'. Note that a similar voice is heard in Isa. 1.17, 10.2 and Zech. 7.9-10.

126. Dupont, *Bonne Nouvelle*, 69.

127. Ibid., 89-90.

128. Amos 5.14-15; 21-4; Isa. 1.17; 10.2; 58.2-9; Zech. 7.9-10. Fasting, keeping festivals and sacrificial offerings are juxtaposed with their injustice done to the poor. See also Mary Douglas, 'Justice as the Cornerstone: An Interpretation of Leviticus 18-20', *Int* 53 (1999): 347-9.

ἡ βασιλεία τοῦ θεοῦ. At the centre lies God's justice tied to his compassion and mercy especially towards the powerless.

> Render true judgments (מִשְׁפָּט), show kindness (חָסֶד) and mercy (רַחֲמִים) to one another;
>> do not oppress the widow, the orphan, the alien or the poor;
>> and do not devise evil in your hearts against one another. (Zech. 7.9-10)

Chapter 6

WHAT MUST WE DO?: HUMAN EMBODIMENT OF DIVINE MERCY I (LK. 3.1-20)

6.1 Introduction

Having examined the salvation of the poor in terms of divine mercy and justice, I will now turn to their human embodiment in the next three chapters (6, 7 and 8), following the question: 'What must we/I do?' in Luke's Gospel. This chapter examines Luke's unique account of John the Baptist's teaching in Lk. 3.10-14 in its immediate context (3.1-20). This account, shaped by the threefold question, Τί ποιήσωμεν (Lk. 3.10, 12, 14),[1] sets an example for the later accounts where the question is raised in the Gospel (10.25-37; 18.18-30; cf. 12.16-21; 16.1-9). Also, it plainly incorporates Luke's socio-economic concerns into his message of salvation by expressing repentance (μετάνοια) as the human embodiment of divine mercy and justice.

The significance of John the Baptist's ministry and baptism in Luke-Acts is evidenced at several points. Not only is his message of μετανοίας εἰς ἄφεσιν ἁμαρτιῶν (Lk. 3.3) continued by Jesus and his followers throughout Luke-Acts,[2] but his baptism is also regarded as the beginning of Jesus' ministry[3] and is affirmed repeatedly as the one initiated by divine authority.[4] Moreover, his preaching resonates with the message of salvation of which he gives knowledge to people as

---

1. Fitzmyer, *Luke*, 469.

2. See Lk. 4.18; 5.20, 23, 32; 7.47-49; 15.7; 24.47; Acts 2.38; 3.19; 5.31; 10.43; 11.18; 13.38; 20.21; 22.16; 26.18-20.

3. Acts 1.22; 10.37; 13.24. Especially note Acts 1.22 where Jesus' earthly ministry begins from the baptism of John (ἀρξάμενος ἀπὸ τοῦ βαπτίσματος Ἰωάννου) and ends with the ascension of Jesus (ἕως τῆς ἡμέρας ἧς ἀνελήμφθη ἀφ' ἡμῶν).

4. Note Lk. 3.2; 7.24-29; 20.4. See also Tannehill, *Unity: Luke*, 48–50; Bovon, *Luke 1*, 127; Marshall, *Luke*, 132; Green, *Luke*, 166, 603. Contra Conzelmann argues, 'John no longer marks the arrival of the new [era], but the division between two epochs in the one continuous story, such as is described in Luke xvi, 16.' *Theology*, 22–3.

he proclaims repentance for ἀφέσει of sins (Lk. 1.77). What marks his ministry is not separation from that of Jesus and of his followers, but its 'archetypal' role and its continuation in the Lukan narratives.[5]

I will first suggest a chiastic reading of Luke's account of John the Baptist's ministry (Lk. 3.1-20). This will provide the contexts for his teaching (Lk. 3.10-14) and illuminate its character. Next, I will examine (1) the historical–political (Lk. 3.1-2, 19-20), (2) soteriological (3.3-6, 18) and (3) eschatological contexts (3.7-9, 15-17) of the teaching (3.10-14). Lastly, I will further explore John's teaching (Lk. 3.10-14) of showing mercy and doing justice in the light of its scriptural background and in view of its enactment in Lk. 19.1-10 and in Acts 2.37-47 and 4.32-37.

6.2 A Chiastic Reading of Lk. 3.1-20

Scheffler argues that it is essential to analyse Lk. 3.10-14 within its immediate context (3.1-20) despite his failure to recognize the structural significance of its context.[6] Most commentaries divide Luke's account of John's ministry in Lk. 3.1-20 into three sections under the heading of 'The Ministry of John the Baptist': John the Baptist (3.1-6), his preaching (3.7-18), his imprisonment (3.19-20) with a few variations.[7] Bovon and Radl divide the middle section into two: preaching (3.7-14) and the Messiah (3.15-18).[8] Some suggest subsections, noting different aspects of John's preaching (3.7-18). Fitzmyer's outline of the middle section (Lk. 3.7-18) is typical: 'eschatological, ethical and messianic'.[9] However, this section division fails to illuminate Luke's account of John the Baptist's teaching. Instead, a chiastic reading of Lk. 3.1-20 sheds light on the teaching (3.10-14).[10]

---

5. Joel Green, 'From "John's Baptism" to "Baptism in the Name of the Lord Jesus": The Significance of Baptism in Luke-Acts', in *Baptism, the New Testament and the Church: Historical and Contemporary Studies in Honour of R.E.O. White*, ed. Stanley E. Porter and Anthony R. Cross, JSNTSup 171 (Sheffield: Sheffield Academic, 1999), 159, 162.

6. E.H. Scheffler, 'The Social Ethics of the Lucan Baptist (Luke 3:10-14)', *Neot* 24.1 (1990): 21, 30.

7. Typical of this structure are Fitzmyer's in *Luke*, 449–78 and Nolland's in *Luke 1–9:20*, 136–57; Green differs only in specifying John's preaching as 'good news' (3.7-18). *Luke*, 165–83.

8. Bovon, *Luke 1*, 119–28; Radl, *Lukas 1,1–9,50*, 145.

9. Fitzmyer, *Luke*, 463. See also Marshall, *Luke*, 132–50; Neale, *Luke 1–9: A Commentary in the Wesleyan Tradition*, NBBC (Kansas: Beacon Hills, 2011), 89–101.

10. Note that Green suggests a structural development of the middle section (Lk. 3.7-18). *Luke*, 174.

    A Judgment in 3.7-9,
        B Instruction in 3.10-14,
    A′ Judgment in 3.15-17,
        C Summary in 3.18.

6. Human Embodiment of Divine Mercy I

The suggested chiastic structure of the passage is as follows:

A. Historical–Political Context (Lk. 3.1-2)
    B. Message of Salvation: Prepare the Way (Lk. 3.3-6; cf. Isa. 40.3-5)
        C. Impending Judgement (Lk. 3.7-9)
            D. What Must We Do?: Bearing Fruits Worthy of Repentance (Lk. 3.10-14)
        C′. Impending Judgement (Lk. 3.15-17)
    B′. Message of Salvation: Exhortations and Good News (Lk. 3.18)
A′. Historical–Political Context (Lk. 3.19-20)

This chiastic structure discloses the ways in which each section (A, B, C) corresponds to the other (A′, B′, C′) and at the same time points to the central section (D). Thus, John's teaching in Lk. 3.10-14 (D) stands as the crux of the passage (Lk. 3.1-20). Several observations are worth noting here. First, Luke introduces John's ministry in the context of the powers of his day (A), particularly mentioning Herod the tetrarch of Galilee (τετρααρχοῦντος τῆς Γαλιλαίας Ἡρῴδου Lk. 3:1), and concludes with Herod's imprisonment of John (3.19-20) (A′).[11] Luke refers to Philip as Herod's brother (Φιλίππου ... τοῦ ἀδελφοῦ αὐτοῦ Lk. 3:1) (A) and Herodias as his brother's wife (Ἡρῳδιάδος τῆς γυναικὸς τοῦ ἀδελφοῦ αὐτοῦ Lk. 3.19) (A′).

Second, John's preaching of μετανοίας εἰς ἄφεσιν ἁμαρτιῶν in Lk. 3.3 and the citation from Isa. 40.3-5 LXX in Lk. 3.4-6 (B) match up with the exhortations (παρακαλῶν) and the preaching of the good news (εὐηγγελίζετο) in 3.18 (B′). Third, John's warnings with a metaphor of tree and fruit in Lk. 3.7-9 (C) and wheat and chaff in 3.15-18 (C′) correspond although the one who brings judgement differs. Lk. 3.9 indicates God as the judge whereas the Messiah (ὁ Χριστός 3.15) is the one who judges in 3.17.

The wider context of the salvific message (B, B′) highlights the nature of John's ministry as alluded to in the birth narratives (Lk. 1.16, 17, 76, 77) despite the presence of impending judgement. Moreover, in relation to the central section (D), note the threefold question asked by the people who come to be baptized (D) in response to John's message of salvation (B) and to his warning of impending judgement (C). While John's teaching (D) primarily expounds the meaning of his exhortation in Lk. 3.8 (ποιήσατε ... καρποὺς ἀξίους τῆς μετανοίας), the question also assumes: 'What must we do to be saved?' Hence this chiastic reading of the passage (Lk. 3.1-20) illuminates the meaning and the significance of John's teaching in Lk. 3.10-14 (D) by providing the historical–political, soteriological and eschatological contexts.

---

11. Josephus, *Ant.* 18.136.

6.3 The Historical–Political Context of John's Teaching
(Lk. 3.1-2, 19-20)

The style of Luke's detailed introduction in Lk. 3.1-2 places John the Baptist close to the prophets in the HB.[12] The subject, ῥῆμα θεοῦ in association with Ἰωάννην τὸν Ζαχαρίου υἱὸν and ἐν τῇ ἐρήμῳ (Lk. 3.2), comes last after a lengthy introduction of the historical–political settings.[13] Lk. 3.1-2 locates John's ministry within the geopolitical powers of the day as noted (see Chapter 2). In fact, Luke opens his first three chapters in a similar pattern.[14]

The whole narrative begins in the days of King Herod (Lk. 1.5). Jesus' birth is announced in the context of a census under Augustus (27 BCE–14 CE) and Quirinius, the governor of Syria (6–12 CE) (Lk. 2.1). Luke's reference to a census by Quirinius in connection with Jesus' birth has been contested with respect to dating.[15] The reason for mentioning the census, however, is not to be so much chronological as drawing attention to the significance of a census in relation to Jesus' birth. Luke's repeated reference to a census (ἀπογράφω, ἀπογραφή Lk. 2.1, 2, 3, 5; Acts 5.37) which was tied to the direct Roman taxation *tributum capitis* explains both the political and the socio-economic background of Jesus' birth and ministry (see Chapter 2).[16]

John the Baptist launched his ministry (Lk. 3.1) during the reigns of Caesar Tiberius (14–37 CE), Pontius Pilate the governor of Judaea (26–36 CE), Herod Antipas the tetrarch of Galilee (4 BCE–39 CE), Philip the tetrarch of Ituraea and Trachonitis (4 BCE–34 CE) and of the high priesthoods of Annas (6–15 CE) and

---

12. Green, *Luke*, 163. See Jer. 1.1; Zech. 1.1 LXX.

13. Michael E. Fuller suggests that stress might be given to 'in the wilderness' rather than to John in that the word of God comes not 'in Rome' or 'in the Temple', but 'in the wilderness'. 'Isaiah 40.3-5 and Luke's Understanding of Wilderness of John the Baptist', in *Biblical Interpretation in Early Christian Gospels*, vol. 3: *The Gospel of Luke*, ed. Thomas R. Hatina, LNTS 376, SSEJC 16 (London: T&T Clark, 2010), 50.

14. Lk. 1.5 (ἐν ταῖς ἡμέραις Ἡρῴδου βασιλέως τῆς Ἰουδαίας); 2.1 (ἐν ταῖς ἡμέραις ἐκείναις ... Καίσαρος Αὐγούστου). See Pyung Soo Seo, *Luke's Jesus in the Roman Empire and the Emperor in the Gospel of Luke* (Eugene: Pickwick, 2015), 23–30. He argues that Luke intentionally compares John the Baptist and Jesus particularly in Luke 1 and 2 to highlight Jesus' authority. He also compares the powers, Caesar Augustus and King Herod of Judaea, which provide the settings of Jesus' and John's births (see 27–9). For the general discussion of parallelism between John the Baptist and Jesus in Luke 1–4, see Farris, *Hymns*, 99–107; Talbert, *Literary*, 44–8; Green, *Theology*, 51–5.

15. There is at least a decade gap in the historical dating (Mt. 2.1-22; Lk. 1.5). For further discussion, see Brown, *Messiah*, 547–55 (Appendix VII: The Census under Quirinius); Stanley E. Porter, 'The Reasons for the Lucan Census', *Luke*, 165–88; A.N. Sherwin-White, *Roman Society and Roman Law in the New Testament* (Grand Rapids: Baker Book, 1978), 162–71.

16. Green, *Luke*, 124–5; Josephus, *Ant*. 17.354; 18.1-2. In relation to the census, Josephus refers to the rebellion of Judas the Galilean (*Ant*. 18.6, 23) which Luke also mentions in Acts 5.37.

Caiaphas (18–37 CE).[17] In a wider narrative context of the Gospel, these rulers play a significant role in the deaths of John the Baptist and Jesus.[18] A negative portrayal of Herod is clearly recorded (Lk. 3.19-20). John's reproval of Herod over Herodias is noted. Luke adds to it: Πάντων ὧν ἐποίησεν πονηρῶν ὁ Ἡρῴδης. After all, Herod imprisoned John (Lk. 3.20) and later killed him (9.7-9).[19]

In the immediate context, however, John the Baptist's message (Lk. 3.10-14) directly points to the socio-economic issues of the time – food and clothing for basic subsistence, tax collection and the extortion of money by soldiers. The historical–political settings in which Luke posits his whole story are closely linked to the socio-economic framework of the time. Luke also marks the crowd who come to be baptized by 'their economic status'.[20] Taking the economic exploitation by Roman governors, the Herodians and the ruling class of Judaea, particularly the high priestly families into account (see Chapter 2), it is not coincidental that Luke mentions tax collectors (τελῶναι)[21] and soldiers (Lk. 3.12, 14) instead of the Sadducees and Pharisees (Mt. 3.7).[22] They are most likely of Jewish origin as the locals are usually engaged in collecting indirect taxes in Roman Palestine.[23] The involvement in tax farming by the Jews is attested in Josephus.[24] Soldiers here are suggested to be Herod's forces. They often assist tax collectors in collecting taxes.[25]

17. See Josephus, *Ant.* 18.26, 34, 95 for the appointment and deposition of the high priesthood of Annas and Caiaphas and *Ant.* 20.198 for the remark about Annas who had five sons in the high priesthood, in addition to Caiaphas his son-in-law and Matthias his grandson. Hence Annas must have had huge influence on the high priesthood. Jeremias, *Jerusalem*, 157, 194–5.

18. See Lk. 9.9, 22; 13.31; 19.47; 20.1, 19; 22.2, 4, 52, 54; 23.1-25; Acts 4.6, 27.

19. For Luke's portrayal of Herod Antipas, see Jensen, *Antipas*, 115–16.

20. While the Pharisees and the Sadducees come to be baptized in Mt. 3.7 (cf. 16.1, 6, 11), Luke instead has the crowd (ὄχλοι) including tax collectors and soldiers.

21. This term, 'τελώνης', only occurs in the Synoptic Gospels, but none in the LXX or Apocrypha. See John R. Donahue, 'Tax Collectors and Sinners: An Attempt at Identification', *CBQ* 33.1 (1971): 45–8, 54, 58–9. He notes that they are toll collectors who work within the tax farming system, collecting indirect taxes, such as customs and tolls.

22. Lk. 3.10-14; Mt. 3.7. See Laurie Brink, *Soldiers in Luke-Acts: Engaging, Contradicting, and Transcending the Stereotypes*, WUNT 362 (Tübingen: Mohr, 2014), 98.

23. Fitzmyer, *Luke*, 470; Green, *Luke*, 179–80; Marshall, *Luke*, 143. The narrative context of John's message, particularly in reference to Abraham's descendants in Lk. 3.8, points to their Jewish origin. Contra Brink, *Soldiers*, 100–101; Bovon, *Luke 1*, 124; Radl, *Lukas 1,1–9,50*, 175–6. They suggest that they are Roman soldiers based on Luke's positive portrayal of Roman soldiers in Luke-Acts (Lk. 7.1-10; 23.47; Acts 21.31-40; 22.22-30; 23.10, 12-35; 27.1-44).

24. Josephus, *Ant.* 12.169-178. He gives an account of a tax bidding and Ptolemy grants Joseph to farm taxes. Also in *J.W.* 2.287. John, a tax collector (Ἰωάννης ὁ τελώνης), was with other Jews to solve the trouble over the synagogue in Caesarea.

25. Fitzmyer, *Luke*, 470; Marshall, *Luke*, 143; Joan E. Taylor, *The Immerser: John the Baptist within Second Temple Judaism* (Grand Rapids: Eerdmans, 1997), 118. Josephus, *Ant.* 12.180. Joseph took two thousand foot soldiers for assistance in tax collecting.

In the time of John's ministry, it was Herod Antipas who oversaw the collection of taxes and tolls in Galilee as the tetrarch.²⁶

Two aspects of Josephus's portrayal of John the Baptist provide interesting parallels to Lk. 3.10-14.²⁷ First, he depicts John's teaching ethically. John urged the Jews (τοῖς Ἰουδαίοις) to practise virtue (ἀρετήν) and justice/righteousness (δικαιοσύνῃ) towards one another and piety (εὐσεβείᾳ) towards God (*Ant.* 18.117). Second, he recounts that some people (τῶν ἄλλων) gathered with excitement upon hearing his words (τῇ ἀκροάσει τῶν λόων) and with readiness to follow his counsel (συμβουλῇ). Here John P. Meier suggests that tax collectors and soldiers are τῶν ἄλλων among John's adherents in Josephus's account (*Ant.* 18.118).²⁸ Thus, Herod may have considered John the Baptist as a possible threat not only politically but perhaps also economically.²⁹ This suggests that one of the contributing factors to Herod's killing of John is his influence on tax collectors and soldiers who are 'important props of Antipas's financial and military power'.³⁰

As examined, Lk. 3.1-2, 19-20 provides the historical–political context for John the Baptist's teaching in 3.10-14 with the introduction of the powers and the presence of tax collectors and soldiers. It also reflects the abuse of power and economic exploitation.

6.4 *The Soteriological Context of John's Teaching (Lk. 3.3-6, 18)*

Lk. 3.3 sums up John's ministry as proclaiming a baptism of repentance for the forgiveness of sins (κηρύσσων βάπτισμα μετανοίας εἰς ἄφεσιν ἁμαρτιῶν). It is interpreted as a fulfilment of Isaiah's prophetic message.³¹ Lk. 3.4-6, a citation from Isa. 40.3-5 LXX, is of particular importance in answering in what sense John the

---

26. Emil Schürer, *The History of the Jewish People in the Age of Jesus Christ (175 B.C.–A.D. 135)*, ed. Geza Vermes and Fergus Millar, vol. 1 (London: T&T Clark, 1973), 372, 374.

27. Josephus's portrayal of John in a positive light is intriguing (*Ant.* 18.117-118), considering his harsh criticism of other prophet-like figures (Theudas in *Ant.* 20.97-99; an Egyptian Jew in *Ant.* 20.167-170; *J.W.* 2.259-263; an imposter in *Ant.* 20.188).

28. John P. Meier, 'John the Baptist in Josephus: Philology and Exegesis', *JBL* 111.2 (1992): 236–7. cf. Feldman footnotes that the identity of τῶν ἄλλων is not clear but suggests that they might be 'the unjust men' (Josephus, *Ant.* 18.118 [Feldman]).

29. Meier, 'Baptist', 237.

30. Ibid. Concerning Herod's imprisonment and killing of John the Baptist, Josephus explains that it was due to fear (δείσας) and suspicion (ὑποψίᾳ) of possible insurrection (ἀποστάσει) (*Ant.* 18.118-119). See also Lk. 3.19. However, Luke does not give a detailed account of John's death unlike Mt. 14.3-12 and Mk 6.17-29.

31. Fitzmyer, *Luke*, 460–1. He notes that ὡς in Lk. 3.4 indicates a fulfilment of Isa. 40.3-5 in John's ministry. Similarly, ὡς is used in Acts 13.33, indicating fulfilment of the scripture.

Baptist's preaching is summarized as good news (εὐαγγελίζω) in Lk. 3.18.³² Moreover, the reverberating echoes of Isa. 40.3-5 in Luke's birth narratives mark the significance of this citation in Luke.³³ Not only do Lk. 1.16-17 and 1.76-77 strongly allude to Isa. 40.3 along with Mal. 3.1 and 4.5-6,³⁴ but they also anticipate and prepare for John the Baptist's ministry in Lk. 3.3-6. I will briefly examine Lk. 1.16-17 and 1.76-77 in three aspects: (1) Ἐπιστρέφω (Lk. 1.16, 17), (2) Ἑτοιμάζω (1.17, 76) and (3) Δίδωμι γνῶσιν σωτηρίας (1.77).

Ἐπιστρέφω is a most frequently translated word for שוב in the HB in the LXX.³⁵ שוב means 'turn' or 'return' to the point of departure and is used for a physical, moral and religious change.³⁶ When it is used with 'to God', it conveys the idea of conversion or repentance. Although שוב is rarely rendered as μετανοέω in the LXX,³⁷ Luke's use of ἐπιστρέφω appears synonymous with μετανοέω.³⁸ Luke uses them together to describe related concepts in Lk. 17.4 and in Acts 3.19 and 26.20.³⁹

---

32. Luke's repeated uses of σώζω related terms which occur in the beginning of the Gospel (Lk. 1.47, 69, 71, 77; 2.11, 30) culminate in Lk. 3.4-6.

33. Klyne Snodgrass, 'Streams of Tradition Emerging from Isaiah 40:1-5 and its Adaptation in the New Testament', *JSNT* 8 (1980): 36. He particularly notes that Isa. 40.3-5 is heard in the Lukan birth narratives (1.17; 1.76-79; 2.30-33). See also Tannehill, *Unity: Luke*, 47.

34. John's role as Elijah in Luke's Gospel has been disputed. Although Lk. 1.17 strongly reflects Mal. 3.22-23 LXX and mentions that John is to come in the power and spirit of Elijah, it seems less likely that Luke portrays John the Baptist as Elijah. Unlike Matthew, Mark and Luke does not mention John the Baptist's diet and clothing nor associates him with Elijah. cf. Mt. 3.4, 11.14, 17.10, Mk 1.6, 9.11. Rather Jesus is described as a great prophet like Elijah in Luke's Gospel (Lk. 4.25-27; 7.11-17). See Walter Wink, *John the Baptist in the Gospel Tradition* (Cambridge: CUP, 1968), 42-4; Marshall, *Luke*, 59. Contra Fitzmyer strongly argues that Luke identifies John as Elijah. *Luke the Theologian: Aspects of His Teaching* (London: Geoffrey Chapman, 1989), 103, 108-9.

35. William L. Holladay, *The Root ŠÛBH in the Old Testament* (Leiden: Brill, 1958), 20. His survey shows that about 70 per cent of *šûbh* is rendered as compound verbs of στρέφω in the LXX.

36. Nave, *Repentance*, 112.

37. נחם is often translated as μετανοέω in the LXX and frequently denotes changes in God's intention. See 1 Sam. 15.29; Amos 7.3, 6; Joel 2.13, 14; Jon. 3.9,10; 4.2; Zech. 8.14; Jer. 4.28; 18.8, 10. However, Jer. 8.6 LXX renders שוב as μετανοέω referring to human repentance from wickedness. Also see Jer. 31.19 and Isa. 46.8.

38. Tannehill, *Shape*, 86-7. Contra Nave argues that ἐπιστρέφω and μετανοέω are not synonymous. The meaning of μετανοέω has changed from the idea of remorse or regret to that of 'a change in thinking and behaving' in that later Greek translators of the HB increasingly render שוב as μετανοέω. *Repentance*, 112-18 (118).

39. Luke's use of ἐπιστρέφω closely reflects that of the LXX. Lk. 17.4 interestingly combines a change of physical direction with an idea of repentance.

Hence ἐπιστρέφω (Lk. 1.16, 17) anticipates John the Baptist's preaching of repentance (μετάνοια) in Lk. 3.3.[40]

John's role is most typically depicted as a preparer, yet interestingly Luke adds the idea of preparing a people (λαός) for the Lord (Lk. 1.17) to preparing the way (ὁδός) of the Lord which is attested in all the Synoptic Gospels.[41] Ἑτοιμάζω in Lk. 1.17 follows repeated occurrences of ἐπιστρέφω (1.16, 17). Hence the idea of 'turning' as an expression of repentance is strengthened and suggests that a people will be prepared for the Lord through repentance. Furthermore, ἑτοιμάζω is reminiscent of Isa. 40.3 and Mal. 3.1 and is reiterated in Lk. 3.4 and 7.27. Ἑτοιμάσαι ὁδοὺς αὐτοῦ in Lk. 1.76 is linked with τοῦ δοῦναι γνῶσιν σωτηρίας in 1.77 as they form a structural parallel. Both seem to draw ideas from Isa. 40.3-5 LXX which is cited in Lk. 3.4-6.[42]

While to give knowledge of salvation draws an explicit connection between John the Baptist and salvation, the nature of this knowledge is not clear in the first instance. Farris suggests that ἐν ἀφέσει ἁμαρτιῶν αὐτῶν (Lk. 1.77) defines the meaning of the knowledge of salvation although no precedence for this expression is found in other contemporary writings.[43] Significantly, knowledge which leads to salvation is closely related to ἀφέσει ἁμαρτιῶν which John's baptism of repentance is also concerned with (Lk. 3.3).[44] Σωτηρία in Lk. 1.77 is a recollection of the Davidic Messiah in 1.69 (κέρας σωτηρίας) and of God's deliverance in 1.71 and of an anticipation of σωτήριόν in 2.30 and 3.6. Hence prophetic pronouncements concerning John's work in Lk. 1.16-17 and 1.76-77 harbinger the ways in which John turns, prepares and gives knowledge of salvation to people in Lk. 3.1-20, particularly alluding to Lk. 3.3-5.

Concerning Luke's citation of Isa. 40.3-5 LXX, the influence of Isa. 40.1-11 on Lk. 3.3-6, 18 is worth noting. A broader context of Isa. 40.1-11 LXX which introduces themes of God's comfort and restoration to Isaiah 40–66 provides a thematic background behind Lk. 3.3-6, 18.[45] Isa. 40.1-11 LXX opens up with the

---

40. See Taylor, *Immerser*, 107–10. Taylor argues that repentance for John means 'a turning back to God in obedience and trust' (107). Thus, it means following Torah and doing good.

41. In both uses of ἑτοιμάζω, it portrays John's relationship to the Lord. See Mt. 3.3; 11.10; Mk 1.2, 3; Lk. 3.4; 7.27. Here in Lk. 1.17 and 1.76, whether 'the Lord' refers to God or the coming Messiah is ambiguous and disputed. Although the parallelism between John and Jesus in the Lukan birth narratives points to John as a forerunner and preparer of Jesus, it is not clear whether 'the Lord' in Lk. 1.15-17 refers to Jesus or God. However, it becomes explicit in Lk. 1.76-77 with the reference to Jesus as the Lord in 1.43 and with a change of tone in 1.76-77. See Rowe, *Christology*, 57–70.

42. Snodgrass, 'Isaiah 40:1–5', 37.

43. Farris, *Hymns*, 139.

44. Taylor, *Immerser*, 106–7.

45. Snodgrass, 'Isaiah 40:1–5', 25.

message of comfort (παρακαλέω) (vv. 1, 2)⁴⁶ and urges the prophet to prepare the way of God's coming so that all flesh shall see the salvation of God (σωτήριον τοῦ θεοῦ) (vv. 3-5).⁴⁷ This is once again highlighted as the preaching of good news (εὐ αγγελίζω), which is God's advent (Ἰδοὺ ὁ θεὸς ὑμῶν 40.9).⁴⁸ Similarly, after citing Isa. 40.3-5 LXX, Lk. 3.18 summarizes John the Baptist's ministry as the exhortation (παρακαλέω) and preaching of good news (εὐαγγελίζω).⁴⁹

Luke colours John's ministry with three major themes from Isa. 40.1-11 LXX: (1) the message of comfort (παρακαλέω), (2) salvation (σωτήριον) and (3) good news (εὐαγγελίζω) upon the Lord's coming. However, Luke's passage brings a significant change as the coming Lord, for whom John the Baptist prepares, now points to the Messiah, rather than God.⁵⁰ While the identity of the Lord appears ambiguous with Luke's change of τοῦ θεοῦ ἡμῶν to αὐτοῦ in Lk. 3.4 (Mt. 3.3//Mk 1.3) as αὐτοῦ refers to κυρίου, it becomes clear later in the passage (3.15-17) that John anticipates the Messiah's (ὁ Χριστός) coming.⁵¹

The structure of Lk. 3.4-6 closely follows Isa. 40.3-5 LXX with a few variations.⁵² Luke alters πεδία (Isa. 40.4 LXX) to ὁδοὺς λείας (Lk. 3.5), and thus adds ὁδός once again. Here the meanings of ὁδός and Luke's extended citation are worth noting to

---

46. It is noteworthy that the LXX adds παρακαλέω (נחם in Hebrew) in Isa. 40.2, 11, and thus stresses the message of comfort.

47. Σωτήριόν is inserted in Isa. 40.5 LXX. Perhaps this insertion is influenced by Isa. 52.10. See Snodgrass, 'Isaiah 40:1-5', 27.

48. In Tg. Isa. 40.9, it is 'the kingdom of God' instead of 'God' that is to be revealed. Although Luke does not directly link the message of the coming kingdom with John the Baptist like Matthew (3.2), Luke reports John's preaching of good news which is closely related to the kingdom of God in Luke's Gospel (4.43; 8.1; 16.16; 9.2, 6). See Knox Chamblin, 'John the Baptist and the Kingdom of God', *TynBul* 15 (1964): 12; Bruce D. Chilton, *The Glory of Israel: The Theology and Provenience of the Isaiah Targum*, JSOTSup 23 (Sheffield: Sheffield University, 1983), 77-8.

49. Lk. 3.18 summarizes John's ministry as proclaiming good news, and anticipates Jesus' ministry in Lk. 4.18. Taking Isa. 40.1-11 LXX into account, the good news which John preaches is not much different from the one which Jesus preaches. Moreover, a close relation among good news, salvation and the kingdom (God's reign) in Isaiah LXX and Luke suggests, though indirectly, that John's preaching may be understood in a similar context. Thus, Nolland aptly states that any difference between John and Jesus lies not in 'the message', but in 'the state of fulfilment'. *Luke 1:9-20*, 141. See also Wink, *Baptist*, 52-3.

50. Marshall, *Luke*, 132.

51. In addition, Luke's previous accounts which refer to Jesus as Lord (Lk. 1.43), a saviour (2.11) and God's salvation (2.30) also give more weight to the Lord as the Messiah. Rowe, *Christology*, 71-7.

52. Thomas R. Hatina, 'The Voice of Northrop Frye Crying in the Wilderness: The Mythmaking Function of Isaiah 40.3 in Luke's Annunciation of the Baptist', *Interpretation*, 68-9.

illuminate John's teaching in Lk. 3.10-14.[53] First, ὁδός conveys several significant meanings in the Lukan narratives. Ὁδός in Lk. 3.4 denotes the physical way of the Lord whose coming is imminent. However, Luke's citation of the LXX which renders מְסִלָּה as τρίβος may suggest an ethical understanding of ὁδός.[54] Hence the meaning of ὁδός in Lk. 3.4 is closer to τὴν ὁδὸν τοῦ θεοῦ in 1.79 and 20.21.[55] Ὁδός in these references points to the way of life, that is, the way of conforming to God, and thus leading to life. It is both soteriological and ethical.[56]

Also, the uses of the way (דרך) and wilderness (מדבר) in 1QS (The Community Rule) are instructive in understanding Luke's use of ὁδός and of Isa. 40.3.[57] Isa. 40.3 plays a significant role for the self-understanding and life of the Qumran communit(ies). George J. Brooke observes that the use of Isa. 40.3 in 1QS indicates both literal and metaphorical understanding of דרך and מדבר. 1QS 8.13-18 and 9.17-20 interpret 'prepare the way' in Isa. 40.3 metaphorically as 'the study of the Torah' while indicating a literal movement to the wilderness.[58] Luke is somewhat similar in that both literal and metaphorical meanings of ὁδός and perhaps of ἔρημος[59] are suggested. Ὁδός indicates a physical way for the Lord's coming as well as a way of God in ethical and soteriological terms. Moreover, it alludes to preparing a people for the Lord's coming as foretold in Lk. 1.17.[60]

---

53. Pao, *Exodus*, 37–41, 52-9. Pao asserts that Isa. 40.3-5 functions 'as a hermeneutical lens without which the entire Lukan program cannot be properly understood' (37). He argues for the significance of Isa. 40.1-11 in relation to the whole narrative of Acts, particularly highlighting the use of the term ὁδός, in relation to 'the exodus paradigm' in Isa. 40–55 LXX (52).

54. John Goldingay and David Payne, *Isaiah 40–55*, vol. 1, ICC (London: T&T Clark, 2006), 76.

55. Also in Acts 2.28; 13.10; 16.17; 18.25, 26; cf. 14.16. See George J. Brooke, 'Isaiah 40:3 and the Wilderness Community', in *New Qumran Texts & Studies: Proceedings of the First Meeting of the International Organization for Qumran Studies, Paris 1992*, ed. George J. Brooke (Leiden: Brill, 1994), 132; *Isaiah at Qumran: Updating W.H. Brownlee's the Meaning of the Qumrân Scrolls for the Bible*, OPIAC 46 (Claremont: IAC, 2004), 18–19.

56. Snodgrass, 'Isaiah 40:1-5', 37-9.

57. See James Dunn, 'John the Baptist's Use of Scripture', in *The Gospels and the Scriptures of Israel*, ed. Craig A. Evans and W. Richard Stegner, JSNTSup 104, SSEJC 3 (Sheffield: Sheffield Academic, 1994), 45.

58. Brooke, 'Isaiah 40:3', 124–6.

59. While both terms are directly attached to John the Baptist in Luke's Gospel (ὁδός in Lk. 1.76, 79; 3.4, 5; 7.27; ἔρημος in Lk. 1.80; 3.2, 4; 7.24), Luke's use of wilderness primarily points to the location of John the Baptist. A theological use of wilderness which expresses an exilic status of Israel as captivity in sin may lie behind Luke's use of Isa. 40.3-5. Yet, a more cautionary approach seems necessary.

60. The Targum suggests that the way is being prepared for the people to return to Jerusalem. Snodgrass observes the influence of Isa. 52.14 and 62.10 on the Targum rendering of Isa. 40.3. 'Isaiah 40:1-5', 27–8.

6. Human Embodiment of Divine Mercy I

Another intriguing use of ὁδός may be suggested from 1QS 9.18 which uses דרך as the self-designation of the community.[61] Prepare the way (דרך) (1QS 9.19; Isa. 40.3) follows a technical use of דרך (1QS 9.18). It may indicate that the understanding of the way in Isa. 40.3 is adapted to the self-understanding of the community.[62] Similarly, Luke uses ὁδός as a technical term with reference to a believing community in Acts.[63] This illuminates Luke's use of ὁδός in view of Acts.

Most importantly, however, what follows immediately specifies and elaborates the meaning of ὁδός in Lk. 3.4. The words, describing a transformation of the way such as ταπεινόω, εὐθεῖα and σκολιός (Lk. 3.3-5), recur in the context of salvation in the Lukan narratives.[64] In the beginning of Luke's Gospel, Mary praises God the Saviour for lifting the humble (ταπείνωσις Lk. 1.48, ταπείνοω 1.52) while the powerful are brought down. It is (the intention of) Simon's heart which Peter rebukes and speaks of repentance for not being right (εὐθεῖα Acts 8.21) before God, but full of wickedness and bitterness. Later in Acts, Paul confronts Elymas, the magician, who perverts τὰς ὁδοὺς [τοῦ] κυρίου τὰς εὐθείας (Acts 13.10) while he was proclaiming the word of God to the proconsul. Moreover, σκολιός, which is rarely used in the NT,[65] occurs in Peter's sermon. Peter exhorts people: Σώθητε ἀπὸ τῆς γενεᾶς τῆς σκολιᾶς ταύτης (Acts 2.40). It alludes to transposition and demands transformation.

Second, Luke's citation extends to and climaxes in τὸ **σωτήριον** τοῦ θεοῦ (Lk. 3.6; Isa. 40.5 LXX emphasis added).[66] It advances from the preparing of the way (Lk. 3.4) to the unfolding of the nature of its preparation (3.4-5) to meet the supreme goal of salvation (3.6). The significance of salvation in the Lukan narratives is also attested in the long citation from Joel in Acts 2.17-21 which ends with καὶ ἔσται πᾶς ὃς ἂν ἐπικαλέσηται τὸ ὄνομα κυρίου **σωθήσεται** (Acts 2.21; Joel

---

61. Michael Wise, Martin Abegg, Jr and Edward Cook, *The Dead Sea Scrolls: A New Translation* (London: HarperCollins, 1996), 140. cf. Florentino García Martínez and Eibert J.C. Tigchelaar, eds, *The Dead Sea Scrolls Study Edition*, vol. 1 (1Q1–4Q273), 2nd edn (Leiden: Brill, 1999), 93. Whether דרך refers to the self-designation of the community is not clear from the translation of Martínez and Tigchelaar.

62. Snodgrass, 'Isaiah 40:1–5', 28.

63. Acts 9.2; 19.9, 23; 22.4; 24.14, 22. Note Pao's discussion of the 'Way' in Acts as the identity of the early Christian community. *Exodus*, 59–69.

64. See Tannehill, *Unity: Luke*, 48; Nave, *Repentance*, 147.

65. Σκολιός is frequently used to describe a wicked generation, one's way of life, one's condition of heart and one's speech in the LXX. See Deut. 32.5; Ps. 77.8 (generation); Prov. 2.15; 21.8; 22.5, 14; 28.18; Isa. 42.16 (way of life); Prov. 23.33 (condition of heart); Prov. 4.24; 8.8 (speech). In the NT, see Lk. 3.5; Acts 2.40; Phil. 2.15 (γενεᾶς σκολιᾶς καὶ διεστραμμένης); 1 Pet. 2.18.

66. Lk. 4.18-19 which cites Isa. 61.1-2 LXX omits ἡμέραν ἀνταποδόσεως. With the inclusion of salvation in Luke 3 and the exclusion of vengeance in Luke 4, Luke stresses a salvific aspect while toning down the negative one of the Isaianic message.

3.5 LXX emphasis added).[67] Both citations, coming in the two initial sermons in Luke and Acts, climax in salvation. The combination of ὁράω and σωτήριον in Lk. 3.6 is reminiscent of Simeon's prophecy in 2.30 which also recalls Isa. 40.3 LXX.[68] Simeon's prophecy highlights σωτήριον as what God has prepared. Yet, it is not far from John's ministry in that the ultimate goal of preparation is for all people to see God's salvation, or in other words, to give people knowledge of salvation as in Lk. 1.77. Furthermore, the initial interpretation of Isa. 40.3-5 LXX is offered in Luke's introduction of John the Baptist: Κηρύσσων βάπτισμα μετανοίας εἰς ἄφεσιν ἁμαρτιῶν (Lk. 3.3).

Hence the significance of Lk. 3.3-6, 18 with the citation from Isa. 40.3-5 LXX can be summarized as (1) the announcement of salvation which is observed from the major theme of Isa. 40.1-11 LXX and from Luke's extended citation and (2) the ethical and soteriological interpretation of ὁδός which is suggested by the transformative and transposing words used in Lk. 3.4-5. This interpretation of preparing ὁδός anticipates John's teaching in Lk. 3.10-14 which concretizes its meaning particularly in socio-economic terms.

6.5 The Eschatological Context of John's Teaching (Lk. 3.7-9, 15-17)

While the citation from Isaiah LXX provides an underlying theme for John's ministry, Lk. 3.7 picks up the baptism of repentance in 3.3. The οὖν (Lk. 3.7) 'marks a return to the storyline' and links baptism with repentance as 3.7-8 indicate.[69] John preaches to the crowd (τοῖς ὄχλοις) who came out to be baptized in response to his message of a baptism of repentance (Lk. 3.3). Repentance is highlighted, not baptism itself.[70] His warning on τῆς μελλούσης ὀργῆς (Lk. 3.7) also points to repentance.[71] He calls the crowd γεννήματα ἐχιδνῶν (Lk. 3.7) and renounces their ancestral privilege as Abraham's children.[72] Thus, it is through

---

67. The occurrences of σωτήριον is rare in the NT (three out of four occur in Luke-Acts), but common in the LXX. Luke refers to τὸ σωτήριον τοῦ θεοῦ at the beginning of the Gospel (Lk. 2.30; 3.6) and at the end of Acts (28.28).

68. Snodgrass, 'Isaiah 40:1-5', 38. He also notes the possible influence of Isa. 52.10 LXX where a similar construction of ὁράω and σωτήριον occurs.

69. Martin M. Culy, Mikeal C. Parsons and Joshua J. Stigall, *Luke: A Handbook on the Greek Text*, BHGNT (Waco: Baylor University, 2010), 105.

70. Unlike Matthew (3.6, 13) and Mark (1.5, 9), Luke depicts John more as a preacher of baptism than a baptizer although it is implied that he baptizes people (Lk. 3.16, 21). Also, John's arrest (Lk. 3.20) is noted before the account of baptism of people including Jesus (3.21). After his baptism and while he is praying, the Spirit descends on Jesus, according to Luke. See Marshall, *Luke*, 135.

71. In Lk. 3.7, the meaning of ὑποδείκνυμι is originally 'to show' or 'to give direction'. 'ὑποδείκνυμι', BDAG: 851-2.

72. Green, *Luke*, 175-6.

bearing fruits worthy of repentance (ποιήσατε οὖν καρποὺς ἀξίους τῆς μετανοίας Lk. 3.8) that the crowd avoid judgement and verify their kinship with Abraham.

John's preaching of the coming wrath and of bearing fruit of repentance finds its home in the Jewish prophetic and apocalyptic traditions.[73] However, Luke's use of bearing fruits in relation to repentance in Lk. 3.8 is noteworthy in several aspects. First, bearing fruit means doing (ποιέω) good deeds in Luke.[74] Jesus' teaching on the plain (Lk. 6.43-44) mentions good trees which bear (ποιέω) good fruit. The previous teaching (Lk. 6.27-38) sums up being merciful (οἰκτίρμων) as loving (ἀγαπάω), doing good (ἀγαθοποιέω) and lending generously (δανείζω, δίδωμι) (see Chapter 4). The concluding teaching (Lk. 6.45-49) tackles the issue of 'doing' and of 'not doing' through comparing the heart of a person to a tree and one's speech to fruit.

Similarly, John's teaching in Lk. 3.10-14 specifies the deeds/fruit of worthy of repentance in terms of mercy and justice. John's preaching (ποιήσατε οὖν καρποὺς ἀξίους τῆς μετανοίας) in Lk. 3.8 is consonant with Paul's preaching (ἄξια τῆς μετανοίας ἔργα πράσσοντας) in Acts 26.20.[75] Repentance (μετάνοια) demands changing one's way of life by 'doing' what conforms to God's word and Jesus' teaching as observed in the later narratives.[76]

Second, bearing fruit brings a positive nuance to John's preaching despite the imminent nature of judgement.[77] Luke shifts the emphasis from judgement to bearing fruit as John's teaching (Lk. 3.10-14) continues to expound its meaning.[78] John demonstrates how to flee from the impending judgement and what to do to bear fruit worthy of repentance. Furthermore, the people's (λαός)[79] response to John's teaching (Lk. 3.10-14) demonstrates their expectation of the Messiah (ὁ Χριστός) (3.15).[80] The occurrence of χριστός here recalls the prophetic announcements concerning Jesus in the Lukan birth narratives (Lk. 2.11, 26).

---

73. See Dunn, 'Baptist', 47–9; Scobie, *Baptist*, 81. See Isa. 10.15-16, 33-34; Jer. 46.22-23; Ezek. 15.1-8; Mal. 4.1 for the imagery of God's judgement drawn from axe, tree and fire. Also in Mt. 3.7-10. However, Matthew's accounts differ at two points. The addressees are the Pharisees and the Sadducees and fruit is in a singular form.

74. See Alan C. Mitchell, 'Zacchaeus Revisited: Luke 19,8 as a Defense', *Bib* 71 (1990): 172.

75. Nave points out that an *inclusio* is formed by 'the theme "fruits/deeds worthy of repentance"' in Lk. 3.8 and Acts 26.20. He also notes that both relate ἄφεσιν ἁμαρτιῶν to repentance. *Repentance*, 29.

76. Nave, *Repentance*, 148–9. See also Scobie, *Baptist*, 81. He suggests that John's message of repentance in terms of bearing fruits 'represents the Jewish view exactly'. It essentially means 'good works'.

77. The impending judgement is vividly captured by the combination of expressions, such as ἤδη, δὲ καί and the axe being laid to the root in v. 9.

78. Nave, *Repentance*, 149–50.

79. Note that Luke's ὄχλοι in vv. 7, 10 is now changed to λαός in v. 15 (also in vv. 18, 21).

80. cf. Jn 1.24-27.

Jesus is called σωτήρ and χριστός in Lk. 2.11 and Simeon sees (ὁράω) the Lord's Christ (τὸν χριστὸν κυρίου) and salvation (σωτήριόν) in Lk. 2.26, 30. The messianic expectation is closely linked with a salvific message in both accounts. Similarly, aspects of John's teaching which raise messianic expectations carry a message of hope rather than of doom.

Lastly, the imagery of tree and fruit (Lk. 3.9) in the context of judgement is paralleled with that of grain and chaff (3.17).[81] John speaks of the Messiah in an eschatological context as the imagery of harvest shows.[82] However, Luke uses the future tense for judgement which is the burning (κατακαύσει) of the chaff with fire while the use of infinitives for clearing (διακαθᾶραι) the floor and gathering (σθω αγαγεῖν) the grain suggests 'readiness to carry out the action'.[83] The positive activity of the Messiah is stressed by its imminent happening whereas the judgement is seemingly toned down.[84]

Jesus' parable in Lk. 13.6-9 also echoes John's preaching with the imagery of δένδρον, ποιέω καρπός and ἐκκόπτω.[85] The parable immediately follows Jesus' teaching of repentance (Lk. 13.1-5) in the context of repentance and judgement. Nevertheless, the imminence of the coming judgement in Lk. 13.8-9 is toned down. In both passages, an eschatological context is firmly set by a strong imagery of the impending judgement. Yet it is also coloured by messianic and salvific elements. Hence, with the emphasis on the urgency of repentance, John's preaching in Lk. 3.7-9, 15-17 anticipates salvific aspects of his teaching as the messianic expectation in Lk. 3.15 indicates.[86]

6.6 What Must We Do?: Bearing Fruit(s) of Mercy and Justice (Lk. 3.10-14)

In the study of Lk. 3.10-14, Scheffler contends that Luke employs those who ask the question to communicate his special interest, namely, 'an economic message'.[87]

---

81. As noted earlier, the Messiah is the agent of judgement in Lk. 3.17 while God is implied in 3.9.

82. Dunn, 'Baptist', 53; Scobie, *Baptist*, 60-2. See Isa. 41.15-16; Ps. 1.3-4.

83. Culy, Parsons and Stigall, *Luke*, 113. In Mt. 3.12, clear (διακαθαριεῖ), gather (σθνάξει) and burn (κατακαύσει) are all in the future tense.

84. Scheffler, 'Baptist', 24. Contra J. Liebenberg, 'The Function of the Standespredigt in Luke 3:1-20: A Response to E.H. Scheffler's the Social Ethics of the Lucan Baptist (Luke 3:10-14)', *Neot* 27.1 (1993): 58-66. He strongly argues that John's preaching has nothing to do with salvation, but everything to do with judgement. See also Scobie, *Baptist*, 60-2. Scobie is typical of those who picture John the Baptist as a preacher of 'the imminent approach of the end of days and of the judgement' (60).

85. Jesus' audience is also the crowd (Lk. 12.54) as in Luke 3.

86. Peter Mallen's observation is apt here: There is a 'tension between announcements of salvation and judgment' in Luke's account of John's preaching. *Isaiah*, 71.

87. Scheffler, 'Baptist', 27.

6. Human Embodiment of Divine Mercy I

He thus stresses the social and ethical aspect of the *Standespredigt*. His argument is plausible to the extent that the socio-economic implications of John's teaching are in line with those of Jesus and the significance of salvation provides a supreme context for the teaching.[88] However, his overemphasis on Luke's redactional activities neglects a more significant issue, that is, an intrinsic relationship between John the Baptist's teaching and the message of salvation.[89] Luke's interest in an economic message is essentially a soteriological one as the question, Τί ποιήσωμεν (Lk. 3.10, 12, 14), indicates.

Lk. 3.10-14 is in a dialectical form as the crowd (οἱ ὄχλοι), tax collectors (τελῶναι) and soldiers (στρατευόμενοι) ask the identical question, Τί ποιήσωμεν, in response to John's preaching (3.3, 7-9). John gives practical instructions to this question and his message raises messianic expectations (Lk. 3.15). His preaching is concluded with exhortations (Lk. 3.18).

Following is a simplified form of John's teaching in Lk. 3.10-14.

3.10-11 (οἱ ὄχλοι)	τί οὖν **ποιήσωμεν**; ὁ ἔχων δύο χιτῶνας ***μεταδότω*** τῷ μὴ ἔχοντι, καὶ ὁ ἔχων βρώματα ὁμοίως ποιείτω.
3.12-13 (τελῶναι)	διδάσκαλε, **τί ποιήσωμεν**; ***μηδὲν*** πλέον παρὰ τὸ διατεταγμένον ὑμῖν **πράσσετε**.
3.14 (στρατευόμενοι)	**τί ποιήσωμεν** καὶ ἡμεῖς; ***μηδένα διασείσητε μηδὲ συκοφαντήσητε*** καὶ ***ἀρκεῖσθε*** τοῖς ὀψωνίοις ὑμῶν.

The question can be elaborated in three ways. First, the Codex Bezae (D) adds ἵνα σωθῶμεν to the question in Lk. 3.12, and thus makes its meaning closer to Acts 16.30 (τί με δεῖ ποιεῖν ἵνα σωθῶ). This reflects a broader context of John's preaching as captured in Luke's citation from Isaiah LXX. Next, it narratively responds to John's warning in Lk. 3.7. The question then looks like the following: Τί ποιήσωμεν φυγεῖν ἀπὸ τῆς μελλούσης ὀργῆς. Lastly, considering the repeated use of ποιέω in both bearing fruits (ποιήσατε καρποὺς) and the question (τί ποιήσωμεν), the main thrust of the question is on 'doing'. It expounds what it means to bear fruit worthy of repentance.

John's practical instructions include two positive exhortations: μεταδίδωμι, ἀρκέω[90] and three negative ones: μηδὲν πλέον πράσσετε, μηδένα διασείσητε and μηδὲ συκοφαντήσητε. Sharing (μεταδίδωμι)[91] is demanded of the crowd in general

---

88. Scheffler, 'Baptist', 30–1.

89. Scheffler mentions several times that John's teaching is to be understood as salvation and good news, yet he never develops further.

90. Taylor draws attention to Josephus's advice to his troops, particularly to be content (ἀρκοθμένους). *Immerser*, 118. Josephus, *Life* 244.

91. Note that μεταδίδωμι is used to denote both material and spiritual sharing in the NT. See Lk. 3.11; Rom. 12.8; Eph. 4.28 and Rom. 1.11; 1 Thess. 2.8.

while the rest are directed at tax collectors and soldiers. Notably, John's answer to the theologically directed question is coloured by economic aspects of life: food and clothing which are life essentials, tax, extortion of money and wages. Thus, Green comments, 'Repentance is evidenced in one's socio-economic relations.'[92]

Moreover, John's teaching assumes a general poverty of the crowd in that having two χιτῶνας or βρώματα is hardly an indicator of economic affluence (see Chapter 3). Yet they are told to share with those who have none. Specific instructions to tax collectors and soldiers reflect unjust practices and an abuse of power not only by those individuals but also by the oppressive social–political system in which they live as implied in Lk. 3.1-2, 19-20 (see 6.3). Within this context, John shows them the way (ὁδός) which is portrayed by mercy and justice, and thus proclaims good news. In sum, at the heart of John's teaching lies a genuine concern for the poor and the oppressed and a challenge to unjust social practices.

This is not a new message addressed by either Luke or John but a message which is 'at home within the scriptures and Judaism'.[93] As Wolter shows, John's teaching is in line with common ethical instructions of his day.[94] It is also consonant with Jesus' teaching throughout Luke's Gospel and particularly in Lk. 4.18-19, 6.29-30, 34-36, 10.37 and 18.22 where radical generosity towards those who are in need is demanded. As noted in Chapter 4, Deut. 15.1-18, Lev. 25.13-55 and Lev. 19.9-18, 33-37 aptly provide a rich context for John's teaching in the light of his preaching of ἄφεσις. It carries a 'social dimension'[95] and demands that life essentials are shared and that others are treated justly. Deut. 15.1-18 encourages the Israelites not only to deal mercifully with the needy and the poor but also to give generously and lend freely according to others' needs. Similarly, Leviticus 25 urges people not to oppress their neighbours (25.14, 17), but to be merciful with those who fall into dire situations (25.25, 35, 39, 47, 48).

The use of συκοφαντέω in Lk. 3.14 is also worth noting. While διασείω is attested in relation to the malpractice of soldiers in a first-century Egyptian papyrus,[96] συκοφαντέω mostly occurs in the wisdom literature in the context of socio-economic injustice carried out against the poor and the needy.[97] Συκοφαντέω

---

92. Green, 'Baptism', 164.

93. Green, *Luke*, 174; Marshall, *Luke*, 142–3; Scobie, *Baptist*, 86; Bovon, *Luke 1*, 124–5. Bovon notes, 'John's message for Luke is nothing new, and not even specific, all together, it encompasses the requirement of wisdom, of the prophets, and finally of the law of God' (125). See also Wolter, *Lukasevangelium*, 162. While noting that John's teaching is in line with common ethical instruction of his day, he differentiates Jesus' teaching which is 'ein Vielfaches radikaler' from John's, based on Lk. 16.16.

94. Wolter, *Lukasevangelium*, 162. He differentiates Jesus' teaching which is 'ein Vielfaches radikaler' from John's, based on Lk. 16.16.

95. Green, 'Baptism', 164. He observes, 'The promise of forgiveness has an obvious social dimension.'

96. P.Oxy. II 240. The papyrus is dated 37 CE.

97. Prov. 14.31; 22.16; 28.3 LXX; Eccl. 4.1 LXX; Job 35.9 LXX.

in Lev. 19.11 LXX seems most close to Lk. 3.14 in that a negative command not to συκοφαντέω a neighbour is used in the context of loving one's neighbours and dealing justly with them.[98] Similarly συκοφαντέω[99] in Lk. 19.8 indicates defrauding people of money. Hence John's message of repentance, of salvation and of preparing of the way (ὁδός) is concretized in his teaching of merciful and just dealings with others particularly in socio-economic terms (Lk. 3.10-14).

While John's preaching in Lk. 3.8 (ποιήσατε οὖν καρποὺς ἀξίους τῆς μετανοίας) connects repentance with doing,[100] Zacchaeus's account in Lk. 19.1-10 vividly embodies John's preaching and teaching.[101] It echoes John's at several points. First, Zacchaeus who appears at the final stage of the Lukan TN is a chief tax collector (ἀρχιτελώνης Lk. 19.2).[102] Second, his eagerness to see Jesus (ἐζήτει ἰδεῖν τὸν Ἰησοῦν Lk. 19.3, ἴδῃ αὐτὸν 19.4)[103] and to obey his word is highlighted (19.5-6). Jesus' command to σπεύσας κατάβηθι (Lk. 19.5) is responded to exactly by Zacchaeus's action (σπεύσας κατέβη 19.6). Perhaps these identical phrases reflect not only Zacchaeus's positive response to Jesus but also his willingness to obey Jesus' word.

Third, Zacchaeus's word to Jesus in Lk. 19.8 aptly captures John's teaching in 3.10-14 and Jesus' particularly in 6.27-49:[104] showing mercy and doing justice. Whether what Zacchaeus says is an expression of the defence of his practice against those who accuse him or of the resulting resolution in response to Jesus' acceptance or not[105] makes little difference to the discussion of the embodiment of John's

98. Συκοφαντέω occurs only twice in the NT, in Lk. 3.14; 19.8.

99. Mitchell suggests the meaning of συκοφαντέω in 19.8 as an unintentional act or false accusation by giving examples from Josephus (*Ant.* 10.114-115; 16.170). 'The Use of συκοφαντεῖν in Luke 19,8: Further Evidence for Zacchaeus's Defense', *Bib* 72 (1991): 546-7. However, Luke's use of συκοφαντέω in John's teaching, where Mitchell notes the connection with Zacchaeus and its occurrences in the LXX, provides closer contexts for the understanding of the meaning of συκοφαντέω as defrauding in 19.8.

100. cf. Acts 26.20.

101. Jantsch, *Jesus, der Retter*, 83-4.

102. Ἀρχιτελώνης only occurs here. Luke's τελώνης first appears in Lk. 3.12 and the last one is ἀρχιτελώνης in 19.2.

103. Zacchaeus is in fact seen (ἀναβλέψας) and sought out (ζητῆσαι) by Jesus in Lk. 19.5, 10. There is an interesting parallel between seeing salvation (also in Lk. 2.30; 3.6) and seeing Jesus. Likewise, when Jesus comes to Zacchaeus's house, so does salvation. Note that Jesus is referred to as σωτηρία in 1.69. See William P. Loewe, 'Towards an Interpretation of Luke 19:1-10', *CBQ* 36 (1974): 324-5.

104. See John O'Hanlon, 'The Story of Zacchaeus and the Lucan Ethic', *JSNT* (1981): 18-21. He draws attention to Jesus' sermon in Luke 6 and to Zacchaeus's story.

105. The interpretation of Lk. 19.8 is highly contested on the ground of the present active indicative tense of 'δίδωμι' and 'ἀποδίδωμι', which may be either present or future, and of narratively parallel passages in 5.27-32; 15.1-32. Taking the verbs as present tense, it suggests Zacchaeus's habitual practice of merciful and just acts. Then, Zacchaeus is defending himself against his accusers and Jesus is vindicating him in 19.9. See Richard C. White, 'Vindication

teaching in Lk. 19.8. In either case, what Zacchaeus has done or will do points to the teachings of John the Baptist and Jesus. Also noteworthy is the occurrence of δίδωμι, ἀποδίδωμι (Lk. 19.8) and συκοφαντέω (19.8) in congruence with John's instructions, that is, μεταδότω (3.11), to share with those who have no life essentials: χιτών and βρῶμα, and μηδὲ συκοφαντήσητε (3.14).

Lastly, Jesus pronounces salvation (σωτηρία Lk. 19.9; cf. 1.77) to his household and reaffirms his identity as a son of Abraham (υἱὸς Ἀβραάμ) (19.9).[106] The connection between salvation and promises made to Abraham is alluded to in the birth narratives in the context of the mercy (ἔλεος) of God the Saviour (σωτήρ) (Lk. 1.54-55, 72-75). John's preaching in Lk. 3.7-9 relates the children of Abraham (τέκνον Ἀβραάμ) to bearing fruit (ποιέω καρπός) and his subsequent teaching in 3.10-14 concretizes the characteristics of the fruit/deeds (καρπός/ἔργα). These are linked with Luke's citation of Isa. 40.3-6 LXX which culminates in the salvation of God (τὸ σωτήριον τοῦ θεοῦ). In this respect, Mitchell remarks, 'Luke seems to be saying ... that "salvation" is a matter of doing; that is, what it means to be τέκνον Ἀβραάμ.'[107] Zacchaeus's giving to the poor (τοῖς πτωχοῖς δίδωμι) of half of his wealth and restoring what might have been defrauded (τι ἐσυκοφάντησα ἀποδίδωμι) fourfold[108] confirms not only his identity as τέκνον Ἀβραάμ but also his salvation (σωτηρία).

Also, Peter's first sermon after Pentecost in Acts 2.38-40 and a summary account in 2.42-47 are worth noting. Peter's preaching not only resembles John's in its pattern but also echoes John's message.[109] It opens with the citation from Joel 3.1-5 LXX which extends to the message of salvation (Acts 2.17-21) as mentioned. It is responded to with urgency by the hearers who ask Τί ποιήσωμεν (Acts 2.37).

---

for Zacchaeus?' *ExpTim* 91 (1979): 21; Mitchell, 'Zacchaeus', 153–76; 'συκοφαντεῖν', 546–7; Fitzmyer, *Luke*, 1220–1; Green, *Luke*, 671–2. However, those who read them in a futuristic sense argue that the verbs point to Zacchaeus's resolution and his repentance enacted in almsgiving and correcting injustice. Thus, the account becomes a salvation story. See Marshall, *Luke*, 697–8; Bovon, *Luke 2: A Commentary on the Gospel of Luke 9:51–19:27*, Hermeneia (Minneapolis: Fortress, 2013), 598–9; Dennis Hamm, 'Zacchaeus Revisited Once More: A Story of Vindication or Conversion?' *Bib* 72 (1991): 249–52; 'Luke 19:8 Once Again: Does Zacchaeus Defend or Resolve?' *Bib* 107 (1988): 431–7; Nolland, *Luke 18:35–24:53*, WBC 35c (Dallas: Word Books, 1993), 905–6; Méndez-Moratalla, *Conversion*, 174–5. Taking Luke's narrative development and the culminating effect of Jesus' word in 19.9-10 into account, it is more likely that Zacchaeus is responding to Jesus' acceptance. Thus, what is highlighted is the coming of salvation to Zacchaeus, a rich chief tax collector.

106. See Lk. 3.8.

107. Mitchell, 'Zacchaeus', 172.

108. Lev. 6.1-5 requires one fifth added to the original amount for the recompense.

109. Despite notable similarities between John's preaching and Peter's, the latter centres around works (Acts 2.22), death (2.23), resurrection (2.24-28, 31, 32) and ascension (2.33) of Jesus who is Lord and Christ (2.36). Thus, baptism is preached in the name of Jesus. See Green, 'Baptism', 169; Nolland, *Luke 1–9:20*, 142.

Peter's answer to the question 'Μετανοήσατε ... βαπτισθήτω ... εἰς ἄφεσιν τῶν ἁμαρτιῶν' (Acts 2.38) echoes what John the Baptist proclaims in Lk. 3.3.[110] Jantsch observes that there is a close link between baptism and repentance in both passages.[111] In the opening summary of the work of John the Baptist, John proclaims, 'A baptism of repentance for the forgiveness of sins' (Lk. 3:3). This link is strengthened when the call to repentance and the call to baptism are paralleled in Acts 2:38.[112]

Furthermore, Peter's reference to Ιησοῦ Χριστοῦ and τοῦ ἁγίου πνεύματος in connection to baptism in Acts 2.38 evokes John's anticipation of the Messiah (ὁ Χριστός) and the baptism in the Holy Spirit (πνεύματι ἁγίῳ) in Lk. 3.16. Peter with many other words (ἑτέροις ... πλείοσιν) witnesses and exhorts (παρεκάλει) his hearers, saying the following: Σώθητε ἀπὸ τῆς γενεᾶς τῆς σκολιᾶς ταύτης (Acts 2.40). Likewise, John's preaching is summarized as exhorting (παρακαλῶν) and preaching good news (εὐηγγελίζετο) with many other words (πολλὰ ... ἕτερα) (Lk. 3.18).

The life of the believers in Acts 2.42-47 in which possessions are shared to meet needs (εἶχον ἅπαντα κοινά 2.44, διεμέριζον αὐτὰ ... ἄν τις χρείαν εἶχεν 2.45) mirrors John's teaching on the sharing of clothes and food in Lk. 3.11. Acts 4.32-35 similarly describes sharing everything (ἦν αὐτοῖς ἅπαντα κοινά 4.32) and giving out things according to needs (διεδίδετο ... ἄν τις χρείαν εἶχεν 4.35). As a result, there was no needy person among them (Acts 4.34) which echoes Deut. 15.4 LXX, the wider context of which offers a rich intertextual background for understanding ἄφεσις in Luke.[113] Deuteronomy 15 repeatedly stresses radical generosity in terms of releasing debts and lending generously for the sake of the indebted.[114] Hence John's teaching in Lk. 3.10 and Luke's depiction of the believers in Acts 2.42-47 and 4.32-35 point in a similar direction.[115]

6.7 Conclusion

To sum up, two issues emerge from the examination of John's teaching (Lk. 3.10-14) in its immediate context (Lk. 3.1-20) and its narrative development in the

---

110. The initial preachings of John, Jesus, Peter and Paul cite prophetic messages which are climaxed at salvation and include ἄφεσιν. Lk. 3.3; 4.18; Acts 2.37; 13.38.

111. Jantsch, *Jesus, der Retter*, 81.

112. Ibid.

113. See A. Friedl, 'The Reception of the Deuteronomic Social Law in the Primitive Church of Jerusalem according to the Book of Acts', *AcTSup* 23 (2016): 176–200.

114. Norbert Lohfink, 'The Laws of Deuteronomy: A Utopian Project for a World without Any Poor', *ScrB* 26.1 (1996): 15.

115. Hamilton, *Deuteronomy*, 146–54. He uses Luke as a point of reference in his conclusion on the justice of society, the obligation of the powerful and God's special concern for the dependent in Deut. 15.

wider Lukan narratives. First, John's teaching is not merely ethical. Rather, his teaching encapsulates what he preaches. The messages of salvation, repentance in view of coming judgement and messianic expectations are spelled out in socio-economic terms as the human embodiment of divine mercy and justice. Hence it tackles one of the central issues which flow throughout the Lukan narratives, that is, the message of salvation in terms of being merciful and treating others justly. This is closely related to and derived from God's saving activity depicted as his ἔλεος shown to people.

Second, John's teaching, shaped by the question, Τί ποιήσωμεν, concretizes the human embodiment of divine mercy (ἔλεος). The answer is clear: to share life essentials and deal justly with others. Hence his answer to this question is not theorized or theologized. Rather Luke offers practical answers in terms of 'doing' what the scriptures say. To this issue, I will now turn and examine what the scriptures say (Lk. 10.25-37; 18.18-30).

Chapter 7

WHAT MUST I DO?: HUMAN EMBODIMENT OF DIVINE MERCY II (LK. 10.25-37; 18.18-30)

7.1 Introduction

This chapter, the second on the human embodiment of divine mercy, further explores the passages which begin with the identical question: Τί ποιήσας ζωὴν αἰώνιον κληρονομήσω (Lk. 10.25; 18.18). The two passages, placed at the beginning and the end of Luke's TN (Lk. 9.51–19.44), concern deuteronomic expositions of the law (Deut. 6.4-5; 5.16-21).[1] The ways in which the discourses develop are significant. The discussion of the law (Deut. 6.4-5 and Lev. 19.18) in Lk. 10.25-37 concludes in terms of showing mercy (ὁ ποιήσας τὸ ἔλεος 10.37) to the needy. Keeping the second five of the Ten Commandments (Exod. 20.12-16// Deut. 5.16-20) in Lk. 18.18-21 still demands almsgiving to the poor (πάντα ὅσα ἔχεις πώλησον καὶ διάδος πτωχοῖς 18.22) which promises treasure in heaven.

This chapter examines (1) to what extent mercy (ἔλεος) and almsgiving (ἐλεημοσύνη) are central to Luke's interpretation of the law as the human enactment of divine mercy and (2) in what sense they are related to eternal life. First, I will examine the setting out question: Τί ποιήσας ζωὴν αἰώνιον κληρονομήσω (Lk. 10.25; 18.18). Next, the discourses in Lk. 10.25-37 and 18.18-30 will be examined in their literary and narrative contexts with particular attention given to the law, mercy (ἔλεος), almsgiving (ἐλεημοσύνη) and eternal life (ζωή αἰώνιος). Finally, I will revisit Luke's interpretation of the law in terms of mercy (ἔλεος) and almsgiving (ἐλεημοσύνη) and their implications for eternal life (ζωή αἰώνιος).

---

1. In Luke's TN (9.51–19.44) scholars note a chiastic arrangement. For instance, Goulder suggests 'a deliberate chiastic arrangement' of the TN. 'Chiastic', 196-7, 202 (196). Talbert elaborates Goulder's chiastic pattern and builds eleven parallels between 10.21 and 18.30. *Literary*, 51-3. Both Goulder and Talbert argue that the themes of eternal life and law, prayer, kingdom of God and judgement, wealth and repentance are repeated in reverse order in Luke's TN. Moreover, Luke 12 and 16 neatly correspond to each other within this pattern in the discussion of judgement, wealth and stewardship. See also Moessner, *Banquet*, 124.

7.2 Τί Ποιήσας Ζωὴν Αἰώνιον Κληρονομήσω (Lk. 10.25; 18.18)

A careful reader of Luke's Gospel could hardly miss the repetition of the identical question: Τί ποιήσας ζωὴν αἰώνιον κληρονομήσω (Lk. 10.25; 18.18).[2] Not only does Luke place the question in both episodes but he also shapes it differently from Matthew and Mark despite their use of the same words. Τί, ποιέω, ζωὴν αἰώνιον and κληρονομέω (in Mark and Luke; cf. ἔχω in Matthew) form the question. Ποιήσας is an aorist participle in Luke, and thus makes κληρονομήσω a main verb while ποιήσω is the main verb in Matthew and Mark. Also noted is the omission of ἵνα in Luke.[3]

Τί ἀγαθὸν **ποιήσω** ἵνα σχῶ ζωὴν αἰώνιον. (Mt. 19.16);
Τί **ποιήσω** ἵνα ζωὴν αἰώνιον κληρονομήσω. (Mk 10.17);
Τί **ποιήσας** ζωὴν αἰώνιον κληρονομήσω. (Lk. 10.25; 18.18)

The interrogative pronoun τί with a dependent clause followed by ἵνα in Matthew and Mark suggests aorist subjunctives as the most likely reading of ποιήσω and κληρονομήσω. In Luke, it appears more complicated as to whether the verb κληρονομήσω is an aorist subjunctive or a future indicative. Nevertheless, the combination of present imperative (ποίει) with future indicative (ζήσῃ) in the corresponding response of Jesus in Lk. 10.28 seems to suggest the future indicative as a better reading for κληρονομήσω in 10.25 (also in 18.18).[4] If this is so, then with the use of aorist participle ποιήσας, the future indicative reading highlights the relationship between present action and future reward, that is, eternal life. Hence the grammatical structure of Luke's question stresses the aspects of doing now to inherit eternal life in the age to come.[5]

Luke makes it clear that eternal life will be granted to those who do the law/keep the commandments – Shema (Deut. 6.4-5) and the Decalogue (Exod. 20.12-16//Deut. 5.16-21). The question thus naturally connects the law with eternal life

---

2. Literal translation: 'By doing what will I inherit eternal life?' is suggested in Culy, Parsons and Stigall. *Luke*, 360.

3. See Jon Mark Reeves, 'Inheriting "Eternal Life" in Luke's Travel Narrative: Redaction and Narrative in Luke 9.51–19.44' (MA Thesis, Brite Divinity School, 2011), 19–25. 12 April 2015, https://repository.tcu.edu/bitstream/handle/116099117/4344/ReevesJ.pdf?sequence=1

4. Note Lk. 18.30 in response to 18.18 that the inheritance of eternal life is limited to the age to come. Contra Bailey suggests a present tense reading of the verb ζήσῃ, based on the Syriac version. Yet, it seems unnecessary to read the verb in the present tense. *Peasant*, 38.

5. Luke uses a present tense for entering the kingdom (εἰσπορεύονται 18.24) while eternal life is promised in a future tense. For the present aspect of the salvation, see Lk. 11.20; 17.21; 19.9; 23.43.

while putting an emphasis on doing.[6] The importance of doing in Luke's Gospel in general and in these passages in particular has been noted.[7] Wilson observes that what matters in the passages under discussion is 'doing the Law', not discussing it.[8] William Loader also remarks, 'In both [passages] Luke puts the emphasis on doing.'[9] Deuteronomy provides a rich context to the discussion of inheritance, life and law. Obedience to the law is the key to inheriting the land and to life in Deuteronomy.[10] Ἐντολή, κληρονομέω and ζάω occur together in Deut. 8.1; 11.8; 30.16 LXX.[11] Furthermore, while the notion of inheritance of the land is particularly deuteronomic, Bailey observes that it becomes 'participation in the salvation of the age to come' in the late STP.[12] Inheritance of the land is later interpreted as inheriting eternal life.[13]

What then does eternal life (ζωὴ αἰώνιος) in the question refer to? It appears in Dan. 12.2 (עוֹלָם חַיֵּי, ζωὴ αἰώνιος) in the context of the resurrection of the righteous. Similar uses are also found in the Pseudepigrapha (Pss. Sol. 3.12; 13.11; 14.10; 4 Macc. 15.3; 1 En. 37.4; 58.3) prior to or contemporary with the NT. Luke refers to eternal life only in these two passages (Lk. 10.25; 18.18, 30). In the Synoptic Gospels, eternal life (or life) is relatively rare, compared to its prevalence in John's Gospel.[14] While eternal life is both a present and future reality for John, it is

---

6. Νόμος in Lk. 2.22, 23, 24, 27, 39; 10.26; 16.16, 17; 24.44; Μωϋσέως in reference to the Law in 16.29, 31; 24.27, 44; ἐντολή/in connection to the Law in 1.6; 18.20; 23.56. cf. 15.29. Hence both νόμος and ἐντολή in our passages refer to the Law. See Wilson's discussion on legal terminology in Luke-Acts. *Law*, 1–11.

7. Note the importance of hearing (ἀκούω) and doing (ποιέω) the word of God/Jesus in Lk. 6.47, 49; 8.21; 11.28. For the significance of hearing and doing the Law in Luke's TN, see Moessner, *Banquet*, 125-6.

8. Wilson, *Law*, 56.

9. William Loader, *Jesus' Attitude towards the Law: A Study of the Gospels* (Grand Rapids: Eerdmans, 2002), 327.

10. Deuteronomy 6–8 vividly captures Shema, keeping the commandments, inheriting the land and life.

11. Deuteronomy 4.1 and 6.24 LXX also convey a similar idea as life is promised to those who keep the commandments. cf. In Deut. 32.47 LXX, λόγος instead of ἐντολη is used. Note Lev. 18.5 LXX where keeping (φυλάξεσθε, ποιήσετε, ποιήσας) the commandments is closely related to life (ζήσεται).

12. Bailey, *Peasant*, 34; C.F. Evans, *Saint Luke* (London: SCM, 1990), 465.

13. Marshall, *Luke*, 442; Charles A. Kimball, *Jesus' Exposition of the Old Testament in Luke's Gospel*, JSNTSup 94 (Sheffield: Sheffield Academic, 1994), 125.

14. See Mt. 19.16, 29; 25.46; Mk 10.17, 30; Lk. 10.25; 18.18, 30 (cf. Acts 13.46, 48). Note eternal life occurs sixteen times in John's Gospel. Nine times out of sixteen are used with ἔχω. See Jn 3.36; 5.24; 6.47 for present reality of eternal life. Jn 12.50 equates God's commandments to eternal life. See Wayne G. Rollins, 'Eternal Life in John's Gospel: It's Playing Now', in *Heaven, Hell, and the Afterlife: Eternity in Judaism, Christianity, and Islam*, ed. J. Harold Ellens (Santa Barbara: Praeger, 2013), 13–19.

promised as a reward in the age to come, and thus points to a future reality in the Synoptic Gospels.[15]

In addition to the formation and content of the question, the narrative contexts reveal several points. First, it is posed by the Jewish (religious) leaders (νομικός Lk. 10.25, ἄρχων 18.18) who call Jesus teacher (διδάσκαλε). Religious leaders in Luke are often depicted negatively as those who challenge Jesus' teachings and authority, but claim themselves righteous.[16] However, they are not indiscriminately Jesus' opponents.[17] While Luke reveals that the lawyer's intention is to test (ἐπειράζων) Jesus and to pronounce himself righteous (δικαιῶσαι ἑαυτὸν),[18] the ruler seems to have a more genuine motive in his inquiry to participate in God's kingdom.

Second, the question in both passages points to the two most important Jewish laws – Shema and the Decalogue. While the lawyer's reading of the law combines Shema (Deut. 6.4-5) with Lev. 19.18, Jesus lists commandments (Deut. 5.16-21) which the ruler claims to have kept from his youth. Despite their seemingly acceptable answers, the central issue moves towards one's neighbour (Lev. 19.18) or neighbourly relations (the second table of the Decalogue).

Lastly, it immediately follows short accounts (Lk. 10.17-24; 18.15-17) about the kingdom which is revealed and granted to infants (νηπίοις in Lk. 10.21, βρέφη in 18.15) without any distinct spatial or temporal changes in both discourses.[19] Hence the question carries on the topic of entering the kingdom, and thus the soteriological issues in its narrative contexts. Overall, Luke's formation of the question, its meaning and its narrative contexts centre around doing the law to inherit eternal life. It carries soteriological inquiry (eternal life)

---

15. Rollins, 'Life', 13. He observes that eternal life in the Synoptic Gospels 'reflect[s] the eschatological-apocalyptic perspective of Rabbinic Judaism referring to the future everlasting life promised to the righteous in the life to come'.

16. For Luke's negative depiction of religious leaders, see Lk. 4.21; 5.30; 6.2, 7, 11; 7.30, 39; 10.25, 29, 31-32; 11.38-54; 13.14; 14.7; 15.2; 16.14-15; 18.9-12, 18; 19.47-48; 20.1-2, 19-22; 22.4-5; 23.10. Powell, 'The Religious Leaders in Luke: A Literary-Critical Study', *JBL* 109.1 (1990): 93–110. He argues that religious leaders are not 'hopeless' evil characters in Luke although they are often depicted as those who reject and oppose Jesus and his message.

17. Lk. 7.3-5; 8.40-42; 23.50-51.

18. Except the devil (Lk. 4.10-11) and the lawyer (10.25, 27) who tried to test Jesus, the scriptures are only quoted by Jesus in Luke's Gospel. See Emerson B. Powery, *Jesus Reads Scripture: The Function of Jesus' Use of Scripture in the Synoptic Gospels* (Leiden: Brill, 2003), 215.

19. The lawyer's question follows Jesus' mention of names written in heaven (Lk. 10.21) and God's mystery revealed to little children. Similarly, the ruler comes to Jesus after hearing Jesus' teaching on the kingdom and its recipients as little children. Talbert observes that Luke's use of βρέφη in 18.15 instead of παιδία in 18.16, 17 (also in Mk 10.13-15) makes a clear parallel to Lk. 10.21. *Literary*, 53.

in the context of praxis (doing).[20] I will now turn to each discourse (Lk. 10.25-37; 18.18-30) for further investigation.

7.3 Mercy (Ἔλεος) and Eternal Life (Ζωή Αἰώνιος) (Lk. 10.25-37)

Lk. 10.25-37 with Mt. 22.35-40 and Mk 12.28-34 shares a common interest in a wholehearted love towards God and neighbour (Deut. 6.4-5; Lev. 19.18). Nevertheless, Luke's account notably diverges from those of Matthew and Mark. It is located at the outset of the journey to Jerusalem.[21] More importantly, the pressing issue for Luke is not identifying the greatest commandments, but the law in view of eternal life. Moreover, Luke expands the initial discourse to the Parable of the Good Samaritan (Lk. 10.30-37) to the extent that it provides a kind of midrash on Lev. 19.18.[22] In its immediate preceding episode (Lk. 10.17-24), Jesus assures the disciples that their names are written in heaven (10.20). The lawyer, one among the wise and understanding (Lk. 10.21), asks Jesus about eternal life.[23]

The structural formation of the passage (Lk. 10.25-37) which is coupled with questions and answers underscores the thrust of the discourse. Besides, frequent action verbs in the parable (Lk. 10.30-35) further unveil each character in the light of the initial question posed by the lawyer: Τί ποιήσας ζωὴν αἰώνιον κληρονομήσω (Lk. 10.25). Below is the simplified/highlighted form of the passage (10.25-37).

Q1: νομικός (ἐκπειράζων) τί **ποιήσας ζωὴν αἰώνιον** κληρονομήσω (v. 25);

   Q′1: ἐν τῷ νόμῳ τί γέγραπται; πῶς ἀναγινώσκεις (v. 26);
   A′1: **ἀγαπήσεις κύριον τὸν θεόν σου** ἐξ ὅλης [τῆς] καρδίας σου καὶ ἐν ὅλῃ τῇ ψυχῇ σου καὶ ἐν ὅλῃ τῇ ἰσχύϊ σου καὶ ἐν ὅλῃ τῇ διανοίᾳ σου, καὶ **τὸν πλησίον σου** ὡς σεαυτόν. (v. 27)

A1: **τοῦτο ποίει** καὶ **ζήσῃ**. (v. 28)[24]

Q2: νομικός (δικαιῶσαι ἑαυτόν) τίς ἐστίν μου **πλησίον** (v. 29);
A2: **ἄνθρωπός τις** ... λῃσταῖς περιέπεσεν, ... ἐκδύσαντες αὐτὸν ... ἐπιθέντες ... . ἀφέντες ἡμιθανῆ.

---

20. Powery, Scripture, 221-2.
21. Both Matthew and Mark place this account near the end of the Gospels. The question (Mt. 22.36; Mk 12.28) is this: Which commandment is the greatest?
22. cf. Derrett argues that the parable is a kind of midrash on Hos. 6.6. Law, 227. Craig A. Evans suggests 2 Chron. 28.1-15 as the Hebrew scriptural background of the parable. 'Luke's Good Samaritan and the Chronicler's Good Samaritans', Interpretation, 32-42.
23. Byrne, Hospitality, 99.
24. Jesus' response corresponds to the lawyer's question in terms of ποιέω and ζάω. See Wolter, Lukasevangelium, 391. Furthermore, ποιέω is concretized as ἀγαπάω and doing ἔλεος. cf. Lev. 18.5 LXX.

... ἱερεύς ... ἰδὼν αὐτὸν ἀντιπαρῆλθεν
ὁμοίως ... Λευίτης ... ἰδὼν ἀντιπαρῆλθεν.
Σαμαρίτης ... ἰδὼν ἐσπλαγχνίσθη,
καὶ προσελθὼν κατέδησεν τὰ τραύματα αὐτοῦ ἐπιχέων ἔλαιον καὶ οἶνον, ἐπιβιβάσας δὲ αὐτὸν ἐπὶ τὸ ἴδιον κτῆνος ἤγαγεν αὐτὸν εἰς πανδοχεῖον καὶ ἐπεμελήθη αὐτοῦ. καὶ ἐπὶ τὴν αὔριον ἐκβαλὼν ἔδωκεν δύο δηνάρια τῷ πανδοχεῖ καὶ εἶπεν· ἐπιμελήθητι αὐτοῦ, καὶ ὅ τι ἂν προσδαπανήσῃς ἐγὼ ἐν τῷ ἐπανέρχεσθαί με ἀποδώσω σοι. (vv. 30–35)

Q´2: τίς τούτων τῶν τριῶν **πλησίον** δοκεῖ σοι γεγονέναι τοῦ ἐμπεσόντος εἰς τοὺς λῃστάς (v. 36);

A´2: ὁ **ποιήσας τὸ ἔλεος** μετ᾽ αὐτοῦ. (v. 37)

A1: πορεύου καὶ **σὺ ποίει ὁμοίως**. (v. 37)

The lawyer's question primarily raises the issues of 'doing' and 'eternal life'. First, Jesus let him answer his own question by asking him (νομικός): in the law (ἐν τῷ νόμῳ), what is written and how do you interpret it? (v. 26). In response, he refers to Deut. 6.4-5 and Lev. 19.18 and provides his interpretation by tying them together with the verb ἀγαπήσεις (v. 27). Hence doing the law, which is concretized as loving God and neighbour, leads one to eternal life. Jesus affirms his answer (v. 28) and commands the following: do this (τοῦτο ποίει) and you shall live (ζήσῃ) (v. 28).

Second, the lawyer turns his initial question from 'by doing what' to 'who'. Thus, his second question searches for the identity of the neighbour who deserves wholehearted love. Ironically, Jesus opens the parable with ἄνθρωπός τις.[25] Even the detailed descriptions of the unfortunate incident obscure his identity. This man was left half-dead and naked without leaving any identity markers, namely, language and clothes.[26] Perhaps not only does Jesus deliberately leave the man's identity unspecified but also his unspecified identity is 'absolutely essential' to the thrust of the parable as the story further unfolds.[27]

Lastly, the appearance of a priest and a Levite anticipates an Israelite layperson as in 'the triadic form of popular stories'.[28] The appearance of a Samaritan as the

---

25. Jesus frequently begins the parable with ἄνθρωπός τις. Wilfried Eckey, *Das Lukasevangelium: Unter Berücksichtigung seiner Parallenlen*, vol. 1: Lk. 1,1–10,42, rev. edn (Kempten, Germany: Neukirchener, 2006), 488. However, it is intriguing that this phrase immediately follows the lawyer's question on 'who'.

26. Bailey, *Peasant*, 42–3; John R. Donahue, *The Gospel in Parable: Metaphor, Narrative, and Theology in the Synoptic Gospels* (Philadelphia: Fortress, 1988), 130.

27. Esler, 'Jesus and the Reduction of Intergroup Conflict: The Parable of the Good Samaritan in the Light of Social Identity Theory', *BibInt* 8.4 (2000): 337, 340. See also Michael P. Knowles, 'What was the Victim Wearing? Literary, Economic and Social Contexts for the Parable of the Good Samaritan', *BibInt* 12.2 (2004): 157, 170.

28. Jeremias, *Parables*, 204; Amy-Jill Levine and Marc Zvi Bretter, *The Jewish Annotated New Testament* (New York: Oxford University, 2011), 123.

third character is simply shocking, taking the widely noted animosity between Jews and Samaritans into account.[29] Moreover, the Samaritan in the story is not only ethnically dissimilar from the preceding characters but more significantly his actions also diverge from theirs. While a priest and a Levite see the man and pass by on the other side (ἰδὼν αὐτὸν ἀντιπαρῆλθεν), he sees and has compassion (ἰδὼν ἐσπλαγχνίσθη) which is followed by tangible actions – coming, binding up the wounds, pouring on oil and wine, setting on his animal, bringing to the inn, taking care and giving money. These actions specifically involve considerable economic expense (see Chapter 1 [PS]) and show how much risk the Samaritan is willing to take.

Jesus asks the lawyer a second question which brings him back to his initial one (τί ποιήσας). The lawyer answers the following: 'The one who shows mercy' (ὁ ποιήσας τὸ ἔλεος) becomes a neighbour to the one in need. This apparently changes neighbour as an object to be loved to a subject who shows mercy. The identity of the neighbour becomes irrelevant. Perhaps more crucially, Jesus keeps pressing on illustrating what love looks like, rather than who the neighbour is.[30] Hence the story rejoins the initial question of 'doing' and 'eternal life'. It is the doing of the law which is interpreted as loving (v. 27) and more precisely it is by doing tangible acts of mercy (v. 37) that one will inherit eternal life. The episode climaxes in mercy (ἔλεος) in view of eternal life (ζωή αἰώνιος).

What then is the focal point of the passage? Derrett and Powery suggest that the passage is about Jesus' distinctive interpretation of the law.[31] The right understanding of the scripture which is offered by Jesus as doing mercy is at issue. For Loader and Wilson, what is at stake is not the interpretation of the law but the proper practice of the law.[32] The central issue for them lies in how well one practises the law. Bauckham argues that the episode poses a *halakhic* debate at its centre.[33] The passage demonstrates that concern for people overrides ritual purity. Esler argues that identity and boundary issues form the major thread of the passage, not purity issues, although purity is often a boundary issue.[34] While these suggestions are

---

29. Sir. 50.25-26. Josephus, *Ant.* 18.29-30; *J.W.* 2.232-246. Mt. 10.5; Lk. 9.52-54; Jn 4.9; 8.48. See Timothy Wardle, *The Jerusalem Temple and Early Christian Identity*, WUNT 2.291 (Tübingen: Mohr, 2010), 102–19. He highlights the role of the temple in Mount Gerizim as a main cause of the animosity between Jews and Samaritans. See also Esler, 'Conflict', 329–30.

30. Marshall, *Luke*, 445.

31. Derrett, *Law*, 223; Powery, *Scripture*, 210.

32. Loader, *Law*, 329, 341; Wilson, *Law*, 24.

33. Bauckham, 'The Scrupulous Priest and the Good Samaritan: Jesus' Parabolic Interpretation of the Law of Moses', *NTS* 44 (1998): 485. See also Steve Moyise, *Jesus and Scripture* (London: SPCK, 2010), 54. Contra Amy-Jill Levine, 'Luke and Jewish Religion', *Int* 68.4 (2014): 397.

34. Esler, 'Conflict', 337–45. See also Greg W. Forbes, *The God of Old: The Role of the Lukan Parables in the Purpose of Luke's Gospel*, JSNTSup 198 (Sheffield: Sheffield Academic, 2000), 62–3.

valuable, the lawyer's initial inquiry on inheriting eternal life and his subsequent question culminates in Jesus' call: go and do the acts of mercy to the one in need (Lk. 10.37).[35]

Mercy is indeed an overarching aspect of the law in Luke's Gospel.[36] Jesus' Sermon on the Plain is centred around the call to be merciful (γίνεσθε οἰκτίρμον ες καθὼς [καὶ] ὁ πατὴρ ὑμῶν οἰκτίρμων ἐστίν Lk. 6.36) as previously examined (see Chapter 4).[37] Also noted is Luke's specific use of mercy (ἔλεος) which frequently relates to God's character expressed in his saving activity towards his people (Lk. 1.50, 54, 58, 72 and 78).[38] Ποιῆσαι ἔλεος μετὰ τῶν πατέρων ἡμῶν in Lk. 1.72 is vividly echoed in ὁ ποιήσας τὸ ἔλεος μετ' αὐτοῦ in 10.37. The combination of compassion and mercy (διὰ σπλάγχνα ἐλέους θεοῦ ἡμῶν) in Lk. 1.78 resonates deeply with the parable. In fact, it is the Samaritan who embodies Jesus' call to be merciful just as God is merciful.[39]

Why a Samaritan? Certainly, as Esler argues, the identity of the Samaritan is important and gives a surprising twist to the story. Yet it is mercy which frames the whole episode in view of eternal life as noted. The appearance of the Samaritan over against the Jewish religious leaders may be better understood in the light of Jesus' previous teaching: Ἀγαπᾶτε τοὺς ἐχθροὺς ὑμῶν, καλῶς ποιεῖτε τοῖς μισοῦσιν ὑμᾶς (Lk. 6.27). The enemies in Luke's account are those who hate and curse them, unlike those who persecute them in Mt. 5.44. Josephus's records vividly portray the hatred, the cursing and the violence involved in fights between the Jews and the Samaritans.[40]

By putting the Samaritan as the hero of the story, Jesus embodies his own teaching: do good to those who hate you (Lk. 6.27), taking the rejection of the Samaritans (9.52-53) into account. Despite the lawyer's pressing question on the identity of the neighbour, Jesus' focus remains on loving actions, which are vividly portrayed in his teaching in Lk. 6.27-36. Lk. 10.25-37 evinces the significance of doing tangible acts of mercy (ἔλεος) in view of eternal life (ζωή αἰώνιος). Now I will turn to the second of the law and eternal life inquiries.

---

35. See John Meier who aptly summarizes 10.25-37 as 'It has everything to do with mercy and practical aid shown to a person in need, regardless of race and religion.' *A Marginal Jew: Rethinking the Historical Jesus*, vol. 4: *Law and Love* (New Haven, Yale University, 2009), 525.

36. See Lk. 6.1-5, 6-11; 13.10-17; 14.1-6; 10.25-37; 16.19-31; 18.18-24.

37. The imperatives of both Mt. 5.48 and Lk. 6.36 echo Lev. 19.2 LXX.

38. cf. Lk. 1.58 refers to God's mercy shown to Elizabeth, yet in a communal setting. All the other references to God's mercy are directed towards his people.

39. See the combination of ὁράω and σπλαγχνίζομαι in Lk. 7.13 and 15.20. It, however, is unnecessary to identify the Samaritan with God and Jesus. Sylvia C. Keesmaat, 'Strange Neighbors and Risky Care (Matt 18:21–25; Luke 14:7–14; Luke 10:25–37)', in *The Challenge of Jesus' Parables*, ed. Richard N. Longenecker (Grand Rapids: Eerdmans, 2000), 280–1; Bailey, *Peasant*, 56.

40. Josephus, *Ant.* 18.29-30; *J.W.* 2.232-246.

7.4 Almsgiving (Ἐλεημοσύνη) and Eternal Life (Ζωή Αἰώνιος) (Lk. 18.18-30)

The juxtaposition of the law and eternal life is once again repeated. The ruler's question in Lk. 18.18 echoes the previous one (10.25) and anticipates references to the law. Not surprisingly in the light of the previous discussion (Lk. 10.25-37), Jesus lists the second half of the Decalogue which deals with human relations (18.20). The account in Lk. 18.18-30 follows the episode of little children and the kingdom of God in 18.15-17 as noted. Stephen E. Fowl observes that the theme of this episode, receiving the kingdom as a child, leads to the three following accounts: Lk. 18.18-30, 18.35-43 and 19.1-10 in the context of salvation.[41] Hence Lk. 18.18-30 is aptly placed within the narrative contexts of the kingdom/salvation while the whole section reaches its climax with the story of Zacchaeus (19.1-10).[42]

This account is also attested in all Synoptic Gospels. Yet, Luke's account diverges from the other two in several ways, among which two are germane to our discussion. First, the ruler appears to be present in the previous discussion of the kingdom and children. While a temporal or spatial shift from the episode of the kingdom and children to the inquiry about eternal life is indicated in Mt. 19.15 and Mk 10.17, Luke makes none. This suggests that the ruler is in the audience in the previous episode (Lk. 18.15-17). His presence sheds positive light on his motive on the inquiry (Lk. 18.18).

Likewise, after Jesus' call to 'sell and give' and 'come and follow', he remains and hears what Jesus has to say about wealth and the kingdom.[43] This leaves the ruler's failure to follow Jesus rather inconclusive.[44] In fact, the ruler's response is described as περίλυπος (Lk. 18.23). Bovon sees the ruler's sorrowful response as 'the first act of conversion'.[45] James Metzger also suggests, 'He has accepted Jesus' injunction as a valid requirement for obtaining eternal life and even begun considering its cost.'[46]

---

41. Stephen E. Fowl, 'Receiving the Kingdom of God as a Child: Children and Riches in Luke 18.15ff', *NTS* 39.1 (1993): 153–8.

42. Lk. 19.1-10 functions as the climax of its narrative unit concerning the kingdom/salvation and also of the TN to a large extent. The story covers the issue of hospitality, concern for mercy and justice, use of wealth and salvation.

43. Matthew and Mark not only record that the inquirer went away but also note the change of the audience to the disciples for the subsequent teaching (Mt. 19.22, 23; Mk 10.22, 23).

44. Frequently noted is the failure of the ruler to follow Jesus due to his wealth. Méndez-Moratalla argues that this account epitomizes 'the non-conversion' episode. See *Conversion*, 198–207. Nevertheless, this misses Luke's perhaps deliberate variations in his account in comparison with those of Matthew and Mark. This rather sympathetic tendency towards the rich is not uncommon in Luke's Gospel.

45. Bovon, *Luke 2*, 568.

46. Metzger, *Consumption*, 169. Contra Wolter notes that Luke's use of ἄρχων (18.18) in the beginning of the story indicates the rich man's refusal of Jesus' invitation to follow. *Lukasevangelium*, 600.

Second, in hearing of the ruler, Jesus speaks in the present tense of the difficulty or almost impossibility for the rich to enter the kingdom: Πῶς δυσκόλως οἱ τὰ χρήματα ἔχοντες εἰς τὴν βασιλείαν τοῦ θεοῦ **εἰσπορεύονται** (Lk. 18.24, emphasis added).[47] Inheriting eternal life (Lk. 18.18, 30), entering the kingdom of God (18.24, 29, 35) and being saved (18.26) are used synonymously in this passage. Luke's use of the present tense (εἰσπορεύονται) here suggests the significance of participating in God's kingdom now by caring for the poor to whom the kingdom belongs for the inheritance of eternal life in the age to come.[48] This is affirmed in the following discourse: Leaving what the disciples have for the sake of the kingdom ensures eternal life in the age to come (Lk. 18.28-30).

Structurally, this passage is formulated with question, answer and extended discourse similar to Lk. 10.25-37. The final statement responds to the ruler's initial question on eternal life. A simplified/highlighted form of the passage is as follows:[49]

Q: (τις ... ἄρχων) τί *ποιήσας* **ζωὴν αἰώνιον κληρονομήσω** (v. 18);

    A 1: τὰς ἐντολὰς οἶδας: (v. 20)
    R1: ταῦτα <u>πάντα</u> ἐφύλαξα (v. 21)
    A2: <u>πάντα</u> ὅσα ἔχεις πώλησον καὶ διάδος **πτωχοῖς**,
    καὶ **ἕξεις θησαυρὸν ἐν [τοῖς] οὐρανοῖς**,
    καὶ δεῦρο ἀκολούθει μοι. (v. 22)
    R2: περίλυπος ἐγενήθη·... **πλούσιος σφόδρα** (v. 23)
    A 3: πῶς δυσκόλως οἱ τὰ χρήματα ἔχοντες **εἰς τὴν βασιλείαν τοῦ θεοῦ εἰσπορεύονται**· (v. 24)

    Q´: (οἱ ἀκούσαντες) τίς δύναται **σωθῆναι**; (v. 26)
    A´: τὰ ἀδύνατα παρὰ ἀνθρώποις δυνατὰ παρὰ τῷ θεῷ ἐστιν. (v. 27)
    R´: (ὁ Πέτρος) ἰδοὺ ἡμεῖς ἀφέντες τὰ ἴδια *ἠκολουθήσαμέν* σοι. (v. 28)

A: [ἀπο]λάβῃ πολλαπλασίονα ἐν τῷ καιρῷ τούτῳ καὶ ἐν τῷ αἰῶνι τῷ ἐρχομένῳ **ζωὴν αἰώνιον**. (v. 30)

The issue is again 'by doing what' and 'eternal life' as observed from the frequent occurrence of action verbs: ἐφύλαξα (v. 21), πώλησον (v. 22), διάδος (v. 22), δεῦρο (v. 22), ἀκολούθει (v. 22) and ἀφέντες ἠκολουθήσαμέν (vv. 28, 29), and of

---

47. Both Matthew and Mark use future tenses (εἰσελεύσεται in Mt. 19.23; εἰσελεύσονται in Mk 10.23).

48. Green, *Luke*, 659.

49. Although Lk. 18.19 is omitted in this simplified form partly due to its indirect connection with our discussion, the goodness of God is significant in that it covers the first table of the Decalogue and more importantly postulates that the commandments which follow are built upon God's goodness. See Arseny Ermakov, 'The Salvific Significance of the Torah in Mark 10.17–22 and 12.28–34', in *The Torah in the New Testament: Papers Delivered at the Manchester-Lausanne Seminar of June 2008*, ed. Michael Tait and Peter Oakes (London: T&T Clark, 2009), 22-3.

soteriological terms: ζωὴν αἰώνιον (vv. 18, 30), τὴν βασιλείαν τοῦ θεοῦ (vv. 24, 25, 29) and σωθῆναι (v. 26). Intriguingly though, the ruler claims that he has practised the commandments to which Jesus refers.[50] Yet there still (ἔτι) remains one thing lacking.

Jesus demands selling all that he has, giving to the poor and following him. This is the most contested issue of our discussion here. Is Jesus adding two requirements to keeping the commandments to inherit eternal life? Marshall suggests that Jesus demands two additional steps for salvation[51] while others argue that the two are intrinsically one. For instance, Bailey and Evans highlight the significance of following Jesus, which presupposes dispossession, in addition to keeping the commandments.[52] In a similar vein, Wilson avers that obedience to Jesus' call supplements the demand of the law.[53] Hence it is by following Jesus that one ensures eternal life.

Nevertheless, it appears uncertain whether Jesus attaches an additional demand to keeping the commandments for the inheritance of eternal life. Rather, Jesus' demand implies that the ruler has not kept the commandments fully.[54] Loader aptly notes that the issue is 'how well' one keeps the commandments.[55] His reading draws the lawyer (Lk. 10.25) and the ruler (18.18) closer in their incomplete practices of the law. The point is doing the law properly and fully in order to inherit eternal life. In view of the wider Lukan narratives, as Loader asserts, 'Luke could not think of obedience to the law and obedience to Jesus as separable.'[56]

This particular episode needs further investigation. Despite Luke's combination of renunciation and discipleship elsewhere,[57] the insertion of θησαυρὸν ἐν [τοῖς] οὐρανοῖς (Lk. 18.22) in this account separates almsgiving (διάδος πτωχοῖς 18.22) from a call to follow.[58] In response to the ruler's question and his claim, Jesus expands the meaning of the Decalogue (Lk. 18.20; Exod. 20.12-16//Deut. 5.16-20) in terms of how one, the rich man, relates to the other, namely, the poor. One thing which is lacking is spelled out as πάντα ὅσα ἔχεις πώλησον καὶ διάδος πτωχοῖς (Lk. 18.22). Treasure in heaven is promised for doing so. The structure suggests

---

50. The lawyer appears to know what is written in the Law and to interpret correctly, yet the issue is 'doing' it properly.

51. Marshall, *Luke*, 685.

52. Evans, *Luke*, 652; Bailey, *Peasant*, 163.

53. Wilson, *Law*, 28.

54. Here Matthew's use of εἰ θέλεις τέλειος εἶναι (19.21) may enlighten what Jesus meant in lacking one thing. Note also Matthew's use of ἔτι (19.20).

55. Loader, *Law*, 341.

56. Ibid., 342.

57. Lk. 5.11, 28; 14.33; 18.28. See Green, *Luke*, 656.

58. Hays, *Ethics*, 168. He notes, '"Come and follow me" is not part of the "one thing lacking"'.

that treasure in heaven is synonymous with eternal life.[59] This reading separates Jesus' call to follow from the previous demand of almsgiving in view of the ruler's initial question. Moreover, it is anything but novel that giving to the poor stores up treasure in heaven in the late STP. Almsgiving is a popular theme particularly in Sirach and Tobit. It is rewarded with treasure in heaven in both soteriological and non-soteriological contexts.[60]

In Mt. 6.1-21, treasures in heaven as reward (μισθός) are stored up (θησαυρίζω) for the righteous (δικαιοσύνη) deeds, namely giving alms (ποιέω ἐλεημοσύνη), praying (προσεύχομαι) and fasting (νηστεύω).[61] However, Luke distinctively highlights almsgiving (ἐλεημοσύνη) in relation to treasure in heaven in Lk. 12.33-34 and 18.22. In fact, the narrative contexts in which these two passages are located find several points of contact in the issues of wealth, almsgiving, discipleship, kingdom and life. Most noticeably, the kingdom is linked with almsgiving and with heavenly treasure in their immediate contexts. The ways in which Luke highlights almsgiving in soteriological contexts are particularly intriguing. It is the very nature of almsgiving as tangible acts of love that leads one to participate in the kingdom.[62] At the same time, both accounts make it clear that it is God who grants the kingdom or makes one's salvation possible.

Hence Luke's stress on almsgiving followed by treasure in heaven in the account of the rich (πλούσιος) ruler is twofold. (1) Almsgiving (ἐλεημοσύνη) is a tangible act of mercy by which the ruler fulfils the commandments (ἐντολὰς).[63] Nevertheless,

---

59. Hays notes that they are equivalent terms as seen both from rabbinic materials and from the narrative context of the passage. Hays, *Ethics*, 168. Contra Fitzmyer, *Luke*, 1200; Nolland, *Luke 9:21–18:34*, 887.

60. Sir. 29.9-13; Tob. 4.5-11; 12.8-9; Mt. 6.19-21; 19.21; Mk 10.21; Lk. 12.33-34 (indirectly also 6.32-37). See Garrison, *Almsgiving*, 54–5. The influence of Prov. 10.2 and 11.4 in the light of 'redemptive power of almsgiving' on Tobit and Sirach is noted. See also Anderson, *Charity*, 53–61. He argues that a proximity between almsgiving and a (heavenly) treasury in Tobit and Sirach is influenced by Prov. 10.2 and 11.4.

61. Nathan Eubank, 'Storing Up Treasure with God in the Heaven: Celestial Investments in Matthew 6:1–21', *CBQ* 76 (2014): 77–92 (especially 90–1); *Wages*, 85.

62. Halvor Moxnes, 'Social Relations and Economic Interaction', in *Luke-Acts: Scandinavian Perspective*, ed. Petri Luomanen (Helsinki: Finnish Exegetical Society, 1991), 70. Moxnes summarizes, 'This act of almsgiving is both a precondition in order to have a treasure in heaven, and a reflection of heaven, that is, of the way in which God acts.'

63. Regarding the relationship between almsgiving and commandments, see Anderson, *Sin*, 171, 174. He states, 'The Talmudic declaration that almsgiving is equal to all the other commandments in the Torah is a widespread motif ... in rabbinic literature' (174). See also Saul Lieberman, 'Two Lexicographical Notes', *JBL* 65 (1946): 69–72. His study shows that ἐντολή is also used in the sense of alms in Christian and Jewish Greek sources (particularly in the Testament of Asher 2.8) just as מצוה (ἐντολή) is often used to denote 'charity', 'alms', in Rabbinic Hebrew.

(2) distributing all to the poor (πτωχοῖς) is not a simple admonition to almsgiving or dispossession, but concern for the poor in view of God's goodness.

In this aspect, Jesus' word, Διάδος πτωχοῖς, καὶ ἕξεις θησαυρὸν ἐν [τοῖς] οὐρανοῖς (Lk. 18.22), is not far from 'keep the commandments and you will have eternal life'. In this incident, the crucial lacking aspect of the commandments which leads to eternal life (ζωή αἰώνιος) is almsgiving (ἐλεημοσύνη).[64] Again, Jesus' final answer which corresponds to the initial question of the ruler reaffirms that those who leave what they own for the sake of the kingdom will inherit eternal life. To sum up, the essential issue at stake for the ruler here is that giving of alms to the poor reflects his relations with the other in the light of the Decalogue.

7.5 Law, Mercy and Almsgiving and Eternal Life

I will now revisit the two initial questions posed in the beginning. First, do these passages contend that doing the law is sufficient to lead to eternal life? While scholars generally agree that Luke affirms the validity of the law, whether the law has salvific significance is contested. Wilson thinks that Lk. 10.25-37 and 18.18-30 contradict each other in terms of their portrayal of the salvific significance of the law. He asserts, 'In one the law is sufficient in itself, in the other it is not.'[65]

Unlike Wilson, Powery and Loader argue for salvific sufficiency of the law in both passages. Powery observes, the law 'provides entry into "eternal life"'.[66] Similarly, Loader finds that adherence to the law is crucial for inheriting eternal life.[67] This disagreement is mainly due to the reading of Jesus' demand to the ruler in Lk. 18.22. However, almsgiving to the poor is the one thing that the ruler lacks in keeping the commandments. It is by doing the law that one will inherit eternal life, and thus both passages affirm the salvific significance of fulfilling the law.

Second, to what extent do both passages highlight doing the law as showing mercy (ἔλεος) to those in need and giving alms (ἐλεημοσύνη) to the poor? While Lk. 10.27 refers to Deut. 6.5 and Lev. 19.18, it is Lev. 19.18 which functions as the central axis of the passage. To the ruler's question, Jesus points to Deut. 5.16-20 (// Exod. 20.12-16). Similarly, the context of Lk. 18.19-22 seems to be found in Leviticus 19 as Ermakov convincingly shows.[68] His discussion on the parallel between the goodness of God and the commandments in Mk 10.18-19 and the

---

64. Hays, *Ethics*, 169.

65. Wilson, *Law*, 29, 59, 102. His overall conclusion is 'the law, on its own, is an inadequate vehicle of salvation' (102).

66. Powery, *Scripture*, 224.

67. Loader, *Law*, 345.

68. Ermakov, 'Torah', 23–5. Perhaps it is more true to Luke than to Mark, noting Luke's concern for the poor and his emphasis on being merciful. See Lev. 19.3, 9-10, 11, 13-18, 33-36.

holiness of God and the commandments in Leviticus 19 is particularly helpful.[69] Moreover, taking Leviticus 19 as a 'reworked' Decalogue into account,[70] Jesus' demand to give to the poor in view of God's goodness and in line with the commandments which deal with human relations vividly corresponds to Leviticus 19 and its special concern for the poor. Both Lk. 10.25-37 and 18.18-30 earth their interpretation of the law in Leviticus 19.

The major concern of Leviticus 19 is manifested in the light of God's holiness and human relations in the community. As shown in Chapter 4, Lev. 19.2 is a paradigm-setting expression of the human embodiment of divine mercy. It portrays the ways in which the community embodies God's holiness especially in terms of just dealings with their neighbours. It also features showing concern for the poor and the sojourner, and thus for the weaker members of the community (Lev. 19.9-19, 33-34).[71] In this respect, it is not surprising that the answer to the lawyer's inquiry is summed up as doing merciful acts to those in need and the ruler's as caring for the poor. Luke does not offer a fresh interpretation of the law here, but points to what is written in the law already. Hence both Lk. 10.25-37 and 18.18-30 highlight the law in relation to eternal life by enacting mercy (ἔλεος) towards the needy and the poor.

In a similar vein, Lk. 16.16-31 can also be located in the discussion of the law and salvation as noted (Chapter 5). The law provides an *inclusio* to the Parable of Lazarus and the Rich Man. The validity of the law is affirmed. The destiny of the rich man in the afterlife is interconnected with obeying the law.[72] The rich man's failure to pay attention to the law in his life leads to his life after death in Hades. While asking for mercy (ἔλεος) in Hades, no mercy was given to him who did not show mercy to Lazarus, a poor man at his gate, in his life. All he gets is a firm reminder that the law is sufficient to lead to life. Lk. 16.16-30 is in consonant with 10.25-37 and 18.18-30. The validity of the law in view of salvation is affirmed. The law is interpreted in terms of mercy (ἔλεος) and almsgiving (ἐλεημοσύνη) to the needy and the poor in these accounts.[73]

7.6 Conclusion

In short, Lk. 10.25-37 and 18.18-30 show the human embodiment of divine mercy through acts of mercy (ἔλεος) and almsgiving (ἐλεημοσύνη) in the light of scriptural tradition. This embodiment is closely linked with inheriting eternal life. John the Baptist's teaching (Lk. 3.10-14) specifies mercy and justice in terms of

---

69. For the salvific overtone of Markan episodes, see Ermakov, 'Torah', 21, 26–30.
70. Moshe Weinfeld, *Deuteronomy I–II*, AB (New York: Doubleday, 1991), 250–5 (252).
71. See Michael Fagenblat, 'The Concept of Neighbour in Jewish and Christian Ethics', *Annotated*, 540–3.
72. Stigall, 'Moses', 553–4.
73. Ibid., 553.

sharing life essentials, food and clothing and dealing justly with others. In a similar vein, these two passages highlight tangibles acts of mercy shown to those in need (Lk. 10.30-35) and almsgiving to the poor (18.21). Luke's interpretation of the law expresses not only its concern for the needy and the poor but it also offers practical answers to the inquirers who seek to inherit eternal life.

Furthermore, both discourses draw attention to one's right relationship with the other. To the lawyer's inquiry (Lk. 10.25, 29), it is the Samaritan who stands out, and thus who embodies Jesus' teaching in Lk. 6.36 (γίνεσθε οἰκτίρμονες καθὼς [καὶ] ὁ πατὴρ ὑμῶν οἰκτίρμων ἐστίν). Jesus reminds the extremely rich ruler (πλούσιος Lk. 18.22) of the poor (πτωχός 18.18) to whom he is obliged to give. Here one's use of wealth in view of the other, whether one's enemy or the poor, is featured. In this regard, the proper use of wealth needs further investigation in relation to salvation to which I now turn.

Chapter 8

WHAT MUST I DO?: HUMAN EMBODIMENT OF DIVINE MERCY III (LK. 12.16–21; 16.1-9)

8.1 Introduction

This chapter once again explores the human embodiment of divine mercy in two uniquely Lukan parables (Lk. 12.16-21; 16.1-9) which centre around the following question: Τί ποιήσω (12.17; 16.3). But, unlike the previous instances, Τί ποιήσωμεν (Lk. 3.10, 12, 14) and Τί ποιήσας ζωὴν αἰώνιον κληρονομήσω (10.25; 18.18), the question does not emerge from a theological motivation, but from a very pragmatic one.[1] It primarily concerns socio-economic issues which the characters of the two parables face; however, their actions in response to this question entail theological outcomes. These two parables (Lk. 12.16-21; 16.1-9) show (im)proper use of wealth incorporated into Luke's soteriological message. Hence this chapter examines the third instance of the human embodiment of divine mercy in terms of the proper use of wealth.

I will first propose that juxtaposing these two parables illuminates their meanings and intents by demonstrating their affinities at various points.[2] Next, each parable will be examined in its wider literary and narrative contexts to explore the relationship between (im)proper use of wealth and salvation. Finally, almsgiving (ἐλεημοσύνη), which is offered as the proper use of wealth in the parables under discussion and in the wider Lukan narrative contexts, will be further explored in terms of its redemptive aspects and its implications for Luke's message of salvation.

---

1. R. Daniel Schumacher argues that the question in the two parables points to a moral dilemma; however, this seems less likely. See 'Saving like a Fool and Spending like it isn't yours: Reading the Parable of the Unjust Steward (Luke 16:1–8a) in light of the Parable of the Rich Fool (Luke 12:16–20)', *RevExp* 109.2 (2012): 269.

2. Tannehill, *Unity: Luke*, 247; Nickelsburg, 'Riches', 337; Hays, *Ethics*, 145.

8.2 Points of Contacts: The Parables of the Rich Fool (Lk. 12.16-21) and the Unjust Steward (16.1-9)

The proximity between the Parables of the Rich Fool (Lk. 12.16-21) and Lazarus and the Rich Man (16.19-31) and between the Prodigal Son (15.11-32) and the Unjust Steward (16.1-9) has been noted.[3] Within the wider context of the TN (Lk. 9.51–19.44), Luke's parables are closely tied and correspond to one another dynamically. Still, the structural, thematic and lexical affinities found in the Parables of the Rich Fool and the Unjust Steward are noteworthy.[4]

Structurally, the soliloquies of the main characters lead the plots of both stories.[5] In Luke's parables, soliloquy is common.[6] For instance, the Prodigal Son's thought process is revealed in his soliloquy (Lk. 15.17-19). Jesus invites the audience to hear (Lk. 18.6) what the unjust judge says in his heart (18.4-5). Soliloquies in the parables not only allow the audience/readers to see the inner thoughts of the characters but also lead them to enter the dilemma in the story. In these two parables, the soliloquies disclose troubles and solutions advanced by the main characters. The rich man (Lk. 12.16-17) reasons with himself (τί ποιήσω; 12.17) as to what to do with the abundant produce from the land (χώρα). His concern is where to store the crops (καρπός), and thus his wealth. The steward (Lk. 16.1-3) is at risk of losing his job which may endanger his existence. He reasons with himself (τί ποιήσω; 16.3) as to how he will survive once his job is taken from him. The case proposed in both parables is not on avoiding the impending judgement (Lk. 3.10,

---

3. Nolland avers that closer parallels are found between Lk. 12.16-21 and 16.19-31. *Luke 9:51–18:34*, 684. For the parallels between the parables of the Prodigal Son (15.11-32) and the Unjust Steward (16.1-13), see Donahue, *Parable*, 167-8. Frequently noted is the verb, διασκορπίζω, in Lk. 15.13 and 16.1 in terms of squandering others' possessions. For the parallels between the Parables of the Prodigal Son (15.11-32) and Lazarus and the Rich Man (16.19-31), see Hanna Roose, 'Umkehr und Ausgleich bei Lukas: Die Gleichnisse vom verlorenen Sohn (Luke 15.11–32) und vom reichen Mann und armen Lazarus (Luke 16.19–31) als Schwestergeschichten', *NTS* 56.1 (2010): 1–21.

4. Schumacher, 'Saving', 269–76. Although Schumacher covers only general similarities observed from the two parables, his article suggests that they should be read in the light of each other. See also Gerhard Sellin, 'Lukas als Gleichniserzähler: Die Erzählung vom barmherzigen Samariter (Lk. 10:25–37)', *ZNW* 65 (1974): 182; Bailey, *Peasant*, 58; Dennis J. Ireland notes that Lk. 12.13-34 provides topical and theological contexts of Lk. 16.1-13. *Stewardship and the Kingdom of God: A Historical, Exegetical, and Contextual Study of the Parable of the Unjust Steward in Luke 16:1–13*, NovTSup 70 (Leiden: Brill, 1992), 157–9.

5. Sellin, 'Gleichniserzähler', 182; Carroll, *Luke*, 323. Both list the structural parallels from the two parables.

6. Lk. 5.21; 7.49; 15.17-19; 18.4-5; 20.13. See Philip Sellew, 'Interior Monologue as a Narrative Device in the Parables of Luke', *JBL* 111.2 (1992): 239–53; Bernard Brandon Scott, *Hear Then the Parable: A Commentary on the Parables of Jesus* (Minneapolis: Fortress, 1989), 129.

12, 14) or on inheriting eternal life (10.25; 18.18), but on settling mundane issues as noted.[7]

They begin with problems (Lk. 12.17; 16.3) and move to solutions (12.18; 16.4). The planning of the rich man (Lk. 12.18-19) is contrasted with the rapid actions of the unjust steward (16.5-7). Both parables end with the unexpected responses from God (ὁ θεός Lk. 12.20) and the master (ὁ κύριος 16.8a). One is judged as fool (ἄφρων) while the other is commended for acting wisely (φρονίμως). God speaks directly to the rich man and judges his thoughts (Lk. 12.20, 21). Jesus' comments provide a theological interpretation for the actions of the unjust steward (Lk. 16.8b, 9).

Thematically, the parables concern wealth and its use in view of life, death and life after death. God's direct speech (Lk. 12.20) and Jesus' comment (16.8b, 9) reveal the intents of the parables. Lexically, not only the same words (πλούσιος, τὰ ὑπάρχοντα) and phrase (τί ποιήσω) but also the contrasting ones (συνάγω, διασκ ορπίζω; ἄφρων, φρονίμως) strengthen their ties.[8] The undefined third person plural is used as the ones who demand (ἀπαιτοῦσιν) the ψυχή of the rich man (Lk. 12.20) and who welcome (δέξωνται) those who make friends with wealth into the eternal homes (16.9). Eschatological overtones are present in Lk. 12.1–13.9 within which the Parable of the Rich Fool refers to the death of an individual.[9] The Parable of the Unjust Steward offers an eschatological interpretation at its closing (Lk. 16.8b, 9). These general observations suggest that the two parables may function as foils to each other. I will now turn to each parable to explore the relationship between wealth and salvation.

8.3 Storing up Treasure and the Demise of the Rich Fool (Lk. 12.16-21)

8.3.1 Literary and Narrative Contexts of the Parable of the Rich Fool

Although the Parable of the Rich Fool is found only in Luke and the Gospel of Thomas, it shares a common theme of death and possessions with wisdom traditions.[10] Intertextual parallels are frequently drawn to Sir. 11.14-19 and 1 En.

---

7. Intriguingly though, on the surface, it is merely mundane, but it appears that the consequences of the mundane choices are far from mundane.

8. Note also οἰκονόμος in 12.42 and 16.1, 3, 6, 8. There are even closer lexical parallels when taking the whole chapter of Luke 12 and 16 into consideration. Nolland, *Luke 9:51–18:34*, 806; Tannehill, *Unity: Luke*, 247; Johnson, *Luke*, 245.

9. John T. Carroll, *Response to the End of History: Eschatology and Situation in Luke-Acts*, SBLDS 92 (Atlanta: Scholars, 1998), 53; Christopher Hays, 'Slaughtering Stewards and Incarcerating Debtors: Coercing Charity in Luke 12:35–13:9', *Neot* 46.1 (2012): 43.

10. Matthew S. Rindge, *Jesus' Parable of the Rich Fool: Luke 12:13–34 among Ancient Conversations on Death and Possessions*, SBLECL 6 (Atlanta: SBL, 2011). His study examines the parable of the Rich Fool in the context of the sapiential tradition on death and possessions. However, his focused reading of the parable in the context of the wisdom tradition underestimates its eschatological aspect in relation to use of wealth.

97.8-10.[11] Indeed, the parable is similar to Sir. 11.14-19 in several aspects.[12] Both speak of God who is in charge of wealth, life and death (Sir. 11.14; Lk. 12.17, 20). Enjoying wealth is mentioned in view of the uncertain timing of death (Sir. 11.19; Lk. 12.20). Also, both passages share similar vocabulary: πλοῦτος, ἀγαθός, ἀναπαύω, ἐσθίω. Sirach admonishes the positive use of wealth such as almsgiving which is also a highly significant theme in Luke.[13]

However, Luke's parable is dissimilar from Sir. 11.14-19 at two significant points: (1) the profile of the rich man and (2) the nature of wealth. Sirach refers to the one who becomes rich through diligence and self-denial (ἀπὸ προσοχῆς καὶ σφιγγίας αὐτοῦ Sir. 11.18) while how Luke's rich man becomes rich is not mentioned. In fact, the surplus of wealth is given to the rich man as a gift. It is ἡ χώρα which produced plentifully (εὐφόρησεν) (Lk. 12.16).

Nickelsburg avers that Luke's parable is closer to 1 En. 97.8-10 than Sir. 11.14-19. Both 1 Enoch and Luke mention wealth in the context of judgement and salvation and portray the rich negatively.[14] 1 En. 97.8-10 and Lk. 12.16-21 are concerned with the hoarding of wealth and greed. However, the main issue of 1 Enoch is the unrighteous accumulation of wealth which eventually ascends from the rich man (97.8, 10). Conversely, the rich man's wealth remains even after his life is taken away in Luke (12.20). *Gos. Thom.* 63 also records the rich man's story. John P. Meier strongly argues for Thomas's dependence on Luke's parable as the two share similar wordings, monologue and sudden death.[15] Yet again, the thought in *Gos. Thom.* 63 centres on the accumulation of wealth, and thus on greed while the thrust of Luke's parable moves towards how to use wealth.[16]

In the wider Lukan narrative, the Parable of the Rich Fool (Lk. 12.16-21) is placed within a larger section (12.1–13.9) which deals with several interrelated topics under the umbrella theme of what Nolland calls 'being ready for the

---

11. Rindge, *Fool*, 69–85, 89–102; Snodgrass, *Intent*, 397; Bailey, *Peasant*, 63–4.

12. Bailey suggests that Luke's parable is an expanded form of the story in Sirach. *Peasant*, 63.

13. Rindge, *Fool*, 83; Kim, *Stewardship*, 168–217.

14. Nickelsburg, 'Riches', 335; 'Revisiting', 557, 568.

15. John P. Meier, 'Is Luke's Vision of the Parable of the Rich Fool Reflected in the Coptic Gospel of Thomas?' *CBQ* 74 (2012): 529–47. He argues that *Gos. Thom.* 63 and 72 together reflect the influence of Lk. 12.13-15, 16-21. For the discussion of Luke's influence on the *Gospel of Thomas* in general, see Simon Gathercole, 'Luke in the *Gospel of Thomas*', *NTS* 57 (2010): 114–44.

16. David B. Gowler, 'The Enthymematic Nature of Parables: A Dialogic Reading of the Parable of the Rich Fool (Luke 12:16–20)', *RevExp* 109.2 (2012): 206; Scott, *Parable*, 130. Other than the Jewish and Christian literary contexts of Luke's parable in 12.16-21, Abraham J. Malherbe observes that Luke uses the *topos* on covetousness in Lk. 12.13-34, explicating the Parable of the Sower (8.9-18). 'The Christianization of a *Topos* (Luke 12:13–34)', *NovT* 38.2 (1996): 123–35.

judgment of God'.[17] This section (Lk. 12.1–13.9) begins with the teaching against hypocrisy and introduces the main topics of death, life after death and judgement (12.1-12). A request on the dividing of inheritance brings wealth and possessions in relation to life and death into the discourse (Lk. 12.13-21). The topic continues from life, possessions and God's provision (Lk. 12.22-40) to stewardship, possessions and being ready for judgement (12.41-53). The addressees are changed between disciples (Lk. 12.1-12, 22-53) and crowds (12.13-21; 12.54–13.9). Finally, the last section brings judgement back into the discourse (12.54–13.9). With this broader context in view, the Parable of the Rich Fool (Lk. 12.16-21) encapsulates each topic and the whole section nicely. It weaves the theme of wealth in relation to life and death, and in view of the coming judgement.

8.3.2 Wealth and Death

Several points from the Parable of the Rich Fool (Lk. 12.16-21) are germane to our discussion. First, the repeated uses of the first person singular verbal form (eight times) and of μου attract our attention.[18] The rich man even calls and speaks to his own ψυχή. Other recurring words which carry similar ideas are συνάγω, κεῖμαι, θησαυρίζω and ἀποθήκη; and εὐφορέω, καρπός, σῖτος and πολλὰ ἀγαθά.[19] Two features stand out: (1) the self-centredness of the rich man[20] and (2) storing up of abundant wealth.

Second, the parable interestingly sets ἡ χώρα as the subject in the beginning (Lk. 12.16).[21] It ends with the question concerning wealth (ἃ δὲ ἡτοίμασας, τίνι ἔσται; Lk. 12.20b). The main concern of the parable is wealth, particularly the abundance of possessions (εὐφορέω). The parable is also bracketed by Jesus' teaching in Lk. 12.15 (ὁρᾶτε καὶ φυλάσσεσθε ἀπὸ πάσης πλεονεξίας, ὅτι οὐκ ἐν τῷ περισσεύειν τινὶ ἡ ζωὴ αὐτοῦ ἐστιν ἐκ τῶν ὑπαρχόντων αὐτῷ) and by his comment in 12.21 (οὕτως ὁ θησαυρίζων ἑαυτῷ καὶ μὴ εἰς θεὸν πλουτῶν).[22] The former

---

17. Nolland, *Luke 9:51–18:34*, 683; Tannehill, *Unity: Luke*, 240; Hays, 'Charity', 41–58.

18. For the first person singular verbal form, see ποιήσω, ἔχω, συνάξω, καθελῶ, οἰκοδομήσω and ἐρῶ. For the second person singular to his own soul, see ἔχεις, ἀναπαύου, φάγε, πίε and εὐφραίνου. For the repeated use of μου, note my crop, my barn, my grain, my good things and my soul. Note also that ἀναπαύου and εὐφραίνου (12.20) are used in the present indicative which may imply the habitual actions as a way of life. See Metzger, *Consumption*, 77–8.

19. See also περισσεύω in Lk. 12.15.

20. In his self-centredness, the rich man has forgotten that his soul in fact is a loan from God. See Wilfried Eckey, *Das Lukasevangelium: Unter Berücksichtigung seiner Parallenlen*, vol. 2: Lk. 11,1–24,53, rev. edn (Kempten, Germany: Neukirchener, 2006), 581.

21. Rindge, *Fool*, 2. He notes that this is the only parable of which the opening is not a person.

22. The significance of vv. 15 and 21 in relation to vv. 33 and 34 is noted as they provide a relationship between possession and life in view of God and others. Nolland, *Luke 9:51–18:34*, 687–90; Green, *Luke*, 489; Rindge, *Fool*, 203–4.

(Lk. 12.15) foreshadows the parable (12.16-21) as it concerns life (ζωή),[23] greed (πλεονεξία) and abundance of possessions (περισσεύω). The latter (Lk. 12.21) gives a concluding remark to the parable as it contrasts storing up of wealth (θησαυρίζω) for oneself against being rich towards God (εἰς θεὸν πλουτῶν). The issue is what to do with an abundance of wealth which is given as a gift. While the rich man decides to gather and store it up for entertaining and securing his own ψυχή, the concluding remark of the parable (Lk. 12.21) in line with 12.33 suggests an alternative use of wealth, namely, εἰς θεὸν πλουτῶν[24] and θησαυρὸν ἀνέκλειπτον ἐν τοῖς οὐρανοῖς both of which point to almsgiving (ἐλεημοσύνη).

Lastly, this parable uniquely includes God's direct speech.[25] God's appearance brings a surprising turn and provides an interpretative frame with the extended comment in Lk. 12.21. Whether God's direct talk to the rich man indicates natural death or personal eschatology as divine judgement is open to question (Lk. 12.20).[26] Nevertheless, it seems plausible that the parable has the coming judgement in view as the whole chapter discusses this theme. God is already mentioned as the one in charge of death and life after death (Lk. 12.5). The significance of life, death and life after death is contrasted to the abundance of possessions. The rich man's pragmatic dilemma, Τί ποιήσω, ὅτι οὐκ ἔχω ποῦ συνάξω τοὺς καρπούς μου (Lk. 12.17), is now tuned to serve Luke's theological purpose.

God gives the epithet, ἄφρων, to the rich man (πλουσίου) as he pronounces the impending demise of his ψυχή (Lk. 12.20). The use of ἄφρων here may be drawn

---

23. Luke's use of ἡ ζωή in contrast to the abundance of possessions in Lk. 12.15 is noteworthy. Elsewhere in the Gospel, it usually refers to eternal life (Lk. 10.25; 18.18, 30; cf. 16.25) although it is less likely in 12.15. The ψυχή of the rich man which he tries to secure and entertain is demanded of him (12.19, 20, 22, 23). On the contrary, Jesus teaches not to be preoccupied with ψυχή, but to seek the kingdom and ζωή in 12.22-34. See Seccombe, *Possessions*, 140-1.

24. Joshua A. Noble suggests that '[giving to God' offers a better translation of εἰς θεὸν πλουτῶν in Lk. 12.21. His examination of the grammatical and contextual use of the phrase finds that '[transferring] wealth to God' grasps the meaning of εἰς θεὸν πλουτῶν. Thus, it points to almsgiving. '"Rich Toward God": Making Sense of Luke 12:21', *CBQ* 78 (2016): 302-20 (319).

25. Metzger, *Consumption*, 78.

26. For the coming judgement in view, see Jeremias, *Parables*, 165; Hays, *Ethics*, 127. For the individual eschatology in view, Jacques Dupont, 'Die individuelle Eschatologie im Lukasevangelium und in der Apostelgeschichte', in *Orientierung an Jesus: Zur Theologie der Synoptiker: Für Josef Schmid*, ed. Paul Hoffmann (Freiburg: Herder, 1973), 37-47. For the individual death in view, Snodgrass, *Intent*, 398; Fitzmyer, *Luke*, 971. cf. Carroll, *Response*, 60-71. He argues, 'Luke does indeed accent the role of the individual in relation to eschatology. ... However, it is not the moment of death, but the present situation of the believer'.

from Pss. 14.1, 53.1 and 49.10 LXX.[27] Yet, more convincing is the occurrence of ἄφρων in Lk. 11.40 in its immediate context.[28] Jesus calls the Pharisees ἄφρονες in connection with greed (ἁρπαγή) and wickedness inside (Lk. 11.39-40). Rindge suggests that one of the reasons for the rich man's folly lies in greed (Lk. 12.15, 21).[29] Both Lk. 11.39-41 and 12.15, 21, 33-34 warn against greed (πλεονεξία), but offer almsgiving (ἐλεημοσύνη) as a remedy.[30]

The rich man's major concern, which is his wealth, remains even after his life ends. His folly lies here. He plans to gather (συνάγω) and store up (θησαυρίζω) wealth for his life (ψυχή). In the end, what is at stake is not wealth but his life. He foolishly holds and stores up wealth to secure his life, not realizing God's coming judgement at an unexpected time.[31] Hence the improper use of abundant wealth fails to secure the life of the rich man while giving to God, namely, almsgiving (ἐλεημοσύνη) which stores up unfailing treasure in heaven, is alternatively suggested. Now I will turn to the next parable which also concerns the use of wealth yet offers a positive example.

8.4 Use of Unjust Wealth (Τοῦ Μαμωνᾶ τῆς Ἀδικίας) and Eternal Dwelling (Αἰώνιος Σκηνή) (Lk. 16.1-9)

8.4.1 Various Readings of the Parable of the Unjust Steward

The Parable of the Unjust Steward is indisputably one of the most contested and puzzling parables of Jesus. Far from settling the most complicated issue in Lk. 16.8a, namely, the master's praise of the unjust steward, among many others in the parable, divergent solutions continue to be offered. A short survey of the recent history of scholarship on the parable must suffice for our discussion here.[32]

---

27. Donahue, *Parable*, 178; Bailey, *Peasant*, 68; Forbes, *God*, 85-6; Eckey, *Lukasevangelium*, 581.

28. Rindge, *Fool*, 3, 224–30; Hays, *Ethics*, 126.

29. Rindge, *Fool*, 208–9. He also suggests that his foolishness lies in his failure to recognize the 'precarious' nature of wealth and to use wealth meaningfully in view of inevitable death (see 194, 213–15).

30. The same wording: δότε ἐλεημοσύνην is used in Lk. 11.41 and 12.33. cf. Acts 3.2, 3, 10; 9.36; 10.2, 4, 31; 24.17. Rindge, *Fool*, 191; Anderson, *Charity*, 62–5; *Sin*, 146–7. Here Luke shares a similar idea of almsgiving as a positive and an alternative use of wealth with Tobit and Sirach but diverges from 1 Enoch which consistently sheds a negative light on the rich and wealth (Tob. 1.3, 16; 2.14; 14.2, 10, 11; esp. 4.7-16; 12.8-9; Sir. 3.30; 12.3; 16.14; 17.22; 29.8; 40.17; 40.24; esp. 29.12). See Nickelsburg, 'Revisiting', 578.

31. Rindge, 'The Rhetorical Power of Death and Possessions in Luke's Gospel', *R&E* 112.4 (2015): 562.

32. For a detailed discussion of scholarship, see Dennis J. Ireland, 'A History of Recent Interpretation of the Parable of the Unjust Steward (Luke 16:1–13)', *WTJ* 51.2 (1989): 293–318; *Stewardship*, 7–47.

Adolf Jülicher's interpretation of the parable has been widely accepted and elaborated despite some disfavour. His reading highlights the steward's prompt action in the face of a crisis.³³ However, it lacks an explanation for the master's approval of the unjust steward (Lk. 16.8a).³⁴ Derrett and Fitzmyer fill this gap by justifying the steward's action, arguing that the reduced amount is in fact usurious interest or commission.³⁵ This reading is endorsed by Moxnes and Metzger.³⁶ This solves one problem, and yet it raises another: Why is then the steward called ἀδικίας? With a slightly different view, Jülicher's reading is revived by Ireland, Hays and Forbes, noting that the parable is about the proper use of wealth in view of the impending eschatological crisis.³⁷ Ireland summarizes the parable as 'the faithful stewardship of material possessions' in view of eschatology.³⁸

Against these traditional readings of the parable, social, economic and/or cultural readings have been offered, yet without reaching any consensus. William Herzog critiques a traditional interpretation which is based on 'capitalistic ideology'.³⁹ While he suggests that the steward takes the hidden interest which belongs to the master, the socio-economic world of the parable reconstructed by Herzog sympathizes with the steward who is under the exploitative rich master.⁴⁰ His reading is welcomed by Stephen I. Wright.⁴¹ Similarly John Kloppenborg stresses the economic world of the parable for its better understanding. The social code of honour and shame directs Kloppenborg's reading. He argues, 'What is at stake is the master's honour, not the steward's character.'⁴²

While Kloppenborg sees the master's praise as his 'conversion' despite his further damaged honour due to the steward's action,⁴³ David Landry and Ben May

---

33. Adolf Jülicher, *Die Gleichnisreden Jesu 2: Auslegung der Gleichnisreden der drei ersten Evangelien* (Tübingen: Mohr, 1910), 510-11. He argues that the parable is primarily about the timely action of the steward to the question, Τί ποιήσω, although the parable gives a lesson on the skilful use of earthly goods.

34. Jülicher, *Gleichnisreden*, 512.

35. Derrett, 'Luke XVI', 209-10; Fitzmyer, 'Manager', 36.

36. Moxnes, *Economy*, 140-1; Metzger, *Consumption*, 122.

37. Ireland, *Stewardship*, 214-17; Forbes, *God*, 167-8; Hays, *Ethics*, 141-2. Hays explains the steward's action in terms of reciprocity in addition to those of ethic and eschatology.

38. Ireland, *Stewardship*, 217.

39. Herzog, *Parable*, 245. Contra Bailey, *Peasant*, 94. The cultural world reconstructed by Bailey portrays the rich master as a noble man while the steward's dishonesty is taken for granted.

40. Herzog, *Parable*, 249-55.

41. Stephen I. Wright, 'Parables on Poverty and Riches (Luke 12:13-21; 16:1-13; 16:19-31)', *Parables*, 224-7.

42. Kloppenborg, 'The Dishonoured Master (Luke 16,1-8a)', *Bib* 70.4 (1989): 474.

43. Kloppenborg, 'Master', 493.

aver that the steward in fact restores the master's honour by reducing debts.[44] Most recently John K. Goodrich brings a fresh perspective of 'voluntary debt remission' into discussion.[45] He notes that debt remission was not an uncommon practice for the mutual benefits of landlord and tenants in the Graeco-Roman world. In this respect, the steward's reduction of debts is not unjust but beneficial to himself as he meets his expectation of reciprocity, to the tenants whose debts are reduced and to the master who stands in a better position in relations to his tenants.[46]

Still others illuminate the parable by using its literary parallels. Donahue highlights close parallels between Lk. 15.11-32 and 16.1-8. He shifts the focus from the steward to the master in line with the father in the preceding one. He argues that the master and father are analogous to God in both parables.[47] Somewhat differently, Mary Ann Beavis reads the parable in the light of ancient comedies. While insisting that the steward is in fact a slave, she finds a model for the steward from Aesop, 'the crafty slave'.[48] Various approaches to the interpretation of the parable show that social, economic and/or cultural readings not only shed fresh light on the parable but also show that an interpretation necessarily involves careful investigation of its social, economic, cultural, literary and historical contexts. Nevertheless, one should take them with caution in order not to unduly impose interpretive keys on the text.

As can be seen from the survey above, the parable continues to produce as many questions as answers. Each interpretation seems to raise another issue. Many puzzling issues remain unresolved and the reading of the parable remains challenging. How do we then read the parable for the purpose of this thesis? Here I do not intend to offer another interpretation. Rather I will highlight several significant points for our discussion while generally accepting the traditional reading of the parable.

8.4.2 Wealth and Eternal Dwelling

The parable is part of a larger narrative unit (Lk. 15.1–16.31) which begins at Lk. 15.1. In Lk. 15.1-2, the narrative sets the scene with all the tax collectors and sinners (πάντες οἱ τελῶναι καὶ οἱ ἁμαρτωλοὶ) who keep coming to hear Jesus, and with the Pharisees and the scribes (οἵ Φαρισαῖοι καὶ οἱ γραμματεῖς) who are grumbling against Jesus' welcoming and table fellowship with the former group.

---

44. David Landry and Ben May, 'Honor Restored: New Light on the Parable of the Prudent Steward (Luke 16:1-8a)', *JBL* 119.2 (2000): 301, 308-9.

45. John K. Goodrich, 'Voluntary Debt Remission and the Parable of the Unjust Steward (Luke 16:1-13)', *JBL* 131.3 (2012): 553.

46. Goodrich, 'Remission', 562, 564-5.

47. Donahue, *Parable*, 167-8.

48. Mary Ann Beavis, 'Ancient Slavery as an Interpretive Context for New Testament Servant Parables with Special Reference to the Unjust Steward (Luke 16:1-8)', *JBL* 111.1 (1992): 48-9, 51-2.

Two groups of people are already present and the Parables of Lost and Found in Luke 15 are particularly addressed to the latter group.[49]

In Lk. 16.1, Jesus primarily addresses the disciples; however, the response of the Pharisees (16.14) to the parables and teachings of Jesus (15.3–16.13) is mentioned between the Parables of the Unjust Steward (16.1-9) and of Lazarus and the Rich Man (16.19-31) in 16.14. This links their response to the parable (Lk. 16.1-9) with an intriguing epithet attached to them, φιλάργυροι (16.14). It also initiates the following parable in Lk. 16.19-31.[50] What is noted from this broader narrative unit (Lk. 15.1–16.31) is the issue concerning Jesus' welcoming (προσδέχομαι)[51] and table fellowship (συνεσθίω).[52] It is the underlying theme of the three parables in Luke 15 and of the two parables in Luke 16.

Within this thematic context, the parable (Lk. 16.1-9) features several salient aspects. First, the repeated occurrences of οἰκονόμος group words[53] – οἰκονόμος (Lk. 16.1, 3, 8; cf. 12.42), οἰκονομία (16.2, 3, 4), οἰκονομέω (16.2), οἶκος (16.4) and οἰκέτης (16.13) – and δέχομαι (16.4, 6, 7, 9) in the parable can hardly be missed. They capture two major issues: (1) stewardship in terms of managing entrusted properties[54] and (2) hospitality. Luke's use of the term, 'οἰκονόμος', as distinguished from δοῦλος,[55] ἐπίτροπος (Lk. 8.3) and μίσθιος (15.17, 19), is noteworthy although it was a common practice within Graeco-Roman society that an οἰκονόμος was a slave. The parable also corresponds to Lk. 12.42-48 with its thematic similarities of a steward entrusted with property.[56]

Hospitality is already introduced from the beginning of the section (Lk. 15.1-2) and throughout the preceding parables in multiple layers: (1) Jesus' welcoming (προσδέχομαι) of the tax collectors and sinners (Lk. 15.2), (2) lost ones welcomed by their owners, and thus by angels and God (15.7, 10) and (3) the lost son

---

49. Lk. 15.3 designates the addressees as the Pharisees and the scribes (Εἶπεν δὲ πρὸς αὐτούς). However, εἶπεν δέ which may indicate a broader addressee in view is added at the outset of the Parable of the Prodigal Son.

50. Following Jesus' teaching on making friends with unrighteous wealth (ποιήσατε φίλους ἐκ τοῦ μαμωνᾶ τῆς ἀδικίας), they instead become friends with money (φιλάργυροι). Green, *Luke*, 601.

51. While the repeated use of δέχομαι is significant in Lk. 16.1-13, the use of προσδέχομαι is intriguing. Luke elsewhere uses it in the context of expecting and awaiting the kingdom or *parousia*. Lk. 2.25, 38; 12.36; 23.51; Acts 24.15. cf. Acts 23.21.

52. For the controversial issues of table fellowship, see Acts 11.3; 1 Cor. 5.11; Gal. 2.12; cf. Acts 10.4.

53. Note Luke's addition of οἰκέτης (16.13) in comparison with Mt. 6.24.

54. Perhaps the steward in the parable is a freedman as he worries about losing his job. Contra Beavis, 'Slavery', 49. She argues that not only the steward is a slave but also slavery is in view in the parable.

55. Lk. 7.2, 3, 8, 10; 12.37, 43, 45, 46, 47; 14.17, 21, 22, 23; 15.22; 17.7, 9, 10; 19.13, 15, 17, 22; 20.10, 11; 22.50; cf. 2.29.

56. Hays, 'Charity', 49. Contra Kloppenborg, 'Master', 493.

welcomed by his father (15.20, 24, 31-32). In the Parable of the Unjust Steward (Lk. 16.1-9), the steward is seeking to be welcomed (δέχομαι) when he loses his position (16.4). Also, debt-related words (ὀφείλω, χρεοφειλέτης Lk. 16.5-7) occur at the centre to depict the steward's precise action to fulfil his aim to be welcomed. The steward whose stewardship is in crisis seeks to find hospitality from his master's debtors through reducing debts.

Second, the parable brings an unexpected and puzzling remark from the master.[57] The juxtaposition of ἀδικία and φρονίμως is most troublesome although often noted is the distinction between the steward being ἀδικία and his action being φρονίμως (Lk. 16.8a). Ἀδικία occurs only in Luke among the Synoptic Gospels.[58] Its use in the Parable of the Widow and the Unjust Judge (Lk. 18.2-8) is particularly helpful in understanding ἀδικία in Lk. 16.8a. It is the narrator of the parables who gives this judgement of both characters in Lk. 16.8 (τὸν οἰκονόμον τῆς ἀδικίας)[59] and 18.6 (ὁ κριτὴς τῆς ἀδικίας). They share what Daube calls 'an action laudable in itself but, in circumstances, deliberately injurious'.[60] Both the steward and the judge act rightly, but with wrong motivation. Moreover, both make a similar argument often called *a minore ad maius* (from the lesser to the greater).[61]

With regard to φρόνιμος, Hays observes that it is used in view of eschatology, urging a decisive action in both Matthew and Luke.[62] Luke's repetition of ἀδικία

---

57. This verse indeed has produced countless works to find solutions. Economic solutions argue that the steward's action in 16.5-7 is not unjust, but his squandering of his master's property (16.1-2) is (Derrett and Fitzmyer). Cultural solutions highlight honour and shame in ancient society and offer solutions to the master's praise either from his restored honour (Landry and May) or from his reluctant acknowledgement (Kloppenborg). Comical solutions feature the steward's revengeful action against the powerful master (Scott and Beavis). In addition, solutions are also offered from a theological understanding of the parable, focusing on the master's (analogous to God) mercy and acceptance (Bailey and Donahue).

58. Lk. 13.27; 16.8, 9; 18.6.

59. Although Luke frequently refers to Jesus as κύριος, the context here clearly points to the master (κύριος) of the steward. However, it is the judgement of the narrator that the steward is unjust. Ryan S. Schellenberg brings an interesting perspective to identify ὁ κύριος here. He observes that Luke often blurs the boundaries between the narrative world and the world of the narrator in the parables. Hence the ambiguity of ὁ κύριος in 16.8a allows the audience/reader to 'commingle' the narrative world with their world. 'Which Master? Whose Steward? Metalepsis and Lordship in the Parable of the Prudent Steward (Luke 16.1–3)', *JSNT* 30.3 (2008): 268–73.

60. David Daube, 'Neglected Nuances of Exposition in Luke-Acts', in *ANRW* II. 25.3 (1984), 2329–30.

61. Ireland, *Stewardship*, 90; Metzger, *Consumption*, 131; Francis E. Williams, 'Is Almsgiving the Point of the "Unjust Steward"?,' *JBL* 83 (1964): 295.

62. Hays, *Ethics*, 143. Mt. 24.45; 25.2, 4, 8, 9; cf. 7.24; 10.16; Lk. 12.42; 16.8.

and φρονίμως (Lk. 16.8b, 9) conveys a strong eschatological nuance. Φρονίμως is used to compare sons of this age (οἱ υἱοὶ τοῦ αἰῶνος τούτου) with sons of light (τοὺς υἱοὺς τοῦ φωτός) in Lk. 16.8b.[63] Ἀδικία, which describes the steward, is added to wealth (μαμωνᾶς) in Lk. 16.9. Marshall and Nolland suggest that ἀδικία refers to 'worldly' instead of dishonest in the light of this age in contrast to the age to come (Lk. 16.8-9).[64] Both the steward and wealth belong to this world in contrast to the disciples. The concluding remark of the parable brings eschatological implications to the mundane circumstance and actions of the steward.[65]

Finally, Jesus' additional comment (καὶ ἐγὼ ὑμῖν λέγω Lk. 16.9) to the disciples makes the point of the parable even clearer. Whether Lk. 16.9 is an original part of the parable or not is irrelevant to our discussion.[66] Instead, what is significant is that Lk. 16.9 closely corresponds to 16.4. The steward decides what to do (ποιέω) so that he can be welcomed (δέχομαι) into others' homes (οἶκος) when his job is taken (ἀφαιρέω, μεθίστημι) from him. In response to the steward's action, Jesus tells the disciples to make (ποιέω) friends so that they will be welcomed (δέχομαι) into eternal homes (αἰωνίους σκηνάς) when unrighteous wealth is gone (ἐκλείπω). Hence Lk. 16.9 provides an internal interpretive key to the parable. One's use of wealth is strongly tied to one's eternal destiny.

ἔγνων τί **ποιήσω**, **ἵνα ὅταν** μετασταθῶ **ἐκ** <u>τῆς οἰκονομίας</u> **δέξωνταί** με **εἰς τοὺς** <u>οἴκους αὐτῶν.</u> (Lk. 16.4)
ἑαυτοῖς **ποιήσατε** φίλους **ἐκ** <u>τοῦ μαμωνᾶ τῆς ἀδικίας</u>, **ἵνα ὅταν** ἐκλίπῃ **δέξωνται** ὑμᾶς **εἰς τὰς** <u>αἰωνίους σκηνάς.</u> (16.9)

8.5 Proper Use of Wealth: Is Almsgiving Redemptive?

The examination of the parables in Lk. 12.16-21 and 16.1-9 shows that (im)proper use of wealth appears inseparable from death and life after death. Wealth is not the focal issue of either parable, but its use whether it be righteous or unrighteous.[67] Lk. 12.21 (also in 12.33) and 16.9 capture the main point, providing the concluding remarks for the parables. In Lk. 12.33, which elaborates 12.21, the solution to what

---

63. See Sons of Light in 1QS 1.9; 2.16; 3.13, 24; 1QM (War Scroll) 1.3, 9, 11, 13. Sons of Light is the antithesis of Sons of Darkness in the DSS.

64. Marshall, *Luke*, 621–2; Nolland, *Luke 9:21–18:34*, 801.

65. Eckey, *Lukasevangelium*, 700.

66. The proper ending of the parable is also contested. John D. Crossan says that the adequate ending of the parable is 16.7. *In Parables: The Challenge of the Historical Jesus* (New York: Harper & Row, 1985), 110. cf. For 16.8a as an ending, Fitzmyer, 'Manager', 27; For 16.9 as an ending, Ireland, *Stewardship*, 96.

67. Intriguingly wealth (χώρα, καρπός, σῖτος, ἀγαθός) in Lk. 12.16-21 is portrayed in a positive view while wealth is viewed in the context of debt or referred to as unrighteous mammon (ἔλαιον and σῖτος in the context of debt, μαμωνᾶς τῆς ἀδικίας) in 16.1-9.

to do (ποιέω) with wealth in view of life, death and eternity is cryptically phrased as almsgiving (δότε ἐλεημοσύνην). They are to make (ποιέω) purse which is an unfailing (ἀνέκλειπτος) treasure, by selling possessions (τὰ ὑπάρχοντα) and by giving alms (δότε ἐλεημοσύνην) (Lk. 12.33).

Similarly, what is hinted at in Lk. 16.9 is to make (ποιέω) friends with unrighteous wealth (τοῦ μαμωνᾶ τῆς ἀδικίας) which fails (ἐκλείπω) at an unexpected moment. The essence of this verse is frequently noted as almsgiving.[68] Williams observes the following: the idea in Lk. 16.9 in the light of Jewish piety is 'that a man in practicing almsgiving distributes not his own property, but property which is already God's'.[69] This concluding remark recommends a positive action, which is almsgiving (ἐλεημοσύνην).[70] Hence the significance of almsgiving in these two passages in particular and in Luke's Gospel in general is rarely disputed.[71]

The question remains, however, as to whether Luke suggests redemptive aspects of almsgiving since it is promoted especially in soteriological and eschatological contexts. Redemptive almsgiving is a widespread concept particularly in rabbinic Judaism[72] and in the Apostolic Fathers.[73] It has solid grounds in scriptural traditions before the first century CE.[74] The Greek translation of צְדָקָה into both δικαιοσύνη

---

68. Marshall, *Luke*, 621; Green, *Luke*, 594; Johnson, *Luke*, 248.

69. Williams, 'Almsgiving', 294.

70. Ibid., 297; Johnson, *Luke*, 245; Tannehill, *Unity: Luke*, 247; Nolland, *Luke 9:51-18:34*, 690, 806. Nolland further comments that the unspecified third person plural (δέξωνται) refers to the poor who are the recipients of the alms.

71. See Lk. 3.10-14; 6.30, 34-35, 38; 11.41; 12.33-34; 18.22; 19.8; Acts 9.36; 10.2; 24.17; cf. Lk. 14.13; 16.9; Acts 2.45; 4.34-35.

72. Garrison, *Almsgiving*, 56-9.

73. Ibid., 76-108. His discussion of 1, 2 Clement and the Shepherd of Hermas concludes that redemptive almsgiving is an answer to 'the social conflicts and theological concerns'. See also Justo L. Gonzalez, *Faith and Wealth: A History of Early Christian Ideas on the Origin, Significance, and Use of Money* (New York: Harper & Row, 1990), 94-105; Carolyn Osiek, *Rich and Poor in the Shepherd of Hermas: An Exegetical-Social Investigation*, CBQMS 15 (Washington: Catholic Biblical Association, 1983), 90-1, 124-5; Louis William Countryman, *The Rich Christian in the Church of the Early Empire: Contradictions and Accommodations* (New York: Edwin Mellen, 1980), 103-43; David J. Downs suggests that almsgiving is advanced in 2 Clement not for the rich members but for all members of the congregation as 'communal practices' which represent repentance in view of impending eschatological judgement. 'Redemptive Almsgiving and Economic Stratification in 2 Clement', *JECS* 19 (2011): 493-517 (517).

74. See Garrison, *Almsgiving*, 38-59 (chs 2, 3); Anderson, *Charity*, 53-69 (ch. 4); *Sin*, 164-88 (ch. 11); Hays, 'By Almsgiving and Faith Sins Are Purged? The Theological Underpinnings of Early Christian Care for the Poor', *Economics*, 268-9; Berger, 'Almosen', 182-4. See Prov. 15.27 LXX; Dan. 4.27 LXX; Sir. 29.9-13; Tob. 4.5-11; 12.8-9.

and ἐλεημοσύνη in the LXX is worth noting. Their overlap and proximity of meaning is observed 'as early as the second century BCE'.[75]

For instance, Dan. 4.24 (27) reads, atone for your sins with righteousness (בְּצִדְקָה) and your iniquities with mercy (בְּמִחַן) to the oppressed. The LXX's rendering of ἐν ἐλεημοσύναις conveys the link between righteousness and mercy to the oppressed in the Aramaic text.[76] Moreover, the LXX juxtaposes almsgiving (ἐλεημοσύνη) with redeeming (λυτρόω). Similarly, δικαιοσύνη which delivers from death in Prov. 10.2 LXX (δικαιοσύνη δὲ ῥύσεται ἐκ θανάτου) is understood as ἐλεημοσύνη which delivers from death in Tob. 4.10 (ἐλεημοσύνη ἐκ θανάτου ῥύεται) and 12.9 (ἐλεημοσύνη γὰρ ἐκ θανάτου ῥύεται).[77] A similar idea is carried in Sir. 29.12-13.

Within the early Christian tradition, almsgiving seems beneficial particularly for the Gentile converts as it provides them with access to Israel.[78] Berger suggests that almsgiving has both sociological and soteriological value for the uncircumcised Gentile believers who become Christians.[79] He uses Cornelius in Acts 10 and the Gentile centurion in Luke 7 as examples of those who give alms or do merciful acts towards the Jewish people and express their solidarity with them. Thus, he argues that the Jewish custom of 'alms to Israel' is now applied to new converts or to sympathizers of the church or to the poor.[80]

Several other Lukan passages hint at soteriological implications for almsgiving. John the Baptist's teaching (Lk. 3.10-14) espouses merciful deeds, particularly almsgiving by sharing food and clothing, in soteriological contexts. Yet, an intriguing aspect of almsgiving is raised in Jesus' confrontation with the Pharisees in Lk. 11.39-41 where almsgiving (ἐλεημοσύνη) is directly linked to cleanness (καθαρός).[81] This account relates to the two parables under discussion at significant points. As noted, the Pharisees are called ἄφρονες (Lk. 11.40), just as the rich man is called ἄφρων (12.20), for their ignorance of God. The epithet bears on their use of wealth. The Pharisees are attacked for the discrepancy between the cleanness on the outside and ἁρπαγῆς and πονηρίας on the inside (Lk. 11.39-40). Almsgiving (δότε ἐλεημοσύνην) is proposed as a remedy for ἁρπαγῆς and πονηρίας (11.41).

The use of ἁρπαγή in Lk. 11.39 is worth noting in that the word conveys a meaning of seizing, robbing or extorting properties in the context of injustice and

---

75. Garrison, *Almsgiving*, 51.

76. Dan. 4.27 LXX reads as follows: Πάσας τὰς ἀδικίας σου ἐν ἐλεημοσύναις λύτρωσαι.

77. See Anderson, *Charity*, 53–61; Garrison, *Almsgiving*, 54–5.

78. Garrison, *Almsgiving*, 57. cf. *Jos. Asen.* 9–13.

79. Berger, 'Almosen', 192–5.

80. Ibid., 195.

81. See a recent discussion of Reardon who observes the relationship between almsgiving and cleansing in Lk. 11.37-44, Acts 10.1-18 and 11.1-18. He argues that almsgiving in these passages is particularly efficacious for moral purity. 'Cleansing through Almsgiving in Luke-Acts: Purity, Cornelius, and the Translation of Acts 15:9', *CBQ* 78 (2016): 463–82.

oppression.[82] Moxnes suggests that Jesus accuses the Pharisees of 'robbing' others' property.[83] Their uncleanness in fact results from their 'negative social relations to others'.[84] In this sense, τὰ ἐνόντα (Lk. 11.41) denotes literally ill-gotten wealth rather than a greedy heart.[85] They are to give ill-gotten wealth as alms so that everything will be clean for them.[86] This brings Jesus' exhortation in Lk. 11.41 closer to that in 16.9 particularly in terms of the use of ἁρπαγή or ἀδικίας wealth. Luke seems to suggest a positive use of ill-gotten (ἁρπαγῆς) or unrighteous (ἀδικίας) wealth for the givers' benefit.

Finally, generous giving is highlighted (Lk. 6.27-38) with the promise of a heavenly reward (6.35). Almsgiving is also linked with treasure in heaven (θησαυρός ἐν τοῖς οὐρανοῖς) in view of the kingdom in Lk. 12.31-34 and 18.22-25 as noted in Chapter 7. The Synoptic accounts of the rich ruler (Mt. 19.16-30//Mk 10.17-31//Lk. 18.18-30) promise treasure in heaven to the one who gives to the poor (διάδος πτωχοῖς) in view of inheriting eternal life, entering the kingdom of God and being saved. Hence Luke has little hesitation in relating almsgiving (ἐλεημοσύνη) to being rewarded with treasure in heaven (θησαυρός ἐν τοῖς οὐρανοῖς), eternal life (ζωὴν αἰώνιον) and salvation.

8.6 Conclusion

The two parables examined in this chapter show that the human embodiment of divine mercy concerns the proper use of wealth. At one level, the solutions which the rich man and the steward come up with concerning their pragmatic dilemma, Τί ποιήσω (Lk. 12.17; 16.3), are judged in stark contrasts – ἄφρων (12.20) and φρονίμως (16.8). They result in rather different theological outcomes. The demise

---

82. See Lev. 6.2 LXX; Eccl. 5.7 LXX; Isa. 3.4; 10.2 LXX. Note also the use of ἁρπάζω in the NT. It is either used literally as 'plunder' or 'take something by force' (Mt. 11.12; 12.29; 13.19; Jn 6.15; 10.12, 28; Acts 23.10; Heb. 10.34) or figuratively as 'snatch someone or somebody away' (Acts 8.39; 2 Cor. 12.2, 4; 1 Thess. 4.17; Jude 23; Rev. 12.5).

83. Moxnes, *Economy*, 113.

84. Ibid., 119–23.

85. Kim, *Stewardship*, 180; Moxnes, *Economy*, 111.

86. While Mt. 23.25-26 continues with the idea of cleaning inside as well as outside, Luke combines cleaning of outside with giving what is inside as alms (11.4). Hence it makes better sense that what is inside (τὰ ἐνόντα) refers to wealth accumulated by extortion (ἁρπαγῆς). Concerning a suggested outcome of almsgiving as purity or cleanness (καθαρός), Moxnes argues that Jesus challenges the Pharisaic ritual purity laws which oppress and exploit those who are marginalized but promotes 'the transformation of purity' by social solidarity through almsgiving. *Economy*, 121. Nolland finds a closer connection with Cornelius's account in Acts 10 where giving alms (ποιέω ἐλεημοσύνη), being cleansed (καθαρίζω) and doing works of righteousness (ἐργάζομαι δικαιοσύνη) are intertwined. *Luke 9:21–18:34*, 665.

of the rich man is pronounced by God (Lk. 12.20). The reception into eternal dwellings to which the steward's action leads is suggested by Jesus' remark (16.9). In these two parables, (im)proper use of wealth is intertwined with soteriological reverberations. At another level, Jesus, the narrator of both parables, offers solutions in practical terms. In the first parable, Luke spells out the proper use of wealth by giving it to the poor as almsgiving (ἐλεημοσύνη); in the second, it is by reducing debt.

In the Lukan narratives, almsgiving (ἐλεημοσύνη) not only epitomizes merciful deeds which include acts of justice and caring for the poor but also reflects the essential element necessary to participate in God's kingdom which Jesus brings and embodies. Luke ties the use of wealth with his message of salvation in these passages by offering a practical answer to the question, Τί ποιήσω; that is, almsgiving (Lk. 12.33; 16.9).

Thus far in Chapters 6, 7 and 8, I have shown a close link between the human embodiment of divine mercy and one's socio-economic dealings. Soteriological inquiries are responded to in terms of the enactment of divine mercy, that is, the sharing of life essentials (Lk. 3.11), just economic dealings (3.13-14), tangible acts of mercy which involve radical generosity (10.33-35), cancelling debts (16.5-7) and almsgiving (12.33; 16.9; 18.22). Rich and diverse is the promise: deliverance from the coming judgement (Lk. 3.7), eternal life (10.25, 28; 18.18, 30), the kingdom (12.32; 18.29), treasure in heaven (12.33; 18.22) and the welcoming to eternal dwelling (16.9). Most significantly, however, participating in and eating at the messianic banquet (Lk. 14.15) is yet to come.

Chapter 9

SALVATION OF THE RICH: RESTORED PEOPLE OF GOD (LK. 14.1-24)

9.1 Introduction

This chapter explores salvation of the rich in relation to that of the poor by examining Luke's portrayal of salvation as the messianic banquet of the kingdom. Luke's interest in food and meals (see Chapter 3) ultimately points to the anticipation of the messianic banquet.[1] Lack and abundance of food not only reflect the experience of many in this world but also foreshadow the reversal in the coming world as noted.[2]

In Luke, some luxurious banquets are criticized while other celebrations are anticipated and commended.[3] Servants in readiness will recline at table to be served by the master in the coming kingdom.[4] The Last Supper and the post resurrection meal on the way to Emmaus reaffirm the significance of the meals in Luke's Gospel.[5] Most notably, Jesus' Parable of the Great Banquet (Lk. 14.16-24) draws the imagery of the divine reward as eating bread in the kingdom (14.15). Similarly, being saved and reclining at table in the kingdom are interchangeably

---

1. Johnson aptly puts the significance of the messianic banquet in Luke: 'The banquet is anticipated by the feeding of the multitude (9:12-17), rendered parabolically in 14:15-24, sacramentally in 22:14-30. The meal will continue to be the place where the risen Lord is encountered' (24:28-35, 36-43; Acts 10:41). *Luke*, 217. See also Heil, *Meal*, 312; Craig Blomberg, 'Jesus, Sinners and Table Fellowship', *BBR* 19.1 (2009): 61; Parsons, *Luke*, 223. Besides, the Last Supper (Lk. 22.14-30) also strongly anticipates the coming banquet of the kingdom in a covenant setting. See Brant Pitre's extensive discussion on this subject, *Jesus and the Last Supper* (Grand Rapids: Eerdmans, 2015), 459-81; 'Jesus, the Messianic Banquet, and the Kingdom of God', *Letter & Spirit* 5 (2009): 141-61.

2. Luke 1.52-53; 6.21, 25; 9.10-17; 15.14-24; 16.19-25.

3. The two rich men's feasts in Lk. 12.13-21 and 16.19 are viewed in a negative light while the celebrations in Lk. 15.6-7, 9-10, 23-26, 32 are espoused.

4. Luke 12.35-38; cf. 17.7-10.

5. Luke 22.14-30; 24.28-35. Note the covenant meal in Exod. 24.3-11.

used in Lk. 13.23-30. Hence the coming salvation is portrayed as participating in or eating at the messianic banquet.

In this respect, the Parable of the Great Banquet in Luke 14 is the most pertinent passage for our discussion of salvation of the rich in view of the messianic banquet on two grounds. First, the parable is given as a response to the comment of a meal guest: blessed is anyone who will eat bread in the kingdom of God (Lk. 14.15), which vividly evokes the messianic banquet. Second, the juxtaposition of the two uses of μακάριος (Lk. 14.14, 15) and the double reference to the poor, the crippled, the lame and the blind (Lk. 14.13, 21) are of particular importance. They intertwine the blessedness of the poor to whom the kingdom is granted and good news is preached, the blessedness of the rich who invite them to the banquet and the blessedness of all who participate in the messianic banquet.

For the discussion, I will first examine the anticipation of the messianic banquet within Jewish apocalyptic traditions where Luke's Parable of the Great Banquet shares its thematic affinities.[6] Next, narrative contexts of the parable (Lk. 13.22-30; 15.1-30; 16.19-31) which are resonant with banquet themes will be reviewed.[7] Lastly, the parable will be examined to draw out the ways in which it utilizes the imagery of the messianic banquet to speak of the salvation of the rich in relation to the poor, and thus the restoration of the people.

9.2 The Messianic Banquet in Jewish Apocalyptic Traditions

The term, 'messianic banquet', denotes the presence of the Messiah as the host of the meal whereas eschatological or apocalyptic banquet may be used for the general end time feast which reflects the eschatological hope in ancient Judaism.[8] The ideology which the meals in Luke's Gospel entail finds its home among Jewish apocalyptic traditions reflected in some key texts: Isaiah 25, 1 Enoch 62, 2 Baruch 29 and 1QSa (Rule of the Congregation).[9] Despite the difficulty in proving whether these texts provide the background to Luke's messianic banquet due to controversial

---

6. A strong Hellenistic influence is reflected in the setting or format of the banquet in Luke's Gospel (biblical tradition in general) such as the reclining posture, the placing of the guests and the inviting custom. See Smith, *Symposium*, 261–71; 'Fellowship', 613–38; Steele, 'Luke 11:37–54', 379–94. Contra Blomberg, 'Fellowship', 35–62. He argues, 'Every significant element shared by Jesus' meals and Greco-Roman symposia reappears in the Jewish hope for the eschatological banquet, for which a stronger case can be made as background' (61).

7. Snodgrass finds the 'crucial background' for Luke 14 in Isaiah 25, 1QSa and Lk. 13.22-30. *Intent*, 311.

8. J. Priest, 'A Note on the Messianic Banquet', in *The Messiah: Developments in Earliest Judaism and Christianity*, ed. James H. Charlesworth (Minneapolis: Fortress, 1992), 222; Smith, 'Messianic Banquet', *ABD* 4:788.

9. The above listed texts are the most popular ones which draw the eschatological banquet imagery among the scholarly works on this topic. See Smith, 'Banquet', 789;

issues concerning the late dating of 1 Enoch 37–71 and 2 Baruch,[10] thematic similarities are still instructive in understanding the idea of the messianic banquet in Luke's parable.[11]

The most explicit description of the eschatological banquet is found in Isa. 25.6-8. In Isaiah, the feast (מִשְׁתֶּה) will be given by God to all peoples[12] on Mount Zion on that day (בַּיּוֹם).[13] Several features concerning the feast emerge from the text. First, it is set in the eschatological context of God's coming salvation (Isa. 25.9) and judgement (25.10-12). Second, the universal invitation to the feast is highlighted by the repeated use of all (כָּל) (Isa. 25.6, 7, 8). Third, the imagery of an abundance of food is pictured as a feast of fat things and of wine (Isa. 25.6).[14] Finally, the coming salvation is described in three divine actions:[15] God will provide a feast (מִשְׁתֶּה), ultimately swallow up (בִּלַּע) death and take away the disgrace (חֶרְפַּת) of his people (Isa. 25.7-8).[16] Moreover, the eschatological feast in Isaiah 25 is followed by the reference to the resurrection (26.19) and to the destruction of Leviathan (27.1) in its immediate context. Also, divine reversal is repeatedly pronounced: God will humble the proud (Isa. 25.10b, 12; 26.5-6).

1 Enoch 62 similarly anticipates the messianic banquet in the eschatological context of salvation and judgement.[17] 1 En. 62.13-16 describes the coming salvation of the righteous and the chosen as the following: 'With that son of man they will eat' (62.14).[18] Also, resurrection and the garment of life are promised to the

---

Symposium, 166–71; Pitre, *Supper*, 448–58; Blomberg, 'Fellowship', 38–44; Smit, *Food*, 3–27; Priest, 'Messianic', 223.

10. 1 En. 37–71 can be dated from as early as the first century BCE to the late first century CE. For the earliest dating, see George W.E. Nickelsburg and James C. Vanderkam, *1 Enoch: A New Translation* (Minneapolis: Fortress, 2004), 6; Charlesworth, 'The Date and Provenience of the Parables of Enoch' and Bock, 'Dating the Parables of Enoch: A Forschungsbericht', in *Parables of Enoch: A Paradigm Shift*, ed. James H. Charlesworth and Darrell L. Bock (London: Bloomsbury, 2013), 56, 106. For the late first-century CE dating, see Michael A. Knibb, 'The Ethiopic Book of Enoch', in *Outside the Old Testament*, ed. M. De Jonge (Cambridge: CUP, 1985), 44. The dating of 2 Baruch is from the late first to the early second century CE. cf. For the cautionary use of pseudepigrapha in the NT studies, see James R. Davila, 'The Old Testament Pseudepigrapha as Background to the New Testament', *ExpTim* 117.2 (2005): 56.

11. Lehtipuu, *Afterlife*, 45–53 (45).

12. Note the LXX renders עַם as ἔθνος (Isa. 25.6).

13. Isa. 24.21; 25.9.

14. Pitre notes that the imagery of fat things and wine signifies the 'cultic dimension' of the feast (450). *Supper*, 449–50.

15. John D.W. Watts, *Isaiah 1–33*, WBC 24 (Waco: Word Books, 1985), 331–2.

16. Rev. 21.4.

17. Note on that day in *1 En.* 62.8. Also in 25.4-6.

18. Nickelsburg and Vanderkam, *1 Enoch*, 62–3, 81. See also Priest, 'Messianic', 223. He notes the perpetual eating with the Messiah.

righteous (1 En. 62.14-16) while the kings, the mighty, the exalted and the rulers are condemned (62.9-12).[19] 2 Baruch 29 offers explicit references to the revelation of the Messiah (29.3; cf. 30.1), the consumption of Behemoth and Leviathan (29.4),[20] the abundance of food (29.5, 7) and the descent of the heavenly manna (29.7) in the context of judgement and resurrection (2 Bar. 24–27, 30) at the consummation of time (29.8; cf. that time 29.4). Particularly, the joy in the provision of rich food of those who have hungered is noted (2 Bar. 29.6). Thus, the banquets described in 1 En. 62.12-16 and 2 Bar. 29.1-8 indicate the presence of the Messiah and reflect both 'an occasion of joy for the redeemed' and 'judgment and destruction' for God's enemies.[21]

More illuminating is the messianic banquet envisaged in 1QSa 2.11-22 with its particular remark on those who are excluded from the council, and thus from the banquet at the end of days (1.1).[22] The messianic banquet described in 1QSa, on the one hand, describes a general setting of the meal, such as sitting, not reclining as the posture of the participants at table,[23] and bread and wine as basic elements of the meal.[24] It, on the other hand, reveals the particular concerns of the community, which are, the significance of rank (כבוד)[25] and the ritual and physical purity of the members. The meal participants are to sit at the table by rank (1QSa 2.14, 15, 16, 17) and bless the food and eat by rank (2.21).

With the presence of the two messianic figures, one priestly and the other royal, the higher position is given to the priestly one. Schiffman notes, 'The ultimate perfection of the messianic era would be the realization of the [community]'s

---

19. Pitre, *Supper*, 456.

20. *1 En.* 60.24; *4 Ezra* 6.49-52. For further note on *4 Ezra* 6.49-52, see Smit, 'Reaching for the Tree of Life: The Role of Eating, Drinking, Fasting, and Symbolic Foodstuffs in *4 Ezra*', *JSJ* 45 (2014): 383.

21. Priest, 'Messianic', 227.

22. The introduction of the text locates the 1QSa in the end of days as an eschatological community. Lawrence H. Schiffman, *The Eschatological Community of the Dead Sea Scrolls: A Study of the Rule of the Congregation*, SBLMS 38 (Atlanta: Scholars, 1989), 11–12.

23. Schiffman suggests that the community follows the biblical traditions of sitting, not the Hellenistic custom of reclining. *Community*, 56.

24. Schiffman, *Community*, 56.

25. כבוד is translated as 'rank' here, following Wise, Abegg, Jr and Cook, *The Dead Sea Scrolls*, 147. Yet Charlesworth renders it as 'glory', Schiffman as 'importance', and Martínez and Tigchelaar as 'dignity'. See James H. Charlesworth and L.T. Stuckenbruck, 'Rule of the Congregation (1QSa)', in *The Dead Sea Scrolls: Hebrew, Aramaic, and Greek Texts with English Translations*, vol. 1: *Rule of the Community and Related Documents*, ed. James H. Charlesworth (Tübingen: Mohr, 1994), 116–17; Schiffman, *Community*, 54–5; Martínez and Tigchelaar, *The Dead Sea Scrolls Study Edition*, 103. כבוד is also stressed in 1QS 2.19-23; 6.4, 8-12.

constant striving for total ritual purity.'[26] Not only is the purity of all food elements assumed in any communal meals of the community (1QS 6.16-22), but also the absolute purity of the members is ensured by excluding those with uncleanness or physical imperfections from the eschatological council and banquet.[27]

> No man with a physical handicap – *crippled* in both legs or hands, *lame*, *blind*, deaf, dumb, or possessed of a visible blemish in his flesh – or a doddering old man unable to do his share in the congregation – may en[ter] to take a place in the congregation of the m[e]n of reputation. For the holy angels are [a part of] their congregation. (1QSa 2.5-9 emphasis added)

The excluded persons from the text correspond to those restricted from the priesthood in Lev. 21.18-20 particularly in the light of the important role given to the priest in 1QSa.[28] The rationale for the exclusion in the text is the presence of the holy angels in their midst (1QSa 2.9) because physical imperfection is considered as 'antithetical to the divine presence'.[29] Charlesworth suggests, 1QSa reflects the community living in the end time 'as if the Messiah had already come. Each feast was an enactment of what the messianic banquet would be like.'[30] In this sense, the holy angels are present since heaven is already experienced in the community.

Some shared features emerge from the examination of the selected texts. First, the messianic banquet both conveys the coming salvation and reflects the coming judgement. Second, the Messiah is expected to host the meal.[31] Third, divine action is highlighted in terms of the destruction of death or Leviathan alongside the theme of reversal. The mighty and exalted will be lowered while the hungry will be satisfied. Fourth, alongside the banquet with the imagery of rich food,[32] the

---

26. Schiffman, *Community*, 56. Despite the pursuit of ritual purity and the significance of priests at meals, he argues that the meal in the text is not 'a cultic or sacral meal' (61).

27. The excluded from the eschatological war are similarly classified in 1QM 7.4-7. Also CD (Damascus Document) 15.15-17 restricts a list of people including the physically disabled from entering into the community. Both give the same rationale which is the presence of the holy angels in their midst as 1QSa 2.9 (1QM 7.6; CD 15.17). cf. Lev. 21.17-21.

28. Schiffman, *Community*, 43-9. Note also a seemingly strange parallel in 2 Sam. 5.8 (The blind and the lame shall not come into the house) in relation to David's inauguration banquet which may allude to the messianic banquet in 1 Chron. 12.38-40. Craig A. Evans, 'A Note on Targum 2 Samuel 5.8 and Jesus' Ministry to the "Maimed, Halt, and Blind"', *JSP* 15 (1997): 79.

29. See Aharon Shemesh, '"The Holy Angels Are in Their Council": The Exclusion of Deformed Persons from Holy Places in Qumranic and Rabbinic Literature', *DSD* 4. 2 (1997): 201-2.

30. Charlesworth, 'Rule', 108.

31. It is the Lord of the Host, not the Messiah, in Isa. 25.6-8 who will make a feast.

32. Smit notes that the world to come is frequently associated with 'eschatological nutritional abundance or, alternatively, the abolition of hunger and thirst' in the HB and the

resurrection of the righteous is anticipated. Fifth, exclusion from the banquet is noted either due to wickedness or to ritual or physical imperfection.

Finally, for the later discussion, 1QSa offers an intriguing aspect of the messianic banquet, which is the exclusion of certain persons, particularly those with physical disability due to the presence of the holy angels. The very persons to whom the invitation is given and should be given in Lk. 14.12-14 are those excluded from the messianic banquet in 1QSa. I will now move to the narrative contexts of the Parable of the Great Banquet in Luke 14 to examine the ways in which the anticipation of the messianic banquet unfolds.

9.3 The Messianic Banquet in Luke's Narrative Contexts

The middle section (Lk. 13.10–17.10)[33] of the TN in Luke's Gospel is resonant with the imagery of the great banquets. The meals in this section are placed in the salvific, eschatological and other-worldly settings with the theme of reversal. The banquet with abundance of food is anticipated in stark contrast to the experience of hunger. It invites all, yet exclusion from the banquet is a real possibility. In these aspects and in the light of the previous discussion, the narrative contexts of the parable strongly evoke the messianic banquet. Here three passages are most germane to our discussion: (1) Lk. 13.22-30,[34] (2) Lk. 15.7, 10, 11-32[35] and (3) Lk. 16.19-31.

9.3.1 Reclining at Table of the Kingdom: Lk. 13.22-30

Lk. 13.22-30 explicitly relates salvation to the messianic banquet of the kingdom of God. Following Jesus' teaching on repent (μετανοέω) or perish (ἀπόλλυμι) (Lk. 13.1-5) and on the kingdom of God (13.18-21), the question, Κύριε, εἰ ὀλίγοι οἱ σῳζόμενοι (13.23), is raised.[36] While Jesus' answer redirects the question from how many to what to do (Lk. 13.24), the speculation about the number of those who

---

NT. '4 Ezra', 370–1 (370). See Isa. 55.1-2; Ezek. 35.21-38; Zech. 9.17; Joel 2.18-27; Jn 4.13-14; 6.35; Rev. 7.16-17.

33. Green's outline is helpful. He puts Lk. 13.10–17.10 together under the heading of 'Who will participate in the Kingdom?' and notes that the two phrases in Lk. 13.23 and 14.15 are 'programmatic' in understanding this section. *Luke*, 516.

34. It forms a structural parallel with Lk. 14.15-24. See Nolland, *Luke 9:21–18:34*, 733.

35. Smit suggests that celebrations in Luke 15 are directed more towards 'ecclesiological' than towards 'eschatological'. *Food*, 33. However, the significance of celebrations and juxtaposition of heavenly and earthly banquets in Luke 15 still require discussion in the contexts of eschatological banquets.

36. Green, *Luke*, 529. Highlighting the present tenses, σῳζόμενοι and ἀγωνίζεσθε, he notes, 'Notions of judgment in the future' is tied to 'human behavior in the present'.

will be saved is not uncommon in the STP.[37] For instance, *4 Ezra* states, this age the Most High has made for many, but the age to come for few. Many have been created, but few shall be saved! (8.1, 3).[38] A similar view is reflected in Mt. 7.13-14 and 22.14.

Remarkable is the way in which Luke elaborates and develops the question on being saved in Lk. 13.24-30. Jesus' immediate answer begins with entering the narrow door (θύρα) (Lk. 13.24) which becomes the door of the house (13.25). This house is soon envisioned as the kingdom of God where the banquet takes place for those who are saved (13.28-29).[39]

The metaphor of eating and drinking is used to portray the status of those being saved and the claim of those being condemned. People from every corner of the world[40] are reclining at table (ἀνακλίνω) in the kingdom of God with Abraham, Isaac, Jacob and the prophets[41] while those who claim to have eaten and drunk with the master of the house (οἰκοδεσπότης)[42] will stand (ἵστημι) outside, weeping and gnashing their teeth.[43] The emphatic denial by the master is climaxed with ἀπόστητε ἀπ' ἐμοῦ πάντες ἐργάται ἀδικίας (Lk. 13.27).[44] The use of ἐργάται and ἀδικίας is worth noting. Ἐργάται stresses the doing aspect of salvation.[45] Ἀδικίας, as noted above, qualifies the steward and mammon in Lk. 16.8-9 and the judge in 18.6 (see Chapter 8). The word occurs in the context of the use of wealth and of the exercise of justice. In this respect, the exclusion appears to be based on 'ethical responsibility' as Nolland suggests.[46]

The question of salvation is visualized as reclining at the table in the kingdom on the one hand. The exclusion from the banquet is pronounced to πάντες ἐργάται ἀδικίας (Lk. 13.27) which highlights the necessity of enacting justice to partake in

---

37. Parsons, *Luke*, 221-2; Nolland, *Luke 9:21–18:34*, 733; Green, *Luke*, 529; Fitzmyer, *Luke*, 1024. cf. In response to Jesus' saying about the difficulty of entering the kingdom raises the question Καὶ τίς δύναται σωθῆναι (Lk. 18.26).

38. The question in *4 Ezra* 8.1, 3 emerges from the context where the righteous are few while the ungodly abound (*4 Ezra* 7.45-61). cf. *4 Ezra* 9.15-16.

39. cf. Mt. 8.11-12.

40. Luke most likely has the scattered Jews of the Diaspora and the Gentiles in view here. cf. Mt. 8.11-12. For a detailed discussion, see Michael F. Bird, 'Who Comes from the East and the West? Luke 13.28-9//Matt 8.11–12 and the Historical Jesus', *NTS* 52 (2006): 457; Pitre, *Supper*, 460-5.

41. The allusion to the eschatological banquet in Isaiah 25 is noted. Green, *Luke*, 528, 532; Fitzmyer, *Luke*, 1026.

42. Luke 12.39; 14.21. Οἰκοδεσπότης here reflects an eschatological figure.

43. Note that those who are outside could see the ones reclining at table. See Smit, *Food*, 153.

44. Note Ps. 6.8 (סוּרוּ מִמֶּנִּי כָּל־פֹּעֲלֵי אָוֶן); Ps. 6.9 LXX (ἀπόστητε ἀπ' ἐμοῦ, πάντες οἱ ἐργαζόμενοι τὴν ἀνομίαν).

45. Green, *Luke*, 531.

46. Nolland, *Luke 9:21–18:34*, 733.

the kingdom on the other hand.[47] The reversal which is a most common theme with eschatological overtones is pronounced as a concluding remark of the section: Καὶ ἰδοὺ εἰσὶν ἔσχατοι οἳ ἔσονται πρῶτοι καὶ εἰσὶν πρῶτοι οἳ ἔσονται ἔσχατοι (Lk. 13.30).[48]

9.3.2 Juxtaposition of the Earthly and Heavenly Banquets I (Lk. 15.1-32)

Luke 15 juxtaposes the earthly and heavenly celebrations. Jesus' customary welcoming (προσδέχεται) and table fellowship (συνεσθίει) with sinners (15.1-2) introduces the three parables.[49] They are linked with four common elements: ἔχω (15.4, 8, 11), ἀπόλλυμι (15.4, 6, 8, 9, 17, 24, 32), εὑρίσκω (15.5, 6, 8, 9, 24, 32) and χαίρω, εὐφραίνω (15.24, 29, 32). Each parable progresses and culminates in a communal celebration (Lk. 15.6, 9, 23, 24, 32) which is analogous to a heavenly one (15.7, 10, 32). While joy in heaven and in the presence of the angels of God (Lk. 15.7, 10) is phrased in the first two parables, the use of ἔδει in the concluding remark of the third one (15.32) alludes to the divine necessity of celebration.[50] The joy of finding calls for the great banquets.

Despite the reference to ἑνὶ ἁμαρτωλῷ μετανοοῦντι (Lk. 15.7, 10), it is the overwhelming joy of the shepherd and the woman which is highlighted. The returning of the younger son (15.18, 19) is overshadowed by the father's extravagant welcoming (15.20, 22-24). The stress lies more on 'the joy of finding' than 'of being found'.[51] The focus of the parable is not so much on the repentance of sinners as on the celebration with them.[52]

---

47. Carroll, *Luke*, 292; Smit, *Food*, 153.

48. York, *Last*, 87–92.

49. David A. Holgate places the third parable (Lk. 15.11-32) in line with other Lukan parables which are concerned with the use of possessions. The use of possessions emerges from the parable (Lk. 15.11-32). However, by making it the central issue, he ignores other important thematic, narrative and linguistic flows in the parable. See *Prodigality, Liberality, and Meanness in the Prodigal Son: A Greco-Roman Perspective on Luke 15:11–32*, JSNTSup 187 (Sheffield: Sheffield Academic, 1999), 75–7.

50. Green, *Luke*, 578.

51. Donahue, *Parable*, 151.

52. Marshall, *Luke*, 604; Nolland, *Luke 9:21–18:34*, 791; Green, *Luke*, 575; Donahue, *Parable*, 151. The repentance of the younger son is much contested. While no explicit word, repentance, occurs in the third parable unlike the previous two (15.7, 10), it is assumed from the monologue of the younger son (15.18, 19, 21). However, the emphasis moves quickly to celebration. On the irrelevancy of repentance in this parable, see George W. Ramsey, 'Plots, Gaps, Repetitions, and Ambiguity in Luke 15', *PRSt* 17.1 (1990): 38–42; Sellew, 'Monologue', 246; Scott, *Parable*, 116; Metzger, *Consumption*, 93–5. Conversely, Jeremias notes that Luke 15.18 is 'an expression of repentance'. *Parables*, 130. Similarly, see Bovon, *Luke 2*, 426; Wolter, *Lukasevangelium*, 534; Forbes, 'Repentance and Conflict in the Parable of the Lost Son (Lk. 15:11–32)', *JETS* 42 (1999): 211–29.

With the preponderance of the banquet motif, several features stand out from the third parable of Luke 15. Experience of hunger and scarcity of food are vividly described. The younger son longs to satisfy himself even with the carob which pigs eat. Severe famine (λιμός) strikes where he stays and he is dying of hunger (λιμός). It is this experience of hunger that reminds him of his father and the abundance of food in his father's house. Not only his father but also the feast awaits his return. The fatted calf (Lk. 15.23, 27, 30) illustrates the richness of the coming banquet. The parable is full of food imagery: carob, bread, the fatted calf and a young goat, and full of eating metaphors: feeding (βόσκω), filling (χορτάζω),[53] eating (ἐσθίω),[54] devouring (κατεσθίω) and feasting (εὐφραίνω).[55]

The experience of hunger is acute and the awaiting banquet is opulent. Many are invited, yet the elder son is not willing to come in. While the master of the house in Lk. 13.22-30 would not let some in to the banquet of the kingdom, the father urges the elder son to come in and celebrate together (Lk. 15.32).[56] The invitation remains valid. Whether he accepts or not is inconclusive. The parable stops at the reversed position of the two brothers, yet the door remains open.[57] The younger son who once was away comes back in and the elder son who is always in now stands outside.

The juxtaposition of earthly and heavenly banquets, rich imagery of food and reversed status in the parable convey the eschatological overtones reflecting the messianic banquet.[58] Besides, the use of ἀνίστημι (Lk. 15.18, 20), which indicates the younger son's return, points in a similar direction. The word alludes to resurrection particularly in the light of the father's explanation of the younger son's status: νεκρός (Lk. 15.24, 32) and ἀναζάω (ζάω 15.24, 32).[59]

9.3.3 *Juxtaposition of the Earthly and Heavenly Banquet II (Lk. 16.19-31)*

Another juxtaposition of the earthly and heavenly banquet is observed in Lk. 16.19-31. The daily sumptuous banquets of the rich man are vividly described in stark contrast to the hunger and wretchedness of Lazarus at the gate (πυλών) of the rich man. Death brings the great reversal of their fortunes. Lazarus is escorted by

---

53. The variant reading witnesses γεμίσαι τὴν κοιλίαν αὐτοῦ instead of χορτασθῆναι. Some prefer the former as it carries a stronger expression. See Marshall, *Luke*, 609; Bovon, *Luke 2*, 422; Holgate, *Prodigality*, 42. However, there is little difference in meaning.

54. Luke 20.37.

55. Carroll, *Luke*, 319.

56. Byrne, *Hospitality*, 131.

57. York, *Last*, 151–3.

58. The imagery of the messianic banquet is frequently noted. Forbes, 'Repentance', 221, 227; Crispin H.T. Fletcher-Louis, *Luke-Acts: Angels, Christology and Soteriology*, WUNT 2.94 (Tübingen: Mohr, 1997), 74–5, 92–3; Stephen C. Barton, 'Parables on God's Love and Forgiveness (Luke 15:1–32)', *Parables*, 211; Heil, *Meal*, 127; Blomberg, 'Fellowship', 60.

59. Carroll, *Luke*, 316; Green, *Luke*, 582; Méndez-Moratalla, *Conversion*, 143.

the angels (ἄγγελοι) to the honoured place at the heavenly banquet (εἰς τὸν κόλπον Ἀβραάμ)[60] while the rich man finds himself in torment of Hades. The rich man's distressful condition in Hades (ἐν τῷ ᾅδῃ) is expressed in great detail:[61] torment (βάσανος vv. 23, 28), thirst (asking for water v. 24), flame (φλόξ v. 24) and agony (ὀδυνάω vv. 24, 25). While 'thrown out' or 'weeping and gnashing of teeth' (Lk. 13.28)[62] depicts those who are excluded from the messianic banquet of the kingdom in Lk. 13.22-30, the rich man's torment in Hades (ᾅδης) or possibly Hades itself indicates his exclusion from a future bliss.

Hades is not necessarily the place of eternal punishment, but the place of the dead while awaiting the final judgement.[63] Nevertheless, in the Parable of Lazarus and the Rich Man, Hades is full of negative imagery as a place of agony in contrast to Abraham's bosom, a place of comfort. Abraham's bosom (τὸν κόλπον Ἀβραάμ), an unusual metaphor for a blessed afterlife, appears self-explanatory.[64] Rudolf Meyer suggests that it primarily conveys the imagery of the eschatological banquet where Lazarus takes the closest seat to Abraham. Its secondary meaning simply indicates a close fellowship with Abraham.[65] Bovon prefers the latter in that he does not see any imagery of banquet or an honoured place at a banquet from the passage.[66]

It would, however, be rather odd if this picturesque parable of divine reversal[67] did not use the banquet setting at which the parable began. The banquet moves to the heavenly realm unsurprisingly with the rich man's exclusion.[68] It recalls those who are excluded from the messianic banquet of the kingdom in Lk. 13.22-30, and yet who are still able to see (ὁράω) Abraham and other patriarchs and the prophets reclining at table (13.28). Similarly, the rich man in torment sees (ὁράω) Abraham and Lazarus in his bosom though at a distance (ἀπὸ μακρόθεν) or over the gulf

---

60. Marshall, *Luke*, 636; Green, *Luke*, 607; Smith, *Symposium*, 260-1; York, *Last*, 67; Esler, *Community*, 193. Note also Pieter W. van der Horst's interpretation of the verb, ἀπενεχθῆναι, in 16.22. He suggests that the verb conveys Abraham's bosom as a place 'entitled to' Lazarus. 'Abraham's Bosom, the Place Where He Belonged: A Short Note on ἀπενεχθῆναι in Luke 16.22', *NTS* 52.1 (2006): 144.

61. The scene in the afterlife is described from the rich man's perspective. This intensifies the rich man's agony in Hades. See Lehtipuu, 'Characterization and Persuasion: The Rich Man and the Poor Man in Lk. 16.19-31', *Characterization*, 91.

62. See Mt. 8.12; 13.42, 50; 22.13; 24.51; 25.30. This expression in Matthew almost always relates to judgement, fire and darkness, and thus often depicts the imagery of eternal damnation. See Pitre, *Supper*, 469.

63. Bauckham, 'Hades, Hell', *ABD* 3:14-15; Lehtipuu, 'Reward', 238.

64. Marshall, *Luke*, 636.

65. Meyer, 'κόλπος', *TDNT* 3:825.

66. Bovon, *Luke 2*, 481-2. cf. Lehtipuu, *Afterlife*, 215-20 (215). She suggests that these two meanings are not 'mutually exclusive'.

67. Luke 1.53; 6.20-21, 24-25.

68. Heil, *Meal*, 136.

(χάσμα) (Lk. 16.23). The status is reversed, and the venue of the banquet has changed from the rich man's house to the heavenly realm, yet the banquet continues.

Lazarus's status in the afterlife is taken for granted in a simple statement of divine reversal which fulfils divine justice (Lk. 16.25) (see Chapter 5).[69] To a greater extent, however, the parable highlights the banqueting life of the rich man on earth as well as the tormented situation in Hades where he vainly asks for mercy. The final section of the parable suggests that the rich man's exclusion from the heavenly banquet is closely related to his association with Lazarus in his earthly banqueting life.[70] On the one hand, the need for repentance is acknowledged, based on Moses and the Prophets which frequently point to the care of the poor (Lk. 10.25-37; 18.18-30) in Luke's Gospel (see Chapter 7).

On the other hand, feasting (εὐφραίνω) in Lk. 12.19 and 16.19 is used negatively.[71] The rich fool's imaginary banquet (Lk. 12.19) and the rich man's customary banquets (16.19) result in divine judgement (12.20; 16.25). The underlying element of both banquets is again the concern for the poor. The rich fool's use of wealth concludes with the idea of treasure in heaven which can be stored up by giving alms (Lk. 12.21, 33-34). The rich man's banqueting life constantly ignores Lazarus at his gate. In the light of Lk. 16.9, his exclusion from an eternal dwelling is in fact foreshadowed from the beginning of the parable (see Chapter 8).

These narrative contexts of the Parable of the Great Banquet (Lk. 14.1-24) resonate with the ongoing theme of banquet – lack and abundance of food, invitation and exclusion and reversal in view of the kingdom or the other-world and post-mortem scenes. Particularly intriguing is their anticipation and portrayal of the eschatological banquet which is linked to present action towards the poor and the outcasts. This leads to the culminating Parable of the Great Banquet to which I now turn.

9.4 The Parable of the Great Banquet (Lk. 14.1-24)

Willi Braun's socio-rhetorical reading of Luke 14 locates Jesus' meal with the Pharisees alongside the Graeco-Roman upper-class dinner party. He argues that Lk. 14.1-24 closely follows a popular Graeco-Roman rhetoric pattern in its form of narrative argument.[72] Yet his overemphasis on the Graeco-Roman background of

---

69. Bauckham, 'Lazarus', 233.

70. Luke 16.9 is instructive here as well. As noted, those who welcome others into eternal dwellings refer to the poor. See Lehtipuu, 'Reward', 236.

71. cf. celebrations (εὐφραίνω) in Luke 15.

72. Braun, *Feasting*, 6-7, 42, 127-8. He argues that Lk. 14.1-24 is about 'conversion' of the wealthy host from greed to generosity.

Luke 14 suppresses any eschatological reading of the passage.[73] Particularly the significance of Lk. 14.15, where there is an explicit reference to the messianic banquet and from which the Parable of the Great Banquet (Lk. 14.15-24) emerges in its narrative development, is simply dismissed as a transitional phrase.[74] On the contrary, it is Lk. 14.15 which offers a hermeneutical key to the meal talk in Lk. 14.1-24, put in a question form: Who will eat at the banquet of the kingdom?[75]

9.4.1 Who will Eat at the Banquet of the Kingdom?

Lk. 14.1-24 forms a unified episode with close thematic,[76] structural[77] and verbal[78] parallels. The table talk in the passage fittingly takes place at a Sabbath meal setting (φαγεῖν ἄρτον 14.1) at the house (οἶκος) of one of the leading Pharisees. Lk. 14.1-6 with the presence of a dropsical man at a Sabbath meal forms a parallel to a bent-over woman at the synagogue on the Sabbath in 13.10-17 as noted (see Chapter 5).[79] While the incident is a lot briefer in Luke 14, some of the evident parallels can hardly be missed.[80] The healing takes place on the Sabbath in the presence of either the leader of the synagogue (ἀρχισυνάγωγος) or of the Pharisees (τινος τῶν ἀρχόντων [τῶν] Φαρισαίων). Jesus offers a similar rationale for the healing on the Sabbath (Lk. 13.14-16; 14.3-5).

---

73. Interestingly though, Braun emphasizes the metaphorical reading of dropsy, yet rejects any eschatological reading of the text. See Braun, *Feasting*, 63; Jonathan Marshall, *Jesus, Patrons, and Benefactors: Roman Palestine and the Gospel of Luke*, WUNT 2.259 (Tübingen: Mohr, 2009), 274–5.

74. Braun, *Feasting*, 63.

75. J. Marshall, *Benefactors*, 279; Hans Klein, *Das Lukasevangelium*, KEK (Göttingen: Vandenhoeck & Ruprecht, 2006), 505–7.

76. Not only does the dialogue take place at a meal setting, but its content also concerns the meal etiquette, guests and banquets.

77. Particularly Lk. 14.7-11 and 14.12-14 form a close structural parallel as both develop antithetical arguments.

78. Καλέω is the most predominant and frequent word which occurs in Lk. 14.1-24 (vv. 7, 8, 9, 10, 12, 13, 16, 17, 24 [eleven times]). It is used here to refer to the invitee, the invited and the invitation. Thus, James A. Sanders argues that the passage points to the subversion of the deuteronomic ethic of election from the observation of καλέω. He interprets it as 'apparently elect', or 'those who consider themselves elected'. 'The Ethic of Election in Luke's Great Banquet Parable', in *Luke and Scripture*, 106–20 (113).

79. Nolland, *Luke 9:21–18:34*, 745.

80. In fact, the appearance of the disabled, Jesus' healing as (ἀπο)λύω (13.13, 15, 16; 14.4), the reference to the kingdom of God and the messianic banquet are closely interwoven in Luke 13 and 14. See Nolland, *Luke 9:21–18:34*, 723. For man–woman parallels, see Turid Karlsen Seim, *The Double Message: Patterns of Gender in Luke-Acts* (Edinburgh: T&T Clark, 1994), 15–16. Moreover, Luke elsewhere gives a fuller account for the first incident while making it shorter in the following parallel. Lk. 2.25-35, 36-38; 15.3-7, 8-10.

Dropsy, a rather peculiar illness from which the man suffered in Lk. 14.2, has recently drawn much attention.[81] The metaphorical use of dropsy for insatiable greed or lust for wealth or status is popular among Graeco-Roman and Jewish circles. Thus, the appearance of a dropsical man at a meal gives a proper introduction to the following parable the focus of which lies in the desire for the place of honour at table. More significantly, it anticipates the ideal guests who are to be invited to the banquet later.

Jesus' first parable (Lk. 14.7-11) is addressed to the guests at table, seeking the place of honour (πρωτοκλισία).[82] As discussed earlier from 1QSa, rank at table is not a small matter. 1QSa repeats that each takes a seat according to their rank.[83] Smith also notes 'the issue of ranking' from Plutarch's Table-Talk where he finds a link to Jesus' parable of the place at table (Lk. 14.7-11).[84] However, unlike Plutarch's philosophical and moral concerns, the parable in Luke 14 resolves the issue in terms of 'humility', the foundation of which rests upon scriptural tradition.[85] Prov. 25.6-7 and Sir. 32.1-2 give similar advice against taking the place of honour and self-exaltation at table.[86] Hence this parable, on the one hand, demonstrates the desire for higher honour and status among the guests at table.[87] On the other hand, it points to the divine reversal of status in the kingdom (ὕψωσεν ταπεινούς Lk. 1.52).[88]

Lk. 14.7-11 and 14.12-14 are linked with a structural parallel as both passages develop antithetical arguments.[89] Carroll describes these two sections as Jesus first speaks to 'status-conscious guests' (vv. 7–11) and then to the 'reciprocity-minded host' (vv. 12–14).[90] The passages assume and reflect cultural issues of honour and

---

81. See Hartsock, 'Dropsy', 341–54; Braun, *Feasting*, 31–7; Parsons, *Luke*, 226; Bovon, *Luke 2*, 342; Carroll, *Luke*, 297; Green, *Luke*, 547. See f.n. 68 in Chapter 5.

82. The status of the guests is hinted at in Luke's introduction of the host – one of the leaders of the Pharisees (τῶν ἀρχόντων [τῶν] Φαρισαίων).

83. 1QSa 2.14, 15, 16, 17.

84. Smith, *Symposium*, 254–5; Plutarch, *Mor.* 615.1–2. A similar concern about the place at table is at issue in Plutarch's *Dinner of the Seven Wise Men*, *Mor*.149.

85. Smith, *Symposium*, 255; J. Marshall, *Benefactors*, 258.

86. Prov. 25.6-7 draws a similar idea to Jesus' first parable in Lk. 14.7-11 with several verbal correspondences: τόπος, ἀναβαίνω, ταπεινόω. The advice in Sir. 31.12–32.9 concerns the seating, eating, drinking and humbling at the banquet.

87. See also that Lk. 11.43 and 20.46 criticize the Pharisees and the scribes who seek the seat of honour (πρωτοκαθεδρία) in the synagogues and the place of honour at table (πρωτοκλισία).

88. York, *Last*, 79–80. Note that Jesus brings back the issue of ranking at another meal setting in Lk. 22.24-27 where the messianic banquet of the kingdom is strongly alluded to (Lk. 22.30). Smith, *Symposium*, 256. Priest, 'Messianic', 230; Esler, *Community*, 192.

89. Green also notes linguistic parallels with structural ones: καλέω, φωνέω and ἀντικαλέω. *Luke*, 549; Braun, *Feasting*, 16; Wasserberg, *Aus Israels Mitte*, 169.

90. Carroll, *Luke*, 298.

shame (πρωτοκλισία, αἰσχύνη) and of reciprocity (ἀντικαλέω, ἀνταποδίδωμι).[91] Not only does specific vocabulary indicating the cultural practices occur but also Jesus' teaching in the passages concerns these issues.[92]

What is more significant, however, is that they are adopted and subverted in the light of the kingdom to make a theological point. Lk. 14.7-11 closes with the statement of reversal in v. 11.[93] Those who humble themselves at table will be exalted most likely at the messianic banquet of the kingdom. Lk. 14.12-14 closes with the promise of a divine reward in v. 14. At the resurrection of the righteous, God will reciprocate for what was offered at the earthly banquet to those who could not reciprocate.[94] Thus, with strong eschatological overtones, they point in the same direction. In the expectation of God's reward particularly conjuring up the image of the banquet, they are admonished to take action now on earth.[95]

A further note seems necessary on the list of guests in Lk. 14.12-14 (see Table 9.1). Here the instruction to invite the poor, the crippled, the lame and the blind (Lk. 14.13) is given because they cannot reciprocate unlike the other group of persons (14.12). Their inability to repay is underlined with the promise of the divine reward. In Luke, they are the recipients of the good news (Lk. 4.18-19) and the beneficiaries of Jesus' messianic ministry (7.22). To them, the kingdom is granted and blessings are pronounced with the promise of a future reversal (Lk. 6.20-21).

Lk. 14.13 lists them as ideal guests to the banquet. This listing of the poor, the crippled, the lame and the blind (Lk. 14.13, 21) is in stark contrast to the customary guests: your friends, your brothers, your relatives and your rich neighbours (14.12).[96] Moreover, this list of invitees, as noted earlier, resembles the excluded persons from

Table 9.1 Lists of the Invitees in Luke's Gospel and of the excluded in 1QSa

Lk. 14.12, 21	14.13	4.18	7.22	1QSa 2.5-6
your friends	the poor	the poor	the blind	the crippled
your brothers	the crippled	the captives	the lame	the lame
your relatives	the lame	the blind	the lepers	the blind
your rich neighbours	the blind	the oppressed	the deaf	the deaf
			the dead	the dumb
			the poor	physically blemished

91. Jerome H. Neyrey, 'Ceremonies in Luke-Acts: The Case of Meals and Table Fellowship', *Social World*, 385; Moxnes, *Economy*, 127-38; Green, *Luke*, 550-4. cf. Lk. 6.30, 34. J. Marshall, *Benefactors*, 248-50, 284-5.
92. J. Marshall, *Benefactors*, 262-4.
93. Lk. 14.11; cf. Ezek. 21.31 LXX.
94. Eckey, *Lukasevangelium*, 654; Wasserberg, *Aus Israels Mitte*, 169-70.
95. York, *Last*, 138-40; Klein, *Lukasevangelium*, 507. He notes that the meal scene in Lk. 14.7-14 is an earthly meal with heavenly consequences while the Parable of the Great Banquet in 14.15-24 depicts the heavenly meal.
96. Note the repeated use of σου in Lk. 14.12. cf. 14.26.

the messianic banquet in 1QSa 2.5-6.⁹⁷ While Luke highlights the socio-economic locations of the guest list, the primary concern in 1QSa 2.5-6 is purity.⁹⁸

9.4.2 Blessed are the Rich?

Most intriguing, yet significant, is the first μακάριος which is pronounced to the rich in Lk. 14.14. 'Blessed are the rich' sounds oxymoronic in Luke's Gospel which specifically adds οὐαί to the rich (Lk. 6.24-25) and frequently portrays them in a negative light. Thus, the two instances of 'μακάριος' in Lk. 14.14 and 15 need further investigation. The two blessings are not only at the climax of the meal talk (Lk. 14.1-24) but also they in effect introduce the Parable of the Great Banquet (14.15-24). These two verses correspond to each other closely. Each begins with the pronouncement of μακάριος. Future reciprocity (ἀνταποδοθήσεται) is specified as eating bread (φάγεται ἄρτον). The resurrection of the righteous (ἐν τῇ ἀναστάσει τῶ δικαίων) corresponds to the kingdom of God (ἐν τῇ βασιλείᾳ τοῦ θεοῦ).⁹⁹

μακάριος ἔσῃ, ὅτι οὐκ ἔχουσιν ἀνταποδοῦναί σοι,
   ἀνταποδοθήσεται γάρ σοι ἐν τῇ ἀναστάσει τῶν δικαίων. (Lk. 14.14)
μακάριος ὅστις φάγεται ἄρτον ἐν τῇ βασιλείᾳ τοῦ θεοῦ. (14.15)

The blessedness of the rich should be understood in terms of the divine reward which is intertwined with μακάριος here. First, μακάριος points to a divine action while the reward is eschatological with the use of the future tense (ἔσῃ, φάγεται) and with the references to the eating of bread in the kingdom and the resurrection of the righteous. Hence the reward for the rich is illustrated as participating in the messianic banquet. Second and more importantly, μακάριος is closely tied to the actions done to the poor, the crippled, the lame and the blind. In other words, their association with the poor in this world to whom the μακάριος in Lk. 6.20-21 and 7.23 is announced on the basis of divine reversal and the messianic ministry of Jesus¹⁰⁰ is a determining factor for the participation of the rich in the messianic banquet.

Also, a specific reference to the righteous (δίκαιος) in Lk. 14.14 is intriguing in the light of Luke's general references to the resurrection. He speaks either of the

---

97. 1QM 7.4; CD 15.16. See Johnson, *Luke*, 225; Green, *Theology*, 80-1; Marshall, *Luke*, 584; Fitzmyer, *Luke*, 1047.

98. Moxnes, *Economy*, 132.

99. Bovon, *Luke 2*, 368.

100. Μακάριος in Lk. 7.23 is announced to those who take no offence at Jesus' messianic ministry to the poor and the disabled. Elsewhere, it is pronounced to Mary (Lk. 1.45), the disciples (10.23), those who hear and obey God's word (11.27) and the servants in readiness (12.37, 38, 43).

resurrection of the dead or the resurrection of the righteous and the unrighteous.[101] Perhaps the exclusion of the workers of unrighteousness (ἀδικία) from the messianic banquet in Lk. 13.27 provides a clue to Luke's remark about the righteous (δίκαιος) in relation to resurrection. In this regard, the resurrection of the righteous (Lk. 14.14) draws attention to the righteous actions of those who invite the poor and the disabled.[102] Hence the passage again suggests that the blessedness of the rich and their participation in the messianic banquet rely on their association with the poor.[103] The blessedness of the rich is intrinsically intertwined with that of the poor. This is largely in line with being welcomed into eternal dwellings in Lk. 16.9 or being condemned to torment in Hades in 16.19-31.

9.4.3 Various Readings of the Parable of the Messianic Banquet

Similar accounts to Luke's Parable of the Great Banquet are found in Mt. 22.1-14 (the Parable of the Wedding Banquet) and Gos. Thom. 64. Despite their shared thematic elements, Luke's parable diverges from both in significant ways. Unlike Matthew 22 and Gos. Thom. 64,[104] Luke's parable responds to 'Who will eat in the kingdom of God?' (Lk. 14.15). Hence it specifies those who eat at the banquet which alludes to the messianic banquet (Lk. 14.21, 23).[105] It also features the host in the light of the previous teaching (Lk. 14.12-14).[106] The parable further unpacks the threefold rejection by those originally invited and the threefold invitation (Lk. 14.18-23).[107] It concludes with the pronouncement on those who will not taste the banquet (Lk. 14.24).[108]

---

101. Nolland, *Luke 9:21–18:34*, 751; Eckey, *Lukasevangelium*, 654. For the resurrection of the dead, see Lk. 20.35; Acts 4.2; 17.18, 32; 23.6; 24.21; 24.15. For the resurrection of Jesus, see Acts 1.22; 4.33; 26.23. For the resurrection of the righteous and the unrighteous, see Acts 24:15.

102. Carroll, *Luke*, 301. He links this reference to 'the righteous' to the act of inviting the poor, that is, the act of performing justice.

103. Esler asserts, 'The rich stand condemned by their wealth and the only means they have of avoiding judgment is by helping the poor.' *Community*, 196.

104. Mt. 22.1-14 is the last parable of the three which Jesus addresses to the chief priests and the Pharisees in Jerusalem and highlights the coming judgement. Not only the neglect of the banquet but also the violent action of the invited (22.5-6) are described and judgement of the king follows twice (22.7, 13). Gos. Thom. 64, although the excuses given are closer to that in Luke 14, simply criticizes the rich (merchants and business people). See Fitzmyer, *Luke*, 1050–2; Jeremias, *Parables*, 64–9; Johnson, *Luke*, 231–2; Bovon, *Luke 2*, 366–8.

105. Donahue, *Parable*, 141; Marshall, *Luke*, 585.

106. Braun, *Feasting*, 98; Smit, *Food*, 162.

107. Eckey, *Lukasevangelium*, 656. He notes the structure of the noun counting which the number three plays a role in Lk. 14.12-24.

108. Smit, *Food*, 161.

The parable has been interpreted from various angles. An allegorical interpretation suggests the rejection of Israel (Jewish leaders) and stresses the two-stage invitation extended to the despised Jews and to the Gentiles.[109] It seems to fit nicely into Luke's bigger agenda in view of Acts. But a question remains: Why are the poor and the disabled not invited till the others turn down the invitation? Others find the parallels between the excuses in Lk. 14.18-20 and the occasions in Deut. 20.5-7 through which soldiers are exempt from the battle. Thus, the parable is read as a midrash on Deuteronomy 20.[110] Also in view of Deuteronomy and noting the frequent use of καλέω, it is read as a subversion of the Jewish concept of election (καλέω).[111] However, the extent to which Deuteronomy 20 is concerned with the eschatological war and the extent to which Luke 14 has that war in view are uncertain. Rather, the excuses offered here may be best understood in terms of their invalidity, the intentional shaming of the host and the socio-economic location of the invited.[112]

Recent readings of the parable aptly draw attention to cultural issues such as reciprocity,[113] patronage,[114] or honour and shame,[115] with emphasis given to socio-economic issues. Braun argues that the thrust of the parable points to the conversion of the host in the process of rejection and invitation, based on the previous teaching in Lk. 14.12-14.[116] Most significantly, however, the parable revolves around the imagery of the messianic banquet in that it begins and concludes with the following remarks: Φάγεται ἄρτον ἐν τῇ βασιλείᾳ τοῦ θεοῦ (Lk. 14.15) and γεύσεταί μου τοῦ δείπνου (14.24).[117]

---

109. T.W. Manson, *The Sayings of Jesus* (London: SCM, 1977), 130; Jeremias, *Parables*, 66-9. Similar interpretation is given with slight variations by Fitzmyer, *Luke*, 1053-4; Bailey, *Peasant*, 110; Johnson, *Luke*, 231-2. cf. Marshall, *Luke*, 584-7. He notes that the later tradition may well have interpreted it for the Gentile mission while it is uncertain whether the parable intends it. See Braun's critique of allegorical interpretation. *Feasting*, 84-6.

110. Paul H. Ballard, 'Reasons for Refusing the Great Supper', *JTS* 23 (1972): 350; Derrett, *Law*, 136-8.

111. Sanders, 'Election', 110-13; Bovon, *Luke 2*, 370-1; Snodgrass, *Intent*, 314.

112. Green, *Luke*, 559-60; Bailey, *Peasant*, 96-8; Braun, *Feasting*, 73-5; Forbes, *God*, 101.

113. J. Marshall, *Benefactors*, 276-80; Green, *Luke*, 559-63; Parsons, *Luke*, 228; Carroll, *Luke*, 304-5.

114. Moxnes, 'Patron-Client Relations and the New Community in Luke-Acts', *Social World*, 263-4.

115. Braun, *Feasting*, 98-131.

116. Ibid., 7; Green, *Luke*, 563; Heil, *Meal*, 109-10.

117. Note the future tense of both verbs – φάγεται and γεύσεταί.

9.4.4 Who are Present at the Banquet?

While the first invitation appears to follow the customary pattern, which invites socio-economic equals as described in Lk. 14.12,[118] the second and third group of persons who actually occupy the banquet are at the opposite end of that spectrum. Luke's parable shifts the focus to the subsequent invitations by elaborating on their socio-economic status and physical location (Lk. 14.21, 23).[119] Rohrbaugh's model of the pre-industrial city is perceptive in mapping the location of those invited.[120] The host and those who are invited first are located at the centre of the city where the urban elite or leading members of the city dwell. Conversely, the second invitation is given at the square where communication between the elite and non-elite takes place and to the poorest persons who dwell along the lanes of the city. The final invitation goes further beyond the city walls. Outside the city walls live those who are not allowed to live inside the city.[121] Among them the commonly noted are 'beggars and prostitutes'.[122]

The distance of socio-economic and spatial location between the host and those subsequently invited explains the use of rather forceful language for the invitation: εἰσάγω (Lk. 14.21) and ἀναγκάζω (14.23).[123] It is very difficult, if not impossible, or even an action fraught with fear, for the poor to cross the socio-economic and spatial boundaries. They need to be brought in and compelled to come.[124]

The process of the subsequent invitations also gives a glimpse of those who are present at the banquet. Although the parable does not extend to the inside of the banquet hall as in Mt. 22.11-13, the servant's report after the second invitation assumes that the poor, the crippled, the blind and the lame are already enjoying the banquet.[125] The final statement of the host, λέγω γὰρ ὑμῖν[126] ὅτι οὐδεὶς τῶν

---

118. Those who are invited, yet refuse to come to the banquet, depict not only those listed in 14.12 but also those mentioned in 14.26, 33. See Smit, *Food*, 198.

119. cf. Scott, *Parable*, 164. He unconvincingly suggests that Lk. 14.15 indicates the delay of *parousia* in Luke's Gospel.

120. Rohrbaugh, 'Pre-industrial', 133–6.

121. Ibid., 142–4.

122. Ibid., 145.

123. Ibid.; Braun, *Feasting*, 88, 96–7; Green, *Luke*, 562; Carroll, *Luke*, 305.

124. Metzger argues that the language used here, εἰσάγω (14.21) and ἀναγκάζω (14.23), reflects the 'stigmatization' of and 'discrimination' against the poor and the disabled. He further observes that the shamed host's subsequent invitations are issued out of his anger to take revenge on those who reject his invitation. Thus, the parable fails to offer good news to them at all. Yet, his reading ignores the statement which Luke strongly endorses throughout the Gospel: Blessed are the poor! 'Disability and the Marginalisation of God in the Parable of the Snubbed Host (Luke 14:15–24)', *The Bible and Critical Theory* 6.2 (2010): 23.6–8.

125. Braun, *Feasting*, 95.

126. Lk. 11.8; 15.7, 10; 16.9; 18.8, 14; 19.26.

ἀνδρῶν ἐκείνων τῶν κεκλημένων γεύσεταί μου τοῦ δείπνου (Lk. 14.24), also points to the initial question: Who will eat bread in the kingdom of God? (Lk. 14.15). Yet, who is speaking to whom here? Whose banquet is it? The identity of 'I' in Lk. 14.24 is ambiguous.[127] First, it may well be the host in the parable speaking to those invited first in its narrative flow.[128] Second, the parable in a sense develops the identity of the host, ἄνθρωπός τις (Lk. 14.16), κύριος (14.21, 22, 23) and οἰκοδεσπότης (14.21), which interestingly corresponds to οἰκοδεσπότης who is the host of the messianic banquet in Lk. 13.25, that is, Jesus.[129]

In fact, whether the speaker is the host or not does not remove the possibility of hearing the voice of Jesus. This ambiguity rather strengthens the links between the banquet in the parable and the messianic banquet with a blurred boundary between the two.[130] The parable at one level depicts those who are present in the banquet (Lk. 14.21, 22; cf. 14.13) and those who exclude themselves from the banquet (14.18-20, 24; cf. 14.12). At another level, it revisits the blessedness of the rich who invite the poor to the banquet (Lk. 14.14) and who will eat in the kingdom of God for his or her association with the poor.

Hence the parable portrays who is in and who is out in the coming messianic banquet. It opens the door for the rich to enter the kingdom in their fellowship with the poor.[131] The possibility for the rich to avoid judgement or to be blessed is explicitly in view here. Blessed are the rich who invite the poor to their banquets, for they will be rewarded in the coming messianic banquet. They will be among the blessed who will eat bread in the kingdom of God (Lk. 14.15).

9.5 Conclusion: Salvation, the Messianic Banquet and the Place of the Poor and the Rich

The examination of the messianic banquet within Jewish apocalyptic traditions and in Luke's Gospel features several common elements. The banquets are set in eschatological settings. The feast takes place in the last day (Isaiah 25; 2 Baruch 29; 1QSa 2), in the kingdom of God (Lk. 13.22-30; 14.15), at the resurrection (2 Baruch 29; Lk. 14.14), in the presence of angels or in heaven (Lk. 15.7, 10) or at Abraham's bosom (Lk. 16.19). Both invitation to and exclusion from the banquets are closely related to the coming salvation and judgement.[132] The rich imagery of

---

127. Jeremias, *Parables*, 177; Bovon, *Luke 2*, 374.
128. Green, *Luke*, 562–3; Braun, *Feasting*, 122–6; J. Marshall, *Benefactors*, 275.
129. Manson, *Sayings*, 129; Bailey, *Peasant*, 89–92, 109–11; Fitzmyer, *Luke*, 1054, 1057; Parsons, *Luke*, 229; Nolland, *Luke 9:21–18:34*, 758; Eckey, *Lukasevangelium*, 663.
130. Jeremias, *Parables*, 177–8; Snodgrass, *Intent*, 316.
131. Luke 16.9; 18.22-25.
132. Isaiah 25; 1 Enoch 62; 2 Baruch 29; 1QSa 2; Lk. 13.22-30; 14.1-24; 15.6, 9, 23, 25-32.

food portrays the 'vindication' of the poor.[133] Thus, severe experiences of hunger anticipate the richness of the messianic banquet in the future. This reversal is most prominently featured in terms of divine justice.

The Parable of the Great Banquet speaks of the salvation of the rich in view of the messianic banquet, and the place of the poor and the rich. The relationship between salvation of the rich and the messianic banquet is noted here as the question of who will eat bread in the kingdom tackles two issues. The significance of accepting the invitation is taken for granted to join the banquet.[134] However, the passage further suggests that table fellowship with those to whom the kingdom is granted, to whom good news is proclaimed and to whom blessings are announced, namely, the poor, the crippled, the blind and the lame, is vital, for, by doing this, the rich themselves will get invited to the banquet and will enjoy the blessing of eating in the kingdom.[135] This is understood as righteous actions over against those who practise unrighteous actions (ἐργάται ἀδικίας) and are excluded from the banquet (Lk. 13.27).[136] The invitation will result in divine reward for the rich who invite the poor who cannot repay them (Lk. 14.14).

A similar impulse is found in Lk. 12.33, 16.9, 19-31, 18.22 where the kingdom (βασιλεία 12.32; cf. 18.24-26) is granted as a reward (12.32; cf. 18.24-26), treasure in heaven (θησαυρὸν ἐν τοῖς οὐρανοῖς 12.33; 18.22) is promised and welcoming to the eternal dwelling (τὰς αἰωνίους σκηνάς 16.9) is anticipated in association with the poor and the use of wealth. Hence the salvation of the rich is intrinsically intertwined with the salvation of the poor and so is their place at the messianic banquet.

---

133. Smit, *Food*, 198.
134. Manson, *Sayings*, 129; Forbes, *God*, 104–5; Parsons, *Luke*, 229; Klein, *Lukasevangelium*, 510.
135. Esler, *Community*, 196.
136. Carroll, *Luke*, 301.

Chapter 10

CONCLUSION

10.1 Summary and Conclusions

In this thesis, I have argued that Luke's message of salvation and Luke's soteriological concerns for the rich as well as the poor are inextricably tied to socio-economic issues. I first examined Luke's socio-economic world, that is, the first-century Graeco-Roman world in which the Gospel appeared. What is stressed is the most crucial element of wealth: land, and life essentials, namely, food and clothing (Chapters 2 and 3). The examination of landholding patterns during this period suggests the growth of large landowners at the expense of landless peasants. The most troublesome cause and result of this pattern centres around debt and indebtedness.

Moreover, the common experience of hunger and shortages of food stands in stark contrast to practices of hoarding grain and surpluses of food. This economic disparity constitutes the primary reason for the indebtedness of the poor. Hence the analysis of socio-economic contexts sheds light on Luke's particular concern for the release (ἄφεσις) of debt, his interpretation of the Law which culminates in mercy (ἔλεος) and almsgiving (ἐλεημοσύνη), the recurring theme of reversal and the rich imagery of food and banquets.

Based on this analysis, I examined salvation in Luke centred on divine ἔλεος under four headings: release, reversal, repentance and restoration (Chapter 4). Then, in the following chapters, I explored the passages where soteriological inquiries are closely tied up with socio-economic concerns. First, I highlighted God's mercy and justice in the discussion of 'salvation of the poor'. Divine mercy and justice towards the poor which are the core characteristics of ἡ βασιλεία τοῦ θεοῦ explain why God's coming and his reign essentially entail 'good news to the poor' (Lk. 4.18-19). The examination of the salvation of the widow and her fatherless son (Lk. 7.11-17), and the poor man, Lazarus (16.19-31), further strengthens the view that it is divine mercy and justice which deliver them and reverse the fate of the poor while their piety or even their faith appears rather irrelevant (Chapter 5).

Second, the study of the passages (Lk. 3.1-20; 10.25-37; 18.18-30; 12.16-21; 16.1-9) which are shaped by Luke's programmatic question, Τί ποιήσωμεν, shifted attention to the human embodiment of divine mercy and justice. The question itself raises a critical issue of whether salvation in Luke's Gospel entails 'doing'. This 'doing' is firmly rooted in Jesus' teaching in Lk. 6.35 (Γίνεσθε οἰκτίρμονες καθὼς [καὶ] ὁ πατὴρ ὑμῶν οἰκτίρμων ἐστίν). In comparison with Matthew's use of τέλειος (5.48), Luke's use of οἰκτίρμων (6.35) highlights the significance of divine mercy and of its human embodiment. It is the reflection of the merciful God particularly in their socio-economic relations with others.[1]

Acts of mercy and justice in John the Baptist's teaching (Lk. 3.10-14) not only encapsulate his message of repentance (3.3, 8) but also embody what 'good news' (3.4-6, 18) looks like (Chapter 6). In a similar vein, the quest for eternal life by the lawyer (Lk. 10.25) and the ruler (18.18) is responded to with the portrayal of mercy (ἔλεος) and almsgiving (ἐλεημοσύνη) both of which the Law and the commandments underscore (Chapter 7). The redemptive aspect of almsgiving in this thesis is twofold: (1) Almsgiving brings about salvation of the poor in this world; and (2) it envisions salvation of the rich as eschatological reward.

Conversely, the (im)proper use of wealth which is given and entrusted contributes to death and eternal destiny in Lk. 12.16-21; 16.1-9 (Chapter 8). The study of the passages (Lk. 3.1-20; 10.25-37; 18.18-30; 12.16-21; 16.1-9) shows that repentance entails radical acts of mercy in terms of transformed socio-economic relations and that the human embodiment of divine mercy and justice towards the needy and the poor is crucial in Luke's understanding of salvation.

Third, I drew attention to 'salvation of the rich' in view of the imagery of the messianic banquet in Lk. 14.1-24. The examination of the banquet imagery in Jewish traditions and Luke's Gospel suggests that participation in the messianic banquet denotes divine vindication and reward. Also noted is the theme of reversal as the rich imagery of food invites the hungry whereas hunger awaits those who are full now. Furthermore, the most significant, and perhaps unexpected, conclusion emerging from the examination of Lk. 14.1-24 is the possible inclusion of the rich in the messianic banquet, and thus the possibility of their salvation. Blessed will be the rich when they invite those to whom the kingdom is granted, to whom good news is proclaimed and to whom blessings are announced, namely, the poor. Their radical transformed relations with the poor are vital for their salvation (Chapter 9).

To sum up, Luke's message of salvation and its incorporation into socio-economic issues is best understood in terms of (1) divine mercy which redresses the injustice of the world, (2) human response by embodying divine mercy and (3) divine reward promised to those who enact mercy. Most importantly, salvation of the rich is intertwined with salvation of the poor. The blessedness of the rich is contingent upon their relation to the poor. At its climax, Luke's Gospel anticipates the messianic banquet where the restored people of God, the poor and the rich, gather around the table.

---

1. Rowan Williams, *God with Us: The Meaning of the Cross and Resurrection. Then and Now* (London: SPCK, 2017), Kindle edn, ch. 2, 'The Sacrifice'.

10.2 Contributions

This thesis challenges long-held views on Lukan soteriology at three points. First, against the overemphasis on individualized and internalized faith and piety, this thesis shows that human appropriation of the offer of salvation is relativized by shifting the focus to divine mercy and justice in Luke's portrayal of salvation of the poor. It cautions, 'The disturbing concern for justice for the innocent person who suffers, which is at the heart of the biblical traditions, was too quickly transformed into concern for the salvation of sinners.'[2]

Second, 'unconditioned' divine mercy[3] is not 'unconditional' as Barclay convincingly argues in his study of 'the gift' in ancient contexts.[4] Despite the fact that divine mercy is 'free of prior conditions regarding the recipient', this thesis challenges the concept that it is 'free of expectations'.[5] The demand of γίνεσθε οἰκτίρμονες καθὼς [καὶ] ὁ πατὴρ ὑμῶν οἰκτίρμων ἐστίν (Lk. 6.36) and the recurring inquiry of τί ποιήσωμεν/ποιήσω (3.10, 12, 14; 10.25; 12.17; 16.3; 18.18) remind us that the reception of divine mercy calls for practices which embody it. This involves an active response in tangible terms, not passive receiving. Thirdly, the message of salvation in Luke's Gospel is replete with promises of divine rewards. They spur on the divine-human and the interpersonal dynamics of salvation in Luke's Gospel.

Finally, and most crucially, this thesis clarifies Luke's notion of salvation of the rich: it is possible, but it is never without the poor. The ways in which Luke portrays the message of salvation primarily highlight the poor to whom the kingdom is granted, blessings are pronounced and good news is proclaimed. It is through merciful and just relations towards the poor that the rich are invited to the kingdom, called blessed and gathered with the poor in the banquet. Thus, the salvation of the rich will happen as they participate in the salvation of the poor.[6] The thesis climaxes at the messianic banquet where the restored people of God, the poor and the rich, recline at the table.

---

2. Johann B. Metz, 'La compasión. Un programa universal del cristianismo en la época de pluralismo cultural y religioso', *RLT* 55 (2002): 28. Cited by Jon Sobrino, *No Salvation Outside of the Poor: Prophetic-Utopian Essays* (Maryknoll: Orbis, 2008), 26.

3. See also Harrison, 'Grace', 413–17. He compares Luke's use of the terms, mercy and compassion (pity), against *clementia* and *misericordia* in the Roman imperial context. While the Romans distinguish the terms according to the worthiness of the recipients, they converge in Luke's Gospel, highlighting unconditioned divine mercy towards both the unworthy and the worthy.

4. Barclay, *Gift*, 562.

5. Ibid. cf. Mt. 18.23-35.

6. Pedro Trigo, 'La misión en la Iglesia latinoamericana actual', *RLT* 68 (2006): 191.

10. Conclusion

10.3 Limitations and Further Studies

While this thesis offers a multifaceted approach to salvation in Luke's Gospel, it is not an exhaustive study on Lukan soteriology. Rather I have construed the texts through the lens of the socio-economic contexts of Luke's Gospel to shed light on his message of salvation in its own context. Salvation in Acts is hardly addressed in this thesis except for some brief discussion in relation to Luke's Gospel. As noted, the theologies of Luke and Acts are not mutually exclusive or incompatible; however, each features salvation in its distinct manner. Thus, salvation in Acts and its distinctiveness in comparison with the Gospel remain a future area of research to see whether the findings in Luke carry over into Acts.

10.4 Implications for the World Today

This thesis assumed the context-specific message of salvation in Luke's narrative world. Then how can we read this message of salvation in a way that is relevant in the twenty-first century? Surprisingly or maybe not so surprisingly, many aspects of the socio-economic world of today resonate with that of the first century. It echoes an unbridgeable gap between rich and poor and an economic disparity due to political oppression and social injustice. Just as land became a place of investment, not a place for living, so housing has become an object of investment, not necessarily a place of living. The vicious cycle of debt remains in many forms today.

Then, how should we read Luke's message of salvation? Readers of this thesis most probably are among the rich. Luke is discomforting reading for the rich since the very nature of Luke's message of salvation challenges those who are in the place of comfort and power. Perhaps Luke's message of salvation is indeed grim news to us without the radical transformation of our socio-economic dealings in personal, communal and national relations. So, we ask with Luke's audience the following: Τί οὖν ποιήσωμεν (Lk. 3.10).

BIBLIOGRAPHY

Primary Sources

Aland, Kurt, Barbara Aland, Johannes Karavidopoulos, Carlo M. Martini and Bruce M. Metzger, eds. *Novum Testamentum Graece*. 28th edn. Stuttgart: Deutsche Bibelgesellschaft, 2012.
The Apocryphal Old Testament. Edited by H.F.D. Sparks. Oxford: Oxford University, 1984.
Athenaeus. *Deipnosophistae*. Translated by Charles Burton Gulick. 7 vols. Cambridge, MA: Harvard University, 1954-69.
Benoit, Pierre, Józef Tadeusz Milik and Roland de Vaux. *Les Grottes de Murabbaât*. DJD 2. Oxford: Clarendon, 1961
Biblia Hebraica Stuttgartensia. Stuttgart: Deutsche Bibelgesellschaft, 1997.
Cato. *On Agriculture*. Translated by W.D. Hooper and Harrison Boyd Ash. LCL. Cambridge, MA: Harvard University, 1934.
Charlesworth, James H. and Loren T. Stuckenbruck. 'Rule of the Congregation (1QSa)'. In *The Dead Sea Scrolls: Hebrew, Aramaic, and Greek Texts with English Translations, Vol. 1: Rule of the Community and Related Documents*, edited by James H. Charlesworth, 108-18. Tübingen: Mohr, 1994.
Cicero. *On Duties*. Translated by Walter Miller. LCL. Cambridge, MA: Harvard University, 1913.
Columella. *On Agriculture*. Translated by Harrison Boyd Ash, E.S. Forster and Edward H. Heffner. 3 vols. LCL. Cambridge, MA: Harvard University, 1941-55.
The Dead Sea Scrolls Study Edition. 2 vols. Edited by Florentino García Martínez and Eibert J.C. Tigchelaar. 2nd edn. Leiden: Brill, 1999.
Dessaw, Hermannus, ed. *Inscriptiones Latinae Selectae*. 3 vols. Berolini Apud Weidmannos, 1892-1916.
Dio, Cassius. *Roman History*. Translated by Earnest Cary and Herbert B. Foster. 9 vols. LCL. Cambridge, MA: Harvard University, 1925.
Fronto. *Correspondence*. Translated by C.R. Haines. 2 vols. LCL. Cambridge, MA: Harvard University, 1919-20.
Gaius. *Digest*. 6 June 2014. http://www.thelatinlibrary.com.
Galen. *On the Properties of Foodstuffs (De alimentorum facultatibus)*. Translated by Owen Powell. Cambridge: CUP, 2003.
Josephus. Translated by Henry St. J. Thackeray et al. 10 vols. LCL. Cambridge, MA: Harvard University, 1926-65.
Juvenal. *The Sixteen Satires*. Translated by Peter Green. Harmondsworth: Penguin, 1967.
The Letter of Aristeas. Translated by H. St. J. Thackeray. London: SPCK, 1917.
Lichtheim, Miria. *Ancient Egyptian Literature: A Book of Readings, Vol. 3: The Late Period*. Berkeley: University of California, 2006.

Livy. *History of Rome*. Translated by B.O. Foster et al. 14 vols. LCL. 1919–59.
Lucian. *The Works of Lucian of Samosata*. Translated by H.W. Fowler and F.G. Fowler. 4 vols. Oxford: Clarendon, 1905.
Nickelsburg, George W.E. and James C. Vanderkam. *1 Enoch: A New Translation*. Minneapolis: Fortress, 2004.
The Old Testament Pseudepigrapha. Edited by James H. Charlesworth. 2 vols. London: Darton, Longman & Todd, 1983–1985.
O'Neill, Eugene, Jr, ed. *Aristophanes* in *The Complete Greek Drama*. 2 vols. New York: Random House, 1938.
Origen. *Homilies on Genesis and Exodus*. Translated by Ronald E. Heine. Reprint edn. Washington: Catholic University of America, 2002.
The Oxyrhynchus Papyri Part II. Edited by B.P. Grenfell and A.S. Hunt. London: The Egypt Exploration Fund, 1899.
Paterculus, Velleius. *Compendium of Roman History. Res Gestae Divi Augusti*. Translated by Frederick W. Shipley. LCL. Cambridge, MA: Harvard University, 1924.
Petronius. *Satyricon*. Translated by Michael Heseltine. London: Heinemann, 1930.
Philo. Translated by F.H. Colson. 9 vols. LCL. London: Heinemann, 1937.
Philostratus. *The Life of Apollonius of Tyana*. 2 vols. LCL. Cambridge, MA: Harvard University, 1912.
Plutarch. *Lives*. Translated by Bernadotte Perrin. 11 vols. LCL. Cambridge, MA: Harvard University, 1914–26.
Plutarch. *Moralia*. Translated by Frank Cole Babbitt et al. 15 vols. LCL. Cambridge, MA: Harvard University, 1927–69.
Sallust. Translated by J.C. Rolfe. LCL. Cambridge, MA: Harvard University, 1921.
Septuaginta. Edited by Alfred Rahlfs and Robert Hanhart. Stuttgart: Deutsche Bibelgesellschaft, 2006.
Soncino Babylonian Talmud. Translated by I. Epstein. AWOL. 10 August 2015. http://ancientworldonline.blogspot.co.uk/2012/01/online-soncino-babylonian-talmud.html.
Suetonius. *Lives of the Caesars*. Translated by J.C. Rolfe. 2 vols. LCL. Cambridge, MA: Harvard University, 1914.
Tacitus. *The Histories and The Annales*. Translated by Clifford H. Moore and John Jackson. 4 vols. LCL. Cambridge, MA: Harvard University, 1937.
Wise, Michael, Martin Abegg, Jr and Edward Cook. *The Dead Sea Scrolls: A New Translation*. London: HarperCollins, 1996.
Yadin, Yigael. *The Finds from the Bar Kokhba Period in the Cave of Letters*. Jerusalem: The Israel Exploration Society, 1963.

Secondary Sources

Achtemeier, Paul J. 'The Lucan Perspective on the Miracles of Jesus: A Preliminary Sketch'. *JBL* 95.4 (1975): 547–62.
Allison, Dale C, Jr. *Constructing Jesus: Memory, Imagination, and History*. London: SPCK, 2010.
Anderson, Gary. *Charity: The Place of the Poor in the Biblical Tradition*. New Haven: Yale University, 2013.
Anderson, Gary. *Sin: A History*. New Haven: Yale University, 2009.

Anderson, Kevin L. *'But God Raised Him from the Dead': The Theology of Jesus' Resurrection in Luke-Acts*. London: Paternoster, 2006.
Applebaum, S. 'Economic Life in Palestine'. In *The Jewish People in the First Century II*, edited by S. Safrai and M. Stern, 631–700. Amsterdam: Compendia Rerum Iudaicarum ad Novum Testamentum, 1976.
Atkins, Margaret and Robin Osborne, eds. *Poverty in the Roman World*. Cambridge: CUP, 2006.
Autero, Esa J. *Reading the Bible across Contexts: Luke's Gospel, Socio-Economic Marginality, and Latin American Biblical Hermeneutics*. BibInt 145. Leiden: Brill, 2016.
Bailey, Kenneth E. *Poet and Peasant and Through Peasant Eyes: A Literary-Cultural Approach to the Parables in Luke*. Grand Rapids: Eerdmans, 1983.
Baker, David L. *Tight Fists or Open Hands?: Wealth and Poverty in Old Testament Law*. Cambridge: Eerdmans, 2009.
Ballard, Paul H. 'Reasons for Refusing the Great Supper'. *JTS* 23 (1972): 341–50.
Barclay, John M.G. *Paul and the Gift*. Grand Rapids: Eerdmans, 2015.
Barclay, John M.G. 'Poverty in Pauline Studies: A Response to Steven Friesen'. *JSNT* (2004): 363–6.
Barton, Stephen C. 'Parables on God's Love and Forgiveness (Luke 15:1–32)'. In *The Challenge of Jesus' Parables*, edited by Richard N. Longenecker, 199–216. Grand Rapids: Eerdmans, 2000.
Bauckham, Richard, ed. *The Gospels for All Christians: Rethinking the Gospel Audiences*. Edinburgh: T&T Clark, 1998.
Bauckham, Richard. 'Paul and Other Jews with Latin Names in the New Testament'. In *Paul, Luke and the Graeco-Roman World*, edited by Alf Christophersen et al., 202–20. JSNTSup 217. London: T&T Clark, 2003.
Bauckham, Richard. 'Response to Philip Esler'. *SJT* 51.2 (1998): 249–53.
Bauckham, Richard. 'The Restoration of Israel in Luke-Acts'. In *Restoration: Old Testament, Jewish and Christian Perspectives*, edited by J.M. Scott, 435–87. JSJSup 72. Leiden: Brill, 2001.
Bauckham, Richard. 'The Rich Man and Lazarus: The Parable and the Parallels'. *NTS* 37.2 (1991): 225–46.
Bauckham, Richard. 'The Scrupulous Priest and the Good Samaritan: Jesus' Parabolic Interpretation of the Law of Moses'. *NTS* 44 (1998): 475–89.
Bauer, Walter. *A Greek-English Lexicon of the New Testament and Other Early Christian Literature*. Edited by W.F. Gingrich. Translated by W.F. Arndt. Chicago: Chicago University, 1952.
Beavis, Mary Ann. 'Ancient Slavery as an Interpretive Context for New Testament Servant Parables with Special Reference to the Unjust Steward (Luke 16:1–8)'. *JBL* 111.1 (1992): 37–54.
Berger, Klaus. 'Almosen für Israel: Zum Historischen Kontext der Paulinischen Kollekte'. *NTS* 23 (1977): 180–204.
Bergsma, John Sietze. *The Jubilee from Leviticus to Qumran: A History of Interpretation*. Leiden: Brill, 2007.
Bird, Michael F. *The Gospel of the Lord: How the Early Church Wrote the Story of Jesus* Grand Rapids: Eerdmans, 2014.
Bird, Michael F. 'The Unity of Luke-Acts in Recent Discussion'. *JSNT* 29.4 (2007): 425–48.
Bird, Michael F. 'Who Comes from the East and the West? Luke 13.28–29//Matt 8.11–12 and the Historical Jesus'. *NTS* 52 (2006): 441–57.

Blenkinsopp, Joseph. *Opening the Sealed Book: Interpretations of the Book of Isaiah in Late Antiquity*. Grand Rapids: Eerdmans, 2006.
Blomberg, Craig. *Contagious Holiness: Jesus' Meals with Sinners*. NSBT 19. Downers Grove: InterVarsity, 2005.
Blomberg, Craig. 'Jesus, Sinners and Table Fellowship'. *BBR* 19.1 (2009): 35–62.
Borg, Marcus J. *Conflict, Holiness, and Politics in the Teachings of Jesus*. Harrisburg: Trinity, 1998.
Botterweck, G. Johannes, Helmer Ringgren and Heinz-Josef Fabry, eds. *Theological Dictionary of the Old Testament*. Translated by David E. Green and Douglas W. Scott. 15 vols. Grand Rapids: Eerdmans, 1977–2006.
Bovon, François. *Luke the Theologian: Fifty-five Years of Research* (1950–2005). 2nd and rev. edn. Waco: Baylor University, 2005.
Bovon, François. *Luke 1: A Commentary on the Gospel of Luke 1: 1–9:50*. Hermeneia. Minneapolis: Augsburg, 2002.
Bovon, François. *Luke 2: A Commentary on the Gospel of Luke 9:51–19:27*. Hermeneia. Minneapolis: Fortress, 2013.
Braudel, Fernand. *The Mediterranean and the Mediterranean World in the Age of Philip II*. Translated by Siân Reynold. 2 vols. Berkeley: University of California, 1995.
Braun, Willi. *Feasting and Social Rhetoric in Luke 14*. SNTSMS 85. Cambridge: CUP, 1995.
Brink, Laurie. *Soldiers in Luke-Acts: Engaging, Contradicting, and Transcending the Stereotypes*. WUNT 362. Tübingen: Mohr, 2014.
Brodie, Thomas L. 'Towards unravelling Luke's use of the Old Testament: Luke 7:11–17 as an imitatio of 1 Kings 17: 17–24'. *NTS* 32 (1986): 247–67.
Brooke, George J. *The Dead Sea Scrolls and the New Testament: Essays in Mutual Illumination*. London: SPCK, 2005.
Brooke, George J. 'Isaiah 40:3 and the Wilderness Community'. In *New Qumran Texts and Studies Proceedings of the First Meeting of the International Organization for Qumran Studies, Paris 1992*, edited by George J. Brooke, 117–32. Leiden: Brill, 1994.
Brooke, George J. *Isaiah at Qumran: Updating W.H. Brownlee's the Meaning of the Qumrân Scrolls for the Bible*. OPIAC 46. Claremont: The Institute for Antiquity and Christianity, 2004.
Brooke, George J. 'Luke-Acts and the Qumran Scrolls: The Case of MMT'. In *Luke's Literary Achievement: Collected Essays*, edited by C.M. Tuckett, 72–90. JSNTSup 116. Sheffield: Sheffield Academic, 1995.
Broshi, Magen. *Bread, Wine, Walls and Scrolls*. JSPSup 36. Sheffield: Sheffield Academic, 2001.
Brown, Peter. *Through the Eye of a Needle: Wealth, the Fall of Rome, and the Making of Christianity in the West, 350–550 AD*. Princeton, NJ: Princeton University, 2012.
Brown, Raymond E. *The Birth of the Messiah: A Commentary on the Infancy Narratives in the Gospels of Matthew and Luke*. New York: Doubleday, 1999.
Brown, Raymond E. 'The Pater Noster as an Eschatological Prayer'. *TS* 22.2 (1961): 175–208.
Brueggemann, Walter. *The Land*. Philadelphia: Fortress, 1977.
Bultmann, Rudolf. *The History of the Synoptic Tradition*. Translated by John Marsh. Oxford: Blackwell, 1972.
Burkett, Delbert. *Rethinking the Gospel Sources: From Proto-Mark to Mark*. London: T&T Clark, 2004.
Byrne, Brendan. *The Hospitality of God: A Reading of Luke's Gospel*. Collegeville: Liturgical, 2000.

Cadbury, Henry J. *The Making of Luke-Acts*. London: Macmillan, 1927.
Carcopino, Jérôme. *Daily Life in Ancient Rome: The People and the City at the Height of the Empire*. Edited by Henry T. Rowell. Translated by E.O. Lorimer. London: Routledge, 1968.
Carroll, John T. *Luke*. NTL. Louisville: WJK, 2012.
Carroll, John T. *Response to the End of History: Eschatology and Situation in Luke-Acts*. SBLDS 92. Atlanta: Scholars, 1998.
Carroll, John T. 'Sickness and Healing in the New Testament Gospels'. *Int* 49.2 (1995): 130-42.
Cave, C.H. 'Lazarus and the Lukan Deuteronomy'. *NTS* 15 (1969): 319-25.
Chamblin, Knox. 'John the Baptist and the Kingdom of God'. *TynBul* 15 (1964): 10-16.
Chancey, Mark Alan and Adam Lowry Porter. 'Archaeology of Roman Palestine'. *NEA* 64.4 (2001): 164-203.
Charlesworth, James H. and Darrell L. Bock, eds. *Parables of Enoch: A Paradigm Shift*. London: Bloomsbury, 2013.
Chilton, Bruce D. *The Glory of Israel: The Theology and Provenience of the Isaiah Targum*. JSOTSup 23. Sheffield: Sheffield Academic, 1983.
Coleridge, Mark. *The Birth of the Lukan Narrative: Narrative as Christology in Luke 1-2*. JSNTSup 88. Sheffield: Sheffield Academic, 1993.
Collins, John. 'The Works of the Messiah'. *DSD* 1.1 (1994): 98-112.
Conzelmann, Hans. *The Theology of Saint Luke*. Translated by Geoffrey Buswell. London: Faber and Faber, 1960.
Countryman, Louis William. *The Rich Christian in the Church of the Early Empire: Contradictions and Accommodations*. New York: Edwin Mellen, 1980.
Crawford, Dorothy J. 'Imperial Estates'. In *Studies in Roman Property*, edited by M.I. Finley, 35-70. Cambridge: CUP, 1976.
Crawford, Michael. 'Money and Exchange in the Roman World'. *JRS* 60 (1970): 40-8.
Crossan, John D. *In Parables: The Challenge of the Historical Jesus*. New York: Harper & Row, 1985.
Crossan, John D. 'Parable and Example in the Teaching of Jesus'. *NTS* 18.3 (1972): 285-307.
Crossley, James G. 'The Semitic Background to Repentance in the Teaching of John the Baptist and Jesus'. *JSHJ* 2.2 (2004): 138-57.
Crowfoot, Elisabeth. 'Textiles'. In *Discoveries in the Wâdī ed-Dâliyeh*, edited by Paul W. Lapp and Nancy L. Lapp. AASOR 41. Cambridge, MA: American School of Oriental Research, 1974.
Culy, Martin M., Mikeal C. Parsons and Joshua J. Stigall. *Luke: A Handbook on the Greek Text*. BHGNT. Waco: Baylor University, 2010.
Daube, David. 'Neglected Nuances of Exposition in Luke-Acts'. *ANRW II* 25.3 (1984): 2329-56.
Davies, Eryl Wynn. 'Walking in God's Ways: The Concept of Imitatio Dei in the Old Testament'. In *In Search of True Wisdom: Essays in Old Testament Interpretation in Honour of Ronald E. Clements*, edited by Edward Ball, 99-115. JSOTSup 300. Sheffield: Sheffield Academic, 1999.
Davies, William David. *The Gospel and the Land: Early Christianity and Jewish Territorial Doctrine*. Berkeley: University of California, 1974.
Davila, James R. 'The Old Testament Pseudepigrapha as Background to the New Testament'. *ExpTim* 117.2 (2005): 53-7.

Degenhardt, Hans-Joachim. *Lukas Evangelist der Armen: Besitz und Besitzverzicht in Den Lukanischen Schriften: Eine Traditions-und Redaktionsgeschichtliche Untersuchung.* Stuttgart: Katholisches Bibelwerk, 1965.
Derrett, J. Duncan M. 'Fresh Light on St. Luke XVI'. *NTS* 7 (1960): 198–219.
Derrett, J. Duncan M. *Law in the New Testament.* London: Darton, Longman & Todd, 1970.
Donahue, John R. *The Gospel in Parable: Metaphor, Narrative, and Theology in the Synoptic Gospels.* Philadelphia: Fortress, 1988.
Donahue, John R. 'Tax Collectors and Sinners: An Attempt at Identification'. *CBQ* 33.1 (1971): 39–61.
Donahue, John R. 'Two Decades of Research on the Rich and the Poor in Luke-Acts'. In *Justice and the Holy: Essays in Honor of Walter Harrelson*, edited by Douglas A. Knight and Peter J. Paris, 129–44. Atlanta: Scholars, 1989.
Douglas, Mary. 'Deciphering a Meal'. In *Implicit Meanings: Essays in Anthropology*, 249–75. London: Routledge, 1975.
Douglas, Mary. 'Justice as the Cornerstone: An Interpretation of Leviticus 18–20'. *Int* 53 (1999): 341–50.
Douglas, Mary. *Purity and Danger: An Analysis of Concepts of Pollution and Taboo.* London: Routledge, 1966.
Downs, David J. 'Redemptive Almsgiving and Economic Stratification in 2 Clement'. *JECS* 19 (2011): 493–517.
Duncan-Jones, Richard. *The Economy of the Roman Empire: Quantitative Studies.* 2nd edn. Cambridge: CUP, 1982.
Dunn, James. 'John the Baptist's Use of Scripture'. In *The Gospels and the Scriptures of Israel*, edited by Craig A. Evans and W. Richard Stegner, 42–54. JSNTSup 104. SSEJC 3. Sheffield: Sheffield Academic, 1994.
Dupont, Jacques. 'Die individuelle Eschatologie im Lukasevangelium und in der Apostelgeschichte'. In *Orientierung an Jesus: Zur Theologie der Synoptiker: Für Josef Schmid*, edited by Paul Hoffmann, 37–47. Freiburg: Herder, 1973.
Dupont, Jacques. *Les Béatitudes.* 3 vols. Paris: J. Gabalda et Cie Éditeurs, 1958, 1969, 1973.
Eckey, Wilfried. *Das Lukasevangelium: Unter Berücksichtigung Seiner Parallelen.* 2 vols. Rev. edn. Kempten, Germany: Neukirchener, 2006.
Edwards, Douglas R. 'Dress and Ornamentation'. *ABD* 2:232–8.
Elliott, Neil and Mark Reasoner, eds. *Documents and Images for the Study of Paul.* Minneapolis: Fortress, 2011.
Ermakov, Arseny. 'The Salvific Significance of the Torah in Mark 10.17–22 and 12.28–34'. In *The Torah in the New Testament: Papers Delivered at the Manchester-Lausanne Seminar of June 2008*, edited by Michael Tait and Peter Oakes, 21–31. London: T&T Clark, 2009.
Esler, Philip Francis. 'Community and Gospel in Early Christianity: A Response to Richard Bauckham's Gospels for All Christians'. *SJT* 51.2 (1998): 235–48.
Esler, Philip Francis. *Community and Gospel in Luke-Acts: The Social and Political Motivations on Lucan Theology.* SNTSMS 57. Cambridge: CUP, 1987.
Esler, Philip Francis. 'Jesus and the Reduction of Intergroup Conflict: The Parable of the Good Samaritan in the Light of Social Identity Theory'. *BibInt* 8.4 (2000): 325–57.
Eubank, Nathan. 'Storing Up Treasure with God in the Heaven: Celestial Investments in Matthew 6:1–21'. *CBQ* 76 (2014): 77–92.
Eubank, Nathan. *Wages of Cross-Bearing and Debt of Sin: The Economy of Heaven in Matthew's Gospel.* BZNW 196. Berlin: De Gruyter, 2013.

Evans, C.F. 'The Central Section of St. Luke's Gospel'. In *Studies in the Gospels: Essays in Memory of R.H. Lightfoot*, edited by D.E. Nineham, 37–53. Oxford: Basil Blackwell, 1955.
Evans, C.F. *Saint Luke*. London: SCM, 1990.
Evans, C.F. 'Uncomfortable Words'. *ExpTim* 81 (1970): 228–31.
Evans, Craig A. 'From Gospel to Gospel: The Function of Isaiah in the New Testament'. In *Writing and Reading the Scroll of Isaiah: Studies of an Interpretive Tradition*, 2 vols, edited by Craig C. Broyles and Craig A. Evans, 651–91. Leiden: Brill, 1997.
Evans, Craig A. 'The Function of the Elijah/Elisha Narratives in Luke's Ethics of Election'. In *Luke and Scripture: The Function of Sacred Tradition in Luke-Acts*, edited by Craig A. Evans and James A. Sanders, 70–83. Minneapolis: Fortress, 1993.
Evans, Craig A. 'Luke's Good Samaritan and the Chronicler's Good Samaritans'. In *Biblical Interpretation in Early Christian Gospels, Vol. 3: The Gospel of Luke*, edited by Thomas R. Hatina, 32–42. LNTS 376. SSEJC 16. London: T&T Clark, 2010.
Evans, Craig A. 'A Note on Targum 2 Samuel 5.8 and Jesus' Ministry to the "Maimed, Halt, and Blind"'. *JSP* 15 (1997): 79–82.
Farrer, Austin. 'Dispensing with Q'. In *Studies in the Gospels: Essays in Memory of R.H. Lightfoot*, edited by D.E. Nineham, 55–88. Oxford: Blackwell, 1955.
Farris, Stephen. *The Hymns of Luke's Infancy Narratives: Their Origin, Meaning, and Significance*. JSNTSup 9. Sheffield: JSOT, 1985.
Fensham, F. Charles. 'Widow, Orphan, and the Poor in Ancient Near Eastern Legal and Wisdom Literature'. *JNES* 21 (1962): 129–39.
Finley, Moses I., ed. *The Ancient Economy*. 2nd edn. London: Penguin, 1992.
Finley, Moses I. *Studies in Roman Property*. Cambridge: CUP, 1976.
Fitzmyer, Joseph A. *The Gospel according to Luke*. 2 vols. AB. New York: Doubleday, 1985.
Fitzmyer, Joseph A. *Luke the Theologian: Aspects of His Teaching*. London: Geoffrey Chapman, 1989.
Fitzmyer, Joseph A. *The One Who Is to Come*. Grand Rapids: Eerdmans, 2007.
Fitzmyer, Joseph A. 'The Story of the Dishonest Manager (Luke 16:1–13)'. *TS* 25.1 (1964): 23–42.
Fletcher-Louis, Crispin H.T. *Luke-Acts: Angels, Christology and Soteriology*. WUNT 2.94. Tübingen: Mohr, 1997.
Forbes, Greg W. *The God of Old: The Role of the Lukan Parables in the Purpose of Luke's Gospel*. JSNTSup 198. Sheffield: Sheffield Academic, 2000.
Forbes, Greg W. 'Repentance and Conflict in the Parable of the Lost Son (Luke 15:11–32)'. *JETS* 42 (1999): 211–29.
Fowl, Stephen E. 'Receiving the Kingdom of God as a Child: Children and Riches in Luke 18.15ff'. *NTS* 39.1 (1993): 153–8.
Foxhall, Lin. 'The Dependent Tenant: Land Leasing and Labour in Italy and Greece'. *JRS* 80 (1990): 97–114.
Freedman, David Noel, ed. *Anchor Bible Dictionary*. 6 vols. New York: Doubleday, 1992.
Freyne, Seán. 'Herodian Economics in Galilee'. 'The Galileans in the Light of Josephus' Vita'. *NTS* 26 (1980): 397–413.
Freyne, Seán. 'Herodian Economics in Galilee'. *Galilee: From Alexander the Great to Hadrian 323 BCE to 135 CE*. Edinburgh: T&T Clark, 1980.
Freyne, Seán. 'Herodian Economics in Galilee'. In *Modelling Early Christianity: Social-Scientific Studies of the New Testament in Its Context*, edited by Philip F. Esler, 23–46. London: Routledge, 1995.

Friedl, A. 'The Reception of the Deuteronomic Social Law in the Primitive Church of Jerusalem according to the Book of Acts'. *AcTSup* 23 (2016): 176–200.
Friesen, Steven J. 'Poverty in Pauline Studies: Beyond the So-Called New Consensus'. *JSNT* 26.3 (2004): 323–61.
Fuller, Michael E. 'Isaiah 40.3–5 and Luke's Understanding of Wilderness of John the Baptist'. In *Biblical Interpretation in Early Christian Gospels, Vol. 3: The Gospel of Luke*, edited by Thomas R. Hatina, 43–58. LNTS 376. SSEJC 16. London: T&T Clark, 2010.
Garland, Robert. *The Eye of the Beholder: Deformity and Disability in the Graeco-Roman World*. London: Duckworth, 1995.
Garnsey, Peter. *Famine and Food Supply in the Graeco-Roman World: Response to Risk and Crisis*. Cambridge: CUP, 1988.
Garnsey, Peter. *Famine and Food Supply in the Graeco-Roman World: Response to Risk and Crisis*. Cambridge: CUP, 1988.
Garnsey, Peter. *Cities, Peasants and Food in Classical Antiquity: Essays in Social and Economic History*. Edited by Walter Scheidel. Cambridge: CUP, 1998.
Garnsey, Peter. *Famine and Food Supply in the Graeco-Roman World: Response to Risk and Crisis*. Cambridge: CUP, 1988.
Garnsey, Peter. *Food and Society in Classical Antiquity*. Cambridge: CUP, 1999.
Garnsey, Peter and Richard Saller. *The Roman Empire: Economy, Society and Culture*. London: Duckworth, 1987.
Garrison, Roman. *Redemptive Almsgiving in Early Christianity*. JSNTSup 77. Sheffield: Sheffield Academic, 1993.
Gathercole, Simon. 'Luke in the Gospel of Thomas'. *NTS* 57 (2010): 114–44.
George, Augustin, Jacques Dupont, Simon Legasee, Philip Seidesticker and Beda Rigaux. *Gospel Poverty: Essays in Biblical Theology*. Translated by Michael Guinan. Chicago: Franciscan Herald, 1977.
Giambrone, Anthony. *Sacramental Charity, Creditor Christology, and the Economy of Salvation in Luke's Gospel*. WUNT 2. 439. Tübingen: Mohr, 2017.
Gil, Moshe. 'The Decline of the Agrarian Economy in Palestine under Roman Rule'. *JESHO* (2006): 285–328.
Goldingay, John and David Payne. *Isaiah 40–55*. Vol. 1. ICC. London: T&T Clark, 2006.
Gonzalez, Justo L. *Faith and Wealth: A History of Early Christian Ideas on the Origin, Significance, and Use of Money*. New York: Harper & Row, 1990.
Goodacre, Mark. *The Case against Q: Studies in Markan Priority and the Synoptic Problem*. Harrisburg: Trinity, 2002.
Goodacre, Mark. *The Synoptic Problem: A Way through the Maze*. Sheffield: Sheffield Academic, 2001.
Goodman, Martin. *The Ruling Class of Judaea: The Origins of the Jewish Revolt against Rome A.D. 66–70*. Cambridge: CUP, 1987.
Goodrich, John K. 'Voluntary Debt Remission and the Parable of the Unjust Steward (Luke 16:1–13)'. *JBL* 131.3 (2012): 547–66.
Goulder, Michael D. 'The Chiastic Structure of the Lucan Journey'. In *Studia Evangelica II*, edited by F.L. Cross, 195–202. Berlin: Akademie-Verlag, 1964.
Goulder, Michael D. *Luke – A New Paradigm*. 2 vols. JSNTSup 20. Sheffield: Sheffield Academic, 1989.
Gowan, Donald E. 'Salvation as Healing'. *ExAud* 5 (1989): 1–19.
Gowan, Donald E. 'Wealth and Poverty in the Old Testament: The Case of the Widow, the Orphan, and the Sojourner'. *Int* 41.4 (1987): 341–53.

Gowler, David B. 'The Enthymematic Nature of Parables: A Dialogic Reading of the Parable of the Rich Fool (Luke 12:16-20)'. *RevExp* 109.2 (2012): 199-216.
Grant, Frederick C. *The Economic Background of the Gospels*. London: Oxford University, 1926.
Green, Joel B. *Conversion*. Grand Rapids: Eerdmans, 2015.
Green, Joel B. 'From "John's Baptism" to "Baptism in the Name of the Lord Jesus": The Significance of Baptism in Luke-Acts'. In *Baptism, the New Testament and the Church: Historical and Contemporary Studies in Honour of R.E.O. White*, edited by Stanley E. Porter and Anthony R. Cross, 157-72. JSNTSup 171. Sheffield: Sheffield Academic, 1999.
Green, Joel B. 'Good News to Whom? Jesus and the "Poor" in the Gospel of Luke'. In *Jesus of Nazareth Lord and Christ: Essays on the Historical Jesus and New Testament Christology*, edited by Joel B. Green and Max Turner, 59-74. Grand Rapids: Eerdmans, 1994.
Green, Joel B. 'Good News to the Poor: A Lukan Leitmotif'. *RevExp* 111.2 (2014): 173-9.
Green, Joel B. *The Gospel of Luke*. NICNT. Grand Rapids: Eerdmans, 1997.
Green, Joel B. 'The Message of Salvation in Luke-Acts'. *ExAud* 5 (1989): 21-34.
Green, Joel B. 'Narrative Criticism'. In *Methods for Luke*, edited by Joel B. Green, 74-112. Cambridge: CUP, 2010.
Green, Joel B. *The Theology of the Gospel of Luke*. Cambridge: CUP, 1995.
Green, Timothy M. *Hosea-Micah: A Commentary in the Wesleyan Tradition*. NBBC. Kansas City: Beacon Hill, 2006.
Habel, Norman C. *The Land Is Mine: Six Biblical Land Ideologies*. Minneapolis: Fortress, 1995.
Hamel, Gildas. *Poverty and Charity in Roman Palestine, First Three Centuries C.E.* Berkeley: University of California, 1990.
Hamilton, Jeffries M. *Social Justice and Deuteronomy: The Case of Deuteronomy 15*. SBLDS 136. Atlanta: Scholars, 1992.
Hamm, Dennis. 'Luke 19:8 Once Again: Does Zacchaeus Defend or Resolve?' *Bib* 107 (1988): 431-7.
Hamm, Dennis. 'Zacchaeus Revisited Once More: A Story of Vindication or Conversion?' *Bib* 72 (1991): 249-52.
Hanson, Kenneth C. and Douglas Oakman. *Palestine in the Time of Jesus: Social Structures and Social Conflicts*. Minneapolis: Fortress, 1998.
Harrison, James R. 'Who Is the "Lord of Grace"?: Jesus' Parables in Imperial Context'. In *Borders: Terminologies, Ideologies, and Performances*, edited by Annette Weissenrieder, 383-417. WUNT 366. Tübingen: Mohr, 2016.
Hartsock, Chad. 'The Healing of the Man with Dropsy (Luke 14:1-6) and the Lukan Landscape'. *BibInt* 21 (2013): 341-54.
Hatina, Thomas R. 'The Voice of Northrop Frye Crying in the Wilderness: The Mythmaking Function of Isaiah 40:3 in Luke's Annunciation of the Baptist'. In *Biblical Interpretation in Early Christian Gospels, Vol. 3: The Gospel of Luke*, edited by Thomas R. Hatina, 59-84. LNTS 376. SSEJC 16. London: T&T Clark, 2010.
Hayes, John H. and Sara R. Mandell. *The Jewish People in Classical Antiquity: From Alexander to Bar Kochba*. Louisville: John Knox, 1998.
Hays, Christopher M. 'By Almsgiving and Faith Sins Are Purged? The Theological Underpinnings of Early Christian Care for the Poor'. In *Engaging Economics*, edited by Bruce W. Longenecker and Kelly D. Liebengood, 260-80. Grand Rapids: Eerdmans, 2009.

Hays, Christopher M. *Luke's Wealth Ethics: A Study in Their Coherence and Character*. WUNT 275. Tübingen: Mohr, 2010.

Hays, Christopher M. 'Slaughtering Stewards and Incarcerating Debtors: Coercing Charity in Luke 12:35–13:9'. *Neot* 46.1 (2012): 41–60.

Hays, Richard B. *The Conversion of the Imagination: Paul as Interpreter of Israel's Scripture*. Cambridge: Eerdmans, 2005.

Hays, Richard B. *Echoes of Scripture in the Gospels*. Waco: Baylor University, 2016.

Hays, Richard B. *Echoes of Scripture in the Letters of Paul*. New Haven: Yale University, 1989.

Heil, John Paul. *The Meal Scenes in Luke-Acts: An Audience-Oriented Approach*. SBLMS 52. Atlanta: SBL, 1999.

Hellerman, Joseph H. *Reconstructing Honor in Roman Philippi: Carmen Christi as Cursus Pudorum*. SNTSMS 132. Cambridge: CUP, 2005.

Herzog, William R. *Parable as Subversive Speech: Jesus as Pedagogue of the Oppressed*. Louisville: John Knox, 1994.

Hirschfeld, Yizhar. 'Ramat Hanadiv and Ein Gedi: Property versus Poverty in Judea before 70'. In *Jesus and Archaeology*, edited by James H. Charlesworth, 384–92. Grand Rapids: Eerdmans, 2006.

Hock, Ronald F. 'Lazarus and Micyllus: Greco-Roman Background to Luke 16:19–31'. *JBL* 106 (1987): 447–63.

Holgate, David A. *Prodigality, Liberality, and Meanness in the Prodigal Son: A Greco-Roman Perspective on Luke 15:11–32*. JSNTSup 187. Sheffield: Sheffield Academic, 1999, p. 221.

Holladay, William L. *The Root ŠÛBH in the Old Testament*. Leiden: Brill, 1958.

Houston, Walter. 'The King's Preferential Option for the Poor: Rhetoric, Ideology, and Ethics in Psalm 72'. *BibInt* 7 (1999): 341–67.

Hoyt, Thomas. 'The Poor/Rich Theme in the Beatitudes'. *JRT* 37 (1980): 31–41.

Ireland, Dennis J. 'A History of Recent Interpretation of the Parable of the Unjust Steward (Luke 16:1–13)'. *WTJ* 51.2 (1989): 293–318.

Ireland, Dennis J. *Stewardship and the Kingdom of God: A Historical, Exegetical, and Contextual Study of the Parable of the Unjust Steward in Luke 16:1–13*. NovTSup 70. Leiden: Brill, 1992.

Jantsch, Torsten. *Jesus, der Retter: Die Soteriologie des lukanischen Doppelwerks*. WUNT 381. Tübingen: Mohr, 2017

Jasny, Naum. 'The Daily Bread of the Ancient Greeks and Romans'. *Osiris* (1950): 227–53.

Jensen, Morten Hørning. *Herod Antipas in Galilee*. WUNT 215. Tübingen: Mohr, 2006.

Jeremias, Joachim. *Jerusalem in the Time of Jesus: An Investigation into Economic and Social Conditions during the New Testament Period*. London: SCM, 1969.

Jeremias, Joachim. *The Parables of Jesus*. London: SCM, 1972.

Johnson, Luke Timothy. 'On Finding the Lukan Community: A Cautious Cautionary Essay'. In *Contested Issues in Christian Origins and the New Testament: Collected Essays*, 87–100. Leiden: Brill, 2013.

Johnson, Luke Timothy. *The Gospel of Luke*. SP. Collegeville: Liturgical, 1991.

Johnson, Luke Timothy. 'Literary Criticism of Luke-Acts: Is Reception-History Pertinent?' *JSNT* 28 (2005): 159–62.

Johnson, Luke Timothy. *The Literary Function of Possessions in Luke-Acts*. SBLDS 39. Missoula, MT: Scholars, 1977.

Johnson, Luke Timothy. 'Social Dimension of Sōtēria in Luke-Acts and Paul'. In *Contested Issues in Christian Origins and the New Testament: Collected Essays*, 183–204. Leiden: Brill, 2013.

Jülicher, Adolf. *Die Gleichnisreden Jesu 2: Auslegung der Gleichnisreden der drei ersten Evangelien*. Tübingen: Mohr, 1910.

Karris, Robert J. *Eating Your Way through Luke's Gospel*. Collegeville: Order of Saint Benedict, 2006.

Karris, Robert J. 'Poor and Rich: The Lukan Sitz im Leben'. In *Perspectives on Luke-Acts*, edited by Charles H. Talbert, 112–25. Edinburgh: T&T Clark, 1978.

Keesmaat, Sylvia C. 'Strange Neighbors and Risky Care (Matt 18:21–25; Luke 14:7–14; Luke 10:25–37)'. In *The Challenge of Jesus' Parables*, edited by Richard N. Longenecker, 263–85. Grand Rapids: Eerdmans, 2000.

Kehoe, Dennis P. *Investment, Profit, and Tenancy: The Jurists and the Roman Agrarian Economy*. Ann Arbor: University of Michigan, 1997.

Kilgallen, John J. 'Forgiveness of Sins (Luke 7: 36–50)'. *NovT* 40 (1998): 105–16.

Kim, Kyoung-Jin. *Stewardship and Almsgiving in Luke's Theology*. JSNTSup 155. Sheffield: Sheffield Academic, 1998.

Kimball, Charles A. *Jesus' Exposition of the Old Testament in Luke's Gospel*. JSNTSup 94. Sheffield: Sheffield Academic, 1994.

Kittel, Gerhard and Gerhard Friedrich, eds. *Theological Dictionary of the New Testament*. Translated by Geoffrey W. Bromiley. 10 vols. Grand Rapids: Eerdmans, 1964–76.

Klein, Hans. *Das Lukasevangelium*. KEK. Vandenhoeck & Ruprecht, 2006.

Klinghardt, Matthias. *Gesetz und Volk Gottes: Das Lukanische Verständnis des Gesetzes nach Herkunft, Funktion und Seinem Ort in der Geschichte des Urchristentums*. WUNT 32. Tübingen: Mohr, 1988.

Klinghardt, Matthias. 'A Typology of the Communal Meal'. In *Meals in the Early Christian World*, edited by Dennis E. Smith and Hal Taussig, 9–22. New York: Macmillan, 2012.

Klink III, Edward W. 'The Gospel Community Debate: State of the Question'. *CurBR* 3.1 (2004): 60–85.

Kloppenborg, John S. 'The Dishonoured Master (Luke 16,1–8a)'. *Bib* 70.4 (1989): 474–95.

Kloppenborg, John S. *The Tenants in the Vineyard*. WUNT 195. Tübingen: Mohr, 2006.

Knibb, Michael A. 'The Ethiopic Book of Enoch'. In *Outside the Old Testament*, edited by M. De Jonge, 26–55. Cambridge: CUP, 1985.

Knowles, Michael P. 'What Was the Victim Wearing? Literary, Economic, and Social Contexts for the Parable of the Good Samaritan'. *BibInt* 12.2 (2004): 145–74.

Kreitzer, Larry. 'Luke 16:19–31 and 1 Enoch 22'. *ExpTim* 103 (1992): 139–42.

Kulandaisamy, Denis S. 'The Tender Mercy of God in the Magnificat (Lk 1:46–55)'. *EphM* 66 (2016): 61–74.

Landry, David and Ben May. 'Honor Restored: New Light on the Parable of the Prudent Steward (Luke 16:1–8a)'. *JBL* 119.2 (2000): 287–309.

Lanier, Gregory R. 'The Curious Case of צמח and ἀνατολή: An Inquiry into Septuagint Translation Patterns'. *JBL* 134.3 (2015): 505–27.

Lehtipuu, Outi. *The Afterlife Imagery in Luke's Story of the Rich Man and Lazarus*. NovTSup 123. Leiden: Brill, 2007.

Lehtipuu, Outi. 'Characterization and Persuasion: The Rich Man and the Poor Man in Lk 16.19–31'. In *Characterization in the Gospels: Reconceiving Narrative Criticism*, edited by David Rhoads and Kari Syreeni, 73–105. London: T&T Clark, 2004.

Lehtipuu, Outi. 'The Rich, the Poor, and the Promise of an Eschatological Reward in the Gospel of Luke'. In *Other Worlds and Their Relation to This World: Early Jewish and Ancient Christian Traditions*, edited by Tobias Nicklas et al., 229–46. JSJSup 143. Leiden: Brill, 2010.

Lenski, Gerhard E. *Power and Privilege: A Theory of Social Stratification*. New York: McGraw-Hill, 1966.
Levine, Amy-Jill. 'Luke and Jewish Religion'. *Int* 68.4 (2014): 389–402.
Levine, Amy-Jill and Marc Zvi Bretter. *The Jewish Annotated New Testament*. New York: Oxford University, 2011.
Liebenberg, J. 'The Function of the Standespredigt in Luke 3:1–20: A Response to E H Scheffler's the Social Ethics of the Lucan Baptist (Luke 3:10–14)'. *Neot* 27.1 (1993): 58–66.
Lieberman, Saul. 'Two Lexicographical Notes'. *JBL* 65 (1946): 69–72.
Litwak, Kenneth D. *Echoes of Scripture in Luke-Acts: Telling the History of God's People Intertextually*. JSNTSup 282. London: T&T Clark, 2005.
Loader, William. *Jesus' Attitude towards the Law: A Study of the Gospels*. Grand Rapids: Eerdmans, 2002.
Loewe, William P. 'Towards an Interpretation of Luke 19:1–10'. *CBQ* 36 (1974): 321–31.
Lohfink, Norbert. 'The Laws of Deuteronomy: A Utopian Project for a World without Any Poor'. *ScrB* 26.1 (1996): 2–19.
Longenecker, Bruce. *Remember the Poor: Paul, Poverty, and the Greco-Roman World*. Grand Rapids: Eerdmans, 2010.
MacMullen, Ramsay. *Roman Social Relations: 50 B.C. to A.D. 284*. London: Yale University, 1974.
Malherbe, Abraham J. 'The Christianization of a Topos (Luke 12:13–34)'. *NovT* 38.2 (1996): 123–35.
Malina, Bruce J. *The New Testament World: Insights from Cultural Anthropology*. Atlanta: John Knox, 1981.
Malipurathu, Thomas. *'Blessed Are You Poor!' Exploring the Biblical Impulses for an Alternative World Order*. Ishvani Kendra, India: SPCK, 2014.
Mallen, Peter. *The Reading and Transformation of Isaiah in Luke-Acts*. London: T&T Clark, 2008.
Manson, T.W. *The Sayings of Jesus*. London: SCM, 1977.
Marshall, I. Howard. 'Acts and the "Former Treatise"'. In *The Book of Acts in Its Ancient Literary Setting*, edited by Bruce W. Winter and Andrew D. Clarke, Vol. 1 of *The Book of Acts in Its First Century Setting*, 163–82. Grand Rapids: Eerdmans, 1993.
Marshall, I. Howard. *The Gospel of Luke: A Commentary on the Greek Text*. NIGTC. Exeter: Paternoster, 1978.
Marshall, I. Howard. 'How Does One Write on the Theology of Acts?' In *Witness to the Gospel: The Theology of Acts*, edited by I. Howard Marshall and David Peterson, 3–16. Cambridge: Eerdmans, 1998.
Marshall, I. Howard. '"Israel" and the Story of Salvation: One Theme in Two Parts'. In *Jesus and the Heritage of Israel: Luke's Narrative Claim upon Israel's Legacy*, edited by David P. Moessner, 340–57. Harrisburg: Trinity, 1999.
Marshall, Jonathan. *Jesus, Patrons, and Benefactors: Roman Palestine and the Gospel of Luke*. WUNT 2.259. Tübingen: Mohr, 2009.
Mason, Steve. *Josephus, Judea, and Christian Origins: Methods and Categories*. Peabody: Hendrickson, 2009.
McComiskey, Douglas S. *Lukan Theology in the Light of the Gospel's Literary Structure*. Carlisle: Paternoster, 2004.
McLaren, James S. 'Corruption among the High Priesthood: A Matter of Perspective'. In *A Wandering Galilean: Essays in Honour of Seán Freyne*, edited by Zuleika Rodgers et al., 141–57. JSJSup 132. Leiden: Brill, 2009.

Mealand, David L. *Poverty and Expectation in the Gospels*. London: SPCK, 1980.
Meggitt, Justin J. *Paul, Poverty and Survival*. Edinburgh: T&T Clark, 1998.
Meier, John P. 'Is Luke's Vision of the Parable of the Rich Fool Reflected in the Coptic Gospel of Thomas?' *CBQ* 74 (2012): 529–47.
Meier, John P. 'John the Baptist in Josephus: Philology and Exegesis'. *JBL* 111.2 (1992): 225–37.
Meier, John P. *A Marginal Jew: Rethinking the Historical Jesus, Vol. 4: Law and Love*. New Haven, Yale University, 2009.
Méndez-Moratalla, Fernando. *The Paradigm of Conversion in Luke*. JSNTSup 252. London: T&T Clark, 2004.
Merenlahti, Petri and Raimo Hakola. 'Reconceiving Narrative Criticism'. *Characterization in the Gospels: Reconceiving Narrative Criticism*, edited by David Rhoads and Kari Syreeni, 13–48. London: T&T Clark, 2004.
Metz, Johann B. 'La compasión. Un programa universal del cristianismo en la época de pluralismo cultural y religioso'. *RLT* 55 (2002): 25–32.
Metzger, James A. *Consumption and Wealth in Luke's Travel Narrative*. BibInt 88. Leiden: Brill, 2007.
Metzger, James A. 'Disability and the Marginalisation of God in the Parable of the Snubbed Host (Luke 14:15–24)'. *The Bible and Critical Theory* 6.2 (2010): 23.1–15.
Mineshige, Kiyoshi. *Besitzverzicht und Almosen bei Lukas: Wesen und Forderung des lukanischen Vermögensethos*. WUNT 163. Tübingen: Mohr, 2003.
Mitchell, Alan C. 'The Use of συκοφαντεῖν in Luke 19,8: Further Evidence for Zacchaeus's Defense'. *Bib* 72 (1991): 546–7.
Mitchell, Alan C. 'Zacchaeus Revisited: Luke 19,8 as a Defense'. *Bib* 71 (1990): 153–76.
Moessner, David P. *Lord of the Banquet: The Literary and Theological Significance of the Lukan Travel Narrative*. Harrisburg: Trinity, 1989.
Morlan, David S. *Conversion in Luke and Paul: An Exegetical and Theological Exploration*. London: Bloomsbury, 2013.
Morley, Neville. 'The Poor in the City of Rome'. In *Poverty in the Roman World*, edited by Margaret Atkins and Robin Osbourne, 21–39. Cambridge: CUP, 2006.
Moxnes, Halvor. *The Economy of the Kingdom: Social Conflict and Economic Relations in Luke's Gospel*. Eugene: Wipf & Stock, 1988.
Moxnes, Halvor. 'Patron-Client Relations and the New Community in Luke-Acts'. In *The Social World of Luke-Acts: Models for Interpretation*, edited by Jerome Neyrey, 241–68. Peabody: Hendrickson, 1991.
Moxnes, Halvor. 'Social Relations and Economic Interaction'. In *Luke-Acts: Scandinavian Perspective*, edited by Petri Luomanen, 58–75. Helsinki: Finnish Exegetical Society, 1991.
Moxnes, Halvor. 'The Social-Context of Luke's Community'. *Int* 48 (1994): 379–89.
Moyise, Steve. *Jesus and Scripture*. London: SPCK, 2010.
Nave, Guy D, Jr. *The Role and Function of Repentance in Luke-Acts*. Atlanta: SBL, 2002.
Navone, John. *Themes of St. Luke*. Rome: Gregorian University, 1971.
Neale, David A. *Luke 1–9: A Commentary in the Wesleyan Tradition*. NBBC. Kansas City: Beacon Hill, 2011.
Neale, David A. *None But the Sinners: Religious Categories in the Gospel of Luke*. JSNTSup 58. Sheffield: Sheffield Academic, 1991.
Newsom, Carol A. and Sharon H. Ringe, eds. *WBC*. London: SPCK, 1992.
Neyrey, Jerome H. 'Ceremonies in Luke-Acts: The Case of Meals and Table Fellowship'. In *The Social World of Luke-Acts: Models for Interpretation*, edited by Jerome Neyrey, 361–87. Peabody: Hendrickson, 1991.

Nickelsburg, George W.E. 'Revisiting the Rich and the Poor in 1 Enoch 92–105 and the Gospel according to Luke'. In *George W.E. Nickelsburg in Perspective: An Ongoing Dialogue of Learning*, edited by Jacob Neusner and Alan Avery-Peck, 547–71. JSJSup 80. Leiden: Brill, 2003.
Nickelsburg, George W.E. 'Riches and God's Judgement in Enoch and Luke'. *NTS* 25 (1979): 324–44.
Noble, Joshua A. '"Rich toward God": Making Sense of Luke 12:21'. *CBQ* 78 (2016): 302–20.
Nolland, John. *Luke*. 3 vols. WBC 35_A, 35_B, 35_C. Dallas: Word Books, 1989, 1993.
Nolland, John. 'Luke's Use of ΧΑΡΙΣ'. *NTS* 32.4 (1986): 614–20.
Nolland, John. 'Words of Grace (Luke 4,22)'. *Bib* 65.1 (1984): 44–60.
O'Hanlon, John. 'The Story of Zacchaeus and the Lucan Ethic'. *JSNT* (1981): 2–26.
Oakes, Peter. 'Constructing Poverty Scales for Graeco-Roman Society: A Response to Steven Friesen's "Poverty in Pauline Studies"'. *JSNT* (2004): 367–71.
Oakes, Peter. 'Methodological Issues in Using Economic Evidence in Interpretation of Early Christian Texts'. In *Engaging Economics: New Testament Scenarios and Early Christian Reception*, edited by Bruce W. Longenecker and Kelly D. Liebengood, 9–34. Grand Rapids: Eerdmans, 2009.
Oakman, Douglas. 'Countryside in Luke-Acts'. In *The Social World of Luke-Acts: Models for Interpretation*, edited by Jerome Neyrey, 151–79. Peabody: Hendrickson, 1991.
Oakman, Douglas. *Jesus and the Economic Questions of His Day*. Queenston, Canada: Edwin Mellen, 1986.
Oakman, Douglas. *Jesus and the Peasants*. Eugene: Cascade, 2008.
Osiek, Carolyn. *Rich and Poor in the Shepherd of Hermas: An Exegetical-Social Investigation*. CBQMS 15. Washington: Catholic Biblical Association, 1983.
Pao, David W. *Acts and the Isaianic New Exodus*. Grand Rapids: Baker, 2002.
Parsons, Mikeal C. *Body and Character in Luke and Acts: The Subversion of Physiognomy in Early Christianity*. Waco, TX: Baylor University, 2011.
Parsons, Mikeal C. *Luke*. Paideia. Grand Rapids: Baker, 2015.
Parsons, Mikeal C. and Richard I. Pervo. *Rethinking the Unity of Luke and Acts*. Minneapolis: Fortress, 1993.
Pastor, Jack. *Land and Economy in Ancient Palestine*. London: Routledge, 1997.
Pervo, Richard. 'Israel's Heritage and Claims upon the Genre(s) of Luke and Acts: The Problems of a History'. In *Jesus and the Heritage of Israel: Luke's Narrative Claim upon Israel's Legacy*, edited by David P. Moessner, 127–43. Harrisburg: Trinity, 1999.
Phillips, Thomas E. *Reading Issues of Wealth and Poverty in Luke-Acts*. Lewiston, NY: Edwin Mellen, 2001.
Pilgrim, Walter. *Good News to the Poor: Wealth and Poverty in Luke-Acts*. Minneapolis: Augsburg, 1981.
Pitre, Brant. *Jesus and the Last Supper*. Grand Rapids: Eerdmans, 2015.
Pitre, Brant. 'Jesus, the Messianic Banquet, and the Kingdom of God'. *Letter & Spirit* 5 (2009): 141–61.
Plich, John J. 'Sickness and Healing in Luke-Acts'. In *The Social World of Luke-Acts: Models for Interpretation*, edited by Jerome Neyrey, 181–209. Peabody: Hendrickson, 1991.
Polanyi, Karl. 'The Economy as Instituted Process'. In *Trade and Market in the Early Empires: Economics in History and Theory*, edited by Karl Polanyi et al., 243–70. Glencoe, IL: Falcon's Wing, 1957.
Porter, Stanley E. 'The Reasons for the Lucan Census'. In *Paul, Luke and the Graeco-Roman World*, edited by Alf Christophersen et al., 165–88. JSNTSup 217. London: T&T Clark, 2003.

Powell, Mark Allen. 'Narrative Criticism: The Emergence of a Prominent Reading Strategy'. In *Mark as Story: Retrospect and Prospect*, edited by Kelly R. Iverson and Christopher W. Skinner, 19–43. Atlanta: SBL, 2011.

Powell, Mark Allen. 'The Religious Leaders in Luke: A Literary-Critical Study'. *JBL* 109.1 (1990): 93–110.

Powell, Mark Allen. 'Toward a Narrative-Critical Understanding of Luke'. *Int* 48 (1994): 341–6.

Powell, Mark Allen. *What Is Narrative Criticism?: A New Approach to the Bible*. London: SPCK, 1993.

Powery, Emerson B. *Jesus Reads Scripture: The Function of Jesus' Use of Scripture in the Synoptic Gospels*. Leiden: Brill, 2003.

Price, Jonathan J. *Jerusalem under Siege: The Collapse of the Jewish State 66–70 C.E.* Leiden: Brill, 1992.

Priest, J. 'A Note on the Messianic Banquet'. In *The Messiah: Developments in Earliest Judaism and Christianity*, edited by James H. Charlesworth, 222–38. Minneapolis: Fortress, 1992.

Radl, Walter. *Das Evangelium Nach Lukas 1,1–9,50*. Freiburg im Breisgau, Germany: Herder, 2003.

Rajak, Tessa. *Josephus: The Historian and His Society*. 2nd edn. London: Duckworth, 2002.

Ramsey, George W. 'Plots, Gaps, Repetitions, and Ambiguity in Luke 15'. *PRSt* 17.1 (1990): 33–42.

Ravens, David. *Luke and the Restoration of Israel*. JSNTSup 119. Sheffield: Sheffield Academic, 1995.

Reardon, Timothy W. 'Cleansing through Almsgiving in Luke-Acts: Purity, Cornelius, and the Translation of Acts 15:9'. *CBQ* 78 (2016): 463–82.

Reardon, Timothy W. 'Recent Trajectories and Themes in Lukan Soteriology'. *CurBR* 12.1 (2012): 77–95.

Reed, Jonathan L. *Archaeology and the Galilean Jesus: A Re-Examination of the Evidence*. Harrisburg: Trinity, 2000.

Reeves, Jon Mark. 'Inheriting "Eternal Life" in Luke's Travel Narrative: Redaction and Narrative in Luke 9.51–19.44'. MA Thesis. Brite Divinity School, 2011. https://repository.tcu.edu/bitstream/handle/116099117/4344/ReevesJ.pdf?sequence=1.

Reinhold, Meyer. *History of Purple as a Status Symbol in Antiquity*. Collection Latomus 116. Bruxelles: Latomus, 1970.

Richardson, Alan. *The Miracle-Stories of the Gospels*. London: SCM, 1948.

Rindge, Matthew S. *Jesus' Parable of the Rich Fool: Luke 12:13–34 among Ancient Conversations on Death and Possessions*. SBLECL 6. Atlanta: SBL, 2011.

Rindge, Matthew S. 'The Rhetorical Power of Death and Possessions in Luke's Gospel'. *R&E* 112.4 (2015): 555–72.

Ringe, Sharon H. *Jesus, Liberation, and the Biblical Jubilee: Images for Ethics and Christology*. Philadelphia: Fortress, 1985.

Robinson, James M., Paul Hoffmann and John S. Kloppenborg, eds. *The Critical Edition of Q*. Hermeneia. Minneapolis: Fortress, 2000.

Rohrbaugh, Richard L. 'The Pre-Industrial City in Luke-Acts: Urban Social Relations'. In *The Social World of Luke-Acts: Models for Interpretation*, edited by Jerome Neyrey, 125–49. Peabody: Hendrickson, 1991.

Rollins, Wayne G. 'Eternal Life in John's Gospel: It's Playing Now'. In *Heaven, Hell, and the Afterlife: Eternity in Judaism, Christianity, and Islam*, edited by J. Harold Ellens, 9–29. Santa Barbara: Praeger, 2013.

Roose, Hanna. 'Umkehr und Ausgleich bei Lukas: Die Gleichnisse vom verlorenen Sohn (Luke 15.11–32) und vom reichen Mann und armen Lazarus (Luke 16.19–31) als Schwestergeschichten'. *NTS* 56.1 (2010): 1–21.

Roth, S. John. *The Blind, the Lame, and the Poor: Character Types in Luke-Acts*. JSNTSup 144. Sheffield: Sheffield Academic, 1997.

Rowe, C. Kavin. *Early Narrative Christology: The Lord in the Gospel of Luke*. Grand Rapids: Baker, 2009.

Rowe, C. Kavin. 'History, Hermeneutics and the Unity of Luke-Acts'. *JSNT* 28 (2005): 131–57.

Safrai, Ze'ev. *The Economy of Roman Palestine*. London: Routledge, 1994.

Sanders, Ed Parish. *Judaism: Practice and Belief, 63 BCE–66 CE*. London: SCM, 1992.

Sanders, James A. 'The Ethic of Election in Luke's Great Banquet Parable'. In *Luke and Scripture: The Function of Sacred Tradition in Luke-Acts*, edited by Craig A. Evans and James A. Sanders, 106–20. Minneapolis: Fortress, 1993.

Sanders, James A. 'Sins, Debts and Jubilee Release'. In *Text as Pretext: Essays in Honour of Robert Davidson*, edited by Robert P. Carroll, 273–81. JSOTSup 138. Sheffield: Sheffield Academic, 1992.

Scheffler, Eben. 'Luke's View on Poverty in Its Ancient (Roman) Economic Context: A Challenge for Today'. *Scriptura* 106 (2011): 115–35.

Scheffler, Eben. 'The Social Ethics of the Lucan Baptist (Luke 3:10–14)'. *Neot* 24.1 (1990): 21–36.

Scheidel, Walter and Steven J. Friesen. 'The Size of the Economy and the Distribution of Income in the Roman Empire'. *JRS* 99 (2009): 61–91.

Schellenberg, Ryan S. 'Which Master? Whose Steward? Metalepsis and Lordship in the Parable of the Prudent Steward (Luke 16.1–3)'. *JSNT* 30.3 (2008): 268–73.

Schiffman, Lawrence H. *The Eschatological Community of the Dead Sea Scrolls: A Study of the Rule of the Congregation*. SBLMS 38. Atlanta: Scholars, 1989.

Schottroff, Luise and Wolfgang Stegemann. *Jesus and the Hope of the Poor*. Translated by Matthew J. O'Connell. Maryknoll: Orbis, 1986.

Schumacher, R. Daniel. 'Saving Like a Fool and Spending Like It Isn't Yours: Reading the Parable of the Unjust Steward (Luke 16:1–8a) in Light of the Parable of the Rich Fool (Luke 12:16–20)'. *RevExp* 109.2 (2012): 269–76.

Schürer, Emil. *The History of the Jewish People in the Age of Jesus Christ (175 B.C.–A.D. 135)*. Edited by Geza Vermes and Fergus Millar. Vol. 1. London: T&T Clark, 1973.

Scott, Bernard Brandon. *Hear Then the Parable: A Commentary on the Parables of Jesus*. Minneapolis: Fortress, 1989.

Seccombe, David P. *Possessions and the Poor in Luke-Acts*. SNTSU 6. Linz: A. Fuchs, 1982.

Seim, Turid Karlsen. *The Double Message: Patterns of Gender in Luke-Acts*. Edinburgh: T&T Clark, 1994.

Sellew, Philip. 'Interior Monologue as a Narrative Device in the Parables of Luke'. *JBL* 111.2 (1992): 239–53.

Sellin, Gerhard. 'Lukas als Gleichniserzähler: Die Erzählung vom barmherzigen Samariter (Lk 10: 25–37)'. *ZNW* 65 (1974): 166–89.

Seo, Pyung Soo. *Luke's Jesus in the Roman Empire and the Emperor in the Gospel of Luke*. Eugene: Pickwick, 2015.

Shemesh, Aharon. '"The Holy Angels Are in Their Council": The Exclusion of Deformed Persons from Holy Places in Qumranic and Rabbinic Literature'. *DSD* 4.2 (1997): 179–202.

Sherwin-White, A.N. *Roman Foreign Policy in the East: 168 B.C. to 1 A.D.* London: Duckworth, 1984.
Sherwin-White, A.N. *Roman Society and Roman Law in the New Testament.* Grand Rapids: Baker, 1978.
Smallwood, E. Mary. 'High Priests and Politics in Roman Palestine'. *JTS* 18 (1962): 14–34.
Smallwood, E. Mary. *The Jews under Roman Rule: From Pompey to Diocletian – A Study in Political Relations.* Leiden: Brill, 1981.
Smit, Peter-Ben. *Fellowship and Food in the Kingdom: Eschatological Meals and Scenes of Utopian Abundance in the New Testament.* WUNT 2.234. Tübingen: Mohr, 2008.
Smit, Peter-Ben. 'Reaching for the Tree of Life: The Role of Eating, Drinking, Fasting, and Symbolic Foodstuffs in *4 Ezra*'. *JSJ* 45 (2014): 366–87.
Smith, Dennis E. *From Symposium to Eucharist: The Banquet in the Early Christian World.* Minneapolis: Fortress, 2003.
Smith, Dennis E. 'Messianic Banquet'. *ABD* 4 (1992): 788–91.
Smith, Dennis E. 'Table Fellowship as a Literary Motif in the Gospel of Luke'. *JBL* 106.4 (1987): 613–38.
Snodgrass, Klyne. 'Streams of Tradition Emerging from Isaiah 40:1–5 and Its Adaptation in the New Testament'. *JSNT* 8 (1980): 24–45.
Sobrino, Jon. *No Salvation Outside of the Poor: Prophetic-Utopian Essays.* Maryknoll: Orbis, 2008.
Sperber, Daniel. 'Costs of Living in Roman Palestine'. *JESHO* 8 (1965): 248–71.
Stanton, Graham. *Jesus and Gospel.* Cambridge: CUP, 2004.
Steele, E. Springs. 'Luke 11:37–54: A Modified Hellenistic Symposium'. *JBL* 103.3 (1984): 379–94.
Stegemann, Ekkehard W. and Wolfgang Stegemann. *The Jesus Movement: A Social History of Its First Century.* Translated by O.C. Dean, Jr. Edinburgh: T&T Clark, 1999.
Stenschke, Christoph W. *Luke's Portrait of Gentiles Prior to Their Coming to Faith.* WUNT 2.108. Tübingen: Mohr, 1999.
Stenschke, Christoph W. 'The Need for Salvation'. In *Witness to the Gospel: The Theology of Acts,* edited by I. Howard Marshall and David Peterson, 125–44. Cambridge: Eerdmans, 1998.
Stern, M. 'Aspects of Jewish Society: The Priesthood and Other Classes'. In *The Jewish People in the First Century II,* edited by S. Safrai and M. Stern, 561–630. Amsterdam: Compendia Rerum Iudaicarum ad Novum Testamentum, 1976.
Stigall, Josh. '"They Have Moses and the Prophets": The Enduring Demand of the Law and Prophets in the Parable of the Rich Man and Lazarus'. *R&E* 112.4 (2015): 542–54.
Tabor, James D. and Michael O. Wise. '4Q521 "on Resurrection" and the Synoptic Gospel Tradition: A Preliminary Study'. *JSP* 10 (1992): 149–62.
Talberts, Charles H. *Literary Patterns, Theological Themes and the Genre of Luke-Acts.* SBLMS 20. Missoula, MT: Scholars, 1974.
Tannahill, Reay. *Food in History.* London: Eyre Methuen, 1973.
Tannehill, Robert C. *The Narrative Unity of Luke-Acts: A Literary Interpretation.* 2 vols. Philadelphia: Fortress, 1986, 1990.
Tannehill, Robert C. *The Shape of Luke's Story: Essays on Luke-Acts.* Eugene: Cascade, 2005.
Taylor, Joan E. *The Immerser: John the Baptist within Second Temple Judaism.* Grand Rapids: Eerdmans, 1997.
Theissen, Gerd. *The Miracle Stories of the Early Christian Tradition.* Minneapolis: Fortress: 1983.

Thompson, Richard P. 'Gathered at the Table: Holiness and Ecclesiology in the Gospel of Luke'. In *Holiness and Ecclesiology in the New Testament*, edited by Kent Brower and Andy Johnson, 76–94. Grand Rapids: Eerdmans, 2007.
Trigo, Pedro. 'La misión en la Iglesia latinoamericana actual'. *RLT* 68 (2006): 161–94.
Tucker, W. Dennis, Jr. 'Democratization and the Language of the Poor in Psalms 2–89'. *HBT* 25 (2003): 161–78.
Turner, Max. *Power from on High: The Spirit in Israel's Restoration and Witness in Luke-Acts*. Sheffield: Sheffield Academic, 1996.
Twelftree, Graham H. *Jesus the Miracle Worker*. Downers Grove: InterVarsity, 1999.
Van Den Bergh, Rena. 'The Plight of the Poor Urban Tenant'. *RIDA* 50 (2003): 443–77.
Van Der Horst, Pieter W. 'Abraham's Bosom, the Place Where He Belonged: A Short Note on ἀπενεχθῆναι in Luke 16.22'. *NTS* 52.1 (2006): 142–4.
Veyne, Paul. *Bread and Circuses: Historical Sociology and Political Pluralism*. Translated by Brian Pearce. London: Penguin, 1990.
Veyne, Paul. 'Vie de Trimalcion'. *Annales. Économies, Sociétés, Civilisations* 16.2 (1961): 213–47.
Vijayaraj, R. John. 'Human Rights Concerns in the Lukan Infancy Narratives (Luke 1:5–2:52)'. *IJT* 46/1–2 (2004): 1–12.
Vogels, Walter. 'Having or Longing: A Semiotic Analysis of Luke 16:19–31'. *EgT* 29 (1989): 27–46.
Vogels, Walter. 'A Semiotic Study of Luke 7:11–17'. *EgT* 14 (1983): 273–92.
Walters, Patricia. *The Assumed Authorial Unity of Luke and Acts: A Reassessment of the Evidence*. Cambridge: CUP, 2008.
Wardle, Timothy. *The Jerusalem Temple and Early Christian Identity*. WUNT 2.291. Tübingen: Mohr, 2010.
Wasserberg, Gunter. *Aus Israels Mitte – Heil für die Welt: Eine Narrativ-Exegetische Studie zur Theologie des Lukas*. BZNW 92. Berlin: De Gruyter, 1998.
Watts, John D.W. *Isaiah 1–33*. WBC 24. Waco: Word Books, 1985.
Weinfeld, Moshe. *Deuteronomy I–II*. AB. New York: Doubleday, 1991.
Weinfeld, Moshe. '"Justice and Righteousness" – משפט צדקה – The Expression and Its Meaning'. In *Justice and Righteousness: Biblical Themes and Their Influence*, edited by Henning Graf Reventlow and Yair Hoffman, 228–46. JSOTSup 137. Sheffield: JSOT, 1992.
Wengst, Klaus. *Humility: Solidarity of the Humiliated*. Translated by John Bowden. London: SCM, 1988.
White, Richard C. 'Vindication for Zacchaeus?' *ExpTim* 91 (1979): 21.
Whittaker, C.R. 'The Poor'. In *The Romans*, edited by Andrea Giardina, translated by Lydia G. Cochrane, 272–309. Chicago: Chicago University, 1993.
Wild, John Peter. 'The Eastern Mediterranean, 323 BC–AD 350'. In *The Cambridge History of Western Textiles I*, edited by David Jenkins, 102–17. Cambridge: CUP, 2003.
Williams, Francis E. 'Is Almsgiving the Point of the "Unjust Steward"?' *JBL* 83 (1964): 293–7.
Williams, Rowan. *God with Us: The Meaning of the Cross and Resurrection. Then and Now*. Kindle edn. London: SPCK, 2017.
Wilson, Stephen G. *Luke and the Law*. SNTSMS 50. Cambridge: CUP, 1983.
Wink, Walter. *John the Baptist in the Gospel Tradition*. Cambridge: CUP, 1968.
Witherington, Ben. 'Salvation and Health in Christian Antiquity: The Soteriology of Luke-Acts in Its First Century Setting'. In *Witness to the Gospel: The Theology of Acts*, edited by I. Howard Marshall and David Peterson, 145–66. Cambridge: Eerdmans, 1998.

Wolter, Michael. *Das Lukasevangelium*. HNT 5. Tübingen: Mohr, 2008.
Woolf, Greg. 'Writing Poverty in Rome'. In *Poverty in the Roman World*, edited by Margaret Atkins and Robin Osborne, 83–99. Cambridge: CUP, 2006.
Wright, Christopher J.H. *God's People in God's Land: Family, Land and Property in the Old Testament*. Grand Rapids: Eerdmans, 1990.
Wright, Nicholas Thomas. *The New Testament and the People of God*. London: SPCK, 1992.
Wright, Stephen I. 'Parables on Poverty and Riches (Luke 12:13–21; 16:1–13; 16:19–31)'. In *The Challenge of Jesus' Parables*, edited by Richard N. Longenecker, 217–39. Grand Rapids: Eerdmans, 2000.
York, John O. *The Last Shall Be First: The Rhetoric of Reversal in Luke*. JSNTSup 46. Sheffield: Sheffield Academic, 1991.

INDEX

abomination 94
Abraham 51, 93 n.76, 96, 97–8, 99, 100, 107 n.23, 114–15, 120, 160, 163–4, 172
afterlife 92–3, 97–8, 136, 162–4
Allison, Dale C. 84
almsgiving 2 n.8, 3, 8, 19 n.113, 66, 138, 143, 144, 153
  and eternal life 123, 131–5
  redemptive aspects of 149–52
Annas (Ananus), high priest 33, 106–7
Antipater 24, 25
Apollonius, raising of dead young girl 86, 87
Applebaum, S. 24 n.8, 25 n.17–18, 27, 29
Augustus 49, 50 n.62, 56, 106

Bailey, Kenneth E. 53 n.88, 124 n.4, 125, 133, 145 n.39, 148 n.57. *See also* food; meal(s); messianic banquet
banquet 10, 161–4
  Hellenistic influences 155 n.6, 164–5
  Herod Antipas's birthday 31
  ranking and ritual purity at 157–8, 166, 167–8
Barclay, John 12 n.74, 75, 79, 176
Baruch 155–6, 157
Bauckham, Richard 17, 18 n.105, 77, 93 n.77, 129
Beavis, Mary Ann 146, 147 n.54, 148 n.57
begging/beggar 6, 7, 171. *See also* Lazarus, poor man
Berger, Klaus 151
Bird, Michael F. 18–19
Boethus, High priest 33, 38
Bovon, François 2, 104, 118 n.93, 131, 163
Braun, Willi 164–5, 170
Brooke, George J. 112
Broshi, Magen 46 n.25, 47 n.37
Byrne, Brendan 78

Caesar, Julius 24, 30
Caiaphas, High priest 106–7
Carcopino, Jérôme 55, 58
Carroll, John T. 166, 169 n.102
Chancey, Mark Alan 29 n.45
Charlesworth, James H. 158
cleanness/uncleanness 29 n.44, 151–2, 158
clothing 10, 16, 19, 20, 43–4, 54, 118
  daily clothing 55–6
  and economic disparity 56–8
  sharing of 59, 121, 136–7, 151
  as status marker 54 n.93, 58
comfort 110–11
commandments. *See* law (commandments)
compassion 66, 129, 130
  and miracles 86–92, 100
Conzelmann, Hans 94, 95 n.90, 103 n.4
Crowfoot, Elisabeth 55

death 156, 142–4. *See also* afterlife
debt 7, 17, 20, 25, 39–41, 52, 53–4, 59
  reduction of 40 n.128, 53, 145–6
  release of 42, 67–9, 70, 82, 121
  voluntary remission of 146
debt slavery 36, 52–3, 68, 82
Degenhardt, Hans-Joachim 3 n.8, 7 n.50
Derrett, J. Duncan M. 127 n.22, 129, 145, 148 n.57
disability/disabled 9–10, 51, 82, 155
  exclusion from banquet 158, 159
  guests at banquet 167–8, 169, 171–2
  Jesus' healing of 70, 91–2
divine justice 5, 8, 20, 80
  and reversal 92–8
  and salvation of poor 100–2
divine mercy 2, 5
  human embodiment of 20, 59, 65–6, 78–9, 123, 135–7, 138, 152–3, 174–5
  and repentance 75
  and restoration 78–9

and reversal   71
and salvation   3, 8, 15, 20, 64–6, 80, 100–2
and suffering   72
doing   2. *See also* what must we/I do?
  God's   70–1
  good deeds   114–16
  the law   95–6, 124–5, 135–7
  mercy and justice   20, 116–21, 174–5
  and one's relation to the needy/poor   76
  salvific sufficiency of   135
Donahue, John R.   107 n.21, 146, 148 n.57
dropsy   91–2, 165, 166
Duncan-Jones, Richard   11, 12
Dupont, Jacques   6, 8, 99, 101

economic disparity   20, 96–7, 174, 177
  and clothing   56–8
  and food   51–4
economy, Roman   38
  cost of living   11–12
  Herodian economics   26–7
  money value   10, 11, 12–14
Elymas, the magician   113
Ermakov, Arseny   135–6
Esler, Philip   7, 70, 129, 130, 169 n.103
eternal destiny
  means to   59
  and wealth   1, 146–9, 153, 175
eternal life   73, 76, 125–6
  and almsgiving   131–5
  and law   95–6, 123, 124–5, 126–7, 131, 135–7
  and mercy   127–30
Eubank, Nathan   67 n.24, 69 n.32
Evans, C.F.   76 n.81, 133
Evans, Craig A.   84 n.19, 127 n.22

faith, vis-à-vis miracle and salvation   90–2, 176
famine   25, 29, 48–51, 162
Farris, Stephen   110
Finley, Moses I.   32, 38
Fitzmyer, Joseph A.   98, 104, 145, 148 n.57
food   8, 10, 16, 19, 20, 23, 43–4, 59, 118, 154, 174. *See also* banquet; meal(s)
  abundance of   17, 45, 156, 157, 162
  costs   12, 13
  crisis   48–51, 52, 58, 162
  daily bread   45–8
  daily calorie intake   12
  defined   44
  and economic disparity   51–4
  functions of   45 n.17, 45 n.19
  hoarding of   51–2, 59
  sharing of   59, 121, 136–7, 151
  shortages of   29
forgiveness   10 n.62, 66–7, 69, 76 n.78, 78 n.90, 108, 121
Foxhall, Lin   29
Freyne, Seán   27, 32
Friesen, Steve J.   10, 12, 13, 14

Gaius (jurist)   43
Galilee
  ethnic identity of population   29
  under Herod Antipas   32 n.68
  Josephus depiction of Galileans   32
  landholding patterns   24, 26–7
  local wealthy aristocrats   31
  royal estates   30
Garnsey, Peter   44, 45 n.19, 47, 48 n.47, 53 n.84
gate   97–8, 100–1
generosity   42, 59, 65, 69, 75, 79, 118, 121, 152
gentiles   19, 29, 74 n.63, 89 n.53, 151
gift   79, 176
God   141. *See also* divine justice; divine mercy
  coming of   110–12, 174
  direct speech of   140, 143
  goodness of   135–6
  imitation of   65, 75
  judgement of   115, 116, 143, 164
  love towards   127, 128
  reign of   82, 84–6, 94, 98–9, 101, 111, 174
  and reversal   71–2
  saving action of   63, 64, 71, 74–5, 83, 89–90, 130
Goodman, Martin   32, 39 n.123
good news
  and John's teachings   105, 108–9, 111
  to the poor   2–3, 5, 6, 65, 81–6, 90, 96, 100, 101
Goodrich, John K.   146
Goulder, Michael D.   123 n.1

grace 67–8
gratitude 87, 91
greed 92 n.68, 141, 143, 144, 152, 164 n.72, 166
Green, Joel B. 6, 70, 74 n.64, 75, 76, 104 n.7, 104 n.10, 118, 159 n.33, 159 n.36

Hades 97, 98, 99 n.118, 136, 163, 164, 169
Hamel, Gildas 49 n.61, 54 n.94, 56
Harrison, James R. 65 n.10, 176 n.3
Hartsock, Chad 92 n.68
Hasmonaean kingdom 24, 25, 28
Hays, Christopher M. 53 n.88, 134 n.59, 145 n.37, 148
Herod Antipas, Tetrarch of Galilee 26, 27, 29 n.44, 30, 31, 32 n.68, 105, 106–7, 108
Herodias 105, 107
Herod the Great 25, 26, 28 n.92, 30, 31, 32, 33 n.76–7, 39, 48 n.50, 54 n.96, 106
Herzog, William R. 145
high priests 32–3, 107
  clothing 56
  land ownership 33–5
Hirschfeld, Yizhar 28 n.92
hoarding 51–2, 59, 141, 142–3, 144
Hock, Ronald F. 92 n.70, 93
honour and shame 145–6, 148 n.57, 166–7, 170
hospitality 78, 131 n.42, 147–8
Hoyt, Thomas 6 n.43
humility 87, 98, 166
hunger/hungry 6, 7, 8, 9–10, 17, 20, 59
  experience of 51, 162
  fulfilment of 66 n.16, 78–9
  and reversal 72, 73
Hyrcanus, John, High priest 24, 25

imitatio Dei 65, 75
interest 53–4, 145
Ireland, Dennis J. 145
Israel
  'alms to Israel' 151
  exilic status of 112 n.59
  poor as 4–5
  rejection of 170
  restoration of 76 n.78, 77–8

Jantsch, Torsten 121
Jensen, Morton Hørning 26, 32
Jeremias, Joachim 98, 99, 161 n.52
Jerusalem
  famine 49–50
  good news to 84
  high priestly families 33–5
  Jesus' journey to 76
  tithes 37
  wealthy aristocrats 32
Jesus Christ 5, 19, 23 n.6, 42, 109 n.34, 111 n.51, 120
  birth of 106
  bringer/enactor of good news 85, 86, 87, 90
  call to follow 131–4
  on clothing 57, 59
  on doing 115
  on faith 91
  on generosity 118
  and grace 67
  healing accounts of 70, 78, 91, 165
  on hoarding food 52 n.73
  hunger experience 51
  identity as messiah 87, 89
  and Israel's restoration 77–8
  and John compared 94–5, 106 n.14
  and law 95–6
  messianic expectations 115–16
  ministry of 8, 20, 66, 67, 73, 81, 82–3, 85, 103
  on money 47 n.40
  physical and theological journey of 76
  plot against 31 n.58, 35
  preparing the way of 110–14
  release of sin 69
  and religious leaders 126
  resurrection of dead 83, 86–90, 91
  reversal in life of 70 n.45
  saving activity 65
  Sermon on the Plain 115, 130
  on sharing 59
  table fellowship 44 n.12, 161
  woman anointing 16
Jews
  clothing 56
  large landowners 29
  and Samaritans 128–9, 130
  taxation 38–9
  tax farming 107

Index

Johnson, Luke T. 4, 17, 94, 154 n.1
John the Baptist 20, 41, 42
   death of 107, 108
   and Jesus compared 94–5, 106 n.14
   on Jesus' identity as messiah 89
   and Lord relationship 110
   Luke's account of 104–5
   on repentance 74, 75–6, 175
   salvific message of 105
   teachings of 103–4, 121–2, 175
      eschatological context 114–16
      historical and political context 106–8
      Josephus on 108
      on sharing 54, 59, 151
      socio-economic aspects 116–21
      soteriological context 108–14
Joseph the Tobiad 107 n.24–5
Judaea 26 n.25
   census 27, 106
   ethnic identity of population 29
   famines 48
   high priestly families 38 n.116, 107
   landholding patterns 24, 27–9
   royal estates 30
   taxation 28, 38–9
judgement 35, 105, 115, 116, 143, 148, 164
Jülicher, Adolf 145
justice 65, 77, 82. *See also* divine justice
   John's teachings 108
   and repentance 103, 116–21

Karris, Robert J. 44 n.14
Kim, Kyoung-Jin 2 n.8
kingdom of God 81–6, 94, 95, 111, 123 n.1, 126, 131–2, 134–5, 143 n.23, 152–3, 154–5, 159–61, 165–8, 169, 172, 173, 176
Klinghardt, Matthias 94–5
Kloppenborg, John 35, 145, 148 n.57
knowledge 110, 113–14

land 10, 16, 19, 20, 41, 68 n.27
   inheritance of 125
   as wealth 23–4
   landholding patterns 24–5
      in Galilee 26–7
      in Judaea 24, 27–9
   landowners/landownership 25
      absentee landlords 31, 32, 38, 53

Herodian family 30
high priestly families 33–5, 38 n.116
hoarding of grains 51–2, 59
Judaea 27–8
large landowners 28 n.92, 29–30
local wealthy aristocrats 31–3
and tenants relationship 39–41
Landry, David 145–6, 148 n.57
law (commandments) 20, 54 n.91, 123, 175
   and eternal life 95–6, 124–5, 126–7, 131, 135–7
   and good news 94–5
Lazarus, poor man 10, 51, 93, 96–8, 100, 162–4
   salvation of 98–9
Lehtipuu, Outi 5, 66 n.16, 73, 99 n.118
lepers
   Naaman, the leper 83, 87
   Samaritan leper 91
Loader, William 125, 129, 133, 135
Longenecker, Bruce W. 13 n.82

Magnificat 64, 70–1, 72 n.52, 73, 76, 93, 100
Malipurathu, Thomas 7, 72 n.54
Marshall, Howard 4, 18 n.109, 91, 133, 149
Mary, mother of Jesus 71, 72, 113
May, Ben 145–6, 148 n.57
McLaren, James S. 34 n.83
meal(s) 8, 155. *See also* banquet; food
   communal meals 44
   gluttonous 58
   price of 10
   Sabbath 165
Meier, John P. 108, 130 n.35, 141
mercy 65–6, 82, 123. *See also* divine mercy
   and eternal life 127–30
   and repentance 20, 103, 116–21
   and righteousness 151
messianic banquet 8–9, 17, 20, 59, 66, 73, 78–9, 85 n.24, 97 n.101, 154–5, 172–3, 175. *See also* food
   and earthly banquet 161–4
   exclusions from 158, 159, 160–1, 163, 169
   invitees to 165–8, 171–2
   in Jewish apocalyptic traditions 155–9
   readings of 169–70
   significance of 154 n.1

Metzger, James   131, 145, 171 n.124
Meyer, Rudolf   163
Micyllus the cobbler (fictitious
    character)   52, 54, 93
Mineshige, Kiyoshi   2 n.8
miracle   15, 81
    and compassion   86–92
Mitchell, Alan C.   119 n.99, 120
Moessner, David P.   76 n.81
money   10
    defraud   119
    denarii   11, 12, 13, 14
    drachmae   11, 13–14
    Jesus' criticism of   47 n.40
    lepta   10, 11, 12
morality   74 n.63, 92 n.68, 93, 98, 99,
    151 n.81
Moses   74, 94, 96, 98, 99, 164
Moxnes, Halvor   5, 18 n.105, 53–4,
    134 n.62, 145, 152

Nave, Guy R., Jr.   74, 109 n.38,
    115 n.75
Neale, David A.   10 n.62, 66–7
neighbour   65, 118–19, 126, 127–130,
    136, 167
Nickelsburg, George W.E.   8, 141
Nolland, John   67, 111 n.49, 139 n.3, 149,
    150 n.70, 152 n.86, 160

Oakman, Douglas   11, 13 n.77, 28 n.33,
    37, 41, 47 n.40
orphans/fatherless   6, 10, 51, 81, 82, 85,
    86, 89, 100 n.124, 102

Palestine (Roman)
    economic situation   35
    landholding patterns in   24–9
    landowners profile   29–35
    socio-economic conditions of   19–20,
       41–2, 107
    taxation   37–8
    tenancy   35–7
parables
    the good Samaritan   11, 13, 14, 42, 57,
       66, 126, 127–30, 137
    the great banquet   154, 155, 159,
       164–9, 173
    the prodigal son   139

the rich fool   51–2, 59, 139–44,
    152–3, 164
the rich man and Lazarus   10 n.63,
    72, 74, 93, 96–9, 100, 136, 139,
    162–4
of tenants in the vineyard   35, 42
of unjust steward   53, 94, 138,
    139–40, 144–9, 153
of widow and unjust judge   148
Parsons, Mikeal C.   18, 65 n.12, 67 n.21,
    92 n.68
Pastor, Jack   26, 28 n.37
Pervo, Richard I.   18
Pharisees   5, 10 n.62, 31 n.58, 45 n.16, 92
    n.68, 94, 95 n.89, 107, 115 n.73,
    144, 146, 147, 151–2, 164, 165,
    166 n.87
Philip the Tetrarch   26, 105, 106–7
Phillips, Thomas E.   1 n.1
piety   87, 89, 92, 98–9, 101, 108, 150,
    174, 176
Pilgrim, Walter   5
Pompey the Great   24, 29
Pontius Pilate   106–7
poor
    blessedness of   155
    clothing of   58
    daily bread   46 n.25
    definition of   9–11
       socio-economic and spiritual
          understanding of   5–7, 8
       socio-economic understanding
          of   4
       spiritual and religious
          understanding of   3–5
    eschatological rewards for   66 n.16
    good news to the   2–3, 5, 6, 65, 81–6,
       87, 90, 96, 100, 101
    John's concern for   117–18
    and messianic banquet   78–9, 167–8,
       169, 171–2
    physical location of   9–10
    and reversal   72, 93
    salvation of   1–2, 3, 8, 20, 81, 98–9,
       100–2, 174, 176
    and salvation of rich   2, 3, 20,
       154–5, 176
    tithes to   37
Porter, Adam Lowry   29 n.45

Possessions. *See also* wealth
  abundance of 142–3
  proper use of 74
  renunciation of 2 n.8, 95
poverty scale 10, 11–14
Powery, Emerson B. 129, 135
price/s
  of clothing 56–7
  of wheat 12–13, 14, 53 n.89, 57
Ptolemy 31, 107 n.24

Quirinius, governor of Syria 27, 106

Radl, Walter 104, 107 n.23
Ravens, David 77, 78 n.90–1
Reardon, Timothy W. 151 n.81
reciprocity 146, 166–7, 168, 170
release 17, 42, 65, 66–70, 77, 79, 80, 81–2, 121
  and physical healing 91–2
rent 23, 36–7
renunciation 2 n.8, 95
  and discipleship 131–4
repentance 8, 65, 73–7, 79, 80, 161 n.52, 175
  baptism of 108, 110, 114–15, 120–1
  bearing fruits vis-à-vis 114–21
  call to 95
  and doing mercy and justice 20, 103, 116–21
  and ethical transformation 74–5
  and good news 84 n.19
  and rich 4, 99
  turning as 109–10
restoration 77–9, 80
resurrection
  of dead 83, 86–90, 91, 10, 169
  of righteous 125, 158–9, 167, 168–9
reversal 59, 65, 70–3, 79, 80, 99
  and justice 92–8
  and messianic banquet 156, 158, 162–4, 166, 167
  and piety 98–9
reward 65, 66, 72–3, 167, 168, 176
  eschatological 66 n.16, 72–3
  in Matthew 67 n.24
  and restoration 79
  treasures in heaven as 133–5, 144, 152, 164, 173

rich
  afterlife of 136, 162–4
  blessedness of 168–9, 172
  clothing of 57, 96 n.98
  definition of
    negative examples 5
    socio-economic understanding of 10
    spiritual and socio-economic understanding of 5–6
  diet of 47, 48
  and messianic banquet 59, 78–9, 172–3
  negative attitude towards 8, 10
  and repentance 4, 99
  and reversal 72, 93
  salvation of 2, 3, 20, 154–5, 175, 176
righteous 125, 126, 134, 149–52, 156–7, 158–9, 167, 168–9, 173
Rindge, Matthew S. 140 n.10, 142 n.21, 144
Roman Empire 17
  clothing in 58
  cost of living in 11–12
  famine 49
  food crisis 48
  taxation 37–8
Roth, John 4–5

Safrai, Ze'ev 58
salvation 19
  aspects of 63, 66–80, 174
  coming 154–5, 156–7, 158, 172–3
  diverse references to 63, 66
  in socio-economic terms 1–2, 63–4, 79–80, 177
Samaria 24, 25, 30
Samaritan/s 77 n.87
  good Samaritan 11, 13, 14, 42, 57, 66, 127–30, 137
  leper 91
Sanders, James A. 37, 165 n.78
Scheffler, Eben H. 10, 104, 116–17
Scheidel, Walter 12, 13 n.82
Schellenberg, Ryan S. 148 n.59
Schiffman, Lawrence H. 157–8
Schottroff, Luise 7
Scobie, Charles H.H. 115 n.76, 116 n.84
Seccombe, David P. 4, 5

Seo, Pyung Soo   106 n.14
Setne Khamwas and Si-Osire (Setne II)
   92–3, 97
sharing   54, 59, 117–18, 121,
   136–7, 151
Shema   124, 126
Simeon's prophecy   114, 116
Simon the Pharisee   69
sinners/sin   6, 10, 95 n.89, 147, 161
   forgiveness of   66–7, 69
   release from   67–70, 77
   repentance of   67
Smallwood, E. Mary   24 n.8, 28 n.33
socio-economic issues   1–2, 16–17,
   19–20, 63–4, 79–80, 138, 170,
   174, 177
   and John's teachings   107, 116–21
   poor/rich defined in terms of   4, 5–7
   and release   70
   and repentance   74
soldiers   107–8, 117–18, 170
soliloquy   139
Stegemann, Ekkehard W.   11
Stegemann, Wolfgang   7, 11, 12, 13 n.81
Stenschke, Christoph   74
stewardship   53, 144–6, 147, 148

table fellowship   44 n.12, 45, 146, 147,
   157–8, 161, 173
Talbert, Charles H.   123 n.1, 126 n.19
Tannehill, Robert C.   75
tax   20, 23, 25, 26
   burden of   37–9
   collection of   107–8
   Herodian   27 n.29
   land tax (*tributum soli*)   28, 37
   poll tax (*tributim capitis*)   28, 37,
      39, 106
tax collectors   6, 10, 95 n.89, 107–8,
   117–18, 147
tenants   35–7, 53 n.88
   and landlords relationship   39–41
   parable of   35, 42
   revolts by   39
Theissen, Gerd   90–1
tithes   34, 37

travel/journey, repentance as   74 n.64,
   75–6
Twelftree, Graham H.   91

Van der Horst, Pieter   163 n.60

Walters, Patricia   18 n.106
Wasserberg, Gunter   77–8
wealth   1–3, 10, 19. *See also* clothing;
   food; land
   and death   142–4
   and eternal dwelling   146–9, 153
   ill-gotten   149, 151–2
   markers of   20
   and repentance   8
   use of   20, 138, 140, 144, 149–53, 164,
      175 (*see also* almsgiving)
Wengst, Klaus   72 n.52
what must we/I do?   2, 8, 15, 20, 103,
   120, 138, 176. *See also* doing
   and debt   53
   and eternal life   127–8, 132–3
   and John's teachings   116–21, 122
   and repentance   74, 76–7
   solution to   149–50
Whittaker, C.R.   45 n.20
widow(s)   6, 51, 81, 82
   at Nain   81, 83, 86–90, 91, 100
   poor widow   10, 11, 12, 14, 42
   protection of   85
   release/deliverance to   86
   Sidonian widow   83, 86, 87
   status of   89
   of Zarephath   12, 50
wilderness   112
Williams, Francis E.   150
Wilson, Stephen G.   95, 125, 129, 133,
   135
Wolter, Michael   17 n.104, 118, 131 n.46
Wright, Nicholas Thomas   76 n.78, 77 n.82,
   78 n.91

Yadin, Yigael   55, 56
York, John O.   70 n.45–6, 73 n.60

Zacchaeus   119–20, 131

ANCIENT INDEX

OLD TESTAMENT
Genesis (Gen)
15	93 n.76
18.8	47 n.43
21.1	89 n.53
41.42	54 n.93
47.13–26	52 n.82
47.15	44 n.7
50.24, 25	89 n.53

Exodus (Exod)
3.16	89 n.53
4.31	89 n.53
13.19	89 n.53
20.12–16	123, 124, 133, 135
21, 23	68 n.27
21.2–3	68
21.2–4	82, 99
22.25	54 n.91
22.25–27	38 n.117
22.26–27	44 n.8, 56
23.6	100 n.124
23.10–1	99
23.10–11	68, 82
24.3–11	154 n.5
28.2–4	59 n.139
28.35	57 n.120
29.5, 21, 29	59 n.139
31.10 LXX	59 n.139
34.6	65 n.11
36.35	57 n.120

Leviticus (Lev)
6.1–5	120 n.108
6.2 LXX	152 n.82
18.5	96 n.94
18.5 LXX	125 n.11, 127 n.24
19	16, 135–6
19.2	75, 136
19.2 LXX	65, 130 n.37
19.3, 9–10, 11, 13–18, 33–36	135 n.68
19.9–10, 13–18, 33–37	65
19.9–18, 33–37	118
19.9–19, 33–34	136
19.11 LXX	118–19
19.15	100 n.124
19.18	123, 126, 127, 128, 135
21.17–21	158 n.27
25	41, 68, 82, 99, 118
25.10	69 n.32, 82
25.13–55	118
25.14, 17	118
25.25–28, 35–54	41 n.130
25.25–28, 35–55	38 n.117
25.25, 35, 39, 47, 48	118
25.25–55	42
25.35–46	82 n.7
25.36–37	54 n.91
25.39–43	53 n.83
25.39–54	68

Numbers (Num)
5.15	46 n.31
18.21–32	37 n.107

Deuteronomy (Deut)
4.1	125 n.11
4.31	65 n.11
5.16–20	123, 133, 135
5.16–21	123, 124, 126
6–8	125 n.10
6.4–5	123, 124, 126, 127, 128
6.5	135
6.24 LXX	125 n.11
8.1	125
10.9	34 n.86
10.17–18	85 n.27
10.18	100 n.124
11.8	125
12.12	34 n.86
14.28–29	37 n.107
15	16, 68 n.27, 121
15.1	69 n.32
15.1–11	82

15.1–18	38 n.117, 41, 42, 65, 68, 69, 82, 99, 118	17.12 LXX	12
		17.17–24	87 n.40
15.4	16, 69 n.37	17.23 LXX	87
15.4–8	99 n.116	18.2	50
15.7–14	82 n.7		
15.7, 9	85 n.27	**2 Kings (2 Kgs)**	
15.11	7 n.50, 16, 69	4.1–2	68 n.28
15.12–18	53 n.83, 68, 82	4.8–37	86 n.31
18.1	34 n.86	4.42–43	46 n.31
18.15, 18	89	5.1–19	83 n.11
20	170		
20.5–7	170	**1 Chronicles (1 Chr)**	
24.4	94	12.38–40	158 n.28
24.6	99 n.116	15.27	57 n.120
24.12, 14, 15	7 n.50	**2 Chronicles (2 Chr)**	
24.14, 19–21	85 n.27	5.12	57 n.120
24.17	100 n.124	28.1–15	127 n.22
25.16	94	28.15	44 n.5
26.12	37 n.107	30.9	65 n.11
27.15	94 n.81		
27.19	100 n.124	**Nehemiah (Neh)**	
29.17	94 n.81	5.1	68 n.28
30.11–14	93 n.76	5.1–5	53 n.84
30.16 LXX	125	5.1–13	52 n.82
32.5	113 n.65	5.2	44 n.7
32.16 LXX	94 n.81	5.3	25 n.19
32.47 LXX	125 n.11	5.11	54 n.91
		9.17, 31	65 n.11
Judges (Judg)		10.37–39	37 n.107
5.8 LXX	46 n.31		
7.13	46 n.31	**Esther (Est)**	
		8.15	54 n.93
Ruth (Ru/Rth)		**Job**	
1.6	89 n.53	22.6–7	44 n.5
1 Samuel (1 Sam)		24.7	44 n.8, 54 n.95
15.29	109 n.37	24.7 LXX	56
28.24	47 n.43	24.10	44 n.5
		35.9 LXX	118 n.97
2 Samuel (2 Sam)			
2.10	64 n.9	**Psalms (Pss/Ps)**	
4.10 LXX	84 n.18	1.3–4	116 n.82
22.3	64 n.9	6.8	160 n.44
		6.9 LXX	160 n.44
1 Kings (1 Kgs)		14.1	143–4
2.26	34 n.86	18.2	64 n.9
11.5 LXX	94 n.81	49.10 LXX	143–4
17.1–24	87 n.40	53.1	143–4
17.7–24	86	68.6–7	85 n.27
17.8–12	12	68.17	65 n.11
17.8–24	83 n.11	76.8–10	85 n.27
17.10 LXX	87 n.36		

77.8	113 n.65	5.1–7	35
77.38	65 n.11	5.5–6	35
82	85 n.27	5.7	35
85.15	65 n.11	5.8–9	35
89.25	64 n.9	10.2	100 n.124, 101 n.128
102.8	65 n.11	10.2 LXX	152 n.82
103.6	85 n.27, 100 n.124	10.15–16, 33–34	115 n.73
107.9	51 n.69	14.30	85 n.27
110.4	65 n.11	24.21	156 n.13
111.4–5	65	25	155, 156, 160 n.41, 172
132.14–18	85 n.27	25.4–5, 8	85 n.27
132.17	64 n.9	25.6	156
140.13	85 n.27	25.6–8	156, 158 n.31
144.8	65 n.11	25.7–8	156
144.8–9	65 n.11	25.9	156
146	82	25.10–12	156
146.5–9	51 n.69	25.10b, 12	156
146.7	100 n.124	26.5–6	156
146.7–10	85 n.27	26.19	156
		26.19 LXX	82 n.8

Proverbs (Prov)

2.15	113 n.65	27.1	156
4.24	113 n.65	29.18	82
8.8	113 n.65	29.19–2	85 n.27
10.2	134 n.60	32.7	100 n.124
10.2 LXX	151	35.2–10	85 n.27
11.4	134 n.60	35.5–6	82
14.31	118 n.97	40–55 LXX (52)	112 n.53
15.27 LXX	150 n.74	40–66	110
19.17	65	40.1–11	110–11, 112 n.53
21.8	113 n.65	40.1–11 LXX	110–11, 114
22.5, 14	113 n.65	40.2, 11 LXX	111 n.46
22.16	118 n.97	40.3	110, 112, 113
23.33	113 n.65	40.3 LXX	114
25.6–7	166	40.3–5	112 n.53, 112 n.59
28.3 LXX	118 n.97	40.3–5 LXX	105, 108, 109, 110, 111, 114
28.18	113 n.65	40.3–6 LXX	75–6, 120

Ecclesiastes (Eccl)

4.1 LXX	118 n.97	40.4 LXX	111
5.7 LXX	152 n.82	40.5 LXX	111 n.47, 113
		40.9 LXX	84

Isaiah (Isa)

LXX	84, 85	40.9–11	85 n.27
1	94, 99	41.15–16	116 n.82
1.5–6, 17, 23	99 n.116	41.17	85 n.27
1.10–23	94 n.82	42.16	113 n.65
1.13 LXX	94 n.82	46.8	109 n.37
1.17	100 n.124, 101 n.128	46.13	85 n.27
3.14	100 n.124, 152 n.82	50.1	68 n.28
		51.5	85 n.27

52.7 LXX	84	**Joel**	
52.10	111 n.47	2.13	65 n.11
52.10 LXX	114 n.68	2.13, 14	109 n.37
52.14	112 n.60	2.18–27	159 n.32
55.1–2	159 n.32	3.1–5 LXX	120
58	41	3.5 LXX	113–14
58.2–9	101 n.128	**Amos (Am)**	
58.6	42, 68, 81–2	2.6	68 n.28
58.6 LXX	68	5	99
58.6–7	44 n.5	5.11 [LXX]	100–1
60.6 LXX	84	5.12 [LXX]	100, 101
61	82	5.12–15	99 n.116
61.1	69 n.32, 70 n.40, 82	5.14–15	101 n.128
61.1 LXX	82, 84	5.15	101
61.1–2	7 n.50, 41, 42, 68	5.15a	101
61.1–2 LXX	113 n.66	7.3, 6	109 n.37
61.1–2a	82	7.17	34 n.86
61.1, 7–8, 11	85 n.27	21–4	101 n.128
61.2b	81	**Jonah (Jon)**	
62.10	112 n.60	3.9, 10	109 n.37
67.1	85 n.27	4.2	65 n.11, 109 n.37
Jeremiah (Jer)		**Zechariah (Zech)**	
1.1	106 n.12	1.1 LXX	106 n.12
1.2 4.28	109 n.37	3.8	64 n.9
5.28	100 n.124	6.12	64 n.9
8.6 LXX	109 n.37	7.9–10	101 n.128, 102
18.8, 10	109 n.37	8.14	109 n.37
22.3	100 n.124	9.17	159 n.32
23.5	64 n.9	**Malachi (Mal)**	
31.19	109 n.37	3.1	109, 110
34.8–16	68	3.5	100 n.124
46.22–23	115 n.73	3.22–23 LXX	109 n.34
Ezekiel (Ezek)		4.1	115 n.73
4.12	46 n.31	4.5–6	109
15.1–8	115 n.73	**Septuagint (LXX)**	4–5, 6, 7, 15, 16, 64 n.9, 87, 107 n.21, 109 nn.35, 37, 39, 112, 113 n.65, 119 n.99, 150–1
18.7	44 n.5		
21.31 LXX	167 n.93		
29.21	64 n.9		
35.21–38	159 n.32		
Daniel (Dan)		**APOCRYPHA**	
4.24 (27)	151	**2 Maccabees (2 Macc)**	
4.27 LXX	150 n.74, 151 n.76	4.7–10, 24	33 n.76
9.27	94 n.81	**Sirach/Ecclesiasticus (Sir)**	
11.31 LXX	94 n.81	2.11	65 n.11
12.2	125	3.30	144 n.30
Hosea (Hos)		4.10	65 n.12
6.6	127 n.22		

Ancient Index

11.14	141	5.40	57 n.129
11.14–19	140–1	5.44	130
11.18	141	5.46	69 n.34
11.19	141	5.48	130 n.37, 175
12.3	144 n.30	6.1–21	134
16.14	144 n.30	6.12	68, 69
17.22	144 n.30	6.19–21	134 n.60
28.2	69 n.33	6.24	147 n.53
29.1–2	65	6.25–34	44 n.6
29.8	144 n.30	7.13–14	160
29.9–13	134 n.60, 150 n.74	8.11–12	160 nn.39–40
29.12–13	151	8.12	163 n.62
29.12	144 n.30	9.16	57 n.126
31.12–32.9	166 n.86	9.35	85 n.25
32.1–2	166	10.5	129 n.29
40.17	144 n.30	10.10	54 n.92, 59 n.138
40.24	144 n.30	11.2–5	82
50.25–26	129 n.29	11.5	84 n.16
		11.10	110 n.41
Tobit (Tob)		11.12	152 n.82
1.3, 16	144 n.30	11.14	109 n.34
1.6–8	37 n.107	11.19	58 n.136
1.17	44 n.5, 56 n.119	12.29	152 n.82
2.14	144 n.30	13.19	152 n.82
4.5–11	134 n.60, 150 n.74	13.42, 50	163 n.61
4.7–16	144 n.30	14.3–12	108 n.30
4.10	151	16.1, 6, 11	107 n.20
4.16	44 n.5, 56 n.119	17.10	109 n.34
5.15	57 n.124	18.21–25	130 n.39
12.8–9	134 n.60, 144 n.30, 150 n.74	18.23–25	37 n.110, 41 n.130
		18.23–35	39 n.124
12.9	151	18.28	11 n.68
14.2, 10, 11	144 n.30	19.15	131
		19.16	124
NEW TESTAMENT		19.16, 29	125 n.14
Matthew (Mt)	14–15, 67 n.24, 84, 95 n.92	19.16–30	15 n.90, 152
		19.20	133 n.54
2.1–22	106 n.15	19.21	133 n.54, 134 n.60
3.2	111 n.48	19.22, 23	131 n.43
3.3	110 n.41, 111	19.23	132 n.47
3.4	55, 109 n.34	20.2	57 n.124
3.6, 13	114 n.70	20.2–7	36
3.7	107	20.2, 9, 13	11 n.68
3.7–10	115 n.73	20.8	30 n.54
3.12	116 n.83	21.28–29	31 n.64, 36 n.101
4.23	85 n.25	21.33–41	31 n.65, 35 n.90, 37 n.106, 39 n.121
5.4	54 n.92		
5.25	37 n.110, 41 n.130	22	169
5.26	39 n.124	22.1–14	169

22.5–6	169 n.104	12.14	27 n.30
22.7, 13	169 n.104	12.15	11 n.68
22.11–13	171	12.28	127 n.21
22.13	163 n.61	12.28–34	15 n.90, 127
22.14	160	12.38	57
22.16	31 n.58	13.14	94 n.81
22.17–18	27 n.30	13.16	55 n.100
22.19	11 n.68	14.3–9 (14.7)	69 n.36
22.34–40	15 n.90	15.24	57 n.127
22.35–40	127	15.43	31 n.59
22.36	127 n.21		
23.25–26	152 n.86	**Luke (Lk)**	
24.14	85 n.25	1	106 n.14
24.18	55 n.100	1–2	77
24.51	163 n.61	1–41	106 n.14
25.15	94 n.81	1.1	14 n.87
25.30	163 n.61	1.2	14 n.87
25.35–38, 42–44	44 n.5	1.5	42, 106
25.36, 43	90 n.53	1.5–2.40	64 n.5
25.46	125 n.14	1.6	125 n.6
26.6–13 (26.11)	69 n.36	1.15–17	110 n.41
27.35	57 n.127	1.16	63 n.3, 65 n.13
		1.16–17	109, 110
Mark (Mk)	14–15, 84, 95 n.92	1.16, 17, 76, 77	105, 110
1.2, 3	110 n.41	1.17	112
1.3	111	1.17, 76	109, 110
1.5–9	114 n.70	1.23, 39–40	34 n.82
1.6	55 n.98, 109 n.34	1.25	71
1.20	31 n.64, 36 n.101	1.43	110 n.41, 111 n.51
2.21	57 n.126	1.45	168 n.100
3.6	31 n.58	1.46–53	93
5.15	54 n.94	1.46–55	64, 70–1
5.34	91 n.63	1.47, 69, 71, 77	109 n.32
6.9	54 n.92, 56 n.110, 59 n.138	1.48	113
		1.48–49	71–2
6.17–29	108 n.30	1.48–54	73 n.60
6.21	31	1.50, 54, 58, 72, 78	2, 130
9.11	109 n.34	1.51–53	2, 71
10.13–15	126 n.19	1.51–54	71 n.50
10.17	124, 131	1.52	113, 166
10.17–31	15 n.90, 152	1.52–53	2, 59, 71, 72, 76, 79, 100, 154 n.2
10.17, 30	125 n.14		
10.18–19	135–6	1.53	9, 10, 17, 45 nn.17–18, 51, 72, 94, 99 n.115, 163 n.67
10.21	134 n.60		
10.22, 23	131 n.43		
10.23	132 n.47	1.53–55	70 n.46
10.52	91 n.63	1.54–55, 72–75	120
12.1–9	31 n.65, 35 n.90, 37 n.106, 39 n.121	1.58	71, 130 n.38
		1.67–79	90
12.13	31 n.58	1.68	63 n.3

Ancient Index

1.68–69	100	3.2, 4	112 n.59
1.68–79	64	3.3	63 n.3, 68 n.25, 103,
1.68, 78	63 n.3, 88 n.42		105, 110, 114, 121
1.69	110, 119 n.103	3.3–5	110, 113
1.69, 78	64 n.9	3.3–6, 18	104, 105, 108–14
1.71	110	3.3, 7–9	117
1.72	71, 130	3.3, 8	63 n.3, 65 n.13, 175
1.74	63 n.3	3.4	108 n.31, 110, 111, 113
1.76	110	3.4–5	113, 114
1.76–77	109, 110	3.4, 5	112 n.59
1.76–79	109 n.33	3.4–6	70 n.46, 75–6, 105,
1.76, 79	112 n.59		108–9, 110, 111
1.77	63 n.3, 103–4, 109,	3.4–6, 18	175
	110, 114	3.5	111, 113 n.65
1.78	90, 130	3.5a	76
1.79	63 n.3, 66 n.15, 112	3.5b	76
1.80	112 n.59	3.6	110, 113, 114,
2	106 n.14		119 n.103
2.1	77 n.88, 106	3.7	114, 117, 153
2.1–2	42	3.7–8	114
2.1–3	42	3.7–9	104 n.10, 105, 120
2.1, 2, 3, 5	106	3.7–9, 15–17	104, 114–16
2.11	111 n.51, 116	3.7–14	59, 104
2.11, 26	115	3.7–18	104
2.11, 30	109 n.32	3.8	74 n.64, 107 n.23,
2.14, 29	63 n.3, 66 n.15		114–15, 119
2.22, 23, 24, 27, 39	125 n.6	3.9	105, 116
2.25–35, 36–38	165 n.80	3.10	121, 177
2.25, 38	147 n.51	3.10–11	81 n.1, 117
2.26, 30	116	3.10, 12, 14	2, 103, 117, 138,
2.29	147 n.55		139–40, 176
2.30	110, 111 n.51, 114,	3.10–14	1, 20, 41, 42, 59 n.137,
	119 n.103		65, 74, 76–7, 79, 103,
2.30–33	109 n.33		104, 105, 107, 108,
2.32	19 n.114, 77 n.88		111–12, 114, 115,
2.34	70 n.46		116–22, 136–7,
2.38	63 n.3		150 n.71, 151, 175
2.40, 52	67	3.11	41, 45 n.17, 54, 59, 117
3	113 n.66, 116 n.85		n.91, 120, 153
3.1	35 n.89, 105, 106	3.12	117, 119 n.102
3.1–2	42, 77 n.88, 105, 106	3.12–13	117
3.1–2, 19–20	104, 106–8, 118	3.12–14	42
3.1–6	104	3.12, 14	107
3.1–14	74 n.64	3.13–14	41, 153
3.1–20	16, 19 n.116, 20, 74,	3.14	117, 118–19, 120
	76, 103, 104, 104–5,	3.15	105, 115, 116, 117
	110, 116 n.84, 121,	3.15–17	105, 111
	174, 175	3.15–18	104, 105
3.2	103 n.4, 106	3.16	121

3.16, 21	114 n.70	5.36	57 n.126
3.17	105, 116	6	119 n.104
3.17–18	89 n.51	6.1	47
3.18	105, 108–9, 111, 117, 121	6.1–3, 21	45 n.17
		6.1–4	51
3.19	105, 108 n.30	6.1–5, 6–11	130 n.36
3.19–20	104, 105, 107	6.2, 7, 11	126 n.16
3.20	107, 114 n.70	6.3, 21, 25	45 n.18
3.21	114 n.70	6.17–49	65
3.23–38	19 n.114, 77 n.88	6.20	9, 85 n.24
4	113 n.66	6.20a	100
4.1–3	51	6.20b	100
4.2	45 n.18	6.20–21	2, 7, 66, 100, 167, 168
4.2–4	45 n.17	6.20–21, 24–25	59, 72, 79, 93, 98, 163 n.67
4.10–11	126 n.18		
4.16, 18	92 n.69	6.20–24	97
4.18	2–3, 6, 9, 17, 68 n.25, 70 n.41, 103 n.2, 121 n.110, 167	6.20, 24	9 n.58
		6.20–26	70 n.46
		6.21	17, 45 n.18, 51, 66 n.16, 73
4.18–19	2, 3, 16, 20, 41, 42, 67, 68, 70, 81–6, 100, 113 n.66, 118, 167, 174	6.21, 25	72–3, 154 n.2
		6.23, 35	69 n.34
		6.24	10, 94
4.19	54	6.24–25	2, 168
4.21	126 n.16	6.25	72
4.22	67, 100	6.27	130
4.24–27	87	6.27–35	75
4.25	9, 45 n.18	6.27–36	130
4.25–26	50, 81 n.1, 87, 89 n.47	6.27–38	16, 42, 115, 152
4.25–27	12, 83, 109 n.34	6.27–49	119
4.25–30	19 n.114	6.29	54 n.92, 57 n.129, 59
4.38–39	45 n.16	6.29–30, 34–35, 38	59 n.137
4.43	85, 111 n.48		
5.1–11	90 n.55	6.29–30, 34–36	118
5.11	74	6.30, 34–35, 38	150 n.71
5.11, 28	133 n.57	6.32, 33, 34	67, 69 n.34
5.12	70 n.41	6.32–35	67 n.24
5.12, 13, 15, 17	91 n.62	6.32–37	134 n.60
5.18–26	70	6.35	65 n.12, 66 n.15, 67, 152, 175
5.20	65 n.13		
5.20, 23, 24	63 n.3	6.35–36	65 n.11
5.20, 23, 32	103 n.2	6.35, 38	65, 79
5.21	139 n.6	6.36	2, 16, 59, 65, 75, 130, 137, 176
5.27–32	119 n.105		
5.28	74	6.43–44	115
5.28, 32	79	6.45–49	115
5.29	45 n.17	6.47, 49	125 n.7
5.29–32	44 n.12, 45 n.16	7	151
5.30	126 n.16	7.1–10	87, 107 n.23
5.32	63 n.3, 65 n.13		

Ancient Index

7.2, 3, 8, 10	147 n.55	8.35	54 n.94
7.3–5	126 n.17	8.40–42	126 n.17
7.3, 7	91 n.62	8.43–44	70 n.41
7.3, 9, 50	87 n.41	8.43, 47, 48, 50	91 n.62
7.9, 50	65 n.13	8.48	63 n.3, 65 n.13, 66 n.15, 91 n.63
7.11–12	88		
7.11–17	2, 4, 20, 81, 83, 86, 86–92, 90 n.55, 91, 98, 100–1, 109 n.34, 174	8.49–56	73
		8.50b	91 n.63
		9.2, 6	85 n.25, 111 n.48
7.13	65 n.10, 89, 90, 130 n.39	9.3	54 n.92, 59 n.138
		9.7–9	107
7.13–15	66 n.16, 88	9.9, 22	107 n.18
7.13–15, 38, 50	73	9.10–17	154 n.2
7.15	87	9.12–17	154 n.1
7.16	63 n.3, 87–8, 90	9.16–17	66 n.16
7.16–17	88	9.17	45 nn.17–18, 51, 73
7.17	89	9.22	35 n.89
7.18–20	89 n.51	9.31	76 n.81
7.21	67, 69, 83, 100	9.51	76 n.81
7.22	2–3, 6, 9, 70, 81–6, 87, 100, 167	9.51–19.44	76–7, 123, 139
		9.52–53	130
7.23	168	9.52–54	129 n.29
7.24	112 n.59	10.5	63 n.3, 66 n.15
7.24–29	103 n.4	10.17–24	126, 127
7.25	57	10.20	127
7.27	110, 112 n.59	10.21	123 n.1, 126, 127
7.30, 39	126 n.16	10.23	168 n.100
7.33	45 n.17	10.25	2, 63 n.3, 66 n.15, 76, 123, 124–7, 131, 133, 138, 139–40, 143 n.23, 175, 176
7.34	58 n.136		
7.36–50	16, 45 n.16, 69, 70 n.46		
7.37–38	69		
7.41	11 n.68, 53 n.86	10.25, 27	126 n.18
7.41–42	16, 39 n.124, 42, 54, 69, 79	10.25–28	15 n.90
		10.25, 28	153
7.41–50	68	10.25, 28, 37	1, 79
7.42	69	10.25–29	95 n.93
7.42, 43	67–8	10.25, 29	137
7.42, 47	69 n.39	10.25, 29, 31–32	126 n.16
7.44–46	69	10.25–37	16, 20, 70 n.46, 95, 96 n.96, 103, 122, 123, 127–30, 131, 132, 135, 136, 164, 174, 175
7.47–49	103 n.2		
7.47, 48, 49	67–8		
7.48, 49	63 n.3		
7.49	139 n.6	10.26	125 n.6
7.50	63 n.3, 66 n.15, 91 n.63	10.27	135
8.1	85, 111 n.48	10.28	72–3, 96 n.94, 124
8.3	30, 42	10.30	57
8.9–18	141 n.16	10.30–35	42, 66, 127, 137
8.10, 12, 14	74	10.30–37	19 n.114, 59 n.137, 127
8.21	125 n.7	10.33–35	153

10.35	11	12.19, 20, 22, 23	143 n.23
10.36	63 n.3	12.20	59, 140, 141, 142 n.18,
10.37	2, 76, 118, 123, 130		143, 151, 152-3, 164
10.38-42	45 n.16	12.20b	142
11.3	45 n.17, 47, 51	12.20, 21	140
11.4	54, 63 n.3, 68, 79,	12.21	142, 143, 149
	152 n.86	12.21, 33-34	164
11.8	171 n.126	12.22-23	45 n.17
11.11-12	47	12.22-24	51
11.20	124 n.5	12.22-31	44 n.6
11.27	168 n.100	12.22-34	143 n.23
11.28	125 n.7	12.22-40	142
11.37-44	151 n.81	12.31-34	152
11.37-52	45 n.16	12.32	66 n.15, 153, 173
11.38	44 n.12	12.32-33	79
11.38-54	126 n.16	12.33	2, 59, 66 n.15, 143,
11.39	95, 151-2		144 n.30, 149-50,
11.39-40	144, 151		153, 173
11.39-41	95 n.87, 144, 151	12.33-34	134, 150 n.71
11.40	144, 151	12.35-38	154 n.4
11.41	2, 144 n.30, 150 n.71,	12.35, 37	55 n.102
	151, 152	12.36	147 n.51
11.43	166 n.87	12.37, 38, 43	168 n.100
12	123 n.1, 140 n.8	12.37, 43, 45, 46, 47	147 n.55
12.1-12	142	12.39	160 n.42
12.1-12, 22-53	142	12.41-53	142
12.1-13.9	140, 141-2	12.42	140 n.8, 147
12.5	143	12.42-48	31 n.64, 147
12.7	53	12.54	116 n.85
12.13-15, 16-21	141 n.15	12.54-13.9	142
12.13-21	31 n.64, 142, 154 n.3	12.58	37 n.110, 41 n.130
12.13-34	139 n.4, 141 n.16	12.59	39 n.124
12.15	142-3	13	92, 165 n.80
12.15, 20-21	1	13.1-5	116, 159
12.15, 21	144	13.4, 11	92
12.15, 21, 33-34	144	13.6-9	116
12.16	10, 42, 141, 142	13.8-9	116
12.16-17	139	13.10, 14, 16	92 n.69
12.16-20	138 n.1	13.10-17	70, 90 n.55, 91,
12.16-21	2, 20, 51-2, 59, 103,		130 n.36, 165
	138, 139-44, 149,	13.10-17.10	159
	174, 175	13.12, 15, 16	92
12.16-31	51	13.13	91 n.67
12.17	2, 76, 138, 139, 140,	13.14	126 n.16
	143, 152, 176	13.14-16	165
12.17-18	10	13.16	92
12.17, 20	141	13.18-21	159
12.18-19	140	13.22	75 n.76
12.19	164	13.22-16.31	78

Ancient Index

13.22–30	155, 159–61, 162, 163, 172	14.16	172
13.23	159	14.16–24	2, 4, 154
13.23–30	154–5, 159	14.17, 21, 22, 23	147 n.55
13.24	159	14.18	31 n.64, 42
13.24–30	160	14.18–20	170
13.25	160, 172	14.18–20, 24	172
13.25–30	17, 78 n.97	14.18–23	169
13.27	148 n.58, 160, 169, 173	14.21	9, 160 n.42, 171, 172
13.28	85 n.24, 163	14.21, 22	172
13.28–29	73, 160	14.21, 22, 23	172
13.28, 29	66 n.15	14.21, 23	169, 172
13.30	161	14.23	171
13.31	107 n.18	14.24	169, 170, 171–2
14	44 n.13, 92, 155, 159, 164–5, 169 n.104, 170	14.26	167 n.96
		14.26, 33	171 n.118
14.1	47, 165	14.33	133 n.57
14.1, 3, 5	92 n.69	15	94, 147, 159 n.35, 162, 168
14.1–6	90 n.55, 91, 92 n.68, 130 n.36, 165	15.1	145
14.1–24	8–9, 45 n.16, 78, 164–72, 175	15.1–2	45 n.16, 146–7, 161
		15.1–16.31	146, 147
14.2	166	15.1–30	155
14.3–5	165	15.1–32	119 n.105
14.4	92 n.69	15.1–42	161–2
14.7	126 n.16	15.2	126 n.16, 147
14.7–11	165 n.77, 166–7	15.3	147 n.49
14.7–14	130 n.39, 167 n.95	15.3–7, 8–10	165 n.80
14.7–24	45 n.17, 70 n.46	15.3–16.13	147
14.11	167 n.93	15.4, 6, 8, 9, 17, 24, 32	161
14.12	10, 167, 171, 172	15.4, 8, 11	161
14.12, 13, 21	9 n.58	15.5, 6, 8, 9, 24, 32	161
14.12–14	78 n.97, 79, 159, 165 n.77, 166–7, 169, 170	15.6–7, 9–10, 23–26, 32	154 n.3
		15.6, 9, 23, 24, 32	161
14.12–15	59	15.6, 9, 23, 25–32	172 n.132
14.12, 21	167	15.7	63 n.3, 65 n.13, 103 n.2
14.12–24	169 n.107		
14.13	150 n.71, 167–8, 172	15.7, 10	147, 161, 171 n.126, 172
14.13–21	95 n.87		
14.13, 21	9, 70 n.41, 155, 167	15.7, 10, 11–32	159
14.14	168–9, 172, 173	15.7, 10, 32	161
14.14, 15	155	15.8–10	11
14.15	17, 20, 47, 66 n.15, 73, 85 n.24, 153, 154, 155, 159 n.33, 165, 168, 169, 170, 171 n.119, 172	15.11–31	31 n.64, 36 n.101
		15.11–32	42, 70 n.46, 139, 146, 161 n.49
		15.12, 15, 17, 25	42
14.15–24	154 n.1, 159 n.34, 165, 167 n.95, 168	15.13	139 n.3
		15.14	50

15.14–17, 23, 27, 30	66 n.16	16.5–7	54, 140, 148, 153
15.14–24	154 n.2	16.6, 7	47
15.14, 17	45 n.18, 48 n.45	16.7	149 n.66
15.16	45 nn.17–18, 50, 51, 73	16.8	148, 152
		16.8a	140, 144, 145, 148
15.16–17	17	16.8b	149
15.17	36	16.8b, 9	140, 148–9
15.17–19	139	16.8–9	149, 160
15.17, 19	147	16.8, 9	148 n.58
15.18, 19	161	16.9	1, 59, 66 n.15, 73, 79, 140, 149, 150, 152, 153, 164, 169, 171 n.126, 173
15.18, 19, 21	161 n.52		
15.18, 20	162		
15.20	130 n.39		
15.20, 22–24	161	16.13	147
15.20, 24, 31–32	148	16.14	4, 5, 147
15.21–22	54 n.93	16.14–15	95, 126 n.16
15.22	147 n.55	16.14–18	95 n.93
15.23	45 n.17	16.15	53 n.86, 94
15.23, 27, 30	162	16.16	85, 94–5, 96, 111 n.48, 118 nn.93–4
15.24, 29, 32	161		
15.24, 32	162	16.16, 17	125 n.6
15.27, 30	47	16.16–18	94, 95
15.29	125 n.6	16.16–30	136
15.31–32	78 n.97	16.17	95
15.32	161, 162	16.18	95
16	94, 123 n.1, 140 n.8, 147	16.19	10, 57, 154 n.3, 164, 172
16.1	10, 42, 94, 139 n.3, 147	16.19, 20	9 n.58
		16.19–23	96–7
16.1–2	148 n.57	16.19–25	154 n.2
16.1–3	139	16.19–26	93 n.77, 96
16.1, 3, 6, 8	140 n.8	16.19–31	2, 4, 5, 20, 59, 70 n.46, 72, 74, 79, 81, 86, 92–8, 101, 130 n.36, 139, 147, 155, 159, 162–4, 169, 174
16.1, 3, 8	147		
16.1–8	31 n.64, 138 n.1, 146		
16.1–9	20, 39 n.124, 42, 53, 59, 94, 103, 138, 139–40, 144–9, 174, 175		
		16.20	10 n.63, 58
		16.20–21	70 n.41
		16.20, 22	10
16.1–13	53 n.90, 139 n.4, 147 n.51	16.21	17, 45 nn.17–18, 51, 73
		16.22	163 n.60
16.1, 19	94	16.22, 23	100
16.1–31	96 n.96	16.23	163–4
16.2	147	16.23–25	10
16.2, 3, 4	147	16.23, 28	97
16.3	2, 53, 76, 138, 139, 140, 152, 176	16.23–31	59
		16.24	2
16.4	140, 147, 148, 149	16.24, 25	97
16.4, 6, 7, 9	147	16.24, 25, 27, 28	97

16.25	94, 98–9, 143 n.23, 164	18.20	125 n.6, 131, 133
		18.21	137
16.27–31	78 n.97, 96, 99	18.22	10, 59, 66 n.15, 73, 76, 96 n.94, 118, 123, 133–4, 135, 137, 150 n.71, 153, 173
16.29, 31	94, 96, 125 n.6		
17.1 (16.14)	94		
17.4	63 n.3, 65 n.13, 109		
17.7	36	18.22, 23	9 n.58
17.7, 9, 10	147 n.55	18.22, 24	10
17.7–10	42, 154 n.4	18.22–25	152, 172 n.131
17.8	55	18.22, 28–30	79
17.11–19	19 n.114, 70 n.41, 83 n.11, 90 n.55, 59, 91	18.23	131
		18.24	132
		18.24, 25	66 n.15, 85 n.24, 95 n.93, 124 n.5
17.13	2, 65 n.10		
17.14	91	18.24–26	173
17.14, 15, 17, 19	91 n.62	18.24, 29, 35	132
17.14, 17	91 n.62	18.25	10
17.15	91	18.26	95 n.93, 132, 160 n.37
17.19	65 n.13, 91	18.28	133 n.57
17.21	124 n.5	18.28–30	132
18.1–8	81 n.1	18.29	153
18.2–8	148	18.30	72–3, 123 n.1, 124 n.4
18.3–5	89 n.47	18.35–43	70 n.41, 131
18.3, 5	89 n.49	18.38	2
18.4–5	139	18.38, 39	65 n.10
18.6	139, 148, 160	18.42	65 n.13, 91 n.63
18.8, 14	171 n.126	19, 8	119 n.99
18.9–12, 18	126 n.16	19.1–10	2, 45 n.16, 104, 119, 131
18.9–14	70 n.46		
18.13	63 n.3, 65 n.10	19.2	119
18.15	126	19.2, 8	9 n.58
18.15–17	126, 131	19.3	119
18.16, 17	126 n.19	19.4	119
18.17	85 n.24	19.5	119
18.18	2, 76, 123, 124–7, 131, 133, 137, 138, 139–40, 175, 176	19.5	10, 119 n.103
		19.6	119
		19.8	10, 119, 150 n.71
18.18–21	123	19.8–9	59
18.18, 22	1	19.9	63 n.2, 119 n.105, 120, 124 n.5
18.18–24	130 n.36		
18.18–25	2	19.11–15	14
18.18–30	15 n.90, 20, 70 n.46, 95, 96 n.96, 103, 122, 123, 131–5, 136, 152, 164, 174, 175	19.13, 15, 17, 22	147 n.55
		19.23	54 n.92
		19.26	171 n.126
		19.44	90 n.53
18.18, 30	66 n.15, 95 n.93, 125, 132, 143 n.23, 153	19.47	35 n.89, 107 n.18
		19.47–48	126 n.16
18.19	132 n.49	20.1, 19	107 n.18
18.19–22	135	20.1–2, 19–22	126 n.16

20.4	103 n.4	**John (Jn)**	
20.9	42	1.18	97 n.101
20.9–16	31 n.65, 35 n.90, 37 n.106, 39 n.121, 42	1.22	103 n.3
		1.24–27	115 n.79
20.9–18	42	3.36	125 n.14
20.10	35 n.89	4.9	129 n.29
20.10, 11	147 n.55	4.13–14	159 n.32
20.13	139 n.6	5.24	125 n.14
20.16	35	6.9, 13	46
20.21	112	6.15	152 n.82
20.22, 24–25	27 n.30	6.35	159 n.32
20.24	11 n.68	6.47	125 n.14
20.35	169 n.101	8.48	129 n.29
20.37	162 n.54	10.12, 28	152 n.82
20.46	57, 59, 166 n.87	12.1–8 (12.8)	69 n.36
20.46–47	42	12.50	125 n.14
20.47	89 n.47	13.23	97 n.101
21.1	10	19.23–24	57 n.127
21.1, 2	9 n.58	21.7	55 n.101
21.1–4	42		
21.2	10, 89 nn.48–9	**Acts**	4–5, 85 n.25, 112 n.53
21.2–4	11	1.22	103 n.3, 169 n.101
21.5–6	42	2.17–21	113, 120
21.11	45 n.18	2.21	113–14
22.2, 4, 52, 54, 66	35 n.89, 107 n.18	2.22	120 n.109
22.4–5	126 n.16	2.23	120 n.109
22.4, 52	33 n.79	2.24–28, 31, 32	120 n.109
22.14–30	154 nn.1, 5	2.28	112 n.55
22.17–19	47	2.29–40	19 n.116
22.18–19	45 n.17	2.33	120 n.109
22.24–27	166 n.88	2.36	120 n.109
22.30	166 n.88	2.37	2, 120
22.50	147 n.55	2.37–47	104
22.51	90 n.55	2.38	63 n.3, 103 n.2, 121
23.1–25	107 n.18	2.38–40	120
23.4, 10, 13	35 n.89	2.40	113, 121
23.10	126 n.16	2.42–47	120, 121
23.34	57 n.127	2.44	121
23.43	124 n.5	2.44–46	19
23.47	107 n.23	2.45	19 n.113, 121, 150 n.71
23.50–51	126 n.17	3.2, 3, 10	144 n.30
23.51	147 n.51	3.2–8	19 n.113
23.56	125 n.6	3.6–9	90 n.58
24.20	35 n.89	3.16	65 n.13
24.27, 44	99 n.120, 125 n.6	3.19	63 n.3, 65 n.13, 103 n.2, 109
24.28–35, 36–43	154 nn.1, 5		
24.30, 35	47 n.38	3.21	89
24.36	63 n.3, 66 n.15	4.1	33 n.79
24.44	125 n.6	4.2	169 n.101
24.47	63 n.3, 65 n.13, 103 n.2	4.6, 27	107 n.18
		4.32	121

4.32–35	121	14.15	63 n.3, 65 n.13
4.32–37	19, 104	14.16	112 n.55
4.33	169 n.101	15.36	90 n.53
4.34	16, 69 n.37, 121	15.7	84 n.17
4.34–35	150 n.71	15.14	63 n.3, 89 n.53
4.35	19 n.113, 121	15.19	63 n.3, 65 n.13
4.37	34 n.86, 121 n.110	16.17	112 n.55
5.25, 26	33 n.79	16.30	2, 117
5.31	63 n.3, 65 n.13, 103 n.2	16.30, 33	90 n.58
5.37	28 n.34, 106	16.31	19
6.1	19 n.113, 89 n.48	17.12	31 n.59
7.23	90 n.53	17.18, 32	169 n.101
8.5–8	19 n.113	18.2	50 n.62
8.21	113	18.25, 26	112 n.55
8.27	72 n.51	19.4	63 n.3, 65 n.13
8.39	152 n.82	19.9, 23	113 n.63
9.2	113 n.63	19.13–20	90 n.58
9.32–35, 40–42	19 n.113	20.21	63 n.3, 65 n.13, 103 n.2
9.33–35	90 n.58	20.24	84 n.17
9.35	63 n.3, 65 n.13	21.28	63 n.3
9.36	144 n.30, 150 n.71	21.31–40	107 n.23
9.36–43	19 n.113	22.4	113 n.63
9.39	19 n.113	22.16	103 n.2
9.39, 41	19 n.113, 89 n.48	22.22–30	107 n.23
10	19 n.113, 151	23.6	169 n.101
10.1–18	151 n.81	23.10	152 n.82
10.2	150 n.71	23.10, 12–35	107 n.23
10.2, 4, 31	144 n.30	23.21	147 n.51
10.4	147 n.52	24.14,22	113 n.63
10.36	63 n.3, 66 n.15	24.15	147 n.51, 169 n.101
10.37	103 n.3	24.17	144 n.30, 150 n.71
10.38	86 n.29	24.21	169 n.101
10.41	154 n.1	26.18	63 n.3
10.43	63 n.3, 103 n.2	26.18–20	103 n.2
11.1–18	151 n.81	26.18, 20	63 n.3, 65 n.13
11.3	147 n.52	26.20	63 n.3, 65 n.13, 74 n.64, 109, 115, 119 n.100
11.18	63 n.3, 65 n.13, 103 n.2		
11.21	63 n.3, 65 n.13	26.23	169 n.101
11.28	49–50	27.1–44	107 n.23
13.10	112 n.55, 113	28.17	63 n.3, 65 n.13
13.10–12	90 n.58	28.28	114 n.67
13.24	63 n.3, 65 n.13, 103 n.3	**Romans (Rom)**	
13.33	108 n.31	1.11	117 n.91
13.38	63 n.3, 103 n.2, 121 n.110	12.8	117 n.91
13.46, 48	63 n.3, 66 n.15, 125 n.14	**1 Corinthians (1 Cor)**	
		5.11	147 n.52
13.50	31 n.59	**2 Corinthians (2 Cor)**	
14.9	65 n.13	12.2	152 n.82

Galatians (Gal)		9.18	113
2.12	147 n.52	9.19	113
Ephesians (Eph)		1QSa	155, 159, 166
4.28	117 n.91	2	172
Philippians (Phil)		2.5–6	167–8
2.15	113 n.65	2.5–9	158
		2.9	158 n.27
1 Thessalonians (1 Thess)		2.11–22	157
2.8	117 n.91	2.14, 15, 16, 17	157, 166 n.83
4.17	152 n.82	2.21	157
Hebrews (Heb)		4Q521	82, 83
10.34	152 n.82	2 II 1	82
James (Jas)			
1.27	90 n.53		
2.15	44 n.5		

JOSEPHUS
Antiquitates judaicae (Ant.)

1.197	47 n.43
3.151–158	59 n.139
3.151–171	57 n.120
3.195	11 n.69
3.320	50 n.62
4.69, 205, 240	37 n.107
4.269	44 n.8
6.339	47 n.43
10.114–115	119 n.99
11.331	56 n.120
12.169–178	107 n.24
13.118	72 n.51
13.395–397	24 n.9
14.163	25 n.11
14.190–195	24 n.9
14.200–204	27 n.29
14.202–212	25 n.10
14.335, 479	31 n.58
15.5–7	30 n.47
15.132	27 n.29
15.229–310	48 n.50
15.296	25 n.15
15.299–300, 302–304	25 n.18
15.299–311	54 n.96
15.303	48 n.51
15.310	44 n.8, 54 n.96
15.314	53 n.89
15.403–405	33 n.75
16.136–149	25 n.14
16.154–155	26 n.25, 27 n.29
16.170	119 n.99
17.274–277	39 n.121

1 Peter (1 Pet)
2.18   113 n.65

Jude
23   152 n.82

Revelation (Rev)
6.6   46
7.16–17 159 n.32
12.5   152 n.82
21.4   156 n.16

JEWISH SOURCES
QUMRAN/DEAD SEA SCROLLS
CD (Damascus Document)

15.15–17	158 n.27
15.16	168 n.97
15.17	158 n.27

1QM

1.3, 9, 11, 13	149 n.63
7.4	168 n.97
7.4–7	158 n.27
7.6	158 n.27

1QS

	112
1.9	149 n.63
2.16	149 n.63
2.19–23	157 n.25
3.13, 24	149 n.63
6.4, 8–12	157 n.25
6.16–22	158
8.13–18	112
9.17–20	112

17.305, 307	30 n.47	*Life*	
17.318	27 n.29	1–2	34 n.86
17.354	27 n.30, 106 n.16	30, 123	32 n.69
18.1–2	27 n.30, 106 n.16	33	31 n.60
18.1–4	28 n.34	64	31 n.61
18.2	27 n.31	244	117 n.90
18.3–4	38–9	346	32 n.67
18.6, 23	106 n.16		
18.26, 34, 95	107 n.17	**PHILO OF ALEXANDRIA**	
18.27, 36–38	26 n.23	*De specialibus legibus (Spec. Leg.)*	
18.29–30	129 n.29, 130 n.40	2.71–85	53 n.83
18.31	30	3.159	40
18.36–38	29 n.44		
18.90–95	33 n.75	**PSEUDEPIGRAPHA**	
18.117	108	***2 Baruch (2 Bar.)***	155–6
18.118	108	24–27, 30	157
18.136	105 n.11	29	155, 157, 172
18.285	49 n.59	29.1–8	157
20.6	33 n.75	29.3	157
20.51–52	32 n.71	29.4	157
20.51–53	49 n.61	29.5, 7	157
20.97–99	108 n.27	29.6	157
20.131	33 n.79	29.8	157
20.167–170	108 n.27	30.1	157
20.188	108 n.27		
20.205–207	34 n.82	***1 Enoch (1 En.)***	8
20.251	32 n.74, 33 n.76	22	93 n.76
263–265	31 n.57	25.4–6	156 n.17
		37–41	155–6
Bellum Judaicum (J.W.)		37–71	156 n.10
1.403	25 n.15	37.4	125
2.57	39 n.121	58.3	125
2.69	31 n.56	60.24	157 n.20
2.232–246	129 n.29, 130 n.40	62	155, 156–7, 172 n.132
2.259–263	108 n.27	62.8	156 n.17
2.282	57 n.121	62.9–12	157
2.287	107 n.24	62.12–16	157
2.426	34 n.83	62.13–16	156
2.426–442	34 n.83	62.14	156
2.427	39	62.14–16	156–7
2.641	31 n.61	97.8–10	140–1
2.652	39 n.121	97.8, 10	141
3.30–32	30 n.45		
3.42, 517–519	30 n.52	***4 Ezra***	
3.506–508	47 n.41	6.49–52	157 n.20
3.516–521	32 n.67	7.45–61	160 n.38
5.427	46 n.26	7.73–104	93 n.76
5.512–514	50	7.102–105	97 n.105
5.549	50	8.1, 3	160
		9.15–16	160 n.37

Jubilees (Jub.)
28–30	82 n.4
32.9–15	37 n.107

4 Maccabees (4 Macc.)
13.17	97 n.101
15.3	125

Psalms of Solomon (Ps. Sol.)
3.12	125
13.11	125
14.10	125

Testament of Abraham (T. Ab.)
20.14	93 n.76

LATER RABBINIC SOURCES
Babylonian Talmud (=b.)
Pesahim (Pesah.)
57a	33 n.81, 34 n.83

OTHER LATER RABBINIC SOURCES
Targumim
Targum Isaiah (Tg. Isa.)
40.9	111 n.48

EARLY CHRISTIAN SOURCES
Gospel of Thomas (Gos. Thom.)
63	141
64	169
65	31 n.65
72	141 n.15

OTHER GRECO-ROMAN SOURCES
Athenaeus
Deipnosophistae (Deipn.)
2.55a, 60c, 60d	46 n.29
16c	47 n.36
129c, 131e, 149f	147 n.42

Cassius Dio
Roman History
42.40.4–5	54 n.93
43.24.2	57 n.130
54.1.1–2	49 n.55
55.26.1–3	49 n.58
55.26.1–5, 27.1, 31.3–4	49 n.57
59.17.2	49 n.60

Cato the Elder
On Agriculture (Agr.)
1.7	52 n.81
56–60	47 n.33
59	57

Columella
De re rustica (Rust.)
1.3.12	53 n.84
1.7.1–3	40 n.129
2.9.14	46 n.28

Corpus Inscriptionum Latinarum
IX 2689	13

Galen
On the Properties of Foodstuffs (De alimentorum facultatibus)
507	46 n.27
686	49 n.53
VI, 481–2	46 n.24
VI, 481–90	46 n.23

Juvenal
Satires (Sat.)
III, 147–150	58 n.134
III, 170	58 n.132
III, 223–5	52 n.76
X. 78	45

Lucian
Cataplus (Cat.)
14	57 n.130
14, 20	93 n.74
20	54 n.95
23	93 n.75
24–8	93 n.75

Fugitivi (Fug.)
14	46 n.29, 47 n.36

Gallus (Gall.)
1	52 n.74
6, 12	57 n.130, 93 n.74
9, 14	58 n.133
14	57 n.131

Origen
Homilies on Genesis and Exodus (Hom. Gen.)
12.5	46 n.28

Petronius
Satyricon (Sat.)
46	47 n.42
48, 53, 76	23 n.4

Philostratus
Vita Apollonii (Vit. Apoll.)
4.45 86 nn.30, 32

Pliny the Younger
Epistulae (Ep.)
3.19.6 40 n.128

Plutarch
Cato Major (Cat. Maj.)
1.4.3 57 n.122
Solon (Sol.)
15 53 n.84

Suetonius
The Life of Augustus (Aug.)
40.5 56 n.114
42.3 49 n.58
82.1 56 n.111

Tacitus
Annales (Ann.)
2.42 26 n.25, 27 n.29
12.43 50 n.63
Historiae (Hist.)
1.86 50 n.64

www.ingramcontent.com/pod-product-compliance
Lightning Source LLC
Chambersburg PA
CBHW052037300426
44117CB00012B/1862